REFLEX ACTION

A STUDY IN
THE HISTORY OF PHYSIOLOGICAL
PSYCHOLOGY

RENÉ DESCARTES

REFLEX ACTION

A Study

IN

THE HISTORY OF
PHYSIOLOGICAL PSYCHOLOGY

By

FRANKLIN FEARING, Ph.D.

Northwestern University

HAFNER PUBLISHING COMPANY

New York   London

1964

Originally published 1930
Reprint 1964

———————

Printed and published by
HAFNER PUBLISHING COMPANY, INC.
31 East 10th Street
New York, N.Y. 10003

Library of Congress card catalog number 63-18167

To
PROFESSOR JOHN EDGAR COOVER

"The farther Advances we make in the Knowledge of Nature, the more probable and the nearer to Truth will our Conjectures approach: so that succeeding Generations, who shall have the Benefit and Advantage both of their own Observations, and those of preceding Generations, may then make considerable Advances. . . . In the Meantime it would but ill become us in this our State of Uncertainty, to treat the Errors and Mistakes of others with Scorn and Contempt, when we cannot but be conscious, that we ourselves see Things *but as thro' a Glass darkly,* and are very far from any Pretensions to infallibility. . . . And even Thus by observing the Errors and Defects of a first Experiment in any Researches, we are sometimes carried to such fundamental Experiments as lead to a large Series of many other useful Experiments and important Discoveries." Stephen Hales, *Statical Essays,* London, 1733.

* * * *

"But the concept of the reflex is not a general master key competent to unlock all of the secrets of brain and mind, as some seem to suppose, and it has of late been subjected to very searching physiological analysis. Into the details of these discussions we cannot here enter, though attention should be especially directed to the futility of attempting to derive intelligence and the higher mental faculties in general from reflexes, habits, or any other form of fixed or determinate behavior. . . . The nervous system is more than an aggregate of reflex arcs and life is more than reactions to stimuli." Judson Herrick, *Neurological Foundations of Animal Behavior,* New York, 1924.

PREFACE

The reflex arc concept has come to play a rôle in modern psychological and physiological theorizing which is comparable with the part played by the fundamental explanatory principles of physics and chemistry. The history of its rise to this pre-eminent position is largely the history of a certain phase of mechanistic physiology. The stimulus-response formula embodied in the reflex is suited admirably to the interpretation of the simpler forms of behavior, as shown, for example, by the artificially isolated spinal segments in the experimental animal. In spite of its apparent simplicity and adequacy, certain difficulties and obscurities have appeared in the application of this principle to the complex behavior patterns of the intact animal. This has been due in part to the tendency to uncritically extend the reflex arc concept to include all forms of animal movement,— an extension which is facilitated, no doubt, by the ease with which the arc may be diagrammed in a text-book,—and by the mechanistic bias which has resulted in the undiscriminating use of the mechanical analogy which the word 'reflex' implies.

A somewhat analogous situation is found in the case of the term 'instinct.' The critical revision to which this concept has been subjected in recent years has resulted in a re-examination of all the phenomena on which such a concept must rest. A similar procedure might be of value in the case of reflex action. In any event an historical survey of the growth of the concept should lay the foundation for an analysis of the behavior-phenomena to which it has been traditionally applied. It has been the purpose in the present volume to trace the development of the theory of reflex action and to record the discoveries of the phenomena which the theory was designed to render intelligible.

The history of the development of the reflex arc concept may be divided, for convenience, into five periods: (1) the pre-scientific period, (2) the speculative period, (3) the period of nascent experimentation, (4) the period of the development of knowledge regarding the structural components of the reflex arc, and (5) the modern period. No attempt has been made to deal in detail with the first period. Chapters II, III, and IV cover the second period; chapters V, VI, and VII deal with the third period; chapters VIII, IX, X, and XI deal with the fourth period; chapters XII, XIII, XIV,

XV, and XVI cover the last period.   That is to say, the first eleven chapters
present the history of the subject from the 17th to the 19th centuries inclusive, and the remaining five chapters present the various phases of the
current problems in the field.

The purpose has been to avoid, so far as possible, the current controversial
literature.   This has been difficult in dealing with such topics as reflex
inhibition, postural reflexes, etc.   These are fields in which only the special-
ist may venture with safety.   They contain material, however, which is
significantly related to the development of reflex theory, and it has been
necessary to undertake the hazardous task of reviewing their basic facts.

The elements which contribute to advance in any field of science are so
inter-dependent, and their ramifications so numerous and intricate, that
an attempt to isolate a particular portion for intensive historical study
results, of necessity, in a certain amount of artificial simplification and
distortion.   This is particularly true of the reflex arc concept which is
based not only upon physiology, but upon anatomy, psychology, philosophy,
and even physics and chemistry.   Not all phases of the subject have been
given attention; only those which are related directly to reflex action as an
explanatory principle in physiological psychology are included.   The
difficult problem of what to exclude was solved in part, of course, by the
accessibility of primary source material—particularly for the 17th and 18th
centuries.   The question of elimination, however, becomes especially acute
as the experimental material accumulates in the latter part of the 19th
century.   Such a study cannot be exhaustive even for the field which it
presumes to cover.   There are doubtless many sources of material which
I have inadvertently ignored; I can only plead the difficulties in attempting
an historical investigation of a field, the phenomena of which appear in such
diversified forms and masquerade under so many different names.

A study of this type would be impossible without the friendly interest and
co-operation of a large number of individuals.   Most of the material
presented was gathered in the Library of Stanford University, the Lane
Medical Library of Stanford University, the Surgeon General's Library
in Washington, D. C., and the John Crerar Library in Chicago.   The study
received financial aid in the form of special grants from the Department of
Psychology at Stanford University where the study was begun in 1925, and
from Northwestern University where it was completed.

I am indebted to Professor Frank Weymouth of the Department of
Physiology and Professor C. S. Stoltenberg of the Department of Anatomy
at Stanford University for their advice and encouragement.   My debt to
my teacher, colleague and friend, Professor J. E. Coover of the Stanford

Department of Psychology is but inadequately expressed in the dedication of the present volume.

I desire to express my appreciation to my colleagues, Professor W. Leopold for assistance with the many German quotations, and Dr. E. L. Clark for assistance with the French material. I am especially indebted to Miss Dorothy Morgan, graduate student in psychology at Northwestern, for editorial and bibliographical assistance, and to Mr. Gordon Barclay, graduate student in psychology at Northwestern and the University of Illinois, for his careful work as typist. I wish to acknowledge my indebtedness to my wife without whose encouragement and help the work would not have been completed.

A substantial part of certain chapters has already appeared in print in the form of articles in the following journals: chapter II in the Psychological Review; chapters III and XV in the American Journal of Psychology; chapter XIII in the Journal of Mental and Nervous Diseases; chapter XIV in the Psychological Bulletin. Acknowledgment is made to the Editors of these Journals for permisssion to reprint all or part of these articles.

FRANKLIN FEARING.

Northwestern University,
August 7th, 1929.

CONTENTS

CHAPTER I

Neuro-muscular adjustment as an historical problem. The early distinction between "voluntary" and "involuntary" action. The modern concept of reflex action. Historical studies of the reflex arc concept. The pre-scientific conceptions of neuro-muscular action. The Greek physicians and the doctrine of "sympathies." The division of the history of the principle of reflex action into five periods as follows: The pre-scientific period, the speculative period, the period of nascent experimentation, the period of increased knowledge of the structural components of the reflex arc, and the modern period.

CHAPTER II

The first half of the 17th century as one of the great epochs of biological science. Vesalius as a forerunner of this period. Descartes' conceptions of reflex action and animal automatism.

CHAPTER III

Influence of Harvey. The iatro-physicists and iatro-chemists. The contributions of Paracelsus, van Helmont, Stahl, Perrault, Mayow, Glisson, Borelli and Stenson. The contributions of Swammerdam to nerve-muscle physiology, voluntary action and experimental method.

CHAPTER IV

Willis, Boyle, DuVerny, Preston and Croone. The foundation of the Croonian Lectures. The conceptions of Boerhaave. Summary of the contributions of the 17th century.

CHAPTER V

The contributions of Astruc of Montpelier, von Haller, Whytt, and Hartley.

CHAPTER VI

La Mettrie, Unzer, Prochaska, Blane, and Cabanis. The first Croonian Lecture.

CHAPTER VII

The work of Porterfield, Farr and the Monros. Summary of the 18th century contributions.

CHAPTER VIII

CHAPTER IX

CHAPTER X

CHAPTER XI

CHAPTER XII

CHAPTER XIII

CHAPTER XIV

CHAPTER XV

phenomena. Temporal relationships in the tendon phenomena. Variability in tendon reflexes. The investigation of Bowditch and Warren. Recent experiments using the Bowditch and Warren techniques. Summary.

CHAPTER XVI

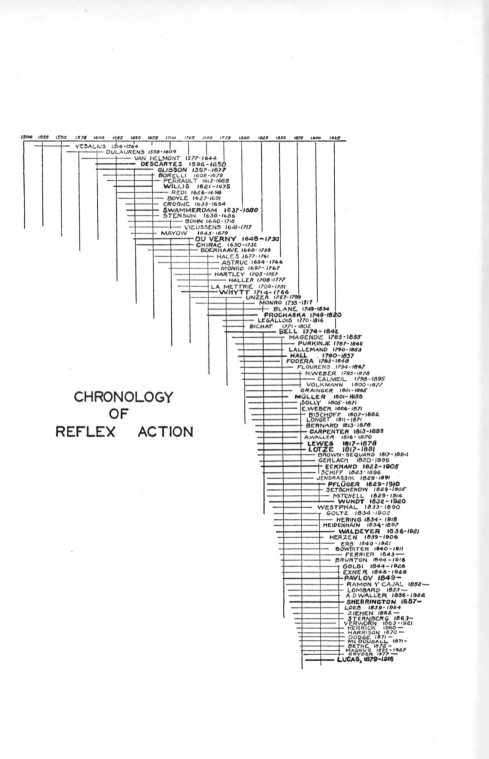

CHRONOLOGY
OF
REFLEX ACTION

| 1500 | 1525 | 1550 | 1575 | 1600 | 1625 | 1650 | 1675 | 1700 | 1725 | 1750 | 1775 | 1800 | 1825 | 1850 | 1875 | 1900 | 1925 |

VESALIUS 1514-1564
DULAURENS 1558-1609
VAN HELMONT 1577-1644
DESCARTES 1596-1650
GLISSON 1597-1677
BORELLI 1608-1679
PERRAULT 1613-1688
WILLIS 1621-1675
REDI 1626-1698
BOYLE 1627-1691
CROONE 1633-1684
SWAMMERDAM 1637-1680
STENSON 1638-1686
BOHN 1640-1718
VIEUSSENS 1641-1717
MAYOW 1645-1679
DU VERNY 1648-1730
CHIRAC 1650-1732
BOERHAAVE 1668-1738
HALES 1677-1761
ASTRUC 1684-1766
MONRO 1697-1767
HARTLEY 1705-1757
HALLER 1708-1777
LA METTRIE 1709-1751
WHYTT 1714-1766
UNZER 1727-1799
MONRO 1733-1817
BLANE 1749-1834
PROCHASKA 1749-1820
LEGALLOIS 1770-1814
BICHAT 1771-1802
BELL 1774-1842
MAGENDIE 1783-1855
PURKINJE 1787-1868
LALLEMAND 1790-1853
HALL 1790-1857
FODERA 1793-1848
FLOURENS 1794-1867
H. WEBER 1795-1878
CALMEIL 1798-1895
VOLKMANN 1800-1877
GRAINGER 1801-1865
MÜLLER 1801-1858
SOLLY 1805-1871
E. WEBER 1806-1871
BISCHOFF 1807-1882
LONGET 1811-1871
BERNARD 1813-1878
CARPENTER 1813-1885
A. WALLER 1816-1870
LEWES 1817-1878
LOTZE 1817-1881
BROWN-SEQUARD 1817-1894
GERLACH 1820-1896
ECKHARD 1822-1905
SCHIFF 1823-1896
JENDRASSIK 1829-1891
PFLÜGER 1829-1910
SETSCHENOW 1829-1905
MITCHELL 1829-1914
WUNDT 1832-1920
WESTPHAL 1833-1890
GOLTZ 1834-1902
HERING 1834-1918
HEIDENHAIN 1834-1897
WALDEYER 1836-1921
HERZEN 1839-1906
ERB 1840-1921
BOWDITCH 1840-1911
FERRIER 1843-
BRUNTON 1844-1916
GOLGI 1844-1926
EXNER 1846-1926
PAVLOV 1849-
RAMON Y CAJAL 1852-
LOMBARD 1855-
A. D. WALLER 1856-1922
SHERRINGTON 1857-
LOEB 1859-1924
ZIEHEN 1862-
STERNBERG 1863-
VERWORN 1863-1921
HERRICK 1868-
HARRISON 1870-
DODGE 1871-
McDOUGALL 1871-
BETHE 1872-
MAGNUS 1873-1927
SNYDER 1877-
LUCAS, 1879-1916

CHAPTER I

Introduction

"L'histoire des doctrines et des théories sur la structure et les fonctions du système nerveux central des Invertebres et des Vertebres, c'est l'histoire naturelle de l'esprit humain."—Jules Soury, *Le Système Nerveaux.*

NEURO-MUSCULAR ADJUSTMENT AS AN HISTORICAL PROBLEM

There are certain problems which, whenever man has attempted to speculate regarding his own actions, have persistently presented themselves. Is the body animated by an immaterial agency called "soul" or "spirit," or does it run like a machine, the functions of which are determined by the parts? The various answers which have been proposed to these and similar questions have furnished a literature of controversy during the last four hundred years which, as it accumulates, threatens to inundate library and laboratory alike.

It is impossible to state when man first began to speculate regarding the nature of the relationship between his own bodily processes and his feelings, sensations, emotions, and thoughts. But we do know that the knowledge of the function and nature of the central nervous system in relation to these mental processes is a very recent development in the history of biology. The idea, however, that they were localized within the body seems to have suggested itself long before the appearance of anything in the nature of proof. It is only necessary to trace the history of the various seats of the soul, of the emotions, and of the intelligence in various parts of the body, to understand that the idea of localization of function was a very ancient explanatory concept.

Even before man speculated about the nature and source of his own experiences, he was probably curious about the agencies by which animal motion was effected. Life and motion are almost synonymous terms. The fact that the living organism moves about in its environment, and that it appears to respond to certain features of that environment, are basic objective data. They are data which at once suggest the fascinating and elusive problems of the "controlling" agency or agencies. Curiosity concerning the nature of this "control" is among the historical antecedents of ethics as well as physiological psychology.

1

At a very early date speculation and self-observation resulted in the distinction between those motions which appeared to be initiated and controlled by the conscious reason and will, and those which ran their course independently of conscious control. The classification of animal movements into *voluntary* and *involuntary* seems to have been accepted by the Greek physicians and appears long before the nature of structures involved in such motion was known.

When the study of muscles and nerves actually began is very difficult to ascertain. As Whewell (536) pointed out, it is probable that the earliest conceptions of man regarding the movements of his members contained no reference to the mechanics by which this motion was brought about. That is, the study of the gross features of movement, the classification of animal movements, and observations of the action of particular limbs preceded the study of nerve and muscle.

Such speculations regarding the source and nature of the control of movement are probably as old as human thought itself. The ideas embodied in the terms *soul, mind, intellect, spirit,* and *will* were not sharply delimited, but they always seem to have indicated an interest in the mechanisms of control of movement. In modern physiological psychology the terms correlation and integration refer to concepts which have a fairly specific connotation. In a very broad sense these terms may be said to refer to the fact that the organism acts as a whole and that this functional inter-dependence is based upon a structural connection between the parts or segments. These conceptions find their historical prototype in the doctrine of "sympathies." By means of "sympathy" the parts of the body were connected—a connection which was not mediated by tissues or by other physical modes of communication. The doctrine that an immaterial psychic principle connected all parts of the body offered an interpretation of integrative movement which was independent of physical structure. Hall (194) has suggested that the widespread acceptance of this doctrine may serve as the explanation for the long delay between the description of the phenomena of involuntary action and their structural interpretation in terms of the reflex arc.

The sixteenth and seventeenth centuries saw the awakening of interest in the structures of the body—an interest which included the spinal cord and brain. With the beginning of anatomy and physiology in the work of Vesalius and Harvey, we may note the appearance of skepticism concerning the doctrine of "sympathy" together with an increasing curiosity regarding the functioning of the nerves and muscles themselves. The time was ripe for the re-interpretation of the phenomena of movement and integration in terms of muscle and nerve.

THE CONCEPT OF REFLEX ACTION

This re-interpretation finds a brilliant and dramatic statement at the hands of Descartes in the middle of the 17th century, and the 18th, 19th and 20th centuries have seen the experimental elaboration of this concept. The importance attached to the concept of reflex action by modern psychology, physiology, and neurology is indicated by the rôle which it plays in current theory in physiology and physiological psychology. It is safe to say that practically all of the theories of neuro-muscular adjustment of the first twenty-five years of the 20th century are related to some form of the reflex action concept. For the so-called "behavioristic" school of psychology, the reflex is the basic type of response.

As recently as 1927 the physiologist, Pavlov, has made the reflex the unit reaction of animal behavior (400). After abandoning psychology as a guide to the study of the higher nervous activity,[1] he finds the path for science already indicated in the study of reflex action. All animal behavior is to be understood in terms of concatenated reflexes. Since the animal organism is a definite circumscribed material system "it can only continue so long as it is in continuous equilibrium with the forces external to it; so soon as this equilibrium is seriously disturbed the organism will cease to exist as the entity it was. Reflexes are the elemental units in the mechanism of perpetual equilibration. Physiologists have studied and are studying at the present time these numerous machine-like, inevitable reactions of the organism—reflexes existing from the very birth of the animal, and due therefore to the inherent organization of the nervous system."[2] Since the foundation of the nervous activities of both men and animals is made up of the "aggregate of reflexes," Pavlov believes that their study is of fundamental importance to physiology. The study of reflexes and instincts[3] may be expected to lead eventually to a complete understanding of the total behavior of the organism.

This position is typical of current physiological theorizing regarding the nature of the "higher" integrations of animals and man. It represents a reaction against the older dualistic and animistic conceptions involving mind, will or any type of conscious process. There are, of course, those among the physiologists who do not find the interpretation of all human

---

[1] Indeed, Pavlov is inclined to question the scientific status of psychology *in toto*. At least, he doubts its claim to be a natural science.

[2] Pavlov, *op. cit.*, p. 8.

[3] For Pavlov instincts are but chain-reflexes. " . . . instincts and reflexes are alike the inevitable responses of the organism to external and internal stimuli." *Ibid.*, p. 11.

behavior in terms of reflex action wholly satisfactory. Herrick (223), for example, points out the "futility of attempting to derive intelligence and the higher mental faculties in general from reflexes, habits, or any other form of fixed or determinate behavior."

For those sciences which are primarily devoted to the study of the integrated responses of living organisms, the concept of reflex action has played, in the 19th and first twenty-five years of the 20th century, a dominating rôle, comparable, perhaps, to the influence of the Newtonian hypotheses in physics. The work of Sherrington with "spinal" animals (441), the studies of Pavlov of the "conditioned" reflexes in intact animals (400, 401) as well as the investigations of Magnus (326), Herrick (223) and Child (88) in the present century, and the work of Pflüger (404), Marshall Hall (196), Bell (28), Goltz (175), Bowditch and Warren (57), and many others in the 19th century have contributed a body of knowledge which has largely determined the direction of theory and research in that branch of biological science which deals with human and animal behavior.

A study of the current usage of the term "reflex" reveals a lack of unanimity as to what is to be included under the term.[4] It is striking that phenomena apparently as simple as those referred to by the term "reflex" should be the occasion for such discrepant interpretation. This difficulty of interpretation suggests that because of the ease with which the reflex "arc" may be diagrammatically represented in a text-book, or demonstrated in isolated form in the "spinal preparation," there has developed a distorted and over-simplified conception of its structural and functional characteristics. Dewey in 1896 (105) pointed out some of the defects of the reflex "arc" idea, especially in connection with the arbitrary separation of the stimulus and response as distinct existences. For the authors of textbooks, however, this warning seems to have had little effect.

A frequent source of confusion in the use of the term "reflex" is found in the failure to distinguish between its application to (1) the neural structures involved in responses to stimulation, and (2) functionally uniform types of response dependent, presumably, upon certain neural connections.

Under the first usage are included all types of response which involve certain structural sequences, e.g., a receptor, afferent neurones, central connections, efferent neurones and an effector mechanism. From this point of view all responses to stimuli involving afferent and efferent conduction may be called *reflex* and the neural structures involved may be referred to as *reflex arcs*.

---

[4] An analysis of the contemporary theories of reflex action is presented in Chapter XVI.

Under the second usage are included only those stimulus-response sequences which possess certain *specific functional and structural characteristics*. The nature of these criteria is a source of disagreement. Inspection of the various definitions reveals that certain criteria are more frequently mentioned than others. The following are arranged roughly in the order of the frequency with which they are mentioned.[5] Reflex action is (1) *involuntary*, (2) a type of behavior which is *unlearned*, *i.e.*, it is based on inherited neural mechanisms, (3) *predictable* and *uniform*, *i.e.*, given a certain stimulus and a certain receptor organ, the response is a necessary and invariable consequence, (4) not conditioned by *consciousness*, (5) the *time* from the reception of the stimulus until the beginning of the response is relatively short as compared with other types of reaction, *e.g.*, consciously conditioned reactions, (6) serves some adjustive or *protective purpose*, (7) involves a *synaptic nervous system* with a receptor, afferent and efferent conduction, and an effector, and (8) a response which *usually does not involve the cerebral cortex*.

The terms of the above list do not designate mutually exclusive categories, nor are they of equal importance. The particular combination of descriptive terms used in a definition depends in part upon certain metaphysical assumptions—implicit or explicit—held by the individual constructing the definition. From the point of view of the following definition, for example, all reactions are reflex, *i.e.*, invariable and machine-like, in nature:

> An external or internal stimulus falls on some one or other nervous receptor and gives rise to a nervous impulse; this nervous impulse is transmitted along nerve fibres to the central nervous system, and here, on account of existing nervous connections, it gives rise to a fresh impulse which passes along outgoing nerve fibres to the active organ, where it excites a special activity of the cellular structures. Thus a stimulus appears to be connected of necessity with a definite response, as cause with effect. It seems obvious that the whole activity of the organism should conform to definite laws.[6]

The key word here is *necessity;* the fundamental reactions of the organism are reflex, *i.e.*, determined responses. As a result of the process of conditioning, the same stimulus may initiate different reactions (reflexes), and, conversely, different reactions may be initiated by the same stimulus. In such a definition there is no room for any kind of psychical process as an explanatory principle in animal behavior.

Sherrington on the other hand (441) discusses the "machine-like fatality" of the spinal reflexes as contrasted with volitional responses. It is "ur-

---

[5] *Cf.* such standard texts as Bayliss (21), Starling (464), Luciani (320), Ladd and Woodworth (277), Nagel (382), Ziehen (552), and Howell (241).

[6] Pavlov, *op. cit.*, p. 7.

gently necessary" however, for physiology to know how volitional control may modify the actions of the reflex machinery. From this point of view, reflex action is not regarded as an all-inclusive principle of animal behavior.

In the same vein, Luciani (320) finds it difficult to make an objective distinction between reflex and volitional actions. In the narrow sense, "as applied to the nervous system, the reflex act is the involuntary transformation of a centripetal into a centrifugal nerve impulse, by means of a central organ." By "involuntary transformation," Luciani means to distinguish the reflex from the voluntary act "which may also follow on, and be evoked by, an afferent impulse."

A still more specific type of definition is that in Baldwin's Dictionary (18). Here a reflex action is defined as a "kinesodic response to aesthesodic stimuli of a regular kind without the intervention of volition or necessary participation of consciousness."

These examples indicate that the concept of reflex action may include responses of widely diversified characteristics. It may be loosely applied to all animal behavior in which afferent, central and efferent elements can be demonstrated. It may be reserved for behavior which has certain specific functional characteristics—the exact nature of which has long been a source of controversy.

Descartes' concept of reflex action stressed primarily its involuntary nature; it was automatic, and therefore machine-like and invariable. Later these terms were applied also to learned or habitual reactions. Thus there appears to be another source of confusion in the use of the term. The broad distinction between voluntary and involuntary is of somewhat uncertain value, in view of the fact that such diversified activities as playing the piano and the beating of the heart may be described by the latter term.

Jennings (261) in discussing the sources of confusion in reflex theory has distinguished three possible conceptions of reflex action: (1) The word reflex may be used to describe the contraction of the muscle when a nerve is stimulated. The nervous impulse is supposed to pass to and be reflected from the spinal cord, back to the muscle. (2) The reflex may be defined as an unconscious or involuntary action. (3) The aspect of uniformity in certain reactions may be the basis for describing them as reflex. It is significant that all of these interpretations refer to phenomena which functionally have much in common, but are unlike from the point of view of their origin and development.

The attempt to make a distinction between voluntary and involuntary action, by introducing some wholly new principle in explaining the complex behavior involving the cortex as contrasted with simple spinal responses, is, as Jennings points out, a pointless proceeding. The distinction is not between conscious action and mechanical reflex, but between movements of which consciousness is adjunct (to use the phrase of Sherrington) and movements which are unconscious. As Titchener (482) has pointed out, all movements, biologically considered, are mechanical in the sense that they are referrable to physico-chemical mechanisms.[7]

The uncertainty and confusion regarding the definition and delimitation of the phenomena included under the term reflex action may be summarized as follows:

(1) The nature of the so-called voluntary actions is largely undetermined. The use of the term "voluntary" as contrasted with "involuntary" is a source of confusion unless objective criteria are available. In this connection the question may be raised as to whether "involuntary" actions are ever wholly so—at least they are modified by the action of mechanisms to which "consciousness is adjunct." The voluntary-involuntary dichotomy is of questionable value.

(2) Learned or habitual actions bear some of the characteristics of the traditional reflex act. They are unconscious and invariable. They have been called "acquired reflexes" or "brain reflexes." The word "automatic" has been used in connection with these reactions, but this word is used by some psysiologists with reference to certain vegetative functions.

(3) The term reflex is frequently used with reference to all types of response involving afferent-efferent conduction in the nervous system.

HISTORICAL STUDIES OF REFLEX ACTION

The study of the theories and phenomena of neuro-muscular integration from the historical point of view might follow several avenues of approach. The theories of the soul, the investigation and theories of cerebral localization, the theories of voluntary action, and the investigations of the structure and function of the muscle and nerve might each be the object of an historical investigation. Research in each of these fields has contributed to the concept of reflex action. The importance of that concept to modern physiology and psychology has been indicated, particularly in the setting given it by such physiologists as Sherrington and Pavlov.

The story of the development of the concept of reflex action and of the phenomena on which it is based, is the object of the present historical survey. Such a study should throw light on the causes of the present lack

[7] The *Gestalt* school of psychologists stresses the distinction between physical and mechanical (machine-like) theories of explanation. *Cf.* the discussion of this interpretation *infra*, Chapter XVI.

of agreement as to the use of the term reflex. At every point we may expect to encounter metaphysical interpretations and points of view, the study of which properly belongs to the history of philosophy. So far as possible, however, the object will be to survey the investigations and theories of neuro-muscular adjustment in chronological order, with particular reference to the theories of reflex action.

The first study devoted exclusively to the history of reflex action is the exhaustive and scholarly monograph of Eckhard in 1881 (125). This study is a comprehensive treatment of the history of the experimental aspects of the subject from the beginning of the 17th century to about 1865.

G. Stanley Hall became interested in the subject of a history of reflex action about 1880. In his "The Life and Confessons of a Psychologist" he refers to his earlier purpose "to publish a comprehensive memoir on the subject" (195).[8] This intention was never completely carried out. Hall's preliminary study (194) in 1890 and that of his colleague at Clark, Professor Hodge (232) in the same year seem to be the only results of Hall's researches in the libraries in Paris and the British Museum. In his memoirs referred to above, Hall refers to the use which Hodge made of the material. Gault, also at Clark University, published in 1904 a paper on the history of reflex action in the 19th century (165).[9]

Historical works of a more general nature which are of fundamental importance in furnishing a general background may be mentioned. Whewell's "History of the Inductive Sciences" (536) and Lange's "History of Materialism" (281) are among the more useful of the older works. The scholarly work of Foster (156)—"Lectures on the History of Physiology during the Sixteenth, Seventeenth and Eighteenth Centuries"—is especially useful because of its copious quotations from source material much of which is

---

[8] I am indebted to Professor W. R. Miles of Stanford University for the opportunity of examining a letter written in 1880 by Hall to the Harvard physiologist, Bowditch, in which Hall refers to his intent to publish a history of reflex action. Professor Miles and Catherine Cox Miles have since published these letters. *Vide* (358) p. 332 for Hall's reference.

[9] Among the important minor studies are those of Monro (365a) in 1787, George (167) in 1837, Jeiteles (257) in 1858, Cayrade (85) in 1864, Stieda (469) in 1899, Gley (169) in 1900, Johnston (263) in 1910, and Harris (205, 206) in 1914. In certain special fields there are important historical summaries. That of Arnold (11) in 1842, Neuburger (384) in 1897, Warden and Warner (519) in 1927, Warden (518) in 1927, and Sternberg (468) in 1893 should be mentioned; the latter is especially important as containing an historical summary of the studies of the tendon reflexes. Griffith's monograph (189) in 1922 is the most comprehensive history of the study of vestibular equilibration available. Ample bibliographies of reflex action may be found in Herrick (223), Child (88), Fulton (161), and Sherrington (441).

not easily available. The chapters on the history of science in the Cambridge Modern History (157) are important. Soury's monumental work (458) and Laehr's exhaustive bibliography (278) are particularly valuable. Garrison's "History of Medicine" (162) is the best of the briefer works in this field, containing as it does an immense amount of factual material.

Many of the more comprehensive physiological treatises contain historical summaries in the field of reflex action. Among these should be noted especially Nagel's *Handbuch* (382), Hermann's *Lehrbuch* (222), Schäfer's "Textbook" (432) and Fulton's recent work (161) on reflex movement.

THE PRE-SCIENTIFIC CONCEPTIONS OF NEURO-MUSCULAR ACTION

In surveying the historical development of a theory or particular field in science, we are impressed with the futility of attempting to attach a date to the "discovery" of any particular idea or fact. Boring (55) has recently pointed out the importance of a healthy skepticism in every case of apparent originality in scientific "discoveries." Thought is not discontinuous, and the development of science is not discontinuous. To determine exactly *when* and exactly *who* "first" discovered the phenomena of involuntary action, the reaction of the pupil to light or the phenomena of neuro-muscular action is as impossible as it is futile. The observations of some of these phenomena, doubtless, are as old as human curiosity itself. The urge to "write it out" or to demonstrate is not equally potent in us and many of these observations may have been made, and their significance noted by unchronicled scientific geniuses. It is unpsychological to attach too much importance to the recorded document; the plan, the observation, the generalization may have been completed months and years before the formal paper.

As has been stated above, it would be very difficult to ascertain when the study of muscles and nerves actually began. There seems to be no doubt but that many of the specific muscular co-ordinations which we now term reflex acts had been observed by the Greek physicians. These were explained on the basis of "sympathy" between various parts of the body. The doctrine of "sympathies," *i.e.*, an immaterial connection between objects, had a very wide application as an explanatory principle. Such an immaterial connection could exist not only between parts of the same body, but also between similar organs in different bodies. As such it was the basis of a crude organo-therapy; a composition of bird's eyes, for example, might be used to treat defective vision in man.[10]

---

[10] *Cf*. Allbutt (7), pp. 150, 152.

In the case of the Greek physicians, the knowledge of the structural basis of the "sympathy" or "consensus" between parts of the body, or of the agencies whereby bodily movements are brought about, was exceedingly primitive. Hippocrates (460–370 B. C.) (230) seems to have held no distinct conception of the muscles and he confused the nerves and tendons.[11] Erasistratus[12], however, seems to have distinguished clearly the arteries, veins and nerves, and to have regarded the latter as carrying the psychic *pneuma* for motion and sensation. This early Alexandrian anatomist also made the distinction between motor and sensory nerves and traced them to their origin in the brain.

The study of bodily movement as distinct from the structural agencies which bring it about, seems in the beginning to have lead to the broad distinction between voluntary and involuntary action. The observations on which this distinction was based may have been both introspective and objective. That is, the individual may have observed in himself that certain movements took place in his body of which he was unconscious and over which he had no control; he, also, may have observed these movements in animals. Proof that the movements in animals are unconscious and involuntary implies certain assumptions regarding the localization of psychic processes, and must rest on the results of surgical elimination of the parts assumed to be associated with mind and will. Such proof was not forthcoming until the latter part of the 17th century.

Aristotle localized the psychic functions in the heart rather than in the brain. Although he made extended observations on animal locomotion, he does not seem to have made clear the means by which the movements were effected. However, he distinguished voluntary from involuntary motion as indicated in the following passage (10):

> We have shown, therefore, after what manner animals are moved by voluntary motions, and from what causes. But some of the parts are, also, moved with certain involuntary motions, and with many which are not voluntary. I call, however, the involuntary motions, such as those of the heart and genital parts. For frequently in consequence of something appearing they are moved; though the intellect does not order them to do so, yet they are not voluntarily moved; and such are the motions of sleep and wakefulness, respiration and others of like kind. (On the common motions of animals. Chapter XI)

Aristotle seems to have been among the first to observe the motions of animals in which the nervous system has been divided, *e.g.*, in the decapitated animal. He divided the animal body into three parts:—that which

---

[11] *Cf.* Whewell (536), II, p. 438.
[12] Allbutt, *op. cit.*, p. 150.

receives food (the head), that which is the recipient of food (the belly), and that which excretes. He noted that the removal of the head segment in certain animals did not result in death, but that certain movements persisted.

For many animals, when deprived of each of these parts, viz., of what is called the head, and of that which is the recipient of nutriment live according to the middle part. But it is evident that this happens to be the case in insects, such as wasps and bees; and many animals that are not insects are able to live when divided according to the nutritive part. For animals that are divided appear to have sense. (On youth and old age, life and death. Chapter II)

Aristotle noted that even in the higher animals there was motion after division.

Animals, however, which are formed in the most excellent manner cannot live when divided, because their nature is as much as possible one; on which account some of the parts of these, when divided, retain a certain imperfect sense, because they possess a certain psychical passion. For the viscera being separated they still move themselves, as is the case with tortoises when the heart is taken away. (On youth and old age, life and death. Chapter II)

In this observation we have perhaps the beginning of the long series of experimental observations on the behavior of animals in relation to certain segments of the nervous system.

In the Syrian "Book of Medicine" (53) a series of lectures by an unknown physician delivered, probably, in Alexandria about the time of Hypocrates and translated into Syriac in the early centuries of the Christian Era, we find certain references that have a modern ring. A clear notion of the nerves and their relation to the spinal cord is evidenced.

And we call nerves those which have many exits from the spinal cord, and they also split up and radiate in all directions throughout the body. In them is located the whole power of sensation . . . . [nerves have] rational powers which give feeling and motion to the whole body. (Vol. II, p. 121)

This unknown lecturer distinguished "voluntary" powers from "natural" powers. The latter are

the power of attraction, power of grasping tightly, the power of digesting and the power of expulsion. These effect the service of the body in all members of the body, great as well as small . . . . This taketh place when the natural powers are in healthy condition, whether we wish it or whether we do not. (p. 122)

The last statement would seem to be a definite anticipation of the idea of reflex action, i.e., a kind of action which is wholly involuntary. The same nerves apparently possess both the voluntary and natural powers, and in injury to the spinal cord, either one or the other may be abolished.

> . . . . for the nerves, beside the natural powers which they possess, possess also the power of performing the wish of the soul, which they effect by means of the various motions of the body, and because of this injuries that happen to them sometimes bring to naught the voluntary functions and sometimes the natural functions also.

The consideration of the location and nature of *pneuma* or *psyche* which played so important a rôle in the speculations of the Greek physicians and philosophers are properly subjects for the history of philosophy. Eckhard (125) has pointed out[13] that the consideration of "sympathies" is not the concern of the history of experimental physiology of the nervous system.

By the time of Galen (131–201 A.D.), however, the structure of the animal frame as composed of bones and muscles was fairly well known. Although Galen still confused tendons and nerves, he recognized the importance of nerves as an essential agency in animal motion. The Greek physician, Rufus of Ephesus,[14] who lived in the reign of Trajan (98–117 A.D.) had described with great precision the state of knowledge up to that time regarding the structure and function of the brain. He distinguished sensory from the motor nerves and noted that sensation and the motor functions are made possible by the agency of the nerves.

Soury (458) points out that in the second century the anatomy of the nervous system was as well advanced as it was at the time of Willis and Vieussens fifteen hundred years later. The rôle of the brain as the seat of sensation, intelligence and voluntary movement, was known, and the motor had been distinguished from the sensory nerves more than a thousand years before the discoveries of Bell and Magendie.

Galen was an experimental neurologist in the sense that he sectioned the spinal cord in order to discover the effects on muscular contraction. He demonstrated that transverse section of the cord destroyed sensibility and movement in the parts of the body below the point of section. He distinguished between voluntary and involuntary motion and included under the latter such integrated movements as the movements of the arteries and heart, and the movements of the stomach and intestines. His treatise on muscular motion is one of the first in the field.[15]

Galen conceived the processes in the nerve in terms of "animal spirits." The blood in going through successive stages of rarefaction in the liver,

---

[13] *Op. cit.*, p. 34.
[14] *Cf*. Soury (458), I, p. 256.
[15] *Cf*. Fulton (161) for a discussion of the various editions of this work.

heart and brain distills in turn "natural spirits," "vital spirits" and "animal spirits." The latter are essential for muscular motion and sensation.

The dogmas and observations of Galen became bound in a body of physiological doctrine which was accepted without modification for nearly fourteen hundred years. Until Vesalius in the middle of the 16th century ventured to study the structure of the body itself, the authority of Galen was unquestioned.

The physiological studies of the Greeks and Romans are difficult to summarize with reference to their contributions to neuro-muscular coordination. The phenomena of involuntary action were described in their broadest aspects, and no doubt many specific neuro-muscular integrations were described which we now would recognize as reflex actions. The agency of the nerves in muscular movement was known to the Greeks, and in part, the functions of the brain and spinal cord were understood. Although the doctrines of "sympathy" and "spirits" were to persist in neural physiology with deadening effect for nearly two thousand years, yet Galen's experimental studies of spinal cord function by the use of operative procedures offered a technique, the revival of which the experimental physiology of the 17th and 18th centuries made efficient use.

The historical development of the reflex arc concept may be divided into stages which are delimited with a fair degree of clearness. We have recognized five such stages, as follows:

(1) The pre-scientific periods (until the 17th century). These include everything until the time of Descartes in the 17th century. The work of the Greek and Roman physicians and philosophers, and the biological speculations of the Middle Ages are of great interest and importance, but no attempt is made to examine them in the present volume.

(2) The speculative period (1650–1750). This includes the era beginning with the description of a certain species of involuntary action by Descartes in the 17th century and ending with the publication in 1751 of Whytt's book on the involuntary motions of animals. Although the work of Willis, Du Verny and others was to some extent empirical, the concept of the reflex arc did not possess a solid foundation in experimental observation until the period which was ushered in by the experiments of Whytt on the spinal cord. The work of Swammerdam in the latter part of the 17th century on the nerve-muscle response was in the nature of an exception to the above characterization, but his work seems to have been neglected by the majority of his contemporaries.

(3) The period of nascent experimentation (1750–1831). This period extended from the time of Whytt until the work of Marshall Hall on the

reflex functions of the spinal cord in 1832.   It was characterized by a certain amount of crude experimentation.   During this time, however, the word "reflex" came into general scientific use.

(4) The period of increased knowledge of the structural components of the reflex arc (1832–1906).   The work of Sir Charles Bell and Marshall Hall gave the concept of reflex action a fixed position in both physiology and medicine.   This is the era of the simple mechanical reflex and includes the discovery of a vast number of separate reflex mechanisms as a result of new experimental techniques.

(5) The modern period.   The publication in 1906 of Sherrington's work on the integrative action of the nervous system is a convenient date with which to mark the change from the hypothesis which regards the reflex as a simple stimulus-response sequence to that which considers it as an integrating unit in the adjustive activities of the organism.

CHAPTER II

The 17th Century. Descartes and Vesalius

"It is necessary that I describe for you first the body, by itself, then the soul, and finally, that I show you how these two natures are to be joined and united to compose men resembling us.

"I postulate that the body be nothing other than a statue or machine of clay which God makes expressly as near like us as possible, not alone giving it on the outside the color and forms of all our limbs, but putting inside as well, all the parts necessary for it to walk, eat, breathe, and in fact, imitate all of our functions which can be imagined to proceed from matter, and to depend only on the arrangement of the organs."—René Descartes, *Traité de l'Homme*, 1662.

The principal sciences of the Middle Ages were astronomy and optics. The one was the study of an "ultimate, immovable reality,"[1] while the other was the mathematical study of refraction and reflection. There was no place in Mediaeval science for the study of man as such. It was the study of the world with man left out.

In the 17th century there was a shift in emphasis. Man himself became an object of study. It is to this shift in emphasis that biology and physiology in the modern sense may be said to owe their origin. A striking aspect of this new curiosity was a great interest in the mechanisms of animal motion. The most significant advance from the point of view of the development of physiological psychology was the fact that *men appeared to be willing to entertain the concept that bodily motions might be explained without reference to a "soul" or other non-material cause.* In this consists the great significance of the 17th century for the history of reflex action.

In 1628 the publication by Harvey (1578–1667) of the results of his investigation of the circulation of the blood contributed largely to the conception that bodily action was to be explained in physical terms. The investigations of Borelli, Glisson, Mayow, Swammerdam, and others carried the attack directly to the neuro-muscular system itself.

The nature and uses of the disturbance transmitted along the nerve, the processes of muscular contraction, and the study of animal responses to specific stimuli were all subjects of observation and experiment. Vesa-

[1] *Vide* Brett (61), II, p. 179 *ff.*

15

lius, in the previous century, had invaded the sacred mysteries of the human body, itself, and as a result an intense curiosity prevailed in the field of the biological sciences regarding the structure and functioning of the bodily mechanisms.

Huxley (247) characterized the first half of the 17th century as "one of the great epochs of biological science."

But, in the 17th century, the idea that the physical processes of life are capable of being explained in the same way as other physical phenomena, and, therefore, that the living body is a mechanism, was proved to be true for certain classes of vital actions; and, having thus taken firm root in irrefragable fact, this conception has not only successfully repelled every assault which has been made upon it, but has steadily grown in force and extent of application, until it is now the expressed or implied fundamental proposition of the whole doctrine of scientific physiology. (p. 199)

The development of these doctrines was possible only because of the revolt against authority in the field of medicine and anatomy which occurred in the 15th and 16th centuries. For more than a thousand years, since the contributions of Galen, there had been no advance in the knowledge of the structure and functions of the living organism. The doctrines of Galen had become enshrined and were accepted not because they were true, i.e., might be verified by competent observation, but because Galen had said they were true.

VESALIUS

The anatomical and physiological teachings of Galen received their first effective challenge at the hands of the most picturesque and dramatic figure in the history of physiology, Andreas Vesalius (1514–1564). This man broke with the authority of Galen in the field of anatomy and substituted for it the descriptions of the human body as he found it by actual examination.

Vesalius was born in Brussels and educated at the University of Louvain. In 1537, after studying under the anatomist, Sylvius, in Paris, Vesalius went to Venice, where he attracted the attention of the rulers; there he was given charge of the public dissections, and held the chair of surgery and anatomy at the University of Padua. Here he abandoned Galen as a source of knowledge and studied the human body at first hand. From this study resulted his great work entitled the "Structure of the Human Body," completed in 1542 and published in the following year. This marks, says Foster,[2] the beginning of modern anatomy and physiology.

[2] Cf. Foster, (156), p. 10 ff.

The primary interest of Vesalius was in the structure of the human body rather than in its functions. In his study of the nervous system, therefore, it was structure rather than the nature of neural action and nervous control that was given attention. Consequently, his contributions to the theories of neuro-muscular integration are indirect. The brain was regarded as the seat of the "chief soul" and the source of "animal spirits." The brain was able to influence any part of the body by means of the animal spirits conducted by the nerves. This concept of nerve function, Vesalius expressed as follows:[3]

And while on the one hand it employs this spirit [animal spirits] for the operations of the chief soul, on the other hand it is continually distributing it to the instruments of the senses and of movement by means of nerves, as it were by cords, the soul never being lacking in this spirit which may be regarded as the chief author of the activity of those instruments, any more certainly than the liver and heart ever leave wholly destitute at least in health, any of the parts on which they bestow their products, although they do not always supply them either in the same quantity or the same quality. Nerves, therefore, serve the same purpose to the brain that the great artery does to the heart, and the *vena cava* to the liver, in as much as they convey to the instruments to which it ought to be sent the spirit prepared by the brain, and hence may be regarded as the busy attendants and messengers of the brain. (Foster, p. 255–256.)

He indulged in little speculation on the mechanism of the relationship between the chief soul and the body, filled, no doubt, as Foster suggests, by a wholesome respect for the doctrines of the Church regarding the soul and its relation to the body. Beyond the fact that the brain was the seat of certain psychical processes and of the origin of movement, and was able to influence the body through the agency of the nerves, Vesalius said but little of the nature of nervous function.

As Foster points out, it is obvious that Vesalius had a distinctly physiological view of the "chief soul" and regarded psychic action as being associated with the operation of the brain. This is clearly stated in the following quotation.

But how the brain performs its functions in imagination, in reasoning, in thinking and in memory (or in what-ever way, following the dogmas of this or that man, you prefer to classify or name the several actions of the chief soul), I can form no opinion whatever. Nor do I think that anything more will be found out by anatomy or by the methods of those theologians who deny to brute animals all power of reasoning, and indeed all the faculties belonging to what we call the chief soul. For as regards the structure of the brain, the monkey, dog, horse, cat, and all quadrupeds which I have hitherto examined, and indeed all birds, and many kinds of fish, resemble man in almost every particular. (Foster, p. 258.)

---

[3] This and the following quotations are taken from Foster's translations. The page citation refers to that work.

The organs of sense and movement are affected by the "animal spirit" through the nerves.

Meanwhile, we will not too anxiously discuss whether the spirit is carried along certain hollow channels of the nerves, as the vital spirit is carried by the arteries, or as light passes through the air.   But in any case it is through the nerves that the influence of the brain is brought to bear on any part, so far I can certainly follow out the functions of the brain by means of vivisections, with great probability and indeed truth.   (Foster, p. 257.)

Vesalius had observed that by experimentally destroying a particular nerve the function of a particular muscle was abolished. And the last sentence in the foregoing quotation is significant to the history of reflex action since it emphasizes the conducting function of the nerves and the dominating influence of the brain.

DESCARTES

After Vesalius, the advances in biological science during the next century were rapid and dramatic. In the previous century, as we have seen, Vesalius had thrust aside the 1500 year-old canons of Galenic physiology and anatomy, and had substituted in their place his own observations of the structures of the human body; in 1628 Harvey had published the results of his observations of the circulation of the blood in living animals; but it remained for Descartes to formulate a statement which described the integrative activity of the animal in terms of automatic, self-acting mechanisms.

It has been pointed out that the agencies by means of which the animal is able to move were the particular objects of biological study in the 17th century. The application of the principles of the "new" physics and mechanics to the problems of muscle and nerve mark the beginnings of physiological psychology in the modern sense. The contributions of Borelli, Swammerdam, Glisson, Stenson, Mayow, and Willis indicate the gradual emergence from speculative obscurity of scientific conceptions of neuro-muscular action. René Descartes, more than any other man, is responsible for concepts of neuro-muscular function which are acceptable in their major outlines to present day physiologists. He had, says Brett (61), "the advantage of coming after Vesalius and being acquainted with the discovery of Harvey."

Although Descartes stands as the most important figure in the development of scientific thought since the Mediaeval period, he was primarily a systematist rather than an original investigator in the field of physiology. It was with the object of confirming a psycho-physical theory of man, that he made dissections and anatomical preparations. He made liberal use of the findings of others, and where attested knowledge was wanting, he did not, in the interests of his theory, hesitate to make assumptions as to structure and function.

Descartes was born in La Haye in Touraine in March, 1596.[4] He was educated in the Jesuit college at La Fleche in Anjou where he spent the years 1604 to 1612. He travelled widely in his youth, visiting Paris, Italy, Hungary, Germany and Holland. He settled in the latter country in 1629 when he was thirty-three years of age. He lived in Amsterdam, Utrecht, Egmond, and Leiden with an occasional visit to Paris. In 1649, at the invitation of Christina, Queen of Sweden, he went to Stockholm where he died on February 11, 1650, at the age of fifty-four years.

Of the four important publications appearing before Descartes' death,[5] the first ("Discourse on Method"), published when the author was forty-one years old, marks, according to Mahaffy (329), "an epoch in the history of human thought." The principal contributions to physiological psychology are contained in "The Passions of the Soul" (103), published in 1649 just before the author's death, and in the *Traité de l'Homme* (102) published in 1662. The latter is regarded by Garrison (162) as the first European text-book on physiology. It is also probably the first attempt to present systematically a coherent description of bodily responses in terms of actual—or hypothetical—neuro-muscular structures.[6] Although this work was not published until after Descartes' death, it was projected by the author in 1634 together with the treatise *On the Formation of the Foetus*.[7] The latter was published in 1664.

[4] The two biographies in English from which material for the present study was drawn are those of Mahaffy (329) and Haldane (192). The most important biography in French is that of Baillet (15), a contemporary of Descartes'. See also Foster *op. cit.*

[5] *The Discourse on Method* (1637), *Meditations* (1641), *Principles of Philosophy* (1644), and the *Passions of the Soul* (1649).

[6] This treatise is divided into five parts as follows: I. On the bodily machine. II. How the machine moves itself. III. On the exterior senses. IV. On the interior senses. V. On the structure of the cerebrum, how the spirits are distributed in order to cause movements and sensations.

[7] It is interesting to note that the time when Descartes was engaged in these physiological researches coincides with the birth of his daughter, Francine, (1635), the mother of whom is unknown. Mahaffy (329) has suggested that there is more than a coincidence in these events. He says, "It is not a little remarkable that this (1634) was the very year when he had peculiar opportunities of making 'observations' concerning the subject of the earliest development of man. There was born to him on the 19th of July, 1635, at Deventer, a daughter, the events of whose brief life he noted on the fly leaf of a book. 'Concepta fuit Amstelodami die Domini 15 Oct. 1634,'—that is to say, while he was specially engaged

AUTOMATIC ACTION

In order to comprehend Descartes' conception of neuro-muscular co-ordination, it is necessary to understand his theory of bodily automatism. Essentially, this theory holds that all motions of animals and man are dependent on the operations of bodily structures. The body acts as a machine and its motions are explicable in terms of the laws which govern all physical machines. Descartes had been impressed by the fountains in the royal gardens which were so constructed that, actuated by water, lay figures moved, made sounds, and played instruments. He conceived the animal body to be actuated on the same principle; instead of pipes and water there are nerves and animal spirits. This conception is made clear in the *Traité de l'Homme* in the following quotation.

> Now as these spirits enter thus into the cavities of the brain, so they pass thence into the pores of its substance and from these pores into the nerves. And according as they enter or even only as they tend to enter more or less into this or that nerve they have the power of changing the form of the muscle into which the nerve is inserted and by this means making the limbs move. You may have seen in the grottoes and fountains which are in our royal gardens that the simple force with which the water moves in issuing from its source is sufficient to put into motion various machines and even to set various instruments playing or to make them pronounce words according to the varied disposition of the tubes which convey the water.
>
> And, indeed, one may very well compare the nerves of the machine which I am describing with the tubes of the machines of these fountains, the muscles and tendons of the machine with the other various engines and springs which serve to move these machines and the animal spirits, the source of which is the heart and of which the ventricles are the reservoirs, with the water which puts them in motion.[8]

Breathing and other such acts depend upon the flow of spirits in the tubes in the same way that the water causes the mill to operate continuously. The effect of an external stimulus on bodily movements is also explained in purely mechanical terms.

> External objects, which by their mere presence act upon the organs of sense of the machine and which by this means determine it to move in several different ways according as the parts of the machine's brain are disposed, may be compared to strangers, who

---

with his physiological researches. . . . Is it possible that he carried his theory of *bêtes machines* a step higher than he confessed in publick, and that this adventure was merely the result of scientific curiosity?" pp. 63–64.

[8] Quoted by Foster (156) pp. 262–3. See also the Tannery edition (101) of Descartes' *Oeuvres, Traité de l'Homme*, vol. 11, p. 130 *ff*. The Tannery edition is the one used in the present translations. The writer is indebted to his colleague, Dr. E. L. Clark, for assistance with the English translation from the *Traité de l'Homme*.

entering into one of the grottoes containing many fountains, themselves cause, without knowing it, the movements which they witness. For in entering they necessarily tread on certain tiles or plates, which are so disposed that if they approach a bathing Diana, they cause her to hide in the rosebushes, and if they try to follow her, they cause a Neptune to come forward to meet them threatening them with his trident.

The *Traité de l'Homme* is a statement of how the human body *might* carry on its functions if it were a machine constructed according to known laws of mechanics. In the "Discourse on Method,"[9] Descartes was careful to note that even though such automata might be constructed which would in all respects simulate the actions and appearances of men, yet it would be possible by the application of "two very certain tests" to determine whether or not they were real men. In the first place, such automata could never use speech appropriately in order to reply to anything that might be said to them. In the second place, inasmuch as these machines do not act from knowledge but from "the disposition of their organs," they could act only in those situations for which they were prepared; that is, it would be "morally impossible that there should be sufficient diversity in any machine to allow it to act in all events of life in the same way as our reason causes us to act." By the application of these two tests it would be possible to distinguish between men who possess souls infused in them by the Deity, and brutes which are to be regarded as clock-like automata.

In a letter to the Marquis of Newcastle (484), Descartes says:

I know, indeed, that brutes do many things better than we do, but I am not surprised at it; for that, also, goes to prove that they act by force of nature and by springs, like a clock, which tells better what the hour is than our judgment can inform us. And, doubtless, when swallows come in the spring, they act in that like clocks. All that honey-bees do is of the same nature; and the order that cranes keep in flying, or monkeys drawn up for battle, if it be true that they observe any order, and finally, the instinct of burying their dead is no more surprising than that of dogs and cats, which scratch the ground to bury their excrements, although they almost never do bury them, which shows that they do it by instinct only, and not by thought . . . . if they [the brutes] should think as we do, they would have an immortal soul as well as we, which is not likely.

The soul in man acts through the bodily mechanisms, that is, the mind can only act indirectly on the body. The soul is located in the "little gland"—the pineal gland—in the center of the brain. At this point the mind, by special arrangement of the Deity, is in contact with the nervous system. The structure of the nerves is described in the following terms (*Traité de l'Homme*):

[9] Haldane Translation (103), I, p. 116 *ff.*

Notice that in each of these little tubes [the nerves] there is something like a marrow composed of several very thin threads (*filet*) which come from the very substance of the brain, and which terminate at one end on the inner side of the brain cavity and at the other end in the skin and flesh where the tubes containing them terminate. But, because this marrow does not serve at all in the movement of members, it is sufficient, for the present, that you know that it does not fill so much the tubes which contain it, as do the animal spirits which yet find here room enough to flow easily from the brain to the muscles, where these little tubes, which here must be considered as so many little nerves, are distributed.

Sensory action is explained by the action of these "delicate threads" which compose the marrow of the nerves. These threads are attached to the sensory organs at one end and to the "orifices of certain pores which exist on the internal surface of the brain" at the other. When the sensory organs are excited by external stimuli they cause a slight pull on these threads which opens the orifices in the brain and permits the animal spirits to flow towards the muscles. These processes were described by Descartes as follows:

In order to understand next how this machine can be incited by the external objects which strike upon its organs of sense to move in a thousand different ways all its members, remember that the little threads, of which I have already spoken so much, coming from the innermost part of the brain and composing the marrow of its nerve, are so placed in all of its parts which serve as sense organs that they can very easily be moved by the objects of its senses. And remember that whenever they are moved, no matter how little, they pull at the same instant the parts of the brain from whence they come, in this way opening the entrances to certain pores, which are on the internal surface of the brain. Through these pores the animal spirits, which are in the cavities, immediately take their course through the nerves to the muscles which serve to make movements in this machine very like unto those we are induced to make when our senses have been touched in the same way.

It is interesting to note that Descartes did not distinguish clearly between sensory and motor nerves, but believed that the nerve tubes both contained the "delicate threads" essential to sensory action and served as a canal through which the animal spirits were conducted to the muscles.

Motor action consisted in the inflation of the muscle by the animal spirits which were conducted to it by the nerve. This is made clear in the following passage:

For you know very well that these animal spirits, being like a wind or very fine flame, cannot fail to flow very quickly from one muscle to another as soon as they find a passageway; although there is no other power to move them excepting only their inclination to continue their movement, according to the laws of nature. And you know, besides this, that as long as they remain very mobile and fine, they do not lose the force to inflate

58   RENATI DES-CARTES

Ubi vero orificium pori feu parvi ductus *d e* ita apertum eft,
fpiritus animales ventriculi F eum ingrediuntur, & hac
via feruntur partim in mufculos, quibus pedem ab igne re-
trahimus, partim in eos quibus oculos & caput obvertimus,

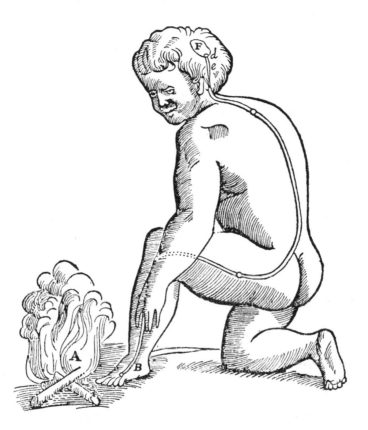

ut refpiciat ignem, & partim in eos quibus manum exten-
dimus, totumque corpus ad ejus defenfionem inflectimus.
Verum fpiritus animales per eundem ductum *d e* etiam
in plures alios mufculos deduci poffunt. Et priufquam ex-
actius explicare aggrediar, qua ratione fpiritus animales per
poros

and make rigid the muscles in which they are enclosed: this happens just as the air in a balloon hardens it and stretches the skins which contain it.

The problem of simultaneous relaxation and contraction of antagonistic muscles, e.g., the coordination of the internal and external recti which turn the eyeball, was explained by assuming the existence of valved channels between the opposing muscles through which the animal spirits were conducted from one to the other. These valves were so arranged that, for example, the inflation of muscle a made impossible the inflation of muscle b and at the same time permitted the spirits of muscle b to flow into muscle a.

In the Traité de l'Homme Descartes has reproduced a kneeling human figure near a fire. In this drawing he has diagrammed the assumed nervous channel from the foot to the brain and described the neuro-muscular events which occur when the foot is withdrawn from the fire.

If, for example, fire comes near the foot, the minute particles of this fire which, as you know, move with great velocity have the power to set in motion the spot of skin of the foot which they touch, and by this means pulling upon the delicate thread which is attached to the spot of skin, they open up at the same instant the pore against which the delicate thread ends, just as by pulling at one end of a rope one causes to strike at the same instant a bell which hangs on the other end. When this pore is opened the animal spirits of the cavity enter into the tube and are carried by it partly to the muscles which pull back the foot from the fire, partly to those which turn the eyes and the head in order to regard it, and partly to those which serve to advance the hands and to bend the whole body in order to shield itself.

Thus we have a more or less complete account of an integrated sensori-motor adjustment expressed in purely mechanical terms and unaccompanied by consciousness. Consciousness appeared when a beneficent Deity equipped man with a soul which could modify bodily action only through the agency of the animal spirits.

The response of the neuro-muscular system to stimulation is dependent upon "six different sorts of circumstances," as follows: (1) The particular sense organ which, by means of the small threads, releases the animal spirits in the brain. (2) The intensity or force of this releasing action. (3) The arrangement of the little threads which compose the substance of the brain, that is, the arrangement may be either "natural" (native) or acquired. (4) The unequal strength possessed by the different parts of the spirits which may be a factor in determining their course. (5) The diverse situation of the exterior members. (6) The organization by means of which co-ordinated action is possible, e.g., walking.[10]

[10] Traité de l'Homme, Oeuvres, vol. 11

In the above list the third item is of particular interest, since it suggests a distinction which is of significance to modern psychology. By the "innate" arrangement of fibres in the brain, Descartes meant that "God had so disposed" them that the animal spirits are sent "toward all the nerves whither they should go in order to cause the same movements in this machine towards which a similar action could excite us following the instincts of our nature."

ANIMAL SPIRITS

The animal spirits, according to Descartes, were a very powerful but subtle fluid, wholly unique, but subject to physical law. Its function was to link the soul with the body, and to inflate the muscles to which it was carried by the nerves. This fluid was distilled from the blood and stored in the brain.

The processes by means of which the food is converted into blood and eventually into animal spirits, occurs in the stomach, liver and brain. It consists essentially in breaking up the food into finer and finer particles. In the heart the blood is expanded and dilated by the "fire without light" which this organ was supposed to contain. From here the "most active, strongest and finest parts of the blood go to the cavities of the brain," at which point it is converted into animal spirits. This refining process was described as follows:

As regards the particles of the blood which reach the brain, they serve not alone to nourish and support its substance, but principally to produce there a certain very quick wind, or rather a very active and pure fire that has been named animal spirits. Now it is necessary to know that the arteries, which carry them from the heart, after being divided into an infinite number of small branches and after composing these little tissues, which are stretched out like a tapestry at the bottom of the cavities of the brain, are assembled around a certain little gland, situated approximately in the middle of the brain substance, at the entrance of these cavities. The arteries have in this place a large number of little holes through which the finest particles of the blood can flow to this gland but which are so narrow that they do not allow the larger particles to pass. . . . . Thus it is easy to see that, as the largest particles go straight up to the external surface of the brain to serve as nourishment, they are the cause for the smallest and most active particles of the blood to turn aside and enter that gland which may be imagined as a very abundant fountain from which these particles simultaneously flow from all sides into the cavity of the brain. And thus without other preparation or change, except that they are separated from the largest particles and that they still retain that extreme swiftness of motion which the heart has given them, they cease to have the form of blood and are called animal spirits.

In addition to an anatomy the details of which were largely imaginary, Descartes committed himself to two major errors in his analyses of neuromuscular function; his "animal spirits" hypothesis, and his conception that the muscle increased in bulk, *i.e.*, it was inflated by the animal spirits, during contraction. He seems to have been in ignorance of the work of his contemporary, the Dutch naturalist Jan Swammerdam,[11] who attacked the problems of neuro-muscular action experimentally, and was able to demonstrate the inadequacy of both the animal spirits and the muscle-inflation hypotheses.

REFLEX ACTION

Descartes is usually credited with making the first descriptive statement of involuntary action which bears a recognizable resemblance to the modern concept of reflex action.[12] Such a concept is implicit, of course, in his hypothesis of the automatism of brutes. The actual use of the word reflex in connection with the action of the nervous system occurs in the following passage, in the "Passions of the Soul."

For in certain persons that [previous associations] disposes the brain in such a way that the spirits reflected from the image thus formed in the gland proceed thence to take their places partly in the nerves which serve to turn the back and dispose the legs for flight, and partly in those which so increase or diminish the orifices of the heart, or at least which so agitate the other parts from whence the blood is sent to it, that this blood being there rarefied in a different manner from usual, sends to the brain the spirits which are adapted for the maintenance and strengthening of the passion of fear, *i.e.*, which are adapted to the holding open, or at least re-opening, of the pores of the brain which conduct them into the same nerves. (Article XXXVI.)

The following excerpt from "Objections and Replies"[13] (Reply to Objection IV), makes clear the mechanical nature of this type of action.

But the greater part of our motions do not depend on the mind at all. Such are the beating of the heart, the digestion of our food, nutrition, respiration when we are asleep, and even walking, singing, and similar acts when we are awake, if performed without the mind attending to them. When a man in falling thrusts out his hand to save his head he does that without his reason counselling him so to act, but merely because the sight of the impending fall penetrating to his brain, drives the animal spirits into the nerves in the manner necessary for this motion, and for the producing it without the mind's desiring it, and as though it were the working of a machine.

The same idea is found again in the following ("The Passions of the Soul," Article XIII).

[11] See Chapter III for a discussion of Swammerdam's contributions, also Fearing (142).

[12] Descartes is usually credited with the "discovery" of reflex action. It is, perhaps, more accurate to say that he was the first to publish a systematic discussion of the phenomena of involuntary action.

[13] See Haldane translation (103).

To follow this example it is easy to conceive how sounds, scents, tastes, heat, pain, hunger, thirst and generally speaking all objects of our other external senses as well as of our internal appetites, also excite some movements in our nerves which by their means pass to the brain; and in addition to the fact that these diverse movements of the brain cause diverse perceptions to become evident to our soul, they can, also, without it cause the spirits to take their course towards certain muscles rather than towards others, and thus to move our limbs, which I shall prove here by one example only. If someone quickly thrusts his hand against our eyes as if to strike us, even though we know him to be our friend, that he only does it in fun, and that he will take great care not to hurt us, we have all the same trouble in preventing ourselves from closing them; and this shows that it is not by the intervention of our soul that they close, seeing that it is against our will, which is its only, or at least its principal activity; but it is because the machine of our body is so formed that the movement of this hand towards our eyes excites another movement in our brain, which conducts the animal spirits into the muscles which cause the eyelids to close.

The reflex type of response cannot be directly controlled by the will, according to Descartes, although it may be indirectly modified by the action of the soul. The following passage from the "Passions of the Soul" is quite remarkable in its agreement with modern interpretations. Descartes is dicussing the dilation of the pupil with far fixation.

At the same time it is not always the desire [volition] to excite in us some movement, or bring about some result which is able so to excite it, for this changes according as nature or custom have diversely united each movement of the gland to each particular thought. Thus, for example, if we wish to adjust our eyes so that they may look at an object very far off, this desire causes their pupils to enlarge; and if we wish to set them to look at an object very near, this desire causes them to contract; but if we think only of enlarging the pupil of the eye we may have the desire indeed, but we cannot for all that enlarge it, because nature has not joined the movements of the gland which serves to thrust forth the spirits towards the optic nerve, in the manner requisite for enlarging or diminishing the pupil, with the desire to enlarge or diminish it, but only with that of looking at objects which are far away or near. (Article XLIV.)

Descartes was concerned primarily with the analogy between mechanical and physiological action. Brett (61) observes that Descartes saw only the points of resemblance between the reflection of light, reflux of water and reflex action, while a modern neurologist would see chiefly the absence of such resemblance. Included under the Cartesian concept were such activities as breathing, singing, walking, swallowing, yawning, bodily accompaniments of emotion, eye movements, intra-ocular adjustments, excretory actions, protective responses to external stimuli, postural responses, etc.,—actions which involve a considerable degree of integrative complexity.

Huxley, who regarded Descartes as a physiologist of the first rank, summarized (247) the latter's contributions to the physiology of the nervous system as follows: (1) The brain was established as the organ of sensation, thought and emotion. (2) Muscular motion is due to change in the form of the muscles which in turn is due to motion of the substance contained in the nerve which goes to the muscle. (3) Sensation is due to change in the substance of the nerves which connect the sense organs with the brain. (4) Reflection of motion from a sensory into a motor nerve may take place without volition or even contrary to it. (5) Motion of the matter in the brain occasioned by the sensory nerve leaves behind a disposition to move again in the same way.[14] While we may not, perhaps, be able to echo Huxley's enthusiastic estimate of Descartes as a physiologist, the significance of the foregoing list of contributions cannot be denied. They had a profound influence upon the attempts of those who followed Descartes to deal with the problems of animal adjustment. Not all of these findings were original with Descartes, but he was responsible for their expression in lucid and systematic form.

With the example of Galileo before him, Descartes had every reason to be extremely cautious in dealing with those topics on which the Mother Church might be expected to be sensitive. He described how the animal body might behave if it were a machine acting in accordance with the known laws of physics and mechanics. In man he retained the soul which through the mediation of the animal spirits could influence and be influenced by the body. He observed, however, that many of the adjustmental activities of the human body could be carried on independently of the soul.

The recognition of the importance of these automatic activities and the principle of reflex action, together with the concept of animal action as dependent upon and explainable in terms of the laws of physical mechanisms, constitute Descartes' major contributions to physiological psychology.

See the *Passions of the Soul*, Article XLII.

CHAPTER III

The 17th Century

"Nor is there here any occasion for a great parade of words to demonstrate the absolute necessity of diligently examining things in themselves; for if our justest reasonings ought to terminate in experiments, to be built upon experiments, and pursue the course prescribed us by experiments, who is there, that would not, in forming his judgement of things, much rather trust to experience, than to the idle fancies of his imagination; nay, I may ask, who will hereafter dare to affirm, that we may depend upon our reason alone, to come at the knowledge of every kind of truth? whereas it is most certain, that by making a proper use of our senses, we may from the things we see, gather sufficient information concerning those that we cannot."—JAN SWAMMERDAM, *Remarks Concerning the Experimental Method*, *The Book of Nature*, 1680 (?).

THE EXPERIMENTALISTS

When, at the beginning of the 17th century, William Harvey found it "absolutely necessary to conclude that the blood in the animal's body is impelled in a circle, and is in a state of ceaseless motion,"[1] he not only demonstrated a principle of enormous importance to physiology, but with one blow demolished the structure, compounded of metaphysics, far-fetched analogy, and mysterious "principles" and "spirits," which constituted the method of mediaeval biology. He showed without appeal to any outside agency or principle, that an important bodily function might be made intelligible in terms of its own mechanisms and, furthermore, he affirmed these conclusions as true, not by appeal to authority, but because *no other conclusions were possible in the face of the observations he had made.*

The rigorous experimental methods of Harvey, characterized as they were by the rigid exclusion of mysterious forces and agencies, were not at once adopted by his contemporaries. Descartes rejected Harvey's conclusions regarding the circulation of the blood, and, as we have seen, the Cartesian method as indicated in *Traité de l'Homme*, was that of the systematist rather than the patient experimentalist. It was Descartes' purpose to present a complete picture of animal behavior in terms of neuro-muscular functions. In order to do this he supplemented the meagre store of facts

---

[1] *Vide* Foster, *op. cit.*, p. 47 for a translation of this passage.

regarding neural anatomy which were available at his time by the liberal use of logical hypotheses. In his exposition he did not distinguish between these hypotheses and the facts established by observation. The picture presented had the merit of being satisfyingly complete, but it was one which could hardly be acceptable to a group of investigators schooled by Vesalius and Harvey. It is not surprising, then, that there should appear in the second half of the 17th century critics of Descartes' conceptions of neuro-muscular action. Of these we shall speak later.

THE IATRO-PHYSICISTS AND THE IATRO-CHEMISTS

There appeared during the 17th century two more or less distinct points of view regarding the nature of bodily processes. Those who were primarily influenced by Harvey interpreted bodily functions in terms of mechanical or physical processes. This school—sometimes called the iatro-physical school—conceived the body as being governed by the laws of mechanics and physics. They expressed in the field of biology the ideas of the "new" physics, optics and mechanics as these sciences were developed by Galileo, Kepler, and Newton.

Representing an older tradition, the so-called iatro-chemical school interpreted bodily operations in terms of fermentative processes. This chemical physiology was applied to the phenomena of digestion, respiration, circulation, neuro-muscular action, etc. The activities of this school seem to have been carried on for a time more or less independently of the investigations of the anatomists and physicists. Indeed, there is no reference to chemical processes in any of Vesalius' work, and it is probable that that forthright anatomist would have been scornful of such occult and mysterious phenomena.[2] Although the origins of this school lie in mediaeval alchemy, it is not until the 16th century that there appears anything in the nature of a chemical physiology.

The distinctions between these two points of view are not clear cut at every point. They tend to diverge from one another most markedly in connection with the interpretation of the phenomena of digestion and the nature of the processes in the nerve and muscle. It is the latter consideration which concerns us here. The doctrine of animal spirits and the phenomena of muscular contraction were interpreted by the iatro-chemical school in terms of processes analogous to fermentation and effervescence. The iatro-physical school, on the other hand, took a purely physical or mechanical view of these events.

---

[2] *Cf.* Foster *op. cit.*, p. 122 *ff.* In Lecture V Foster discusses the iatro-chemical school, in Lecture III the iatro-physical school. *Cf.* Brett (61), II, p. 188 *ff.*

The chemical school begins with the erratic and picturesque genius of the 16th century, Theophrastus Bombast von Hohenheim, called Paracelsus (1490–1541). This man, one of the founders of modern chemistry, seems to have been in conflict with his medical brethren on the question of the relation of chemistry to the orthodox medical teachings of the time. He postulated that all physiological processes were primarily chemical, governed by the *archaei*. These *archaei* were conceived to be spiritual in nature, "the chief *archaeus* being that exalted invisible spirit, that occult virtue which is the artificer of nature in everyone."[3] These ideas brought him into conflict with the teachings of Galen and the orthodox anatomy of the time.

Paracelsus plays but a minor rôle in the history of reflex action. There was born, however, thirty-six years after his death, a man who was profoundly influenced by the half occult and half scientific ideas of Paracelsus, and at the same time was a follower of the physical and mathematical learning of the 17th century. This man was Jean Baptiste van Helmont (1577–1644). Van Helmont died sixteen years after the publication of Harvey's great work, which he does not seem to have accepted, and six years before the death of Descartes, whose ideas he seems to echo. Like Descartes, van Helmont separates the activities of the soul from the operations of the animal spirits and neuro-muscular mechanisms, but unlike Descartes he locates the soul in the pylorus, in the orifice of the stomach.

A significant aspect of van Helmont's physiological conceptions (215) was his theory of *gas* and *blas*.[4] By the former he meant carbon dioxide and by the latter he seems to have had reference to the *archaei* of Paracelsus. He designated by *blas* the various immaterial agencies which he believed presided over physical processes. There was, for example, a *blas meteoron* which governed the heavens, a *blas humanum* which governed the human body, a *blas motivum* which presided over bodily movement. The *blas motivum* was divided into the *blas* which governed voluntary movement and the *blas* which governed natural movements. Like Descartes and those before him, van Helmont maintained that the animal spirits were responsible for muscular action. These spirits were produced at one stage of digestion —the fifth—when the blood in the arteries was changed into the vital (animal) spirits of the *archaeus*.

Van Helmont taught that the "sensitive soul," which was seated in the pylorus, was capable of sensation and movement by means of the brain and nerves. This sensitive soul was possessed by man alone. The plants and

---

[3] Quoted by Foster, *op. cit.*, p. 127.
[4] *Cf.* Foster, p. 133 *ff.*

brutes possessed a "certain vital power, which we may perhaps regard as the forerunner of a soul."[5]

Francois De le Boe (Franciscus Sylvius) (1614–1672) was an intellectual success or of van Helmont and a man of quite different temperament. Where van Helmont was mystical and occult, Sylvius was objective and scientific. Sylvius, like van Helmont, regarded the phenomena of the human body as explainable in terms of chemical processes, but he was unable to accept the immaterial spiritual agencies which his predecessor maintained were in control of these chemical processes.

With the exception of van Helmont's distinction between voluntary and natural movements, which, of course, was not a new distinction, there is little in either van Helmont or Sylvius which contributes directly to the history of reflex action. Their work, however, dealing as it does with the essential nature of the processes within the nerve, muscle and brain, furnishes a background against which later and more exact concepts may be contrasted.

The points of emphasis of the iatro-chemical school which with Sylvius had shifted in the direction of objective experimental science, returned to the conceptions of van Helmont with the advent of Stahl. George Ernest Stahl (1660–1734) was born at Anspach, graduated at Jena, and became Professor of Medicine at Halle. He is the author of the famous phlogiston theory and the founder of modern animistic and vitalistic theories. Stahl believed that between living and non-living things there is a great gap. The former are controlled by an immaterial agent, the sensitive soul. The processes of living bodies resemble only superficially the chemical processes observed in the laboratory among non-living things. The chemical processes in the living body are governed, and *all parts* of the animal body are pervaded by the sensitive soul. This conception of the sensitive soul is in direct opposition to the rational soul of Descartes. In fact, the whole Cartesian conception of automatic action is rejected by Stahl, who believed that the soul was in direct control of all types of bodily action. The following quotation makes this clear.

Vital activities are directly administered and exercised by the soul itself, and are truly organic acts carried out in corporeal instruments by a superior acting cause, in order to bring about certain effects, which are not only in general certain, and in particular necessary, but also in each and every particular adapted, in a special and yet most complete manner, to the needs of the moment and to the various irregularities introduced by accidental external causes. Vital activities, vital movements, cannot, as some recent crude

---

[5] Quoted by Foster, *op. cit.*, p. 143.

CLAUDE PERRAULT,
de l'Academie Royale des Sciences.

speculations suppose, have any real likeness to such movements as, in an ordinary way depend on the material condition of a body and take place without any direct use or end or aim. (Foster, p. 170.)

A forerunner of Stahl was the medical man and architect, Claude Perrault (1613–1688). He published in 1680 his *Essai de Physique* in which the problems of both plant and animal movements are discussed in some detail. He pointed out that, although the movements of plants in turning towards the sun, and the flowing of the river which "seems to seek the valley," appear to indicate choice and desire, in reality these movements are of a wholly different nature than those of animals. In the latter there is a soul which is concerned with sensation and movement. It was necessary for Perrault to consider how it is possible for the soul to be aware of all the movements of the body, especially those internal activities which appear to be imperceptible. He solves this difficulty by assuming two types or levels of movement and consciousness; a clear consciousness which occupies itself with external objects, and a less clear awareness which is concerned with internal states. Perrault discussed (403) the problem in the following terms:

Mais cette difficulté se peut resoudre par l'hypothese, qu'il faut nécessairement faire dans les Animaux de deux connaissances differentes; dont l'une qui s'occupe aux choses de dehors, est claire, expresse & distincte; dont l'autre, qui est employée sur ce que se fait au dedans, est obscure & confuse, l'animal n'y donnant pas d'attention, comme il fait aux choses de dehors, à cause que l'habitude, qu'il a contractée de faire toujours les mêmes choses, lui donne une facilité que l'exempte des soins & de l'application, qu'il faut nécessairement donner aux choses de dehors, qu'il est nécessaire d'examiner pour n'être pas surpris en n'évitant pas les choses nuisibles, on manquant à prendre celles qui conviennent. (p. 519)

We have here a theory which resembles the doctrine of Perrault's contemporary, Leibnitz (1646–1716). The unconscious or unnoticed perceptions of Leibnitz represent from the point of view of metaphysics that which Perrault attempted to establish from the point of view of physiology. For Perrault, then, there are the two types of movement, the *obscur* and the *manifeste*. The former includes the vegetative and intra-organic processes e.g., digestive processes, which modern physiology regards as reflex. From the point of view of Perrault, both were equally under the control of the soul, although the one, through habit, had become unconscious. This species of animism was to appear again in the 18th century neuro-physiology in spite of the Cartesian doctrine of animal automatism and the increasing amount of evidence from experimental neurology.

The explanation of the animal spirits in terms of chemical processes received its most elaborate statement at the hands of John Mayow (1645–

1679).   Mayow was born in London in the year van Helmont died.   He was
educated at Oxford University in law but seems to have found his major
interest in scientific research.   At the age of twenty-five he published a

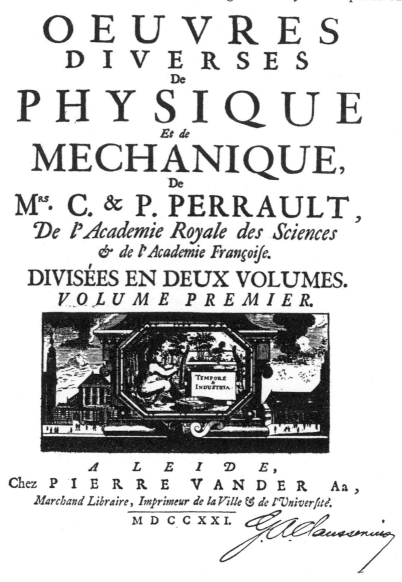

OEUVRES
DIVERSES
De
PHYSIQUE
Et de
MECHANIQUE,
De
M^{rs}. C. & P. PERRAULT,
De l'Academie Royale des Sciences
& de l'Academie Françoise.
DIVISÉES EN DEUX VOLUMES.
VOLUME PREMIER.

A   LEIDE,
Chez PIERRE VANDER Aa,
Marchand Libraire, Imprimeur de la Ville & de l'Université.
MDCCXXI.

TITLE PAGE OF PERRAULT'S WORK

series of four treatises (344) which contain his theory of nitro-aerial spirits. The fourth of these tracts is devoted to muscular motion and animal spirits.

It was Mayow's conception that the air which surrounds us "is impregnated with a certain universal salt, of a nitro-saline nature, that is to say with a vital, fiery and in the highest degree fermentative spirit."[6] These nitro-saline particles are received in the lungs by the act of breathing and there they are separated from the air and introduced into the blood. Here these particles are mixed with the "salino-sulphurous particles of the blood" and they "excite in it a needed fermentation." The nitro-aerial spirits are identical with animal spirits. In the treatise on muscular motion this identity is described as follows:

> For, indeed, nitro-aerial particles seem in a high degree to fit the character of animal spirits, inasmuch as they are very subtle, elastic, and agile. For nitro-aerial particles are suited for entering on very rapid and igneous motion, as we have elsewhere shown. The animal spirits are also of this sort: they pass in a moment through the filaments of the nerves, although they have no visible cavity; and brought at last to the muscles, cause their instantaneous contraction by their own most rapid motion. (p. 252.)

The nitro-aerial spirits are not to be confused with the sensitive soul, which consists of a "special subtle and ethereal matter,"[7] and of which the nitro-aerial spirits serve as the chief instrument. These spirits when brought at last to the muscles unite with the "salino-sulphureous" particles of the blood and "excite an effervescence" which results in contraction.

The nitro-aerial particles, which are received into the blood from the air in the lungs, are separated from it by the meninges which surround the brain. These membranes drive the nitro-aerial particles (animal spirits) into the brain and from thence into the nervous system.[8]

In other words the animal spirits are introduced into the nervous system *via* the brain, and it follows that when the structure is eliminated the supply of activating spirits is cut off. This conclusion is of some consequence to Mayow's theory of neuro-muscular action.

> I think we must allow that the animal spirits in the more perfect animals are elaborated only in the brain, and that they are disseminated from that source to the spinal marrow and to the nerves originating in it; whence it comes about that if the head of such animals is removed, the influx of animal spirits into the spinal marrow is altogether shut off, so that the parts of the decapitated body at once collapse and are deprived of animal motion. (p. 254.)

---

[6] Quoted by Foster, *op. cit.*, p. 186.

[7] *Vide* Mayow, *op. cit.*, p. 259 *ff.*

[8] *Ibid.*, p. 260.

The exceptions to the above rule are found in the case of insects and other "less perfect animals." In these animals it had been noted that movements continued after the head had been removed. Mayow makes the following observations regarding the movements of these mutilated animals:

> But in less perfect animals, such as insects, whose cut-off parts live, the animal spirits are primarily and immediately prepared, not only in the brain but also in the protuberances of the spinal marrow, as it were in so many cerebelli extended through the whole length of the spinal marrow, or rather they are stored as in suitable repositories; and hence it comes to pass that in the cut-off portions of insects, the animal spirits are supplied, for keeping up to some extent life and motion, from the small piece of spinal marrow connected with each portion. (p. 254.)

These statements are highly significant for the history of reflex action. They indicate a recognition of the relative independence of the segments of the nervous system so far as the control of adjacent parts of the organism is concerned. The continued life and motion of headless animals was observed by certain of Mayow's contemporaries of whom we shall shortly speak, but the most convincing experimental demonstration of the relative independence of the nervous segments did not occur until the following century.

In van Helmont, Sylvius, Stahl and Mayow we have a group of men of widely different temperaments, training, and philosophy. Their contributions to neuro-muscular physiology were indirect. They recognized the importance of the brain, spinal cord, and nerves as the essential agencies in the production of animal movement, but their pre-occupation with the nature of "animal spirits" in relation to the mechanisms of control prevented the consideration of the problems of reflex action as such. They assumed that muscular movement depended upon the inflation of the muscle by the animal spirits, which were conveyed to it through the nerves. A possible exception to this point of view was the conclusion of Mayow who seems to have considered the contraction of the muscle to be the result of the chemical combination of the nitro-aerial particles with certain elements already present in the blood of the muscle. These conclusions were reached as the result of a process of reasoning by analogy rather than direct observation. It is to this failure to apply the method of experimentation, that we may attribute in part the lack of progress in the field of neuro-muscular processes which characterized the work of van Helmont and others of this group. In the generalization of Mayow regarding the continued movements of portions of the body after the experimental removal of the brain, we have a significant exception to the foregoing statement. It should be remembered, however, that Mayow did not include the human organism in his generalization, and that he still held a highly speculative conception of the processes in the nerve. Nevertheless we should not minimize the importance of his observation for the history of reflex action, and the ingeniousness of his interpretations.

We may now turn back to a man whose contributions were in striking contrast to those which we have been considering. Francis Glisson (1597–1677) was an Englishman who seems to have been influenced by the work of Harvey. He was a graduate of Cambridge University and one of the founders of the Royal Society. In 1634 he received the degree of Doctor of Medicine, but it was not until the latter part of his life that he published (171) the results of his investigations in the field of neuro-muscular physiology.

Glisson is credited with the first statement of the theory of "irritability." This theory is so general in its implications that Verworn (503) regards Glisson as the founder of general physiology. Glisson believed that animal tissue possessed an inherent property of irritability which manifested itself by the appearance of movement whenever stimulated by external agencies. Stimuli may reach the irritable structures by three different means: (1) stimuli applied directly to the tissue, termed *perceptio naturalis*, (2) excitation in the intact body by way of the sensory nerves, termed *perceptio sensitiva*, and (3) excitation from inner stimuli proceeding from the brain, called *perceptio ab appetitu animali regulata*.[9] In connection with (1) Glisson had noted that the intestines and muscles when removed from the body immediately after death may be stimulated to movement by the application of corrosive fluids and by cold.

Glisson distinguished between *perceptio* and *sensatio*: the former is not sensation, which may arise only through the intervention of the nerves and the brain. Glisson's irritability hypothesis was largely of a speculative nature—the concept of irritability did not take concrete form until the work of Haller, nearly a hundred years later.

It was to the processes in nerve and muscle that Glisson applied direct observation with the result that the hypothesis that the muscle was inflated by the transmission to it of animal spirits, was shown to be inadequate. His description of the experiment in *De Ventriculo* is quoted by Foster as follows:

But indeed this explosion and inflation of spirits has now for some time past been silenced, convicted by the following experiment. Take an oblong glass tube of suitable capacity and shape. Fit into the top of its side near its mouth another small tube like a

---

[9] *Cf.* Verworn (503), pp. 3–4.

funnel. Let a strong muscular man insert into the mouth of the larger tube the whole of his bared arm, and secure the mouth of the tube all round to the humerus with bandages so that no water can escape from the tube. Then pour water through the funnel until the whole of the larger tube is completely filled, and some water rises up into the funnel. This being done, now tell the man alternately to contract and powerfully to relax the muscles of his arm. It will be seen that when the muscles are contracted the water in the tube of the funnel sinks, rising again when relaxation takes place. From which it is clear that the muscles are not inflated or swollen at the time that they are contracting, but on the contrary are lessened, shrunk, and subsided. For if they were inflated the water in the tubule so far from sinking would rise. From this therefore we may infer that the fibres are shortened by an intrinsic vital movement and have no need of any abundant afflux of spirits, either animal or vital, by which they are inflated, and being so shortened carry out the movements ordered by the brain. (Foster, p. 290)

By proving experimentally that the muscle did not increase in bulk during contraction,[10] Glisson was one of the earliest to show the inadequacy of the animal spirits hypothesis in the interpretation of nerve-muscle phenomena.

The iatro-physical school, as we have pointed out, explained the processes in the nerve and muscle from the point of view of mechanics and mathematics. Giovanni Alfonso Borelli (1608–1679) represents this point of view, and, like Glisson, took an agnostic view of the alleged capacity of animal spirits or other immaterial agencies to bring about muscular movement. Borelli was born at Naples and seems to have been largely self-taught. He occupied the Chair of Mathematics of the University of Pisa. He knew many of the learned men of his day including Galileo, Malpighi, and Torricelli. Although primarily a mathematician and physicist, Borelli devoted the last years of his life to writing his great work (54) on animal motion (*De Motu Animalium*), which was published after the author's death in 1680.

In this work Borelli deals with the problems of muscular action from the point of view of mechanics and mathematics. He rejects the conception that the muscle is activated by an incorporeal agency or by air. He seems to regard the processes in the muscle during contraction as chemical in nature. His description of these events is as follows:

Since all muscles, with some few exceptions, do not manifest vital movement otherwise than in obedience to the will, since the commands of the will are not transmitted from the brain which is the instrument of the sensitive, and the seat of the motive soul, by any other channels that the nerves as all confess and as the most decided experiments show, and since the action of any incorporeal agency or of spirituous gases must be rejected, it is clear that some corporeal substance must be transmitted along the nerves to the muscles or else some commotion must be communicated along some substance in the nerves, in such a way that a very powerful inflation can be brought about in the twinkling of an eye.

---

[10] Swammerdam demonstrated this fact before Glisson. *Vide infra* p. 48.

And since the inflation, hardening, and contraction do not take place in the channels which serve for bringing them about and in which the motor influence resides, namely, in the nerves themselves, but takes place outside the nerve, namely, in the muscles, it is evident that the substance or the influence which the nerves transmit is not taken by itself alone sufficient to bring about that inflation. It is necessary, therefore, that something else must be added, something which is to be found in the muscles themselves, or that in the muscles there is some adequate disposition of material so that on the arrival of the influence transmitted by the nerves there takes place something like a fermentation or ebullition, by which the sudden inflation of the muscle is brought about. (Foster, pp. 74–75)

The nerves, Borelli conceived to be canals filled with pith through which the "spirituous juice of the brain" may be transmitted. The action of this juice (*succus nerveus*) is *wholly mechanical* and subject to the laws of physics and chemistry.

. . . . if one of the extremities of the nerve fibre be compressed or pushed, or struck or pinched, forthwith the commotion and concussion or undulation ought to be communicated right to the other end. . . . .
Hence it follows that the fibres or spongy ducts of certain nerves turgid with the spirituous juice can be shaken or pinched by that gentle motion of the spirits by which the acts of the command of the will are in the brain carried out, and then, by concussing the whole length of the nerve through the convulsive irritation, can squeeze out and discharge from their extreme orifices some spirituous droplets into the appropriate muscle, whence the ebullition and explosion follow by which the muscle is contracted and rendered tense. (Foster, pp. 282–283.)

The same chain of events holds also for the sensory portion.

And on the other hand when the extremities of the sensory nerves which end in the skin, nose, ears or eyes, are compressed or struck or titillated, it necessarily follows that forthwith the concussion, undulation, or titillation of the spirituous juice contained within the tubules is conveyed along the whole length of the nerve and reaches the particular part of the brain to which the nerve fibres are joined. (Foster, p. 283.)

Thus we have an explanation of the series of events which underlie sensation and motion which is based on the laws of physics.

Nicolaus Stenson (1638–1686), a Danish contemporary of Borelli, was also a brilliant member of the iatro-physical school. Like Borelli, Stenson was skeptical regarding the doctrine of animal spirits. The references of his contemporaries to the "vapours of the blood," the "juice of the nerves," he regarded as merely "words, meaning nothing."[11] The substance of this fluid, he said, "is unknown to us, so is its movement undetermined, since

[11] *Cf.* Foster, *op. cit.*, p. 284.

neither by sure reasoning nor by experiment has it been ascertained whence it comes, whither it tends, where on its departure it betakes itself."[12]

The critical attitude of the iatro-physicists towards the doctrine of animal spirits was in conflict with the conceptions of Descartes. Stenson in a lecture, published in 1668, (466) delivered in Paris at the house of M. Thévenot, on the anatomy of the brain, took occasion to criticise the anatomical conceptions of Descartes.

M. Descartes knew too well how imperfect an history we have of the human body, to attempt an exposition of its true structure; and accordingly, in his *Tractatus de Homine*, his design is only to explain a machine capable of performing all the functions done by man. Some of his friends have indeed expressed themselves on this subject differently from him; but it is evident from the beginning of that work, that he intended no more than what I have said; and in this sense, it may justly be said that M. Descartes has gone beyond all the other philosophers. He is the only person who has explained all the human actions, and especially those of the brain. The other philosophers describe to us the human body itself. M. Descartes speaks only of a machine but in such a manner, as to convince us of the insufficiency of all that had been said before him, and to teach us a method of inquiring into the uses of the parts with the same evidence with which he demonstrates the parts of his machine called a man, which none had done before him.

We must not, therefore, condemn M. Descartes, though his system of the brain should not be found altogether agreeable to experience; his excellent genius, which shines nowhere more than in his *Tractatus de Homine*, casts a veil over the mistakes of his hypotheses, especially since even Vesalius himself, and other anatomists of the first rank, are not altogether free from such mistakes. And since we can forgive these great men their errors, who passed the greatest part of their lives in dissecting, why should not Descartes meet with the same indulgence, who has happily employed his time in other speculations. . . . . I find myself obliged to point out some parts of his system, without relating the whole, in which they must see, if they have a mind to be instructed, the vast difference there is between Descartes' imaginary machine, and the real machine of the human body.[13]

It will be observed that both the iatro-chemists and iatro-physicists were unable to accept the Cartesian doctrines of neuro-muscular phenomena. The iatro-chemists, at least as represented by Stahl, objected to Descartes' theory of animal automatism, since from the Stahlian point of view the sensitive soul pervades and directly governs every part of the organism. The iatro-physicists, on the other hand, took exception to the accuracy of Descartes' anatomy. Between Borelli and Descartes there was much in common, and as Brett (61) has suggested,[14] a reconciliation might have been possible, but between Descartes and Stahl there was complete opposition.

[12] *Ibid.*, pp. 284–5.
[13] Quoted in Stirling (472), pp. 31–2. Translation is from *Winslow's Works* by G. Douglas.
[14] *Op. cit.*, II, p. 195.

In both the iatro-physical and iatro-chemical schools there was but little attempt to correlate the outer phenomena of integrated behavior with neuro-muscular processes. It was just such a correlation that constituted the unique aspect of Descartes' contribution to neuro-muscular physiology and the history of reflex action. Descartes observed certain total *acts* of the organism and attempted to explain their neuro-muscular basis.

We have seen how in the case of the iatro-chemists, the pendulum had swung from the method, exemplified by Harvey, of precise reasoning from experimental observations. Glisson, Borelli, and Stenson, on the other hand, although filled with a wholesome respect for the value of direct observation, were unable wholly to escape the metaphysical bias of their contemporaries in the field of neuro-muscular physiology. We now turn to a man whose contributions in this field exemplify the rigorous experimental method of Harvey, and the range of whose scientific interests approximate that of Descartes.

SWAMMERDAM

Jan Swammerdam, a Dutch naturalist, using the comparative as well as the experimental method, is perhaps the most important figure of the 17th century in the fields of neuro-muscular physiology and physiological psychology. His studies in the field of comparative anatomy[15] of insects have tended to obscure his contributions to the physiology of muscle and nerve. In these entomological studies—which were not only anatomical but included observations on behavior as well—the comparative point of view is stressed, as indicated, for example, by such chapter headings as "Man himself compared with insects, and with the Frog," and "A particular treatise on the Frog and its young, exhibiting its history, and comparing it with the insects."[16] His insight into the problems of neural physiology, his use of the comparative method in the study of animal behavior, and his vigorous criticisms of the current dogmas regarding "animal spirits" and the agencies

[15] Foster, in *Cambridge Modern History* (157), credits Swammerdam and his contemporary, Malpighi, with being the founders of the science of Comparative Anatomy.

[16] In the introduction to his work Swammerdam indicates his interest in comparative study of behavior in the following terms: "After an attentive examination of the nature and fabrick of the least and largest animals, I cannot but allow the less an equal, or perhaps superior degree in dignity. . . . If, while we dissect with care the larger animals, we are filled with wonder at the elegant disposition of their limbs, the inimitable order of their muscles, and the regular direction of their veins, arteries and nerves; to what an height is our astonishment raised, when we discover all these parts arranged in the least, in the same regular manner." p. 1.

THE

BOOK of NATURE;

OR, THE

HISTORY of INSECTS:

Reduced to diftinct CLASSES, confirmed by particular INSTANCES,
Difplayed in the Anatomical Analyfis of many SPECIES,

AND

ILLUSTRATED with COPPER-PLATES,

INCLUDING

The Generation of the FROG, the Hiftory of the EPHEMERUS, the Changes of FLIES,
BUTTERFLIES, and BEETLES;

WITH THE

Original Difcovery of the MILK-VESSELS of the CUTTLE-FISH, and many other curious Particulars

By JOHN SWAMMERDAM, M. D.

WITH

The LIFE of the AUTHOR, by HERMAN BOERHAAVE, M. D.

Tranflated from the DUTCH and LATIN Original Edition,

By THOMAS FLLOYD.

Revifed and improved by NOTES from REAUMUR and others,

By JOHN HILL, M. D.

LONDON:

Printed for C. G. SEYFFERT, Bookfeller, in DEAN-STREET, SOHO.

MDCCLVIII.

TITLE PAGE OF THE ENGLISH TRANSLATION OF THE "BOOK OF NATURE"

and processes in muscular contraction, place him in the front rank of his contemporaries, if not, indeed, as one of the founders of physiological and comparative psychology.

Swammerdam's principal contributions are collected in a curious and interesting volume entitled "The Book of Nature" (477) (*Biblia Naturae*) which was published by his countryman, Hermann Boerhaave in 1739, over fifty years after the author's death.[17] An English translation of this work appeared in London in 1758, from which the material for the present study is drawn. This work is devoted primarily to the presentation of the author's anatomical and behavior studies of bees, wasps, dragon flies, snails, butterflies, ants, worms, etc., but contains a section devoted to the development, mating behavior and anatomy of frogs. This section contains a separate essay entitled: "Experiments on the particular motion of the muscles of the Frog; which may be also, in general, applied to all the motions of the muscles in Men and Brutes." It is here that Swammerdam has described his fundamental experiments on neuro-muscular action.

The father of Swammerdam was John James Swammerdam, an apothecary, born in 1606.[18] The father was "very studious of natural history, and very well skilled in several branches of it," according to Boerhaave and seems to have made collections of insects, fossils, etc., which attracted much attention in his native city of Amsterdam. Here, also, Jan was born on February 12, 1637. In 1651 he entered the University of Leyden where he was admitted "a candidate in physic" in 1663 and received the degree of Doctor of Physic in 1667. His interest in dissection was indicated during these years by his concern with the methods of preparation and preservation of anatomical material. He succeeded, also, "in nice contrivances to

[17] Swammerdam was "little versed in Latin" according to the biographical preface by Boerhaave in the 1738 edition of the *Biblia Naturae*, and the original works were in Dutch. On the author's death, his original manuscripts were left to Melchisedeck Thèvenot, formerly the French Minister to Genoa. Boerhaave relates the history of these papers as follows: After Thèvenot's death this material was "purchased by Joubert the king's painter whose heirs afterwards sold it at the inconsiderable price of fifty French crowns to the illustrious Joseph du Verny, with whom they lay hid and disregarded for a long time. . . . At last by the assistance of the reverend Mark Guitton, and the eminent William Roell, professor of anatomy at Amsterdam both then residing in Paris, I so far succeeded, that they were purchased for me the twenty-sixth of March, 1727, at the price of one thousand five hundred French florins, and received them complete the same summer."

[18] The chief source of material is the biographical introduction to the *Biblia Naturae* entitled "The Life of John Swammerdam" by Hermann Boerhaave. See also, Locy (305), Duncan (120), Klencke (268), "Anonymous" (477a), and Foster, *op. cit.*

dissect and otherwise manage the minutest insects" and showed "extraordinary skill in dissecting frogs."[19]

Swammerdam's father seems to have been wholly unsympathetic with his son's interest in anatomy. The father "threatened him severely that if he did not immediately exert his talents as a physician" and desist in his "expensive researches after insects, and his experiments of that kind, he would neither supply him with money or clothes; and to show he was in earnest, he immediately deprived him of the means of pursuing what he had begun."

In 1674, when he was thirty-seven years old, Swammerdam finished his treatise on bees. About this time he "conceived a distate for wcrdly affairs" and came under the influence of Antonia Bourignon, the Flemish mystic and Pietist (1616–1680) who seems to have dominated him for the remainder of his life. It was she who advised him to reject the offer of the Grand Duke of Tuscany of 12,000 florins for the purchase of his entomological collections. This offer was made through Swammerdam's life-long friend, Stenson, the Danish physiologist, and was contingent on Swammerdam's removing to Florence where "life would be easy and agreeable" and entering the Catholic Church. But Swammerdam put these Latin temptations behind him and rejected the offer "as the greatest indignity that could be offered him." After 1675 he "renounced all thoughts of human affairs, to think of nothing but his spiritual concerns, which he imagined he could not so well promote in any other manner, as by going to confer personally with Bourignon." He disposed of his collections and retired from the world until his death which occurred on February 17th, 1680, when he was but forty-three years of age.

The friendship for Stenson, the controversy with his father, and the relationship with Antonia Bourignon seem to have been the important external influences in Swammerdam's life. The preoccupation with religion and the tendency towards mysticism which marked the final years of his life, were in conflict with the objectivism of his scientific inquiries. Boerhaave records that Swammerdam possessed a "temperament of the melancholy kind" and gives some indication of his inner struggles.

   . . . . his treatise of Bees was formed amidst a thousand torments and agonies of heart and mind, and self-reproaches, natural to a mind full of devotion and piety. On one hand his genius urged him to examine the miracles of the great Creator in his natural productions, whilst on the other, the love of that same all-perfect Being deeply rooted in

---

[19] Boerhaave, *op. cit.* Unless otherwise indicated all biographical references are to this work.

his heart, struggled hard to persuade him, that God alone, and not his creatures, was worthy of his researches, love and attention. The distress of mind of our author felt upon this occasion, was so severe that as soon as he had finished his book upon Bees, he put it into the hands of another, without knowing or giving himself the least concern about what might become of it.[20]

The enormous industry of Swammerdam is indicated by the magnitude of his collections as described by Boerhaave.

These treasures consisted chiefly of insects and anatomical preparations from human subjects . . . . our author alone had collected near three thousand species of insects, that had no relation one to another, and had examined every one of them, and disposed them all in classes according to their real and natural characters; he had even dissected many of them with that skill and dexterity peculiar to himself, and having with unwearied diligence traced them through every least period of their change from the egg to the Butterfly, faithfully recording all his observations, taking care at the same time to prepare and keep by him the minute originals as incontestable vouchers of his indefatigable industry in examining them . . . . he used himself to hatch, in a manner found out by, and only known to himself, the little eggs of insects, in order to discover the obscure manner of the existence of their first rudiments, the progress of these rudiments to life. (p. x)

CONTRIBUTIONS TO NERVE-MUSCLE PHYSIOLOGY

The conceptions of the majority of Swammerdam's contemporaries regarding the nature of the agencies which effect muscular action, as we have seen, were highly speculative. Few of the phenomena of integrative behavior had been demonstrated before the 17th century; and, although the muscles and nerves were recognized as the chief instruments in this behavior, the mode of their action was mystery.

The existing ignorance and the extreme difficulties of these problems were recognized by Swammerdam. He discusses these difficulties at the beginning of his study of muscular action in the frog.[21]

How important and difficult it is to explain the real causes of muscular motion, is sufficiently evident from numerous experiments; which though made by very ingenious men yet have not hitherto discovered its true nature. The great utility and foundation of further knowledge, which we should acquire from that discovery, lie yet involved in the thickest clouds of obscurity.

He notes the numerous problems, the solution of which was essential to the complete understanding of the nature of neuro-muscular action.

[20] *Op. cit.*, p. ix. In the *Biographie Universelle*, it is recorded that on one occasion Swammerdam burned all his writings on which he could lay his hands. *Cf.*, the anonymous biographical note (477a).

[21] Unless otherwise noted the quotations are taken from the essay on "Experiments on the particular motion of the muscles in the Frog, etc.," which is found in Part II of the *Biblia Naturae*, pp. 122–132.

The chief among these are concerned with the structures involved, *i.e.*, the nature of the neuro-muscular junction,[22] the structure of the muscular fibres, the structure of the veins and arteries attached to the muscle, and the nature of the connective tissue in the muscle. He admits the impossibility of the immediate solution of these difficulties, but, quite properly, he undertakes the task of descriptive observation of muscular *response to stimulation* of the nerve.

He begins by presenting his experiments which demonstrate the essential agency of the nerve in muscular action. After observing that "whenever the nerves of living bodies are handled, there is immediately observed a considerable motion in the muscles to which they are sent," he describes his experiment with an excised frog's muscle.

Another very delicate and useful experiment may be made, if one of the largest muscles be separated from the thigh of a Frog in such a manner as to remain unhurt. For if, after this, you take hold of each tendon with your hand, and then irritate the propending nerve with scissors, or any other instrument, the muscle will recover its former motion, which it had lost. You will see that it is immediately contracted and draws together, as it were, both the hands, which hold the tendons. This I formerly (in the year 1658)[23] demonstrated to the most illustrious and now reigning Grand Duke of Tuscany, when he graciously vouchsafed to pay me a visit. This experiment may be repeated in the same muscle, as long as any part of the nerve remains unhurt; and we can thus make the muscle contract itself, as often as we please. (p. 123)

This experiment, which is illustrated with lettered drawings, is the prototype of the nerve-muscle preparation which has become a standard demonstration of the physiological laboratory. Not content with the mere demonstration of the neuro-muscular response, Swammerdam desired to know "in what degree the muscle thickens in its contraction, and how far its tendons approach toward each other." He developed a technique which closely approaches modern graphic methods of recording muscular contractions.

[22] This phrase is not Swammerdam's, of course. His text runs as follows: " . . . it merits particular consideration in what manner the nerve is actually joined to the muscle; how it is constructed in the muscle; what is its course, entrancè, middle distribution, and end; as also how it communicates with the moving fibre, and what effect it produces in it; also what that very subtle matter properly is which is undoubtedly conveyed to the muscle through the nerve." A truly inclusive list of questions!

[23] It is possible that this date should be 1668. Boerhaave notes in the "Life" that the Duke of Tuscany "being then in Holland with Mr. Thèvenot, in order to see the curiosities of the country, came to view those of our author. . . . On this occasion Swammerdam made some anatomical dissections of insects in the presence of that great Prince." In an anonymous biographical note published in 1884 (447a) 1668 is the date given for the visit of the Duke to Swammerdam.

. . . . we must put the muscle into a glass tube, and run two fine needles through both its tendons, where they had been before held by the fingers; and then fix the points of those needles, neither too loose nor too firmly, in a piece of cork. If afterwards you irritate the nerves you will see the muscle drawing the heads of the needles together out of the places; and that the belly of the muscle itself becomes considerably thicker in the cavity of the glass tube, and stops up the whole tube, after expelling the air. This continues till the contraction ceases, and the needles then move back into their former places: and the belly of the muscle parting again from the tube, affords a free passage for the air through its cavity. (p. 123)

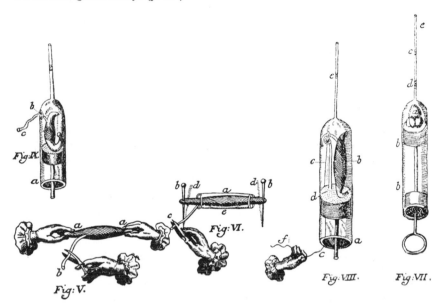

SWAMMERDAM'S FIGURES ILLUSTRATING HIS NERVE-MUSCLE EXPERIMENTS

In explaining Figure V Swammerdan says ("Book of Nature"): "Another very delicate and useful experiment may be made, if one of the largest muscles be separated from the thigh of a Frog, and, together with its adherent nerve, prepared in such a manner as to remain unhurt. For if, after this, you take hold, *aa*, of each tendon with your hand, and then irritate *b* the propending nerve with scissors, or any other instrument, the muscle will recover its former motion, which it had lost. You will see that it is immediately contracted, and draws together, as it were, both the hands, which hold the tendons."

Regarding Figure VI the author says: "If we have a mind to observe, very exactly, in what degree the muscle thickens in its contraction, and how far its tendons approach toward each other, we must put the muscle into a glass tube, *a*, and run two fine needles *bb* through both its tendons, where they had been before held by the fingers; and then fix the points of those needles, neither too loose nor too firmly, in a piece of cork. If afterwards you irritate, *c*, the nerves, you will see the muscle drawing *dd* the heads of the needles together out of the places; and that the belly of the muscle itself becomes considerably thicker *e* in the cavity of the glass tube, and stops up the whole tube, after expelling the air. This continues till the contraction ceases, and the needles then move back into their former places."

Figures VII, VIII and IX illustrate the experiment designed to demonstrate that the muscle does not increase in bulk during contraction.

The next problem which our investigator faced had to do with the nature of the processes in the nerve. He rejected the notion, held by his contemporaries, of a rarified substance, called "animal spirits" on several grounds: (1) The muscle continues to respond when the nerve is stimulated long after the whole preparation is cut off from the spinal cord, although the animal spirits are presumably "dissipated, or grown weak, after many times discharging their duty; and when there is not further communication between the nerve, brain, and marrow." (2) Even after the muscle is cut and the fibres are separated from each other, they continue to move when the attached nerve is irritated. (3) The hypothetical animal spirits would be inconceivably fine to pass through "those very fine fibrillae, which constitute the nerves." (4) The muscle shows no increase in bulk when contracted.

The last point was given experimental proof by Swammerdam. Using both the excised frog's muscle and the excised heart, he demonstrated by the plethysmographic technique that there was no increase in volume of the muscle when the attached nerve is stimulated. As Fulton points out (161), Swammerdam's experiment anticipated that of Glisson by several years, although it is the latter who is usually credited with this discovery.[24]

Swammerdam summarized his conclusions regarding animal spirits together with his hypothesis regarding the nature of nervous action as follows:

> Therefore, I would have it seriously considered, that it cannot be demonstrated by any experiments, that any matter of sensible or comprehensible bulk flows through the nerves into the muscles. Nor does anything else pass through the nerves to the muscles; all is a very quick kind of motion, which is indeed so rapid, that it may be properly called instantaneous. There the spirit, as it is called, or that subtile matter, which flies in an instant through the nerves into the muscles, may with the greatest propriety be compared to that most swift motion, which, when one extremity of a long beam or board is struck with the finger, runs with such velocity along the wood, that it is perceived almost at the same instant at the other end; nay, that it is further propagated through the nerves into our muscles; and thus produces various motions in them. (p. 124)

Swammerdam confesses his inability to explain the exact nature of the action of the nerve on the muscle. He suggests, however, a "coarse similitude" between the action of muscles and that of certain plants.

---

[24] Fulton, in his "Historical Introduction" (161) says: "Swammerdam's use of an excised muscle was, in addition, more convincing than Glisson's demonstration with the intact human arm; moreover, the method employed by Swammerdam is that still used in physiological class rooms."

I might conceive it effected in the same manner with the alterations visible on handling, or touching ever so gently the parts of the Herba Impatiens, called Touch me not, or podded Ars Smart, or the Balsamita alteria of Fabius Columna; the part of which plant being extended according to the course of two or three nervous or herbaceous fibres, in consequence of any momentary irritation, most suddenly contract, and the pods burst. (p. 129)

Swammerdam next concerned himself with the question of the origin of nervous action, *i.e.*, where is the "beginning of that natural irritation, stimulus or provocation of the motion, thus communicated to the muscles through the nerves?" The principle of this irritation is regarded as being in the spinal cord and all the nerves of the body. They are in a state of perpetual irritation and the muscles are in a state of continuous contraction[25] brought about, according to Swammerdam, by the "continual impulse of the arterial blood upon the marrow and nerves."

ON VOLUNTARY ACTION

Swammerdam did not indulge in metaphysical speculation, and pious dogmatizing, so dear to the hearts of his contemporaries, regarding the nature of the "soul" as a seat of reason and the source of voluntary action. He dealt with the problem from a point of view which will be recognized as distinctly modern.

I would have it particularly observed, that I admit no essential difference between the natural and spontaneous contraction of the muscles, and that performed by the will. I consider this difference as merely accidental; but, because we move all these muscles which we move voluntarily, in a contrary direction; that which is said to be essential in the contraction of all muscles, is a natural contraction. (p. 125)

Voluntary motion is impossible unless we "have the power of determining the natural motion of the antagonists to the contrary side." Where there are no antagonistic muscles voluntary motion is impossible. The nature of this "determination" gives rise to a discussion of the involuntary action which is significant in the light of the concept of reflex action presented by Descartes a few years before.[26]

. . . . wherever the power of the antagonist is equal, there is observed no motion of the muscles, and all things are in both in equilibrio, until there arises another determination, which, causing one muscle, to be contracted somewhat more strongly than another, at length moves our limbs. Such a determination may proceed from various causes.

---

[25] Borelli and others had referred to the phenomenon of tonus.
[26] *Passions of the Soul*, 1649.

If, for example, a man's skin be very gently rubbed and irritated with a hair doubled several times; I often observed, that the motion of the antagonist muscles of the arm and hand was immediately determined; so that the person instantaneously, as it were, unknown to him, has put his hand to the place where he felt the titillation, and then scratched the skin until he made it red, imagining that was probably occasioned by a Flea, or some other insect. But when I stopt, his hand and arm rested likewise, because the natural con-traction was then equal in all the muscles. If the same experiment be made on sleeping dogs and cats, it is likewise observed, that a determinate motion is produced in the muscles which move their skin; and therefore it is pleasant to see them suddenly draw it up, pricking up their hairs, and sometimes shaking them in their sleep. (pp. 125–126)

The contraction of the pupil of the eye when it is irritated by a "particle of light," and the peristalsis of the intestines "in proportion to their contents" so that their contractions "resembles that of the sea, whose waves follow and mutually press upon one another," belongs to the same category of action.

All manner of motor automatisms may make place without the will "as manifest in our walking, standing, and making use of our hands; for we certainly move our limbs almost every moment, without reflecting in the least upon what we do." These actions are explained in mechanical terms, *i.e.*, without any metaphysical "cause."

It is for a similar reason, that, when we find ourselves too near the fire, we retire to a greater distance from it, and put our limbs, by means of various motions, into their former posture, without attending in the least to what we do; but merely in consequence of the impression made upon us by the irritating object. From hence it appears, that we can never be truely said to move voluntarily, *unless when the will is put in motion by the object*,[27] and then by its own motion produces a third; for whenever the light happens to be too strong, we shut our eyes, turn our head aside, and give ourselves many other motions, as we are variously excited to them by the objects that present themselves. (p. 131)

These facts "abundantly prove" that a voluntary movement is never pro-duced except as it is preceded by a "determining principle." Since the muscles are in a "perpetual state of contraction," the "least degree of determination" is sufficient to actuate the body in a "thousand different ways." This "determining principle" may be a thought "merely casual," a dream "presenting itself before us in the night," or some pattern of physical stimuli (the "object" in Swammerdam's terminology).

Swammerdam draws a parallel between the train of our images and the continuity of muscular motions. He says:

[27] Italics not in original.

Thus, with regard to external objects, we often salute a person we meet, merely because another in our company takes off his hat, or because we are affected by such external object, though we do not know who the person is we have saluted, nor so much as think of our saluting him. For this reason therefore it is plain, that as our memory is local, and is assisted by the image of one thing in passing to that of another, and so on without end, the contractions of our muscles are in like manner natural; and the muscles themselves are urged by one cause of motion to another, and from this to a third, and so on without any interruption. (p. 131)

We are, perhaps, scarcely justified in interpreting Swammerdam's Principle of Determination in terms of present day "determining tendencies," but his discussion of volition is vigorous and, on the whole, consistent with the point of view of modern psychology.

In Swammerdam's discussion of the direction of the motion in nerves, he foreshadows developments in neural physiology a hundred years later. He notes that the "motion produced in the muscle by irritating the nerve, is always propagated out of the larger into the smaller branches, and goes afterwards continually descending." The nerves issuing from the spinal cord above a stimulated point are not affected when a lower point is stimulated—the twitching of the muscles serving as an indicator. This is a partial recognition of the principle of segmentation in the spinal cord. The functioning of the sensory nerves is also discussed.

The nerves designed for the senses are circumstanced in a quite different manner; for in these, the sensitive motions, doubtless, tend upwards. In order to contract any muscle, it is necessary that its nerve be irritated in the region above the muscle, or at its insertion into it; since that motion never tends upwards, but always downwards. (p. 125)

We have here a vague anticipation of the nervous arc—a concept elaborated by Descartes, Whytt, and Bell.

Swammerdam concluded his essay by pointing out the complexity of the factors involved in every muscular contraction.

. . . . it would be necessary for us to consider the atmosphere, the nature of our food, the blood, the brain, marrow, and nerves, that most subtile matter which instantaneously flows to the moving fibres, and many other things, before we could expect to attain a sight of the perfect and certain truth. (p. 131)

Throughout Swammerdam's studies the comparative point of view is apparent. This is illustrated in his observations on the sex behavior in insects, the phenomena of metamorphosis and life cycles of insects, and the anatomical studies. The following quotation illustrates his mode of interpretation of insect behavior.

From these considerations it therefore follows, that among Bees there is no wiser regulation than among domestic fowls, for they have their natural desire to sit; they make nests, and nourish their young, being compelled thereto by such laws as they cannot avoid nor surpress by any rational principle; because they are impressed on them by the eternal law of nature. These little insects are under as great necessity to perform all these actions, as the winter is to follow the summer. The only difference among several kinds is, that some execute these functions in a manner more convenient, more orderly, and more agreeable to reason than others. This appears chiefly in the Bees, and hence there is no authority for the prevalent and common opinion that the government of Bees is carried on with the scepter of prudence and judgment, under law, and with rewards and punishments; for in truth all that order which we so much, and not without reason admire, is impelled by nature, and is only designed for the propagation of their species. (Book of Nature, Part I, p. 170)

ON THE EXPERIMENTAL METHOD

Swammerdam's discussion of the nature and limits of the experimental method at the conclusion of Part Two of the "Book of Nature" is so striking in language and significant in its psychological implications, that it is worth reproducing as an indication of the growing interest in direct observation as a source of scientific truth. He points out that we cannot know "first causes" but only appearances in nature.

I may hence, for certain, conclude, that all the knowledge and wisdom of philosophers, consists merely in an accurate perception of these elegant appearances or effects. For this reason, we should strenuously endeavor to make ourselves well acquainted with these appearances, and then draw from them firm rules and principles; otherwise as I have hinted in my preface, we may easily lose our way, and stray into the paths of error, as disputing on nature, which is quite inexhaustible, without sufficient experiments, which, on such an occasion, are as necessary to find us a path, considering with what darkness of ignorance we are surrounded, as a staff to the blind.

Reason, alone, is an inadequate guide to truth. Reasoning which does not terminate in experiment is "idle and vain," whatever "syllogisms and enumerations people may think proper to build upon them." Reasoning follows observation, but the individual may be said only to have true knowledge when he can *reproduce* what he has observed.

I believe we shall find it not unjust to dignify with the name of reason that faculty of our minds, by the assistance of which, we form clear and distinct notions of things, whilst we make proper use of our senses in sufficient experiments, so as to be able afterwards to effect exact copies of the originals we have thus endeavoured to be thoroughly acquainted with. For this reason it is, that our idea of any thing is said to be more or less clear and distinct, according as we can produce another thing more or less like it; and are therefore said to have more or less the power of it. This being granted, it should follow, that we have no clear, distinct or perfect knowledge of any things, except of such as we can truly and effectually produce.

By making the proper use of our senses, we may "from the things we see, gather sufficient information concerning those that we cannot."

Swammerdam reflected the spirit of his time in that he regarded the body of man as a machine and he was filled with an intense enthusiasm to exemplify the findings of physics and mechanics in its structure and functioning. Boerhaave states that Swammerdam often "wished for a year of perpetual heat and light to perfect his inquiries, with a polar night to reap all the advantages of them by proper drawings and descriptions." It is, perhaps, no small loss to science that such energy was submerged in the struggle with the "practical" minded father and found eventual outlet in the sterile fanaticism of religion. From the point of view of physiological psychology, Swammerdam's most important contributions are in the field of neuro-muscular mechanisms in relation to voluntary and involuntary movement. These may be summarized as follows:[28]

(1) The essential agency of the nerve in muscular contraction received careful experimental verification. That the stimulation of the nerve causes the muscle to contract, was not, of course, an original discovery of Swammerdam's. This investigator, however, introduced a quantitative, graphic method for the study of the response of the excised nerve-muscle preparation.

(2) Swammerdam showed experimentally the inadequacy of the animal spirits hypothesis.

(3) He was probably the first to show experimentally, using an excised muscle, that there is no increase in bulk during the muscle contraction.

(4) He discussed voluntary action from an objective and comparative point of view rather than as a problem in metaphysics. This is remarkable in view of the contemporary discussions and in view of his own later preoccupation with religious mysticism.

(5) He attempted to bring both the phenomena of voluntary and involuntary action under a single neuro-muscular principle. He pointed out that both were determined by some previous event or stimulus.

(6) He suggested the importance of the spinal cord in neuro-muscular action, especially in connection with segmentation. Implied in this there was a rather vague idea of the nervous arc concept.

[28] No attempt has been made, of course, to evaluate the notable contributions of Swammerdam to entomology and general physiology. He was, for example, the first to describe the red blood corpuscles, the valves of the lymphatics, etc.

CHAPTER IV

LOCALIZATION OF FUNCTION

"For as in general it is scarce possible to learn the true nature of any creature, from the consideration of the single creature itself; so particularly of divers parts of an human body it is very difficult to learn the true use, without consulting the bodies of other animals, wherein the parts inquired after is by nature either wholly left out as needless, or situation, or figure, or connection with, and relation to other parts, may render its use more conspicuous, or at least more discernable."—ROBERT BOYLE, *The Usefulness of Natural Philosophy.*

During the last fifty years of the 17th century a brilliant array of men were working on problems in connection with the function and structure of the nervous system. No attempt will be made to determine questions of priority so far as their specific discoveries are concerned. In the case of the group under discussion in the present chapter, the basis of classification has been the similarity in the problems attacked and the methods used.

These problems have to do in the main with the differential nature of the functions of the gross divisions of the nervous system. It is particularly important from the point of view of the development of the theory of reflex action to determine which division of the central nervous system is involved. In the modern usage, the term reflex is reserved for those neural arcs which do not involve the so-called higher or cortical centers.

Thomas Willis (1621–1675), celebrated English anatomist and physician, and Sedleian Professor of Natural Philosophy at Oxford University, attempted the difficult task of collecting and ordering the then known facts regarding neuro-muscular physiology and anatomy. This man, who seems to have been an able clinician rather than an original investigator in physiological science,[1] published in 1664 his *CerebriAnatome.* This book, which was illustrated by Sir Christopher Wren, was regarded as the most complete account of the nervous system which had hitherto appeared.[2] In neural anatomy Willis' name is associated with numerous contributions to our knowledge of cerebral structures and, on the side of physiology, he is to be

---

[1] He was, for example, the first to note the sweetish taste of diabetic urine and to describe and name puerperal fever. *Vide* Garrison (162) p. 194.

[2] *Vide* Garrison *op. cit.*, p. 194, and Foster *op. cit.*, p. 270 *ff.*

Æ·TATIS SVÆ. 45.

THOMAS WILLIS. FROM "SOME APOSTLES OF PHYSIOLOGY"

credited with the clearest statement, after Descartes, of the theory of reflex action and the principle that the involuntary actions are presided over by the lower rather than the higher nervous centers.[3]

In the treatise "Of Muscular Motion" (541), Willis distinguished between two primary faculties of the "corporeal soul," the sensitive and the motive; the former was concerned with sensory impressions and the latter with muscular motion. The motive and sensitive faculties were discussed in the following terms.

The motive Faculty of the bodily Soul is wont to be exercised with another kind of Action than the sensitive, viz. with a diverse aspect and tendency of animal Spirits. For that every Sense is a certain passion, wherein the Soul, or some portion of it, being outwardly struck, is forced to nod and shake, and a wavering of the Spirits being inwardly made to look back towards the Head; but on the contrary, every Motion is a certain Action wherein the Soul seems to exert itself whole, or part of itself, and by a declination or fluctuation of Spirits being made to bring forth a Systasis, and to extend something as it were its member. Further, whilst the Soul so exerts itself, or some part of itself, that the works then designed might be performed, an heap of animal spirits being everywhere disposed in the motive parts, sometimes one, sometimes more are raised up by the Soul, which by that means being expanded with a certain force, and as it were exploded, they blow up the containing bodies, and so the same being increased as to their thickness, and made short as to their length, are made to attract the adjoyning member, and stir up local motion. (p. 34)

Willis accepted the orthodox doctrine of his time with regard to animal spirits which he regarded as a "nimble and elastic" substance conveyed to the muscles by the nerves.

Therefore as to the Muscular Motion in general, we shall conclude after this manner, with a sufficiently probable conjecture, viz. that the animal Spirits being brought from the Head by the passage of the Nerves to every Muscle, and (as it is very likely) received from the membranaceous fibrils, are carried by their passage into the tendinous fibres, and there they are plentifully laid up as in fit Store-houses; which Spirits as they are naturally numble and elastick, wherever they may, and are permitted, expanding themselves, leap into the fleshy fibres; then the force being finished, presently sinking down, they slide back into the Tendons, and so vicissively. But whilst the same animal Spirits, at the instinct given for the performing of motion, do leap out of the tendinous fibres into the fleshy, they meet there with active Particles of another nature, supplied from the blood

---

[3] Neuburger (384), regarding Willis, says: "Die Willisiansche Theorie was die erste, welche den Zusammenhang des Centralnervensystems mit dem Vital-organen schärfer präcisirte und hiedurch zu prüfenden Thierversuchen anregte, zumal sie in einer Zeit veröffentlich wurde, in der das Experiment auf dem Gebiete der Physiologie des Kreislaufs und der Respiration bereits zur Herrschaft gelangt war; letzteres moment gab auch den Ausschlag, das die Frage, welcher Hirnabschnitt zum Leben unbedingt nöthig sei, in das genauer präcisirte Problem: Welcher Hirnabschnitt steht mit der Fortdauer der Herzaction in unmittelbaren Zusammenhange? verwandelt wurde."

and presently they grow mutually hot; so that by the strife and agitation of both, the
fleshy fibres, for that they are lax and porous, are stuffed up and driven into wrinklings
from all which being at once wrinkled or shrivell'd up, the contraction of the whole
muscle proceeds; the contraction being finished, the sincere or clear Spirits; which reside
or are asswaged, go back for the most part into the tendinous fibres, the other Particles
being left within the flesh; the loss or wasting of these the blood supplies, as the Nerves
do those. (p. 42)

Willis clearly distinguished between the seats of the voluntary and involuntary motion, a distinction which applied not only to the structures
in the central nervous system but to the differentiation between the animal
spirits distilled in the brain and those produced by the cerebellum. The
conception of the localization of the higher and lower centers is a unique
aspect of Willis' theory and serves to distinguish him from the majority
of his contemporaries.

When sometime past I diligently and seriously meditated on the office of the Cerebel
and revolved in my mind several things concerning it, at length, from the Analogy and
frequent Ratiocination, this (as I think) true and genuine use of it occurred; to wit, that
the Cerebel is a peculiar Fountain of animal Spirits designed for some works, and wholly
distinct from the Brain. Within the Brain, Imagination, Memory, Discourse, and other
more superior Acts of the animal Function are performed; besides, the animal Spirits flow
also from it into the nervous stock, by which all the spontaneous motions, to wit, of which
we are knowing and will, are performed. But the office of the Cerebel seems to be for
the animal Spirits to supply some Nerves; by which involuntary actions (such as are the
beating of the Heart, easie Respiration, the Concoction of the Aliment, the protrusion of
the Chyle, and many others) which are made after a constant manner unknown to us,
or whether we will or no, are performed. As often as we go about voluntary motion, we
seem as it were to perceive within us the Spirits residing within the fore part of the Head
to be stirred up to action, or an influx. But the Spirits inhabiting the Cerebel perform
unperceivedly and silently their works of Nature without our knowledge or care. Wherefore whilst the Brain is garnished as it were with uncertain Meanders and crankling turn-
ings and windings about, the compass of this is furnished with folds and lappets disposed
in an orderly series; in the spaces of which, as in designed Orbs and Tracts, the animal
Spirits are expanded according to the Rule and Method naturally impressed on them.
For indeed those in the Cerebel, seem orderly disposed after that manner within certain
little places and boundaries, that they may flow out orderly of their own accord one series
after another without any driver, which may govern or moderate their motions. Wherefore forasmuch as some Nerves perform some kind of motions according to the instincts
and wants of Nature, without consulting the government of the will or appetite within
the Brain, why may it not be imagined, that the influence of the Spirits is derived wholly
from the Cerebel for the performing of these? (p. 11)

Voluntary and involuntary motion originate, then, in the brain and
cerebellum respectively, but reflex action may occur in either of these
structures.

Either of these [voluntary or involuntary motion] is either direct, which is stirred up of itself, or primarily from this or that beginning, as often as the appetite requires this or that thing, out of a certain proper, and as I may say intestine deliberation, and chuses out respective motions; so in like manner, when the ordinary offices of the natural and vital Function are performed, according to the solemn Rite of nature; *or the motion of either kind is reflected,*[4] to wit, which depending on a previous sense more immediately, as an evident cause or occasion, is presently retorted, so a gentle titillation of the skin causes a rubbing of it, and the more intense heats of the Praecordia stir up the Pulse and Respiration. (p. 34)

Although the higher (brain) and lower (cerebellar) centers were regarded by Willis as being relatively autonomous, he believed that under certain conditions they manifested a degree of inter-dependence. The conditions under which there occurred a "spread" of effects from the lower to the higher center was described as follows:

More instances might be here brought of all the other acts of the vital or merely natural function: of which besides it may be observed, that when a sense of the trouble is immediately conveyed from the *Praecordia* or *Viscera* to the Cerebel, this affection, like the waving of waters, is either stopt or terminated there, from whence a motion, as the business requires, unknown to the Brain, is presently retorted, as when the actions of the *Praecordia* are altered by a feaverish distemper without our knowledge: or secondly, that sense of the trouble being transmitted to the Cerebel, for that it is more vehement, it unfolds itself more largely and like a stronger waving of waters, passing through the Cerebel, goes forward further even to the Brain, and warns its inhabitants of the evil; by which they being incited to oppose the enemy, cause a motion of another kind: So (as hath been said) when the *Praecordia* grow cruelly hot, the Cerebel feeling this, makes the Pulse and Respiration stronger. But further, the Brain being warned of the same trouble, seeks and diligently requires cold drink and other remedies to moderate the heat. (p. 115)

Willis discussed in some detail the manner in which the animal spirits were distributed to the muscles; especially the manner in which a specific action or muscular motion could be brought about. The problem that concerned him was—How is it that the animal spirits can go to a particular muscle or group of muscles rather than spreading through all the nerves? The possibility of "little doors" in the nerves was considered and rejected on the ground that the problem would still remain of accounting for the differential action of the "little doors." He finally concluded that each nerve kept a separate course from its point of origin to the particular muscle in which it was inserted.

But in truth, this may rather be said, that all the shoots of the Nerves and lesser branches remain distinct and singular among themselves from the parts to which they are inserted, even to their beginnings; so that a peculiar tract of the spirits or way of passage lyes

---

[4] Italics not in original.

open, from the Brain and its medullary Appendix, to every Muscle and nervous part; for in truth, although the Nerves, according to their beginnings, may seem to arise from the greater Trunks, yet it will be easily appear, if you shall open the trunk and those branches, that in them many little Nerves, only like hairs, for the sake of a better conduct, are collected together in the same bundle; yea, the coverings being separated, you may follow oftentimes the little Nervulets, and those single to the respective parts and members, to which they are destinated. (p. 48)

Although most nerves remained anatomically distinct until the muscle was reached, yet in certain cases there was a peripheral connection or anasto-mosis of the nerves which permitted the transmission of the animal spirits from one nerve tract to another. This hypothesis of peripheral fusion of the nerve tracts permitted Willis to account for certain types of intergra-tive activity in which there was some degree of muscular coördination. He discussed this in the treatise "Of Muscular Motion" as follows:

But in the meantime, although there be singular passages or chanels of the animal Spirits of most Nerves, distinct among themselves; yet some do variously communicate with others through the branches and shoots sent on either side; which indeed ought to be so made, that when many Nerves together, are required to some motion of a Muscle equally, all these, by reason of the commerce mutually had between themselves, might conspire in the same action; hence in some motions of the members, as in the striking of a Harp or Lute and other complicated actions, many Muscles co-operate with admirable celerity; so that, although many be employed at once, they perform their task severally without any confusion. Besides, there is need for the Nerves to communicate mutually among themselves, because of the Sympathetical motions of the members and of some of the parts, for neither for any other cause is the Nerve of the Diaphragma inserted into the brachial branches, or those belonging to the Arms, than that the exercise of living Creatures, especially, in running or flying, might be proportionate to the tenour of Respiration. Hence it also proceeds, that in any passion, the Praecordia being bound up or dilated, the countenance and aspect of the face, yea and the gestures of the hands and members are pathetically figured. (p. 48)

With Willis the general concept of reflex action presents indications of growth. It was more precise, anatomically speaking, than that of Descartes and the way was opened for a mode of experimental study. The fact that Willis still clung to an hypothesis of animal spirits which resembled that of Descartes, should not obscure the importance of his attempt to account for integrated and coördinated muscular action—an attempt which led him to the theory of peripheral nerve connections.

The method of the experimental isolation or removal of a portion of the central nervous system for the purpose of observing the effect of such inter-ference on behavior, had not been employed to any large extent before the middle of the 17th century. The idea of Willis that the higher and lower centers[5] (the brain and cerebellum) presided over voluntary and involuntary motion respectively, opened up a fertile field of physiological experimentation in connection with the experimental destruction of parts of the central nervous system.   Mayow's contribution in this connection we have already noted in the previous chapter.   During the latter half of the 17th century a number of other investigators studied the relative effects on animal activities of the removal of the brain, cerebellum, and medulla.

The English physicist, Robert Boyle (1627–1691) in his "Essay on the Usefulness of Natural Philosophy" (58), for example, noted that in the case of a chick the heart continued to beat "above a full hour" after the removal of the head.   He described another experiment as follows:

Upon what conjectures we expected so lasting a motion in the heart of a chick, after it had lost the head, and consequently the brain, would be more tedious and less fit to be mentioned in this place, than the strange vivacity we have sometimes, not without wonder, observed in vipers; since not only their hearts clearly sever'd from their bodies may be observed to beat for some hours (for this is common with them to divers other cold animals) but the body itself may be, sometimes, two or three days after the skin, heart, head, and all the entrails are separated from it, seen to move in a twining or wriggling manner: nay (what is much more) may appear to be manifestly sensible of punctures, being put into a fresh and vivid motion, when it lay still before, upon being pricked, especially on the spine or marrow, with a pin or needle. (p. 467)

This author then comments on the significance of these results to certain theories regarding the brain.

Now although I will not say, that these experiments prove, that either it is in the membrane, that sensation resides (though I have sometimes doubted, whether the nerves themselves be not so sensible, chiefly as they are invested with membranes) or that the brain may not be confined to the head, but may reach into the rest of the body, after another manner than is wont to be taught; *yet it may be safely affirmed, that such experiments as these may be of great concernment in reference to the common doctrine of the necessity of unceasing influence from the brain, being so requisite to sense and motion,*[6] especially if to the lately mentioned particulars we add, on this occasion, what we have observed of the butterflies, into which silkworms have been metamorphosed; namely, that they may, not only, like common flies, and divers other winged insects, survive a pretty while the loss of their heads, but may sometimes be capable of procreation after having lost them. (p. 467)

Perrault (1613–1688) found that in dogs the animal survived after the removal of the brain, but that the animal perished after the removal of

[5] It may be noted that Willis' system of brain localization anticipated to some extent that of Gall.

[6] Italics not in original.

the medulla oblongata or small brain. Like results were obtained by Vieussens (1641–1717) and Bohn (1640–1718).[7]

The former, according to Soury (458)[8] distinguished between the following classes of movements: (1) Intrinsic movements of the heart, thorax, and intestines, (2) intrinsic movements accompanying the affective states, and (3) mixed movements or habitual acts which might be modified by the will. Bohn experimented on decapitated frogs, and declared against the current of "vital spirits."[9] These investigations[10] made evident the fact that *various vital functions persisted after the removal of part or all of the cerebrum.*

In addition to the observations on the post-operative effects of the destruction of the brain, there were observations on the behavior of acephalous "monsters"—infants born without a brain. Both these lines of evidence pointed to the possibility of the persistence of vital organic functions in the absence of the brain provided the cord was intact.

Du Verny (1648–1730) (124) and Chirac (1650–1732)[11] reported observations in connection with these two lines of evidence. Charles Preston (412) in 1697 reported the results of these two investigators together with the results of his own observations.

April 3d, 1695. I was called to a woman aged about 28 years, six months and a half gone in her third child. She was feverish, and raved a little; on examination, I found the Orificium uteri Internum dilated about the largeness of a crown. . . . . One hour after I delivered her happily of a male child, that lived half an hour, and received baptism; this child was big and strong, and all parts of the body well proportioned, as they ought to be naturally, except the head, the hinder part whereof was flat, as if it had been taken off with the stroke of some weapon, even to the Os Sphoenoides; there was neither brain, cerebellum, nor medulla oblongata; the cavity which ought to contain these was very superficial. . . . .

The great motion of the eyes of this child, during the time it lived, gave me the curiosity to search the cause. . . . .

There has passed under my hands three subjects like unto this, all males, and who lived some time. (pp. 458–9)

One of these subjects was submitted to Du Verny, Professor of Anatomy in the Royal Garden at Paris, for dissection with the following results:

He traced the eighth and ninth pairs of Nerves and intercostal. Having cut up the canal of the vertebres, discovered the medulla spinalis all along the cavity, and traced all

---

[7] *Vide* Neuburger, *op. cit..* p. 22.

[8] P. 448.

[9] *Vide* Garrison, *op. cit.*, p. 196.

[10] *Cf.* Neuburger for a discussion of *Das Kleinhirnexperiment, op. cit.*, p. 7 *ff.*

[11] Neuberger, *op. cit.*, p. 21.

the veretebral nerves proceeding therefrom; as also the sciatick nerve considerable enough: it is true, the medulla spinalis was not here of that consistence as in adult persons; but one could with some pains observe all the four tunicks, and the two substances as in the brain, to wit, the cortical or glandulous substance, and the fibrous or white, but with this difference, that the brown substance is exterior in the brain, but interior in the medulla spinalis. . . . . (p. 460)

Preston came to the following significant conclusion:

In a word, one can say all of it that they can of the brain, and more, for it appears more sensible and necessary for the life, for you can take the brain or cerebellum from an animal, and yet the animal shall live sometime thereafter; but a wound or compression of the medulla spinalis will cause sudden death. And the generation, or filtration, and distribution of animal spirits, is performed the same way as in the brain; and Monsieur Du Verny has observed, that all subjects of this nature, that he has had occasion to dissect, never one of them was found wanting the medulla spinalis; so that from what is above observed, I take for a sufficient demonstration. It was not wanting in this subject, being so necessary for the life of animals, and without which it is impossible to conceive how they can subsist; . . . . (pp. 460–1)

Preston then proceeded to review the experiments of Du Verny and Chirac on animals.

Monsieur Du Verny, in the year 1673, ... took the brain and cerebellum from a pigeon, and in place thereof, filled the crainium with flax, notwithstanding which it lived some time, searched for aliment, did the ordinary functions of life, and had the use of sense; and Monsieur Chirac, Professor of Anatomy at Montpelier, by several experiments he has made upon dogs, has clearly proved, an animal may live some time wanting the brain, and even sometimes the cerebellum, as you'l see by the following experiments. The first was upon a dog, from whom he had taken the brain, yet he lived some time, but when the cerebellum was taken out he died immediately: but he has observed, that by blowing into the lungs, the animal has lived an hour altho' wanting the cerebellum. The second experiment was upon a dog from whom he took half the cerebellum, but he died immediately. The third upon a dog, from whom he took half of the brain, after he continued to have the motion of all the parts, and could walk about; then he took all the brain from the same dog, he had yet sense and respiration. A fourth experiment upon a dog, by introducing a pair of scisars betwixt the first vertebre and the Os Occipitis, to separate the medullar oblongata from the medulla spinalis, the animal had died immediately, but by blowing into the lungs, the motion of the heart continued, and the animal could move its body. The fifth experiment upon a dog, from whom he took the cerebellum, but he lived twenty four hours, and his heart beat well.

All these experiments let you see an animal may live some time, tho' imperfectly wanting the brain, and even the cerebellum, but there is no experiment where ever they lived wanting all; therefore I humbly conceive, the medulla spinalis was not wanting, for it has supplied the defect of the brain and cerebellum and the animal spirts have been separated and distributed for continuing the circulation of the blood. . . . . (pp. 461–2)

The foregoing experimental observations foreshadow that aspect of the reflex respones which concerns actions that take place independently of the

brain.   Descartes' formulations had to do with involuntary action in the
intact individual; the observations just quoted supplement and substantiate
those formulations by apealing to vivisection.   These experiments were in
the physiological tradition of Harvey and Swammerdam and the results are
among the most significant achievements of the 17th century in the field
of reflex action.

The whole field of general physiology was cultivated by Hermannn Boerhaave (1668–1738), who is significant, not so much because of his original
contributions, but because, like Willis, he summarized the physiological
and anatomical knowledge and point of view of his day with regard to
medico-physiological problems.   Coming as he did at the end of the 17th
and at the beginning of the 18th centuries, his point of view represented the
ideas and "best" opinion prevailing in scientific circles at the time of this
transitional period in the history of neuro-muscular physiology.   Boerhaave's *Institutiones Medicae* published in 1708 was a widely used text in
the schools, and its author was an influential and widely know teacher.[12]

Boerhaave spent most of his professional life at the University of Leyden,
holding simultaneously the professorships of Medicine, Botany, and Chemistry at that institution.   He was in contact with the best scientific thought
of his time and knew as friends many of the learned men of his day.   As a
teacher he attracted many students, the most famous of whom was Albrecht
von Haller, the great physiologist of the 18th century.

In the second and third volumes of the English translation of the *Institutiones* (51) we find discussions of the "Structure and Action of the vital
and sanguificative Organs" which includes the brain, nerves and muscles.
In these discussions we find that the author accepts (1) the animal spirits
hypothesis, (2) the distinction between voluntary and involuntary action,
(3) the differential function of the brain and cerebellum, and (4) the experimental results of Du Verny.

Boerhaave followed Willis in distinguishing between the spirits produced
by the brain, which are called "animal," and those produced by the cerebellum, which are called "vital."   He described as follows the nature of the
"juice of the brain:"

Tho' the nervous Juice or Spirits separated in the Brain are the most subtile and move-
able of any Humour throughout the whole Body, yet are they formed like the rest from
the same thicker Fluid and Blood, passing thro' many Degrees of Attenuation, till its
Parts become small enough to pervade the last Series of vessels in the Cortex, and then it
becomes the subtile Fluid of the Brain and Nerves.   But as far as we can perceive, all

---

[12] *Cf.* Foster, *op. cit.*, p. 203.

HERMANN BOERHAAVE. FROM "SOME APOSTLES OF PHYSIOLOGY"

the circulating Juices in the Body consist of spherical Particles and therefore this circulating Juice of the Nerves probably consists of such figured Particles, only simple, or the least compounded of other smaller Spherules of any Humour in the whole Body; and therefore such simple or least compounded Spherules will be the most solid, or the least apt to divide and breack into less. (II, pp. 290–1)

The action of the spirits is described in purely physical terms.

But it does not follow, that because the Motion of this Juice is slow that therefore its Action must be so, for we are assured to the contrary, by its instantaneous Obedience to the Will in dancing and other Exercises; the Mind no sooner wills the Extension of the Arm but it immediately follows; not because a certain Quantity of the nervous Juice is impell'd at that time all the way from the Brain into the extended muscles, but because the Nervous Tubuli being full, an Impulse communicated to the Liquor at one End of that Tube will thrust out its Globules at the other End in the very same Instant of Time; as we know by placing a Row of ivory Balls close to each other upon a Table, and then by striking upon the outermost Ball at one End, the furthermost at the other End will instantly recede or run off with the Velocity first communicated, without any possible succession through the intermediate Balls; and if a Tube be full of Liquor, you no sooner urge more in at one End but it instantly runs out at the other. (II, p. 317)

Boerhaave was particularly impressed with the "celerity" of the action of the "nervous fluid;" this is expressed in the following passage.

I no sooner will the Extension of my Arm, but the Action instantly follows without any sensible Interval: but this Action of the Mind must be first exerted in the Brain, notwithstanding M. Perrault's Opinion to the contrary. We are furnished with innumerable Experiments which argue against him, and demonstrate that the Brain being obstructed or destroyed, the voluntary Motions are thence suppressed; and that by intercepting the Commerce betwixt the Brain and any Part, that Part immediately ceases to be governed and actuated by the Mind. But if the muscular Motion of a part so immediately follows the determinate Action in the Brain, it is evident that no Juice can suffice for the Office, but what is apt to move the swiftest and easiest of any. (II, p. 290)

That Boerhaave was an admirer of his countryman, Swammerdam, is indicated by the fact that he collected and published the latter's scientific papers. Nevertheless, he rejected Swammerdam's demonstration of the inadequacy of the animal spirits hypothesis.

I am not ignorant that Swammerdam has oppos'd Experiments to this Opinion, and has demonstrated that by compressing of the Nerve belonging to any Muscle of an Insect, that Muscle will be convuls'd; and Steno having divided the crural Nerve in a Dog, found that by vellicating and pulling the same the Foot was directly convuls'd. Add to this that Vipers and Snakes of all kinds continue their reptile Motion after the Heart has been pull'd out; and a Frog that has had its Heart and Lungs cut out will swim upon being thrown into cold Water, also an Eel being cut into several Pieces continues to move about for a long time after; but all these are in Reality no Objections to the Existence of a nervous Fluid; for the two first Experiments make nothing against us, and the rest only shew that the Fabric of the Nerves in cold amphibious Animals is different from that of the Nerves in Quadrupeds and hot Animals; so that no argument of Force can be thence drawn to make any Conclusions with regard to the human Body. (II, pp. 312–13)

Although our author clung to the classic conception of animal spirits—as did, indeed, most of his contemporaries—nevertheless, his statement of the structural-functional relations of the brain, cerebellum, spinal marrow, and muscles represented the best experimental evidence available at the time. It may be regarded, in fact, as an excellent summary of the best scientific opinion on these matters at the close of the 17th century.

. . . . hence therefore they [the muscles] appear to be continually kept in a State of Violence or distention, with respect to themselves, always resisting Elongation, and always endeavouring to contract or shorten themselves; but this much more in the living than in the dead animal, and therefore one Muscle requires to have this antagonized by another Muscle acting in a contrary Direction.

If the Brain be violently compressed, contused, totally obstructed, suppurated, or cut out in such a Manner as to let the Injury extend into the Medulla, then the Actions of all the voluntary Muscles cease instantly, together with all the senses and Memory; but on the other hand, the spontaneous Motions of the involuntary Muscles still continue both in the Heart, Vessels, Viscera, and vital Parts; but nothing of all this happens when the Brain which is opened remains free and sound.

If the same Injury be offered to the Cerebellum, the Action of the Heart immediately ceases, together with all the Senses, voluntary Motions, Respiration, and Life itself; but vermicular Motion remains a long time after in the Stomach and Intestines, which may be again restored in these Parts after it has ceased, and when these Injuries are removed in time.

If the Nerve of a Muscle be compressed, tied with a strict ligature, corrupted or cut asunder, all the vital and voluntary Motion of that Muscle is then quite abolished; and if the Trunk of a Nerve is injured in the same manner, supplying its Branches to different Muscles, they will all of them be in like manner deprived of their Motion; but the Injury being moved without destroying the Continuity of the Nerve, the Functions of all the Muscles return as at first.

The same Injury being offered to any Part of the Spinal Marrow, then the Action of all those Muscles is destroyed, whose Nerves arise from the spinal Medulla below the Part affected, while the actions of those remain intire, which have their Nerves from above. (III, pp. 192–93)

Complete as this statement is, it contains no reference to the principle of reflex action as expressed by either Descartes or Willis; "involuntary motions" as used by Boerhaave is scarcely synonomous with reflex, although the two expressions refer to activities which have elements in common. In another place Boerhaave referred to a certain type of animal response which the modern psychologist might recognize as habitual and which suggests the principle of reflex action.

There is no room to doubt, but that there are several voluntary muscles in the Body which operate only from Custom by the Influence of the Mind, of which by continued Use we are insensible; which Muscles taking their first Action from the Command of the Will, do nevertheless afterwards continue to operate in a manner as if it was spontaneously. We often walk at the same time that we are thinking or talking upon divers Affairs; and when we first wake out of our sleep in a Morning, we sit up in Bed, and throw our Muscles into that Posture to which they have been accustomed through the whole Course of Life, without giving them any sensible Command by the Will. (III, pp. 215–16)

This description of automatized actions "of which by continued use we are insensible" is one of the earliest references to this type of response. It is evidently Boerhaave's intention to point out that, although the voluntary muscles are under the control of nerves whose origin is in the brain, the action of these muscles may, under certain conditions, appear to resemble that of the involuntary muscles. This is equivalent to a type of process which later was to be described by the term "acquired reflex."

SUMMARY OF THE CONTRIBUTIONS OF THE 17TH CENTURY

The enormous increase of interest in the study of the phenomena of muscle and nerve is perhaps the most significant development of 17th century physiology. The intensity of this interest appears particularly in the last half of the century in those brilliant investigations associated with the names of Borelli, Mayow, Stenson, Glisson, Swammerdam, Du Verny, and Descartes.

An interesting manifestation of this interest is found in the plan of William Croone (1633–1684) providing for a series of lectures on muscular motion to be delivered before the Royal Society. Croone was a physiologist whose treatise (95) on muscular motion, published in 1664, reflects the same spirit that is shown in the works of Borelli, Stenson, and others of this period. His will made no provisions for carrying out the plan for the lectureships on muscular motion. In the *Record of the Royal Society* (419) we find, however, that his widow remedied the situation.

His widow who subsequently became Lady Sadleir . . . . in her will, dated September 25, 1701, bequeathed to the Society one fifth of the clear rent of the King's Head Tavern, in or near Old Fish Street, London, at the corner of Lambeth Hill, 'for the purpose of a lecture and illustrative experiment for the advancement of natural knowledge on local motion, or (conditionally) on such other subjects as, in the opinion of the President for the time being, should be most useful in promoting the objects for which the Royal Society was instituted,' the remainder being paid to the Royal College of Physicians, also for the support of a lecture to be delivered before them. (p. 176)

In 1728 a decree in Chancery permitted the Society to devote the entire profits accruing from the legacy to the payment for a single lecture, but it was not until 1738 that the first Croonian Lecture was delivered.[13]   These lectures have been the medium through which many important developments in the field of nerve-muscle physiology have been presented to the world. Fulton (161) points out that the history of "muscle physiology in the 18th, 19th and 20th centuries has been largely developed at these annual occasions."

It is clear that in the 17th century the study of the processes in the nerve and muscle received an impetus which resulted in the next century in a well-defined theory of reflex action.   In this connection it is necessary to mention two important influences:—Vesalius and William Harvey.   Vesalius in defying the Galenical tradition laid the foundations of a sound knowledge of human anatomy including the anatomy of the nervous system.   Harvey in his work exemplified a method of which the essence was that sound knowledge regarding the processes in the living body could result only from the observations of those processes themselves.

In spite of the example of Harvey and the agnosticism of Stenson, Borelli, Swammerdam, and Glisson, it is apparent that doctrines involving mysterious non-material "principles" and "spirits" still persisted as explanatory theories in the field of neuro-muscular action and control.   The summaries of Willis and Boerhaave, admirable as they are, reflect this tendency to make the nervous system the seat of mysterious agencies of control, the nature of which was essentially unknowable by the method of observation and experiment.

In its advancement science does not maintain an even front of achievement.   Against a background of uncertain speculation and vague generalization concerning the nature of nervous control, the cautious statement and quantitative experiments of Swammerdam reveal a brilliance which is equalled by but few of his contemporaries.   His point of view was objective and his contributions reveal an unexpected quantitative aspect.   The demonstration that the muscle does not increase in bulk during contraction was a positive contribution of importance and the observation regarding the essential similarity between voluntary and involuntary muscular contractions was unique in the 17th century.

While Descartes' discussions of nerve-muscle physiology were not free from the speculative pre-conceptions of his contemporaries, and although his

---

[13] *Vide* the *Record* (419) p. 195.   From 1786 to 1885 the property referred to in the will returned an income of fifteen pounds per annum, of which sum the Society's share was three pounds.   Since 1885 the return has increased and the Society now receives fifty-six pounds yearly.   On page 216 of the *Record* will be found a list of the Croonian lectures and subjects from 1738 to 1912.

conceptions of neural anatomy were more imaginary than real, yet his effective description of automatized behavior, involving as it does a theory of reflex action, raised his work to front rank as a contribution to physiological psychology. His hypothesis that the body was a machine demands the principle of reflex action to make it intelligible, and this hypothesis was the very heart of physiological and psychological theorizing of the next two hundred years. It is this that constitutes the significance of Descartes' contribution to physiological psychology.

The demonstration that the vital processes of the body might continue after the experimental removal of the brain doubtless had been anticipated by innumerable casual and unrecorded observations. Willis' conception of the relative independence of centers in the brain and cerebellum received experimental proof at the hands of Boyle, Perrault, Bohn, Chirac, DuVerny, Preston, and others. It is significant that these experiments were based on the assumption that similar results would be obtained in the case of man. This attack on the problems of neuro-muscular functions from the comparative point of view, while, historically considered, was not new, was a logical product of the conception that the laws of the bodily mechanism were universally applicable.

The contributions of the 17th century to development of theories of reflex action and automatized behavior may be summarized as follows:

(1) The theory of bodily automatism as stated by Descartes, and elaborated by Willis. This theory involved the specific statement of the principle of reflex action, and included the description of numerous specific automatic acts which modern physiology would recognize as reflex.

(2) The contributions of Swammerdam especially in the use of the nerve muscle preparation as a technique in the study of neuro-muscular phenomena.

(3) The contributions of Swammerdam, Borelli, Glisson, Stenson, and Mayow which tended to show that the traditional concept of animal spirits was inadequate insofar as neuro-muscular processes were concerned.

(4) The study of the effects on behavior of the experimental destruction of various segments of the central nervous system. The theories and contributions of Willis, Perrault, DuVerny, Chirac, Preston, Mayow, and others should be mentioned in this connection.

CHAPTER V

The 18th Century

"We can never indeed want matter for new experiments; and tho' the History of Nature as recorded from almost innumerable experiments, which have been made within the compass of a Century, be very large, yet the Properties of Bodies are so various, and the different Ways by which they may be examined so infinite, that it is no wonder that we are as yet got little farther than the Surface of Things: Yet ought we not to be discouraged, for tho' we can never hope to attain to the compleat Knowledge of the Texture, or constituent Frame and Nature of Bodies, yet may we reasonably expect by the Method of Experiments to make farther and farther Advances abundantly sufficient to reward our Pains."—STEPHEN HALES, *Statical Essays*, 1733.

The "innumerable experiments" to which Stephen Hales referred reflected the intense and almost childlike curiosity which prevailed during the 17th and 18th centuries regarding the newly discovered marvels of the natural world. These marvels included discoveries in the field of physiology as well as in the fields of mechanics and physics. The agency of the brain and nerves in sensation and motion, the gross functional distinctions between the brain and spinal cord, and the chief objective phenomena of involuntary motion had been determined by the beginning of the 18th century as a result of procedures which were acceptable to experimental physiology for a hundred years.

That concept of reflex action which referred to a type of neuro-muscular response with certain specific objective characteristics was formulated by Willis, Descartes, Swammerdam and others in the 17th century, and elaborated by a series of experimental investigations during the 18th century. The statements of Descartes regarding involuntary actions were based on the interpretation of the bodily processes in terms of a mechanism; by the use of the word "reflex" he took advantage of a serviceable analogy merely,—an analogy which has colored nearly all of the subsequent speculation and theorizing in this field. This analogy did not specify the anatomical structures involved, although its author attempted to improvise a neuro-physiology to account for the observed phenomena. The absence of adequate techniques for the investigation of the finer anatomy of the brain and cord delayed until the 19th century the statement of the reflex arc concept in terms of specific structure.

68

In spite of the lack of knowledge as to the exact nature of the nervous structures at the basis of the reflex act, the conception itself persisted. The disagreements regarding the localization of the reflex center reflect the dearth of anatomical knowledge. Two points of view were in evidence regarding the *locus* of the center of muscular control; the one placed it in the cerebro-spinal portion of the nervous system, the other located it in the peripheral nerve plexuses and ganglia. The resolution of this controversy was one of the contributions of the 18th century.

ASTRUC OF MONTPELIER

The 18th Century was, says Garrison, "aside from the work of a few original spirits like Morgagni, Hales, Hunter, Wolff, and Jenner, essentially an age of theorists and system-makers." This tendency to systemize and classify may be noted in the work of Astruc of Montpelier (1684–1766) whom Cayrade (85), writing in 1864, credited with being the first to use the word "reflex."[1] Astruc was interested in the structural basis of the "sympathies," which he grouped into several classes, showing that they could be explained by the theory of anastomosis of the veins, by the continuity of the tissues, or by the intervention of the nervous system. He recognized the nervous system as the sole agent in the last named, and Cayrade believed that Astruc included in this class of nervous sympathies the phenomena which we now call reflex. Astruc says of them:

Je ne m'occuperai, que de cette espece de sympathie qui se montre entre deux parties éloignées, qui n'ont entre elles aucune communication des vaisseaux sanguins, aucune similitude dans les humeurs, aucune parité d'usage; cette espèce de sympathie dans laquelle une partie étant stimulée ou en état de souffrance, une autre partie éloignée est sollicitée à la contraction ou bien est ébranlée par des convulsions. Rien n'est plus fréquent que cette sympathie. Dans l'état normal de l'économie, le mouvement rhythmique du coeur, l'alternance des mouvements respiratoires, le clignement des paupières, l'acte de la déglutition, de la défécation, de la mixtion, de l'éjaculation de la semence, de l'accouchement, etc., sont sollicités sympathiquement par des stimuli particuliers et propres à chacun d'eux. (Quoted by Cayrade, p. 13)

Astruc rejected the theory of peripheral nerve anastomoses as a basis of sympathy on the following grounds: (1) parts of the body entirely distinct are united by "sympathy," (2) the fibres of the nerve trunks parallel each other and remain distinct throughout their entire course, there being no communication between them.[2]

[1] Both Eckhard (125, p. 41) and Hodge (232, p. 157) have pointed out Cayrade's error in failing to credit Descartes with being the first to make use of the analogy of the reflex.

[2] *Cf.* Cayrade, *op. cit.*, p. 13.

Cayrade describes the mechanism which Astruc believed to be the basis of the "nervous sympathy."

Alors il supposa que les impressions extérieures mettent en mouvent les esprits animaux, qui, reflues dan le tube nerveux, viennent frapper une des colonnes du cerveau; là ils sont *réfléchis* suivant un angle égal à l'angle d'incidence, vont porter un ébranlement, et, comme conséquence, le mouvement dans un tube nerveux place sur la ligne de réflexion. Suivant que les esprits réfléchis viendront frapper le tube nerveux directement (a plein canal) ou obliquement, la sympathie, quoique provenent d'un même point, sera différente. Enfin l'intensité du stimulus, la force avec laquelle coulent les esprits, faisant varier, d'après lui, l'angle de réflexion, donnera lieu à une sympathie differente, quoique ce soit sur le même organe qu'ait porté l'impression première. (Quoted by Cayrade, p. 14)

We have here a very literal interpretation of the concept of reflexion. The explanation is wholly mechanical; it is elaborated, however, in somewhat greater detail than that of Descartes and makes use of known facts regarding the structure of the nervous system. It should be noted that Astruc assumed that other kinds of "sympathies" than those dependent on the nervous system existed in the organism.

ALBRECHT VON HALLER

"We may now approach," says Garrison (162),[3] "with all due reverence, the greatest systematist after Galen, and one of the most imposing figures in all medical history, Albrecht von Haller (1708–1777), the master physiologist of his time."

Foster would make the year 1757 a "red letter year,"[4] since it is the date of the appearance of the first volume of Haller's *Elementa Physiologiae*, thus marking the "dividing line between modern physiology and all that went before."

Haller was born at Bern and educated at the Universities of Tübingen and Leyden. He was attracted to the latter institution in 1725 by the growing fame of Boerhaave whose most famous pupil he became. He took his degree in 1727 and spent the next three years in travel. In 1736 he became Professor of anatomy, botany and medicine at the University of Göttingen, where he remained for 17 years, retiring in 1753.

The contributions of Haller to general physiology were extraordinarily numerous; they included a reassertion of the myogenic theory of the heart's action, a recognition of the use of bile in the digestion of fats, and others of fundamental importance.[5] His most important contribution to nervous physiology was the elaboration of Glisson's theory of irritability.[6]

[3] P. 246.
[4] *Op. cit.*, p. 204.
[5] Garrison, *op. cit.*, p. 247 *ff.*
[6] *Ibid.*, p. 246, see also Verworn (503) p. 5.

Irritability was due, according to Haller, to the *vis insita*, a capacity possessed exclusively by the muscles. His discussion (202) of the kinds of muscular action in this connection is illuminating.

A muscle is endowed at least with a threefold power. First the dead one, common to it with other animal fibres. Then another, which we have called the vis insita, possessing different phenomena. For, in the first place, it is peculiar to life, and to the first hours after death, and it disappears much sooner than the dead one. Again, in most cases, its action consists in alternate oscillations; so that moving to and fro, at one moment it contracts itself towards the middle; and at the next extends itself from the middle towards the extremities, and so on successively for several times. Moreover, it is manifest quick, and performs very considerable motions; the dead force only such as are small and scarcely apparent. It is excited both by the touch of a sharp instrument, and in the hollow muscles by inflated air, by water, and every kind of acimony, but more powerfully than by any other stimulus by electricity. Lastly, it is peculiar to the muscular fibre, and in no other part of the human body is it found possessed of the qualities above mentioned. (Par. 400, p. 190)

The *vis insita*, which was clearly distinguished from the capacity of the muscle to act as a result of stimulation *via* the nerves, is inherent in the muscle, while the stimulation *via* the nerves—or *vis nervosa*—is adventitious.

The former (*vis nervosa*) ceases along with life; whereas the latter (*vis insita*), according to certain experiments, subsists long after it. The former is suppressed, by tying a ligature upon the nerve, by injuring the brain, or by the exhibition of opium. The latter is not affected by these circumstances, but continues after the nerve is tied or cut, and even in the intestines, though taken out of the body; it also exists in animals destitute of brain: parts of the body possess motion, which are destitute of sensation, while others possess sensation, which are destitute of motion. The will excites and removes the nervous action, but has no power over the vis insita (par. 404, p. 192)

He described his experiments in connection with the demonstration of the *vis insita*.

I (by my experiments published first in 1739, and again in 1743) separated this irritable nature on the one hand from a mere dead force, and on the other from the nervous force and from the power of the soul. I showed that the movement of the heart and the irritable nature of the intestines depended on it alone. I confined it entirely to the muscular fibre, in which the Batavian school does not agree with me, but they will I hope do so when they are willing to distinguish the contractile force common to all animal fibre from the irritable force proper to the muscle alone. I also showed that that force was something perpetually living, and that it often broke out into movement though no external stimulus as such could be recognized by us was acting. By a stimulus, however, it could at any time be called back from rest into action. In a movement produced through it I distinguished between the stimulus which might be very slight, and the movement called forth by the stimulus which might be very powerful. (Quoted by Foster, p. 293)

As we have already indicated, Glisson's theory of irritability, which Haller revived in his *vis insita*, was much broader in its application. The *vis insita* of Haller was limited rigidly to the muscles and was a capacity, as Verworn points out,[7] which we today refer to as "contractility."

What is the relation of Haller's conception of neuro-muscular activity to reflex action? In examining the functions which he included under the *vis insita*, it becomes apparent that he was referring to a kind of function which resembles in certain particulars that which is included under the modern term reflex.

The intestines are exceedingly tenacious of their *vis insita;* they continue to contract, after they are taken out of the body, and even after they are cold. The heart is even more tenacious than these, if you consider all things; as is most evident in the chick, and in cold-blooded animals. Different muscles are most readily excited, by different stimuli; as the bladder by urine, the heart by blood, and the intestines by air. . . . This power is totally different from any other known property of matter, and is new. It does not depend either upon gravity, or attraction, or elasticity, for it is inherent in soft fibres, and is destroyed, when they become indurated. (Par. 402, p. 191)

It is a kind of involuntary action, but differs from the modern concept of the reflex in at least one important particular; *it is wholly independent of the nerves*. Haller, however, referred to another kind of action, involving the nerves and dependent upon a stimulus, which, also, resembled the reflex. This he discussed in connection with his consideration of the will.

If we may add anything to the phenomena, we may suppose the nervous liquor to be of a stimulating nature, forcing the elementary particles of the muscular fibre to approach nearer to each other. The motive cause which occasions the influx of spirits into the muscle, so as to excite it into action, *seems not to be the soul, but a law established by the Creator*. For animals, newly born, or newly transformed, *without any attempt, or exercise, know how to perform compound motions*, very difficult to be defined by calculation. But the soul learns those things which it performs, slowly, imperfectly, and experimentally. Muscles, therefore, contract, which in a given time receive more of the nervous fluid, whether that be occasioned by the will, or *by some irritating cause arising in the brain, or applied to the nerve*.[8] (Par. 408, p. 195)

We have here one of the earliest references to *unlearnedness* as an aspect of a certain type of animal action. The action of the soul has no relation to the *vis insita*, however.

Though the soul may be supposed to act in nervous motions, it cannot be admitted in those arising from the *vis insita*. The heart and intestines, also some organs of the venereal

---

[7] *Vide* Verworn *Op. cit.*, p. 6. Verworn believes Haller's distortion of Glisson's concept retarded progress of knowledge in this field.

[8] Italics not in original.

appetite, are governed by the *vis insita*, and by stimuli. These powers do not arise from the will; nor are they lessened, or excited, or suppressed, or changed by it. No custom or art can subject these organs of inherent motion to the will, or cause a satellite of voluntary motion to forget to obey the commands of the soul. It is so certain that motion is produced by the body alone, that we cannot even suspect any motion to arise from a spiritual cause, except that which the will seems to excite in animal volition; a stimulus will occasion the most excessive actions, in direct opposition to the will. (Par. 409, p. 195)

We are able to see in the *vis insita* and in the vaguely characterized class of nervous action governed "by a law established by the Creator," references to a type of action which resembles the reflex. Even more definite are Haller's references to certain actions not under the control of the mind in the following.

From these affections of the mind, not only the pure will appears to direct the action of the body to a foreseen purpose, in order to attain good, and avoid evil, but also in the body itself, neither willing them nor capable of opposing them, various changes happen in the pulse, respiration, appetite, strength, and other functions of the heart, nerves, stomach, and other parts, which both immediately follow and indicate the passions of the mind. Thus anger violently excites the motion of the pulse, and the strength of the muscles; forces the blood into the ultimate and pellucid vessels, and even out of the vessels; accelerates the excretion of bile, terminates chronic diseases, and removes obstructions. (Par. 565, p. 276)

Haller proceeded to discuss whether any motions arise from the mind, a discussion which lead him into larger problems of the relation of the body and mind. His conclusion that all motions do not arise from the mind marks him as an opponent of Stahl and his followers.

But it is evidently false, that all motions arise from the mind, and that without it matter would be an immoveable inert mass: for the contractility exciteable by every stimulus, to which the motion of the heart, intestines, and perhaps all the other motions in the human body, belong, does not require the presence of the mind; it continues in the dead body; it is excited by mechanical causes, heat, and inflation; and it does not desert the fibres, until they become stiff and cold, although the mind, which perceives and wills, may have been a long time expelled by the destruction of the brain and heart, and even although the muscle, by being taken out of the body, has been separated from every imaginable connection with the mind. (Par. 575, p. 282)

In this connection Haller referred to the absence of consciousness in the "obscure perceptions" in walking, winking, and the like. He concluded, however, that even on the basis of "obscure perceptions" we cannot explain certain kinds of motion; they are not under the control of the mind. In the "obscure perceptions" we have an hypothesis which resembles the modern psychological conception of automatisms.

The idea of "the sympathy of parts, so famous in the practice of physic" received serious attention. The sympathy may depend upon a variety of non-neural structures; the blood vessels, the "similiture in their fabric" of parts, *e.g.*, the sympathy between the womb and the breasts, the continuity of membranes, *e.g.*, the "itching of the glans penis from calculus," and finally, the sympathy based upon the nerves. The relation between body and mind is a sympathy of the latter sort.

Regarding Haller's other neurological concepts, we may merely state that he believed that the same nerves served both sensation and motion,[9] and that the nerves conveyed an imponderable fluid "very thin and invisible, and destitute of all taste and smell."[10] His view of the seat of the soul or mind was distinctly neurological. Neither the medulla, the corpora striata, thalami, pons nor medulla oblongata[11] could be regarded as the exclusive abode of the soul.

No narrower seat can be allotted to the soul than the conjoint origin of all the nerves; nor can any structure be proposed as its seat except that to which we can trace all the nerves. For it will be easily understood that the sensorium commune ought to lack no feeling of any part of the whole animated body nor any nerve which can convey from any part of the body impression of external objects. And the same may be said of the nerves of movement. Wherefore, even quite apart from the experimental results described above, we cannot admit as the exclusive seat of the soul, either the corpus callosum on the septum lucidum or the tiny pineal gland, or the corpora striata or any particular region of the brain. (Foster, p. 298)

Although Haller's conception of the nervous base of involuntary action was to some extent confused and obscure, his ideas of neuro-muscular control were as clear-cut as the state of neurological knowledge permitted. He empahsized the unlearned and innate aspect of involuntary action, and though he did not elaborate the idea, it seems that the *vis insita* was a very simple primitive form of involuntary action, roughly analogous perhaps to the modern conception of the tropism.

ROBERT WHYTT

The most significant contribution of the 18th century to the physiology of involuntary action was made by Robert Whytt (1714–1766) of Edinburgh. His monograph "On the Vital and Other Involuntary Motions of Animals" (537) begun in 1744 and published in 1751, seems to have been the first extended treatise devoted exclusively to the consideration of those animal

[9] Haller (202) par. 384, p. 183.
[10] *Ibid.* par. 381, p. 182.
[11] *Ibid.* par. 372, p. 172.

ROBERT WHYTT

responses which today we call reflexes. Eckhard (125) refers to Whytt's work as being "full of significance" to the study of reflex movements, and regards him as having contributed the *Fundamentalversuch* in connection with the experimental physiology of reflex action.

Whytt seems to have been precocious in his intellectual development; he received the M.A. degree from St. Andrew's when he was but 16 years of age.[12] He studied medicine at the University of Edinburgh and Leyden, receiving his medical degree at Rheims in 1736. In 1738 he was elected fellow of the Royal College of Physicians of Edinburgh, and in 1747 he was made Professor of the Theory of Medicine at the university there. His published papers cover a wide range of medical and physiological topics and the dates of their publication indicate that he was engaged in scientific activities until the year of his death.

Whytt abandoned at the outset a terminology which had played an important rôle in the quasi-scientific, quasi-metaphysical neurology of his predecessors.

> The immediate cause of muscular contraction, which, from what has been said, appears evidently to be lodged in the brain and nerves, I chuse to distinguish by the terms of the *power* or *influence of the nerves;* and if, in compliance with custom, I shall at any time give it the name of *animal* or *vital spirits*, I desire it may be understood to be without any view of ascertaining its particular nature or manner of acting; it being sufficient for my purpose, that the existence of such a power is granted in general, though its peculiar nature and properties be unknown. (pp. 11–12)

Thus Whytt refused to be drawn into controversies regarding the nature of a substance about which he had little actual knowledge.

Three varieties of animal motion were distinguished; voluntary, involuntary and mixed.

> The voluntary motions are such as proceed from an immediate exertion of the active power of the will. The involuntary and mix'd motions (which last, though subject to the power of the will, yet are not ordinarily directed by it) may be aptly enough comprehended under the general denomination of SPONTANEOUS; since they are performed by several organs as it were of their own accord, and without any attention of the mind, or consciousness of an exertion of its active power; such are the motions of the heart, organs or respiration, stomach, intestines, etc., which have been, also, distinguished by the name AUTOMATIC; though perhaps there is an impropriety in this term, as it may seem to convey the *idea* of a mere inanimate machine, producing such motions purely by virtue of its mechanical construction: a notion of the animal frame, which ill agrees with the inactivity and other known properties of matter. (pp. 1–2)

---

[12] *Cf.* Seller (436) and Carmichael (79) for biographical details. The latter author gives a bibliography of Whytt's writings.

All muscular contraction is due to a "power or influence lodged in the brain, spinal-marrow and nerves."[13] Muscular contractions are of three kinds: natural, voluntary and involuntary.

The natural contraction refers to the constant state of tension in muscles which have antagonists, due to the fact that they "are constantly endeavouring to shorten or contract themselves."[14] This tension of the muscles is due to the influence of the nerves "which is perpetually operating upon them, though in a very gentle manner. . . . ."

The natural contraction of the muscles arising from the constant and equable action of the nervous power on their fibres, and of the distending fluids on their vessels, is very gentle, and without any such remarkable hardness or swelling of their bellies, as happens in muscles which are contracted by an effort of the will. And although the sphincters and those muscles, whose antagonists are paralytic or hindered from acting, do always remain in a state of contraction; yet at any time, by an effort of the will, they can be much more strongly contracted. (p. 16)

This distinction of an especial type of muscular contraction is significant since it marks an early attempt to describe muscle tonus.

Voluntary contractions proceed immediately from the "power of the will." Involuntary contractions, on the other hand, are "strong but suddenly followed by a relaxation," and are the *necessary consequence of the action of a stimulus upon the muscle* and "cannot be affected, either as to [their] force or continuance, by the power of the will."[15] A stimulus, Whytt defines as any irritating substance applied to the "bare muscles" which produces a contraction in them.[16] Although the action of the stimulus is limited to the "bare muscle" by this definition, Whytt by implication later makes it clear that the stimulus may be applied to the nerve which is attached to the muscle.

Whytt's idea of the stimulus is important both to his hypothesis and to the development of the reflex theory. This capacity to react to stimuli which is peculiar to involuntary or "vital" motions of animals is not "owing to any effervescence, explosion, ethereal oscillation, or electrical energy excited" in the fibres or membranes of the muscle.[17] Whytt also objects to Haller's *vis insita* which he regards as "no more than a refuge of ignorance, which nothing but the despair of any success in their inquiries into this

[13] *Op. cit.*, p. 5.
[14] *Ibid.*, p. 14.
[15] *Ibid.*, p. 30.
[16] *Ibid.*, p. 18.
[17] *Ibid.*, p. 265.

AN
ESSAY
ON THE
VITAL and other INVOLUNTARY
MOTIONS of ANIMALS.

By ROBERT WHYTT, M.D. F.R.S.

Physician to his MAJESTY,

Fellow of the Royal College of PHYSICIANS,

AND

Professor of Medicine in the University of *Edinburgh*.

*Inanimum est omne quod pulsu agitatur externo ; quod autem est
animal, id motu cietur interiore et suo. Nam hæc est propria
natura animi atque vis. ———— Quæ sit illa vis, et unde sit in-
tellegendum puto. Non est certè nec cordis, nec sanguinis,
nec cerebri, nec atomorum.*
CICERO. Disput. Tuscul. lib. 1.

The second Edition, with Corrections and Additions.

EDINBURGH

Printed for JOHN BALFOUR.

M,DCC,LXIII.

TITLE PAGE FROM WHYTT'S "ESSAY"

matter"[18] can have caused Haller and his followers to propound this theory. In a word this action is not due to any mechanical cause, but is to be explained on the basis of a "sentient principle,"[19] operating through the body by means of the brain and nerves. Whytt held that this sentient principle is co-extensive with mind. Its relation to consciousness and the relation of consciousness to involuntary or vital motion, will be discussed in a later section.

It is the sentient principle which makes possible the response of the muscle to stimuli which is the special mark of involuntary or vital motion.

If it were constantly observed, that such muscles only as had their fibres immediately acted upon by *stimuli*, were excited into contraction, then indeed it might be suspected with greater shew of reason, that such motions were no more than a necessary consequence of the mechanical action of those *stimuli* upon the muscular fibres: but as we find the muscles of animals brought into action without any irritation of their fibres, whenever a *stimulus* is applied to the coats or membranes covering them, to the nerves which are sent to them, or to some neighbouring or even distant part, it seems absurd to imagine such motion owing to the mechanical action of the *stimulus* upon the fibres of the muscle, and not to the impression it makes on the sentient principle. Thus the contraction of the *sphincter pupillae* arising from the action of light on *the retina*, with which it has no communication of nerves, cannot possibly be explained mechanically, but must be owing to some sentient principle in the brain, which, excited by the uneasy sensation, increases the action of the nervous system upon that muscle. (pp. 276–277)

This "sentient principle" is non-rational. The contraction of the heart, for example, cannot be due to "any previous deduction of reason."[20] The involuntary motions, due to the presence of the sentient principle, *take place too rapidly for the intervention of reason.*

Add to this, that the motions excited by any pain, or irritation are so instantaneous, that there can be no time for the exercise of reason, or a comparison of ideas in order to their performance; but they seem to follow as a necessary and immediate consequence of the disagreeable perception. And the DEITY seems to have implanted in our minds a kind of SENSE respecting *morals* whence we approve of some actions, and disapprove of others, almost instantly, and without any previous reasoning about their fitness or unfitness; a FACULTY of singular use if not absolutely necessary for securing the interests of virtue among such creatures as men! so, methinks, the analogy will appear very easy and natural, if we suppose our minds so formed and connected with our bodies, as that, in consequence of a *stimulus* affecting any organ, or of an uneasy perception in it, they shall immediately excite such motions in this or that organ, or part of the body, as may be most proper to remove the irritating cause; and this, without any previous rational conviction of such motions being necessary or conducive to this end. Hence, men do not

---

[18] *Ibid.*, p. 266.
[19] *Ibid.*, p. 321 *ff.*
[20] *Ibid.*, p. 316.

eat, drink, or propagate their kind, from deliberate views of preserving themselves or their species, but merely in consequence of the sensations of hunger, thirst, etc. (pp. 318–19).

The final statement in the above passage marks an extension of the idea of involuntary motion to many modes of response, which is most significant in the history of the development of theories of reflex action; it marks also an important step in the development of a non-rational, non-purposive psychology.

Whytt believed the "sentient principle" co-extensive with mind, although not dependent on the will. It is true that we do not always perceive the stimulus, however.

> The stimulus occasioning the vital motions is unperceived by us, not only on account of its gentleness, but also because we have been accustomed to it from the earliest period of our lives. The force of custom is prodigious and unaccountable; what we have long been used to, we become scarcely sensible of, while things which are new, though much more trifling, and of weaker impression, affect us remarkably. . . . Few persons in health feel the beating of their heart, although it strikes against the ribs, and that too with a considerable force every second or oftener. . . (pp. 327–328)

It is at this point that we have a crucial test of Whytt's theory, so far as the modern conception of reflex action as a mechanical series of events in the nervous system, is concerned. The Stahlians in opposing the Cartesian conception of the animal body as a machine, postulated a rational, thinking, provident, conscious principle which directs the phenomena of animal behavior. Whytt may be charged with lending support to this animistic view by the introduction of his theory of the "sentient principle" which lies behind involuntary motions. However, his biographer, Seller (436) was at great pains to deny that Whytt was a Stahlian or even a "semianimist." Seller says:

> He [Whytt] does not say that the animal is necessarily unconscious of the stimulus; neither does he say that the animal is unconscious of the muscular contraction which constitutes the movement; what he enforced is, that there is no consciousness of anything interposed between the consciousness of the impression, and the consciousness of the muscular contraction excited.

In other words, there is no act of will. Nevertheless, there can be no doubt but that Whytt did not wholly escape the Stahlian influence. The "sentient principle," although it does not involve consciousness or will seems to be, in part at least, a convenient verbal substitute for an all-pervasive soul.

Whytt found other reasons for accepting the hypothesis that the mind may control motions which are outside the field of consciousness.

But, the objection against the mind's being concerned in the vital and other involuntary motions, drawn from our not being conscious of its interposing for this end, is quite overturned, by considering that a great variety even of the voluntary motions are many times performed, when we are insensible of the power of the will exerted in their production. Thus, while in walking we either meditate by ourselves, or converse with others, we move the muscles of our legs and thighs, without attending to, or knowing anything of the matter. We are not sensible of the eyelids being kept open by the continued operation of the will. . . . The same thing is true of the action of the muscles which support the head. . . . We not only acquire, through custom and habit, a faculty of performing certain motions with greater ease than we were wont to do them, but also, in proportion as this facility is increased, we become less sensible of any share or concern the mind has in them. Thus a young player upon the harpsicord or a dancer, is, at first very thoughtful and solicitous about every motion of his fingers, or every step he makes while the proficients or masters of these arts perform the very same motions, not only more dexterously, and with greater agility, but almost without any reflexion or attention to what they are about. (pp. 334–335)

We have here a fairly clear description of the phenomena of automatisms, together with a remarkably penetrating analysis of the psychological aspects of habit formation. For the history of the theories of reflex action, a significant aspect of Whytt's discussion is the recognition of a resemblance between purely involuntary action i.e., reflexes, and those actions the control of which has dropped from the conscious to the unconsicous level, i.e., automatisms.

Whytt completes his system by making habit acquired as described in the foregoing passage, a link between voluntary and involuntary motion.[21]

Further, it appears, that as in all the works of nature, there is a beautiful gradation, and a kind of link, as it were, betwixt each species of animals, the lowest of the immediately superior class, differing little from the highest in the next succeeding order; so in the motions of animals . . . the mix'd motions, as they are called, and those from habit, being the link between the voluntary and involuntary motions. (p. 360)

In further support of his hypothesis that motion is controlled by the mind although below the level of consciousness, he pointed out that many sensory impressions reach us but are outside the field of clear attention, that is, impressions, "which are in themselves, or lost amidst far stronger ones, are frequently neither attended with consciousness when present."[22] He thus anticipated theories of attention as a factor in psychical inhibition and facilitation.

Whytt pointed out that involuntary motions are under the control of

[21] Whytt objects to the idea of Dr. Porterfield that all vital motions are in the beginning voluntary. Cf. the discussion of Porterfield's position infra, Chapter VII.

[22] Op. cit., p. 323.

the mind, *i.e.*, are not wholly mechanical in nature, since the mere idea of
the adequate stimulus may have as much effect as the stimulus itself.

> Thus the sight, or even the recalled *idea* of grateful food, causes an uncommon flow of
> spittle into the mouth of a hungry person; and the seeing of a lemon cut produces the
> same effect in many people.   (p. 280)

This would seem to be a remarkable anticipation of an observation which
physiologists of 150 years later were to recognize under the term "conditioned
reflex." Whytt believed that all or nearly all involuntary motions are
subject to this kind of control; a control which modern physiological
psychology identifies as cortical and recognizes as a fundamental principle.

The presence of "feeling" in involuntary or vital motion apparently does
not necessarily imply consciousness, since the latter is a power of the "soul"
and is associated with the brain.   Whytt was aware of the experiments of
his predecessors in connection with the persistence of motion after the
removal of the brain.   However, the following passage seems to indicate
that there may have been a low order of consciousness in the case of
vital motion.

> It has been objected, that the separated members of animals, though they continue
> to move for sometime, are nevertheless neither animated nor endowed with *any kind* of
> sensibility, otherwise the animal to which those members belonged, ought to feel pain when
> they are irritated.
> . . . . we have reason to believe that the motions excited by *stimuli* in the muscles
> of animals, after they are separated from their bodies, are owing to *some kind* of feeling or
> *simple* sensation (such as oysters and other animals of the lowest class, who have no brain,
> are endowed with) in those muscles or their nerves, which though not attended with any
> *reflex consciousness*, a power the soul only exercises in the brain, is nevertheless the imme-
> diate occasion of all those motions which arise from the irritation of the fibres of the
> muscles, whether they be connected with the other parts of the body, or newly separated
> from them.   (footnote, p. 432)

Vital motions under certain conditions may be modified by the will;
under most circumstances, however, the motion follows the stimulus
of necessity.

> When the organ is not extremely sensitive, or when the stimulus is very slight, or is
> applied to some distant part, and not immediately to that which is to be moved, we
> can by an effort of the will, restrain those motions, which otherwise would follow. . . .
> (p. 343).

In regard to the center controlling vital motion, Whytt reviewed the
results of Vieussens and others on this point and concluded that it was not
the cerebrum, since that organ may be destroyed without disturbing vital
function.   The cerebellum, however, played a more important rôle.

. . . . since various experiments concur in shewing the cerebellum to be more concerned in the vital motions than the cerebrum, while none at all can be produced in proof of the cerebrum being more immediately necessary to these than the cerebellum, it follows, that the vital organs have their nerves, either wholly or principally, from the latter. (pp. 366–7)

The cerebellum may be destroyed without immediately stopping vital motion for the reason that,

The branches from the spinal marrow which join the intercostals together with the spirits (if I may be allowed to call the influence of the brain by that name) remaining in the trunks of the nerves and fibres of the heart, are sufficient to keep up these motions for some time: in man, perhaps, only for a few pulsations, in young dogs or cats for several hours, and in a tortoise for several months; which last animal, not to mention other differences, has its spinal marrow remarkably large. . . . (p. 367).

This points to the spinal marrow as the essential structure for vital motion. In other experiments Whytt satisfied himself on the basis of experimental observations that,

There is no sympathy between the different muscles or other parts of the body as was observed while the spinal marrow was entire; from whence it seems to follow that the nerves distributed to the several parts of the body have no communication but at their termination in the brain or spinal marrow, and that to this, perhaps, alone is owing the consent or sympathy between them. (Quoted by Hodge, p. 159)

This is the *Fundamentalversuch* of Eckhard.[23] The observations of Preston and DuVerny,[24] however, would seem to have in part anticipated Whytt in this regard. A reference to Preston's paper can leave no doubt but that he fully appreciated the fundamental significance of the spinal cord to vital function.

Whytt added to the evidence regarding the functioning of the spinal cord an important supplementary experiment.

A frog lives, and moves its members, for half an hour after its head is cut off; nay, when the body of a frog is divided in two, both the anterior and posterior extremities preserve life and a power of motion for a considerable time. (p. 427)

---

[23] Eckhard makes the following reference to Whytt's experiment: "Wir finden hier zum ersten Male den Versuch verseichnet, den wir heute in der Experimentalphyiologie als den Fundamentalversuch über die Reflexbewegungen verzuführen pflegen, wenn es sich darum handelt, zu beweisen, dass jene ihre Entstehung dem willenlos wirkenden Rückenmark verdanken, den nämlich, dass decapitirte Frösche, die sich noch auf ihre Haut bewegen, dies nicht mehr thun, wenn man vorher das Rückenmark zerstört hat." *Op. cit.*, p. 43.

[24] That is, the observation that animal motion persists after removal of the brain, but that the presence of the spinal cord is essential. *Cf. supra* Chapter IV.

In other words, *not the cord as a whole, but only a segment is necessary for vital functioning.*

The list of specific motions which Whytt included under the vital or involuntary functions is remarkably complete. Among the specific mechanisms are (1) motions of the alimentary canal especially during the digestive processes, (2) coughing, (3) sneezing, (4) erection of the penis, (5) ejaculation of semen, (6) various genital responses in the female during coition, (7) blushing—arterial changes, (8) secretion of saliva, (9) emptying of the bladder, (10) action of the heart, (11) reaction of the pupil to light[25] and accomodation to distance, (12) reaction of muscles in inner ear in adapting to sound, (13) respiration.

Whytt made it quite clear that all involuntary or vital motions serve a purpose in the animal economy.

> The general and wise intention of all the involuntary motions, is the removal of everything that irritates, disturbs, or hurts the body. . . . So this endeavour to free the body or any of its parts, from what is noxious, becomes unhappily, sometimes, so strong and vehement, as to threaten the entire destruction of the animal fabric. But, in the main, this faculty must be confessed highly useful and beneficial. . . . (p. 320).

In emphasizing the protective function of the vital motions, Whytt again anticipates an important criterion of reflex action. It is true that Descartes' example of a reflex—the winking of the eyes on the sudden approach of a foreign object—implies a protective purpose, but this seems to be incidental to Descartes' description.

SUMMARY OF WHYTT'S CONTRIBUTION

Whytt may be regarded as the most important figure in the history of reflex action up to his time. Brett credits him with being one of the founders of the doctrine of reflex action. Though Descartes is frequently credited with being the originator of the doctrine of reflex action, this is based largely on his chance use of an analogy in support of his theory of the human body as a material machine directed by a rational soul. He did not elaborate the implications in his generalization or offer experimental proofs of the fact itself. In contrast, Whytt, under involuntary motion, as a result of a penetrating psychological and physiological analysis, recognized a separate class of animal action.

[25] Whytt demonstrated that this was due to the *effect of light on the retina,* and not the result of a stimulus acting on the iris as Haller and de la Hire (231) had believed. Whytt discovered also that the destruction of the anterior corpora quadrigemina would abolish the pupillary response. *Cf.* Garrison, *op. cit.,* p. 256.

Eckhard lists[26] Whytt's contributions to reflex theory as follows:

(1) Whytt performed the *Fundamentalversuch* in nerve physiology, in demonstrating experimentally that the spinal cord is essential to reflex action. Eckhard points out that it had already been demonstrated that the brain was essential, and that Whytt presented the final link in the evidence by showing that reflex functions disappeared when the cord was extirpated.[27]

(2) The movements in response to skin stimulation in the decapitated frog do not begin for several minutes after the operation. Thus Whytt presented the first observation in connection with the inhibitory mechanism.

(3) Whytt showed that not the whole cord, but only a segment was necessary to vital function.

(4) Whytt pointed out the protective function of the involuntary motions in man.

(5) Whytt described a number of responses which we today know as reflexes, that had not been recognized before.

To these might be added:

(1) The "Essay on Vital Motions" is the first extensive monograph devoted exclusively to the consideration of reflex action.

(2) Whytt recognized a type of muscular action which bears a close resemblance to that which we now know as tonus.

(3) Whytt pointed out that in involuntary motion a stimulus is essential and that the motor response is a necessary consequence of the stimulus.

(4) Whytt described a class of motor responses controlled by subliminal processes, i.e., automatisms, and pointed out their resemblance to involuntary (reflex) motions.

(5) He suggested the possibility of modifying vital functions by the will, and pointed out the possibility of the *ideational control* of these functions. His observations in connection with the latter anticipate to some extent the principle of the so-called conditioned reflex.

DAVID HARTLEY

David Hartley (1705–1757), a contemporary of Whytt's, published in 1749 a seven hundred page treatise entitled "Observations on Man, His Frame, His Duty, and His Expectations" (209). Hartley is known to psychology as an expounder of Association psychology, and association plays an important part in his theory of animal motion. Hartley was interested in the operations of both the body and the mind, and he has been

---

[26] *Op. cit.*, p. 43 *ff*.

[27] We have already indicated that Preston and DuVerny seem to have anticipated Whytt in this connection.

credited with being the originator of the science of physiological psychology. The doctrine of association and "vibrations" is at the base of all of Hartley's physiological and psychological theories. Applied to the nervous system, this doctrine assumed that the impression of an object gives rise to vibrations which travel along the sensory nerves to the brain where they meet and interact, and then descend from the brain to the muscles causing motion. The sequence of events in this series is physical and mechanical. The vibrations run along the nerves in some such manner "as sound runs along the surface of rivers, or an electrical virtue along hempen strings."[28]

With the vibrations in the nervous system were associated sensations and ideas. Hartley divided motions into automatic and voluntary; the former depended upon sensation and the latter upon ideas. Vibrations in sensory nerves ascended towards the brain; when they arrived at the origins of the motor nerves they descended to the muscles. Some of the sensory vibrations, however, continued to the brain and were diffused over the "whole medullary substance."[29] These left-over vibrations, also, descended to the motor nerves and excited some "feeble vibrations" in the muscles. If the vibrations in the brain were repeated frequently they generated ideas. The heat of the blood passing through the medullary substance, also, excited vibrations which descended to the muscles. These together with the feeble vibrations of the "left-over" vibrations from the brain "account for that moderate degree of contraction, or tendency thereto, which is observable in all the muscles, at least in all those of healthy adults, during vigilance."[30] This seems to be a vague reference to tonus. Sensations are due to vibrations in the brain and cord excited by external objects impressed on the senses.

Voluntary action is dependent upon association in every day life, although theoretically, there may be a kind of pure volition.

If it follows that idea, or state of mind . . . which we term the will, directly, and without our perceiving the intervention of any other idea, or of any sensation or motion, it may be called voluntary, in the highest sense of the word. If the intervention of other ideas, or of sensations and motions (all of which we are to suppose follow the will directly), be necessary, it is imperfectly voluntary; yet still it will be called voluntary, in the language of mankind, if it follow certainly and readily upon the intervention of a single sensation, idea or motion, excited by the power of the will: but if more than one of these be required, or if the motion do not follow with certainty and facility, it is to be esteemed less and less voluntary, semi-voluntary, or scarce voluntary at all, agreeable to the circumstances. (p. 59)

---

[28] Hartley, *op. cit.*, p. 50.

[29] *Ibid.*, p. 52.

[30] *Ibid.*, p. 52.

After actions which have been rendered "most perfectly" voluntary by one set of associations they may

by another, be made to depend upon the most diminutive sensation, ideas, and motions, such as the mind scarce regards, or is conscious of; and which therefore it can scarce recollect the moment after the action is over. Hence it follows, that association not only converts automatic actions into voluntary, but voluntary ones into automatic. (p. 59)

These actions which follow upon "diminutive sensations" are called automatic, or rather "secondarily automatic," to distinguish them from the originally automatic and voluntary motions.

Hartley described the process of transmutation of motions from voluntary to automatic and the reverse, and in the case of what we now know as the grasping reflex, offered an example of this transmutation. By repetition of the original automatic motion, other vibrations are generated which become associated with objects presented to the infant's sight.

By pursuing the same method of reasoning, we may see, how, after a sufficient repetition of the proper associations, the sound of the words grasp, take hold, etc., the sight of the nurse's hand, in that state, and innumerable other associated circumstances, i.e., sensations, ideas, and motions, will put the child upon grasping, till, at last, that idea, or state of mind which we may call the will to grasp, is generated, and sufficiently associated with the action to produce it instantaneously. (p. 60)

Thus the originally automatic act has become voluntary. It may by a similar process of repetition become again automatic—secondarily automatic—on "many occasions" while still voluntary in others.

We have here an attempt at a theory of learning based on association. We may also note an anticipation of the idea of the conditioning of reflexes. Hartley points out that the evident powers of the will in the actions of swallowing, breathing, coughing, expelling the urine and faeces, sneezing, hiccoughing and vomiting, may be explained by the same process of transmutation.

The process of automatization—the transmutation from an originally voluntary action to an automatic action—is described in distinctly modern terms.

Suppose a person who has a perfectly voluntary command over his fingers, to begin to learn to play upon the harpsicord: the first step is to move his fingers from key to key, with a slow motion, looking at the notes, and exerting an express act of volition in every motion. By degrees the motions cling to one another, and to the impressions of the notes, . . . the act of volition growing less and less express in the time, till at last they become evanescent and imperceptible. . . . Whence we may conclude, that the passage from the sensory ideal, or motory vibrations which precede, to those motory ones which follow, is as ready and direct, as from the sensory vibrations to the original automatic motions correponding to them; and consequently, that there is no intervention of the idea, or state of mind, called will. (p. 62)

In Hartley's presentation of the various special senses, he systematically appends a section to each presentation describing the automatic motions which arise from that particular sense. In other words he recognizes each receptor mechanism as an initiating member for a series of reflex responses—to use modern terminology. The list of reflex responses attached to each sense includes a wide variety of specific responses.

Special sense	Automatic motion
1. "Feeling"—touch, pain	Crying, distortion of face, laughter following tickling, grasping, putting muscles into contraction following painful stimulation.
2. Taste	Sucking, mastication, deglutition, distortion of mouth, peristaltic motion of stomach and bowels, vomiting, hiccough, expulsion of faeces, spasms.
3. Smell	Inspiration of air to "increase" odor, contraction of the fauces and gullet, sneezing.
4. Sight	Motions of globe of eye, motions of the eyelid, contractions of the lacrymal glands, contractions of the muscular rings of the iris, and the ciliar ligaments.
5. Hearing	Contraction of small muscles of the auricle in adjusting to sound, contraction of muscles belonging to small bones of the ear.

In Hartley as in Whytt we note that a resemblance exists between involuntary motion (Whytt), or originally automatic motion (Hartley) and habits which have become automatized. There is no reason to believe that Hartley was aware of Whytt's work; in the main their lines of reasoning diverge widely. So far as the development of theories of neuro-muscular action are concerned, Whytt's work is the more suggestive and seems to posses greater vitality. This is due in part to the fact that Hartley is engaged primarily in forcing his ideas into the mold of a system, i.e., he is engaged in establishing the doctrine of associationism. Hartley makes a most interesting contribution to the theory of automatisms in his suggestion that there are motor reactions to "diminutive sensations, such as the mind scarce regards."

Significant also is Hartley's suggestion regarding the sensory-motor conduction of "vibrations." This implies a reflex arc which does not involve the cerebral cortex. However, it should be noted that Hartley does not make any statement regarding the necessity of a relation between the sensory and motor arms. Finally, Hartley's discussion of automatic actions in connection with the various receptor mechanisms marks a distinct advance in the analysis and classification of these types of animal motion.

CHAPTER VI

THE EXTENSION OF MECHANISTIC PHYSIOLOGY—LA METTRIE, UNZER, PROCHASKA AND BLANE

"The soul is therefore but an empty word, of which no one has any idea and which an enlightened man should use only to signify the part in us that thinks. Given the least principle of motion, animated bodies will have all that is necessary for moving, feeling, thinking, repenting, or in a word for conducting themselves in the phys'cal realm, and in the moral realm which depends upon it."—LA METTRIE, *Man a Machine*, 1748.

For Descartes, man and the lower animals, although distinct from each other in the all important matter of the soul, nevertheless had in common one characteristic; they both possessed a capacity for responses in which mind or consciousness did not share. The body of man insofar as it was concerned with these involuntary functions, was a machine and differed only in complexity from that of the lower animals. If animals are self-activating machines, and if man is a machine in all respects except that of the soul, then it would seem that animism was in the process of being eliminated from physiological psychology. As we have seen, this was not the case; animism persisted in one form or another in both 17th and 18th century physiology. It was present in the writings of both Whytt and Hartley, and we shall meet it in a modified form in Unzer and Prochaska.

Whether Descartes was sincere in his retention of a soul in the body of man, or whether "purely for the sake of the parsons"[1] he thought it expedient to include a non-material agency of control, nevertheless his conception of a bodily machine with the soul left out left an ineffaceable imprint on the physiological theorizing of the 17th and 18th centuries. The mechanical flute player of Jacques de Vaucanson, which was exhibited in Paris in 1738, is a reflection of this interest in the human body as a machine.[2]

[1] *Vide* Lange (281) p. 246.

[2] Jacques de Vaucanson (1709–1782) in 1738 presented to the French Academy his mechanical flute player. He also made a duck which could eat, swim, digest, etc. In 1746 Vaucanson was admitted to the Academy of Sciences. *Cf.* Lange *op. cit.*, p. 75 and LaMettrie (280) p. 203. *Cf.* also *infra* Chapter XVI, p. 285 ff. for a discussion of similar contemporary attempts.

The contrivances of Vaucanson were mechanical forerunners of the speculations of the great French materialist, Julien Offray de la Mettrie, whose *L'Homme Machine* published in 1748 made its author a point of attack by the ecclesiastical world. La Mettrie (1709–1751) was born at Saint Malo in the early part of the 18th century. He studied natural philosophy, rhetoric and medicine, taking his doctor's degree in the latter field at Rheims in 1725. He was a student of the great Boerhaave at Leyden and translated many of the master's medical works. His theological and medical enemies forced him to leave France and he took refuge in Prussia where he received a pension from Frederick the Great. Here he spent the remaining years of his life.

La Mettrie criticized Descartes' assumption that the body and soul were distinct, but the Cartesian doctrine that animals were mere machines was extended to include man as well. La Mettrie pointed out all points of anatomical resemblance between man and the animals with a view to showing that the Cartesian dichotomy was not justified. In other words, if it could be demonstrated that the lower animals are mere machines, the same evidence must be used with equal effectiveness to show that man is but a more finely constructed mechanism. In the following passage taken from "Man a Machine" (280), the author makes it clear that there is but one principle of motion in both man and the lower animals.

Grant only that organized matter is endowed with a principle of motion, which alone differentiates it from the inorganic (and can one deny this in the face of the most incontestable observation?) and that among animals, as I have sufficiently proved, everything depends upon the diversity of this organization; these admissions suffice for guessing the riddle of substances and of man. It (thus) appears that there is but one (type of organization) in the universe, and that man is the most perfect (example). He is to the ape, and to the most intelligent animals, as the planetary pendulum of Huyghens is to a watch of Julien Leroy. More instruments, more wheels and more springs were necessary to mark the movements of the planets than to mark or strike the hours; and Vaucanson, who needed more skill for making his flute player than for making his duck, would have needed still more to make a talking man, a mechanism no longer to be regarded as impossible, especially in the hands of another Prometheus . . . . The human body is a watch, a large watch constructed with such skill and ingenuity, that if the wheel which marks the seconds happens to stop, the minute wheel turns and keeps on going its round, and in the same way the quarter-hour wheel, and all the others go on running when the first wheels have stopped because rusty, or, for any reason, out of order. (p. 141)

The mechanical or motive principle is found in every part of the body; La Mettrie reviewed the evidence in connection with the movements of the body after decapitation to show that each part of the organ contains within itself all that is necessary to explain its movements.   The involuntary or reflex movements were explained in mechanical terms.

Let us now go into some detail concerning these springs of the human machine.   All the vital, animal, natural, and automatic motions are carried on by their action.   Is it not in a purely mechanical way that the body shrinks back when it is struck with terror at the sight of an unforeseen precipice, that the eyelids are lowered at the menace of a blow, as some have remarked, and that the pupil contracts in broad daylight to save the retina, and dilates to see objects in darkness?   Is it not by mechanical means that the pores of the skin close in winter so that the cold can not penetrate to the interior of the blood vessels, and that the stomach vomits when it is irritated by poison? . . . . that the heart, the arteries and the muscles contract in sleep as well as in waking hours. . . .?   (pp. 131–2)

It should be noted that La Mettrie does not deny feeling and consciousness to the body; the organism is none the less a machine though it may think and feel.   These capacities depend upon the organization of the brain which "had its muscles for thinking, as the legs have muscles for walking."[3]

In La Mettrie we have a logical development of the doctrine enunciated by Descartes.   The body is but a machine and all its movements are explainable in terms of its own structure.   Although La Mettrie's contribution to the development of the theory of reflex action is indirect, his discussion of what the modern physiologist would call integrative activities in terms of mechanism rather than in terms of non-material powers, bears a striking resemblance to the conception of the organism as a congeries of reflexes—a conception which we recognize as characteristic of modern physiological psychology.

A countryman of La Mettrie who was born six years after his death has been referred to as the "father of materialistic physiology."[4]   Pierre Jean George Cabanis (1757–1808) was not himself a Materialist, but he approached the problems of physiology from the mechanistic point of view. His principal work (75) on physiology was begun in 1795 and was concerned in part with the problem of whether the victims of the guillotine suffered after decapitation.   He assumed three neural levels corresponding to the reflex, semi-conscious, and completely conscious or volitional types of reaction.   The brain only was involved in the latter.   In this connection his famous dictum that the brain is "a special organ whose particular function it is to produce thought just as the stomach and intestines have the special function of carrying on the work of digestion, the liver that of filtering the bile, etc.," indicates that the mental functions were governed by mechanical principles also.   Beginning with the reflex, Cabanis attempted

[3] LaMettrie, *op. cit.*, p. 132.
[4] *Vide* Lange *op. cit.*, II, p. 293.   *Cf.* Brett (61), II, p. 375.

to trace the development of the adjustive reactions of the organism in terms of neural levels of increasing complexity. From this point of view he may be regarded as one of the founders of physiological psychology.

UNZER AND PROCHASKA

Johann August Unzer (1727–1799), born in Halle and educated at the university there, did not, as Hodge points out, contribute much that was new to nervous physiology, but he systematized and presented that which was already known. He did this in his "Principles of Physiology" (501) which was published in 1771 after it had been a quarter of a century in preparation.[5] The "Principles" is a closely knit, monumental work rather heavily burdened with the author's own terminology. A strikingly large proportion of the work is given over to a presentation of the physiology of the nervous system.

Unzer distinguished animal and mechanical machines; the former are the brain and nerves and the latter the other structures of the body. External impressions supply the mind (*via* the nerves) with sensations, provided the impressions reach the brain. The impression may or may not go to the brain; in the latter case animal movements may be exicted which are non-conceptual and unconscious. These latter movements may not be distinguished by the observer from conceptual movements originating in the brain. The movements are either brought about by the *conceptive force* or the *vis nervosa* or nerve force. Those impressions which involve the brain are termed sentient impressions and result in sentient actions as distinguished from purely animal actions.

> By virtue of the *vis nervosa*, the animal body becomes capable of functions, which cannot be explained either by the mechanical and physical laws of motion, or by the laws of the animal-sentient forces, but which are performed by the animal machines, supplied according to special laws with vital spirits. To these belong the purely animal movements caused by an external impression on the nerves before it excites a material external sensation in the brain, with which the muscular irritability of Haller must be classed, as well as those excited by internal impressions on the medulla of the nervous system and which excite no conceptions: or by other stimuli than conceptions including many actions attributed to nervous irritability by Haller. (Par. 354, p. 188)

This would seem to be a slight extension of Haller's doctrine. The two properties possessed by the nervous system are clearly stated in the following:

[5] *Vide* Translator's Introduction, p. ii.

The following irrefragable truth follows from these two leading principles: While the animal machines are endowed by nature with the property of conducting external impressions to the brain, so that they may there excite material idea, giving rise to sensations, and of receiving internal impressions caused by conceptions, they also possess another and entirely different property, and are intended by nature to effect by means of external impressions they receive, whether the latter reach the brain and are felt or not, the same movements which are effected when they do reach the brain and are felt; and to effect by means of an internal impression, which they receive from a touch or irritant caused by no conception whatever, the same movements as are effected by means of the cerebral forces, when the same internal impressions are produced by a conception. The animal machines are mysteriously and inscrutably endowed by the Creator with these two distinct motor forces derived from impressions, in addition to the equally inscrutable animal force originating also from them, partly that they may put the animal sentient forces into action, and partly that through these, they may move the organism animally; and the greater proportion of animal movements are so closely dependent upon them, even when these are at the same time sentient action, that they must be considered as the most fundamental and most general principium of the whole animal mechanism. (Par. 361, p. 193)

The distinction between voluntary and involuntary motion made in the foregoing was based largely on physiological and anatomical criteria. The physiological mechanisms involved in the non-cerebral motions were described in detail.

. . . . the impression is transmitted along the nerve upward to the brain; but ere it reaches there, it is turned from its course, and so reflected downwards, that it excites (as in internal impressions) the nerve of the other remote parts, or the nerve twigs or efferent nerve-fibrils of the part receiving the impression; and this internal impression, which is nothing else than the reflected external impression, thus reaches the mechanical machine which has to perform the nerve-action. (Par. 415, p. 224)

Unzer then gave the experimental proof.

If the toe of a frog at rest be pricked, the external impression thus made goes to the brain. From thence it is reflected upon the limbs, and the animal rises up and springs forward. But if the head be cut off, and the toe be again pricked, the same motions take place. In this case, the external impression on the toe, must pass upwards towards the brain, although it cannot reach it, for if the nerve be divided in the thigh, so as to prevent its transmission, the motion does not take place. Further, it is obvious that it is reflected on the nerves of the limbs as an internal impression, and along their twigs to their muscles, because no other part of the body, except this single toe which was pricked, receives an external impression. Again, supposing while one toe is pinched, that the nerve of the other leg be divided; in this case, the movements will be repeated in all the parts except that whose nerve is cut through. This explains what takes place in similar circumstances, when an impression is made on the spinal cord, and spasms and convulsive movements are excited in all parts below the point of irritation, except those the nerves of which are cut through. The reflected external impression passes as an internal impression to, and only excites movements in those muscles to which it can be transmitted from the point of reflexion. (Par. 415, p. 224)

The completeness of the proof of the generalizations involved may be questioned, but shrewdness of the physiological observations cannot be doubted. In other sections Unzer has made it clear that he regarded consciousness as an adjunct of brain action; hence, the action described above is unconscious. The concept of reflexion seems firmly established in Unzer, and implies an element of necessity. The conversion of an afferent impulse into an efferent impulse by a mechanism of reflexion gives us a concept of reflex action which is adequate even in the modern sense.

Unzer found—as had his predecessors for a hundred years—many data which offer material for neurological study in the motions of decapitated animals.

If a nerve, which certain external impressions, when felt, usually stimulate to produce certain movements in the organism, be cut off from its connection with the seat of the conceptive force, namely, the brain, or in other words, if it be cut or tied, or the head of the animal be entirely separated from the body, undoubtedly observations prove, that the same external impression from the point of impression to the point of division acts as a stimulus to the same movements so long as any traces of life remain in the body, although the external impressions never arrive at the brain, but only as far as the point of division, and, consequently, is neither felt nor excites material external sensations in the brain. This is the first fundamental principle, on which the doctrines to be taught in this Second Part of the Physiology of Animal Nature, are based. (Par. 357, p. 190)

Unzer discussed the complex nature of the acts of the brainless animal and pointed out that the prevision observed was apparent and not real. The animals simulated volitional actions.

. . . . everything, in short, that is effected sensationally and volitionally they effect by means of the organic forces of the impressions; and since they can act as orderly, judiciously, and rationally as it were, as if they thought, it has been inferred erroneously, that the apparent voluntariness of these acts depended on sensational conceptions, even although they might be only external sensations. That which is termed voluntary motion, we term so only in *ourselves;* the voluntariness is not in the movements—which remain the same whether sensational conceptions produce them or not—but simply in this, that *we* produce them by spontaneous sensational conceptions . . . . and nature has so provided when their adapted acts should take place, or their instincts ought to be in operation, that certain external impressions are imparted in a naturally necessary manner, which pass along their nerves, and are so reflected and changed into internal impressions, that the animal must perform those apparently adapted and volitional movements; . . . . (Par. 439, p. 236)

In the opinion of Unzer it was just as erroneous to infer that the complex acts of animals—bees, ants, flies, polypes, etc.,—which are not in a headless condition, are due to volition. Unzer considered the problem of the location of the center where the "reflexion" takes place. He believed that it could occur in the brain.

In the nerves, however, there is no place in which it can occur, except the ganglia of the motor nerves, and at their separation into branches and fibrils. According to all probability, these ganglia and points of division of the nerves, perform in the motor nerves the office of the brain in relation to the external impressions, since they deflect these from their course upwards, and communicate an internal impression, either to other nerves and their branches, or to different fibrils in the same nerve, conducting in the direction from the brain downwards; whereby these twigs and fibrils are suitably stimulated, and such muscular movements excited, as would have been caused if the external impression had reached the brain and had been turned back or reflected from thence by the intervention of an external sensation. (Par. 399, p. 215)

The most important contribution made by Unzer, in addition to his systematic presentation of already known facts, was the discussion of the path of the afferent and efferent impulses together with the physiological mechanisms involved. The proof of his conceptions was perhaps inadequate and could not be complete until the development—nearly a hundred years later—of proper physiological and histological techniques. Unzer's method of attack on his problems is ponderous, deductive, and rational, while that of his able contemporary, Whytt, is brilliant, inductive and psychological.

George Prochaska (1749–1820) was born in Moravia, graduated from the University of Vienna, and became Professor of Anatomy and Diseases of the Eye, there and at Prague.[6] Throughout his life he was interested in neurological problems, especially as they pertained to function. He was acclaimed by his contemporaries and physiologists of the first half of the 19th century as the founder of the doctrine of reflex action. Jeiteles (257)[7] and Longet (314)[8] credit Prochaska with being the first to state the principle of reflexion. Eckhard[9] and others, however, have pointed out that Prochaska's claims in this matter were exaggerated by his contemporaries.

Prochaska's "Dissertation on the Functions of the Nervous System" (416) which was published in 1784 contains his views on the physiology of the nervous system. Two important concepts, neither of which were new, are fundamental in Prochaska's system. The first is the *vis nervosa*, a latent power possessed by the nerves. In the opening pages of the "Dissertation," Prochaska described the *vis nervosa* in a passage in which he also stated his adherence to the inductive method.

[6] *Vide* Translator's Introduction, p. ix *ff*.
[7] P. 64.
[8] I, p. 307 *ff*.
[9] *Op. cit.*, p. 48 *ff*.

At length we abandon the Cartesian method of philosophizing in this part of animal physics also, and adopt the Newtonian, being persuaded that the way to truth through hypotheses and conjectures is tedious and altogether uncertain, but far more certain, more excellent, and shorter, through the inductive method. Newton designated the mysterious cause of physical attraction by the term *vis attractiva*, observed and arranged its effect, and discovered the laws of motion; and thus it is necessary to act with reference to the functions of the nervous system: we will term the cause latent in the pulp of the nerves, producing its effects, and not as yet ascertained, the *vis nervosa:* we will arrange its observed effects which are the functions of the nervous system, and discover its laws; and thus we shall be able to found a true and useful doctrine, which will undoubtedly afford a new light, and more elegant character to medical art. The illustrious Haller has already used the phrase *vis nervosa*, in designating the agent which the nerves employ in exciting muscular contractions; but the celebrated and ingenious J. A. Unzer has thrown the greatest light on the subject. . . . (Chapter I, sec. 8, p. 380)

The second important concept which is basic in the doctrine of Prochaska is the *sensorium commune* which he defined as the point of reflection between sensory and motor nerves. Both of these concepts were necessary to the development of Prochaska's theory of reflex action.

The *vis nervosa* alone is not capable of producing muscular action.

Although this *vis nervosa* is a property inherent in the medullary pulp, it is not the chief and sole cause that excites the actions of the nervous system, but is ever latent, and exists as a predisposing cause, until another exciting cause, which we term stimulus, is brought to bear. As the spark is latent in the steel or flint, and is not elicited, unless there be friction between the flint and steel, so the *vis nervosa* is latent, nor excites action of the nervous system until excited by an applied stimulus, which continuing to act, it continues to act, or if removed, it ceases to act, or if re-applied, it acts again. (Chapter II, sec. 3, p. 390)

This idea of neural action bears a close resemblance to the modern conceptions of the nervous impulse. The stimulus may be applied internally or externally, and may be either mechanical or mental. The *vis nervosa* has in addition two important properties: it is graded in strength and it is divisible. In regard to the first it is important to note that the "strength" is dependent on the intensity of the stimulus and is indicated by the strength or amount of the resultant muscular response. The relationship between the intensity of stimulus and the response here implied was later to become one of the important attributes of the stimulus-response psychology of which the reflex arc is presumably the functional unit.

The divisibility of the *vis nervosa* is important with reference to reflex theory since Prochaska thought that this property explained the experimental observation that a portion of the nervous system, although separated from the rest of the nervous system, still retained its functional activity. The assumption was that when a portion of the nervous system is cut off some of the *vis nervosa* remains in the severed part, thus allowing it to function. The brain does not supply the *vis nervosa*; hence, we may have nervous action independently of the brain.

This *vis nervosa*, which remains in the nerves when separated from the brain, is not exhausted by one or two muscular contractions they excite when irritated, but is equal to the production of numerously repeated movements, as I observed in a frog, the spinal cord of which I divided in the back. It survived this wound several days, and during the whole of that period, by irritating that portion of the spinal cord which was below the section, I excited innumerable convulsions in the lower extremities, nor did these die sooner than the whole frog. . . . Moreover, the *vis nervosa* not only continues in the spinal cord and nerves long separated from their connection with the brain, but exists in nerves that never had any connection with the brain whatever. This is proved by the histories of acephalous foetuses, which lived during the whole period of intrauterine life, were nourished, increased in growth, and when born evinced no obscure signs of vitality, without having a brain, and by the sole *vis* of the nerves and spinal cord, if the latter was not also defective. Animals which have nerves but no cerebrum also demonstrate the same fact. (Chapter II, sec. 3, p. 399)

Prochaska's *vis nervosa* differs from the *vis nervosa* of Haller in one important particular: in the case of Prochaska it persisted in any segment of the neuro-muscular system long after the death of the animal. Haller's conception was confused, of course, by his idea of the *vis insita* which was the exclusive property of the muscle and acted independently of the nerves.

In the idea of the *sensorium commune* we have, perhaps, the most important development of Prochaska's theory. It is the basis of the consensus between the motor and sensory arms of the reflex arc.

The external impressions which are made on the sensorial nerves are very quickly transmitted along the whole length of the nerves, as far as their origin; and having arrived there, they are reflected by a certain law, and pass on to certain and corresponding motor nerves, through which, being again very quickly transmitted to muscles, they excite certain and definite motions. This part, in which, as in a centre, the sensorial nerves, as well as the motor nerves, meet and communicate, and in which the impressions made on the sensorial nerves are reflected on the motor nerves, is designated by a term, now adopted by most physiologists, the *sensorium commune*. (Chapter IV, sec. I, p. 429)

The location of the *sensorium commune* becomes an important problem. Prochaska discussed various possibilities and came to the conclusion that it "extends through the *medulla oblongata*, the *crura* of the cerebrum and cerebellum, also part of the *thalami optici*, and the whole of the *medulla spinalis*,"[10] *i.e.*, it is co-extensive with the origin of the nerves. The reflexion which takes place in the *sensorium commune* is automatic and not under the control of the will.

[10] *Op. cit.*, Chapter IV, sec. 1, p. 429.

The reflexion of sensorial into motor impression, which takes place in the *sensorium commune*, is not performed according to mere physical laws, where the angle of reflexion is equal to the angle of incidence, and where the reaction is equal to the action; but that reflexion follows according to certain laws, writ, as it were, by nature on the medullary pulp of the *sensorium*, which laws we are able to know from their effects only, and in no wise to find out by our reason. The general laws, however, by which the *sensorium commune* reflects sensorial into motor impressions is the preservation of the individual; so that certain motor impressions follow certain external impressions calculated to injure the body, and give rise to movements having this object, namely, that the annoying cause be averted and removed from out the body; and vice versa, internal or motor impressions follow external or sensorial impressions beneficial to us, giving rise to motions tending to the end that the agreeable condition shall be still maintained. (Chapter IV, sec. I, p. 429)

The reflexion may take place with or without consciousness. In the latter case belong the motions of epileptics, movements of the body during sleep, movements of decapitated animals, etc.

All actions flow from the organism, and by physical laws peculiar to the *sensorium commune;* and are, therefore, spontaneous and automatic. The actions taking place in the animal body, with accompanying consciousness, are either such as are independent of volition, or such as the mind can restrain and prohibit at pleasure; the former being governed by the *sensorium commune* alone, independently of the mind are as much automatic as those which the soul is unconscious. Of this character are sneezing from an irritant applied to the nostrils, etc. (Chapter IV, sec. 1, p. 431)

Prochaska devoted some space to the discussion of the function of the ganglia. He finally decided that they act as a sort of "gentle ligature or compress" which may interrupt the passage of the nervous impulse under certain conditions.

. . . . yet the communication of all impressions is apparently not altogether interrupted; for if they be powerful, they appear to pass through the ganglia, and to be transmitted forward along the length of the nerves, but with broken and diminished force. From this it appears to be possible to understand, why the mind has no immediate control over the movements of the heart, stomach, and intestines, namely, because the impressions made by the will on the origins of the nerves do not appear to pass through the ganglia of the inter-costal, or great sympathetic nerve, to the parts mentioned, which derive their nerves principally from the intercostal. (Chapter IV, sec. 3, p. 436)

Prochaska revived the theory of nerve anastomoses, and reviewed the evidence pro and con. He came to the conclusion that while the *sensorium commune* is the principle location of the consensus, "it is not possible to deny some share in connecting and combining the functions of the nerves to their anastomosing and communicating branches."[11]

[11] *Op. cit.*, Chapter IV, sec. 2, p. 435.

It is interesting to note that the man who presented so cogently the evidence for the dominance of the spinal cord as the coördinating center in all nervous activity, should be misled in this important structural detail.

Like Unzer, Prochaska did not make distinctive original contribution to reflex theory, his most important service being a systematic presentation and discussion of already known materials. His discussions have greater clarity than those of Unzer. Under the hypotheses of the *vis nervosa* and *sensorium commune* he was able to include many hitherto dissonant conceptions. Since the value of any scientific hypothesis may be tested only by its inclusiveness, we may grant Prochaska an important place in the history of reflex theory. Whytt anticipated Prochaska's observations in connection with the independent functioning of segments of the spinal cord, and Whytt's analyses are perhaps more penetrating than those of Prochaska, but the latter was able to present clear formulations—perhaps the clearest up to his time—of the doctrine of reflex action.

OTHER CONTRIBUTIONS OF THE 18TH CENTURY.   THE CROONIAN LECTURES

At the hands of Haller, Whytt, Unzer and Prochaska the concept of reflex action had made the most rapid advance in its history. A general awakening of interest in neuro-muscular problems was manifest throughout the century. In England the first Croonian Lecture on muscular motion was delivered in 1738 under the aegis of the Royal Society. We have already described the establishment of these lectures,[12] the purpose of which is described in the Preface to the first lecture (474) as follows:

The late learned and famous Dr. Croune having observed how much the knowledge of the animal oeconomy depends upon the doctrine of the nerves and muscles, and how far the rational practice of physic might be improved by a more perfect acquaintance with the animal oeconomy, did for the encouragement of these studies, form a plan for instituting certain Lectures to be read on such subjects, in the Royal College of Physicians on the nerves and muscles, and in the Royal Society on muscular motion.

The first lecturer on this foundation was Alexander Stuart, who described (474) his experiments on the frog. He suspended the animal whose head had been removed "at the first vertebra of the neck" and stimulated the exposed spinal cord with a probe. The resulting contraction of the legs he explained as follows: (1) motion excited is voluntary and spontaneous motion, (2) the effect of the probe is the same as that produced by the mind or the will, (3) fluid is sent through small tubes (nerves) to muscles by the action of the probe, (4) voluntary motion is produced in the same way,

[12] *Supra*, p. 65.

except that the mind is the cause. Stuart conceived the antagonistic action of muscles to be due to independent impulses sent to the muscles by the mind.

In 1744 James Parsons (395) gave an excellent review of the work of Croune, Stenson, Willis, Mayow, Borelli and others on muscular motion. In this paper, which was read as a Croonian Lecture, Parsons disagreed with these authors in so far as they supported a theory of animal spirits. His own theory was that the muscle's cells are inflated by an "elastic aura" and he denied that any blood or spirits can get into them. The nerves serve as "pipes to convey it (the elastic aura) to the muscles." The distinction is made between voluntary and involuntary motion; the former is initiated by impulses and the latter is carried on mechanically.

The Croonian Lectures for the most part do not offer any material of consequence for the theory of neuro-muscular phenomena during this period. George Fordyce in a lecture read on November 22, 1787, says (152) with regard to his subject, "I should be inexcusable in taking up their [the Royal Society's] time, if the subject was not annually to be discussed before them." Fordyce, after dismissing the three doctrines regarding the cause of muscular motion, viz., (1) that a fluid passes along the nerves to the muscle, (2) that there is a vibration communicated by the nerve to the muscle, and (3) "that the nerves are surrounded with something like electric matter, in which motion runs from the brain to the moving parts," presented the novel theory that it is not necessary for any motion or communication "to pass through any other matter" in order to bring about muscular contraction. This is the result of the fact that muscular motion is an "original motion," that is, it is of the type of gravitation and magnetism; motions which are not dependent upon physical channels of communication.

An exception to this sterile type of theorizing is found in the paper of William Cruikshank (96) also delivered as a Croonian Lecture, in which the author described an experiment on the spinal cord of a dog.

I divided the spinal marrow of a dog, between the last vertebra of the neck and first of the back. The muscles of the trunk of the body, but particularly those of the hind legs, appeared instantly relaxed; the legs continued supple, like those of an animal killed by electricity. The heart, on performing the operation, ceased for a stroke or two, then went on slow and full, and in about a quarter of an hour after, the pulse was 160 in a minute. . . . . About seven in the evening, the pulse was not above twenty in a minute, the diaphragm acting strongly, but in repeated jerks. Between twelve at night and one in the morning, the dog was still alive; respiration was very slow, but the diaphragm still acted with considerable force. Early in the morning he was found dead. This operation I performed from the suggestion of Mr. Hunter: he had observed in the human subject, that when the neck was broke at the lower part . . . . the patient lived for some days, breathing by the diaphragm.   This experiment showed, that dividing the spinal marrow at this place on the neck, if below the origin of the phrenic nerves, would not for many hours after, destroy the animal.   (p. 184)

This is faintly reminiscent of Whytt's experiment performed nearly twenty years earlier.   Lorry, a French investigator, in 1760 also reported (315) an experiment in which he observed that compression or division of the spinal cord produced a paralysis in the portions of the body inferior to the lesion.

The work of Whytt was confirmed by Sir Gilbert Blane (1749–1834) who performed experiments on kittens and insects.   The results of these experiments were reported in his dissertation "On Muscular Motion" (48) which was also one of the Croonian Lectures.   He emphasized the importance of *stimuli*.

I have already acknowledged my ignorance of the manner in which *stimuli* in general operate, and that this must be admitted as an ultimate fact in nature.   But the operation of the will through the nerves, seems involved in double obscurity; for as it depends on the nature of thought, it cannot be made a subject of experimental investigation.   For this reason I shall decline the inquiry, as not being adapted to the ends of this Society; and it seems impossible for human sagacity to penetrate the connection of matter with sensation and volition.   (p. 258)

Although Blane refused to undertake an investigation of volitional action, he was willing to devote his attention to the simpler matter of automatic action.   He especially marked the innate character of these responses.

There is a connection established between the impression of certain external bodies and the action of certain muscles, analogous to what has already been noticed with regard to the internal motions excited in vessels by the peculiar stimulus of their fluids, Nature having instituted certain habitudes between outward stimuli and the moving powers, whereby natural propensities are established equally necessary to the support of life as the internal functions.   (p. 260)

It will be noted that he applied the word "instinctive" to these actions.

Thus in a newborn animal, the first contact of the external air excites the act of respiration and the contact of the nipple excites the act of sucking; both of which actions are absolutely necessary to the maintenance of life, and require the nice cooperation of a great number of muscles, prior to all experience.   Actions of this kind are called instinctive, and differ from voluntary motions in this respect, that the latter are the result of memory and experience, whereas the former are the immediate effect of external impression, in consequence of an established law of nature, and independent of consciousness.   The actions of instinct and those of volition, nevertheless, run imperceptibly into each other, so that what was at first instinctive, may afterwards come to be a matter of deliberate choice. The same muscles are the instruments of both, and they differ from the muscles obeying the internal stimuli, such as the heart, in this respect, that they are liable to fatigue, and thereby concur with the exercise of sensation and of thought, in rendering sleep necessary. (p. 260)

All this has a distinctly modern sound. More than any investigator of his time, he seems to have emphasized the *unlearned* character of automatic action. In regard to his experiments, he said:

I took a live kitten, a few days old, and divided the spinal marrow, by cutting it across the neck. The hind paws being then irritated by pricking them, and by touching them with a hot wire, the muscles belonging to the posterior extremities were thrown into contraction, so as to produce the motion of shrinking from the injury. The same effects observed in another kitten, after the head was entirely separated from the body. In repeating this experiment, I found that when the spinal marrow was cut through, between the lumbar vertebrae and os sacrum, the posterior extremities lost their irritability, but the part below it, the tail, retained it. . . .

The like takes place with regard to insects; for, after the head of a bee is separated from the body, the hinder part will sting, upon the application of such stimulus as would excite the same action in the animal in a perfect state. These facts shew clearly that instinctive, or rather automatic motions may be exerted, without the intervention of the *sensorium commune*, and therefore, without sensation or consciousness. (p. 260)

It is evident that Blane made no clear distinction between instinctive action and automatic action. It is notable that the acts described in the foregoing are all complex, rather than simple, *i.e.*, a coordination of muscles is required.

Blane, as did Whytt, observed the similarity between habit and true (unlearned) automatisms.

It is the nature of a voluntary muscle to perform any motion with greater ease, the more frequently it is repeated, and to act most readily with those muscles, or in company with those sensations with which it has been used to combine its action either at once or in succession. This is the foundation of habit, and is the principle by which all the practical attainments of man acquire facility and perfection. It has been mentioned that some actions, originally instinctive, may afterwards be performed as acts of pure volition; so inversely, all actions, which are the result of reason and reflection, may be brought by habit to resemble instinctive action, and thereby to performed with greater expedition and effect. (p. 263)

It is interesting to note that Blane under the term imitation, included phenomena which we now include under the term suggestion.

In the early part of human life, imitation seems equally independent of reason and reflection, as in mere animals. It takes place not only without the operation of the will, but in opposition to it; for yawning is an involuntary spasm of the muscles of the jaw, which is frequently excited by a sight of the same action in others. . . . The only objects of imitation are gestures and sounds, and by these are also transferred from one individual to another, the emotions of the mind of which they are the natural expressions.   (p. 263)

The acts which he included under imitation seemed to him apparently to bear a close resemblance also to the phenomena of automatic action. This is a strikingly shrewd observation which has been left to modern psychological work on automatisms to verify and develop. In the last sentence of the above quotation there is a suggestion which has been developed by modern social psychology.

Finally, we may note in the following passage comment on what we now refer to as muscle tonus.

There still remains to be mentioned, that important property of living muscular fibres, which consists in a perpetual state of tension taking place at all times, in a greater or less degree, independent of any temporary stimulus. . . . A certain degree of this tension is necessary for the performance of the natural motions of the muscles, whether voluntary or involuntary, and the vigour with which the several actions are performed, depends on the fibres possessing a due degree of this constant tone giving scope to motion.   (p. 270)

Marie Francois Zavier Bichat (1771–1802), a French physiologist, classified the "sympathies." Bichat was uncertain (42) to what extent these phenomena were dependent on nerve action. He classified the sympathies as follows: (1) *Les sympathies de sensibilité animale*, sensations occurring in one part of the body because of disturbance in another; (2) *Les sympathies de contractilité animale*, the convulsion of the voluntary muscles after a dislocation or after stretching (distension) of the ligaments; (3) *Les sympathies de contractilité organique sensible*, the action of the involuntary muscles is accelerated by any affection of an organ or group of organs, *e.g.*, the increased action of the heart when one feels pain; (4) *Les sympathies de sensibilité organique et de contractilité insensible, i.e.*, tonicity— here are included sympathetic absorptions, secretions, exhalations, etc.

CHAPTER VII

THE REACTION AGAINST A MECHANISTIC PHYSIOLOGY

"It has been the misfortune of almost all the functions, to have met with
advocates in the mechanical school; and some have been confident enough
to assert, that they are the actions of a simple machine, instigated by no
spiritual agent, and influenced by no stimulus.   Truth, evidence and reason
are so much in favour of the contrary, that we shall endeavour to vindicate
them from such a character.   The more ingenious have long ago confuted
these principles by showing that the effect was not equal to the Cause, and
that the same rules could not possibly take place as with Matter in general."
—SAMUEL FARR, *A Philosophical Enquiry into the Nature, Origin, and
Extent of Animal Motion*, 1771.

La Mettrie, who was forced to take refuge in Prussia in 1848 because of
the opposition of the religionists to his mechanistic doctrines; wrote a
treatise on lust, and another in which he compared man to a machine; and
met a fitting end, from the point of view of the pious, from over-eating.[1]
It was at this period a topic of discussion whether such an atheist could
live a moral life or die in peace,[2] but as Lange (281) points out, "men could
with virtuous indignation condemn this sinner, while they were gradually
absorbing his ideas; later, too, they could with impunity sell as their own
manufacture what they had learned from La Mettrie—because they had
separated themselves from him with a unanimity and an energy that quite
set at fault the judgment of their contemporaries."[3]

The mechanistic theory of bodily functions, although supported by an
increasing body of evidence from experiments, did not receive universal
acceptance.   Repercussions of the doctrines of Stahl and his followers
bearing a more or less recognizable resemblance to the original appeared
from time to time.   The conception of the body as a mechanism, so bril-
liantly established and supported by Descartes, Borelli and the iatro-
physicists in the 17th century was not accepted without reservations by
Whytt, Hartley, Perrault and others.   We see the pendulum swing still
farther in the direction of a non-mechanistic conception, especially insofar

[1] *Cf.* Lange (281), II, p. 53 *ff.* and 91.
[2] *Ibid.*, II, p. 90.
[3] *Ibid.*, II, p. 49.

as it is applied to the interpretation of involuntary motions of animals, in the case of William Porterfield, an English contemporary of Whytt.[4]

Porterfield's "Treatise on the Eye," (411) published in 1759, contains an illuminating discussion of the subject of involuntary movements in connection with the topic of the motions of the pupil of the eye.   In contradistinction to Whytt, Descartes and the mechanistic school in general, Porterfield maintains that the mind presides over all the movements of the body.   He denies that any necessity exists in the body whereby any motion or series of motions must occur as a consequence of any given set of conditions.   Those motions which appear to be mechanical are so as a result of habit.

Thus when the eyes are turned up or down, the eyelids always follow their motion, and keep the same distance from the pupil; and if a body be hastily moved towards our eyes, they will shut without our being conscious thereof: neither is it in our power to do otherwise, because we have accustomed ourselves to do so on the like occasions; for such is the power of custom and habit, that many actions which are no doubt voluntary and proceed from our mind, are in certain circumstances rendered so necessary, as to appear altogether mechanical and independent on our wills; but it does not from thence follow that our mind is not concerned in such motions, but only that it has imposed upon itself a law, whereby it regulates and governs them to the greatest advantage.   In all this there is nothing of intrinsical necessity; the mind is at absolute liberty to act as it pleases, but, being a wise agent, it cannot but choose to act in conformity to this law, by reason of the utility and advantage that arises from this way of acting.   (II, pp. 16–18)

Examples of these types of motion are the turning of the ear towards different sounds, the accomodation of the eye to objects at different distances, the change in size of the pupil in response to different intensities of light.   These movements, Porterfield believed to have been originally conscious, since the mind acted originally "from a principle of interest" and later, through use to have become habitual and unconscious.   Learning to walk, talk, and sing are examples of this process.

It were easy to illustrate and confirm this doctrine by many familiar examples; observe but children when they first begin to walk, and you'll find, that the whole mind is employed in conducting the motions necessary for their progression, insomuch that if anything shall divide the mind, and draw off its attention, they presently tumble down, by reason of the difficulty that attends the government of these motions, which cannot be rightly conducted, while the mind gives attention to anything else, but when use and custom have once made these motions easy and familiar, then they need but little attention, and allow the mind to employ its most serious and anxious thoughts about other matters.   And what has

---

[4] Whytt takes issue with Porterfield in connection with involuntary motion.   *Cf. supra*, Chapter VI, p. 79.

been said of walking is in like manner also true of speaking, singing, playing on musical instruments, and many other exercises, whose difficulty is only overcome by habit and custom.   (II, p. 34)

Porterfield referred in passing to the "impius attempt" of Descartes to explain animal motion in terms of mechanics, and postulated the existence of a "vital" or "active" principle or "archaeus" which presides over bodily functions.

In like vein is the treatise (133) of Samuel Farr (1741–1795) published in 1771, entitled "A Philosophical Enquiry into the Nature, Origin, and Extent, of Animal Motion, Deduced from the Principles of Reason and Analogy."   Farr refers to the animal body as a "very curious and a very complex machine, calculated in every motion for receiving impressions from external Bodies, and for reacting again upon them, in consequence of their action."   But it is a machine governed by a soul which is not entirely occupied with the conscious direction of the bodily processes.   As a result of a "wise provision of nature," consciousness is freed from the necessity of directly presiding over those types of activity which are essential to the animal economy but which are involuntary.

A similar doctrine is supported by Alexander Monro, the elder, (1697–1767) although he believed that a certain necessity was imposed on the mind in the case of involuntary acts.   Monro was a student of Boerhaave at Leyden in 1718 and was the first professor of anatomy at the University of Edinburgh.   His writings were published by his son, Alexander Monro *secundus* (1733–1817) in 1781 (364).   The elder Monro accepted the hypothesis that the nerves contained a fluid which was the "principal instrument which the mind makes use of to influence the actions of the body, or to inform itself of the impressions made on the body." He discussed the necessity which is imposed on the mind as follows:

Whenever the uneasy sensation, pain, is raised by the too strong application of objects, a sort of necessity is as it were imposed upon the mind to endeavor to get free of the injuring cause, by either withdrawing the grieved part of the body from it, as one retires his hand when his finger is pricked or burnt; or the injuring cause is endeavoured to be forced from the body, as a tenesmus excites the contraction which pushes acrid faeces out of the rectum.   In both these operations, a convulsive contraction is immediately made in the lesed part, or in the neighborhood of it; and if the irritation is very strong or permanent, the greater part of the nervous system becomes affected in that spasmodic or convulsive way.   Is it this necessity which obliges the mind to exert herself in respiration, or in the action of the heart, when the lungs or heart are gorged with blood? or the iris to contract the pupil, when the eye is exposed to strong light? or sneezing to be performed when the nose is tickled?   etc.   Will not a stimulus of any nerve more readily affect those with which it is anywhere connected than the other nerves of the body?   May not this sympathy serve as a monitor of the mind, rather to employ the organs furnished with nerves thus connected, to assist in freeing her of any uneasy sensation, than to make use of any organs? Will not this in some measure account for many salutary operations performed in the body, before experience has taught us the functions of the organs performing them? (pp. 339–341.)

The younger Monro discussed the functions of the nervous system in greater detail in his work "Observations on the Structure and Functions of the Nervous System" published in 1783 (365). In a chapter on "The Manner and Causes of the Actions of the Muscles," he discusses the topic of involuntary or "spontaneous" motion. These are the motions in which the conscious will plays no part in determining the contractions of the individual muscles. The examples of this type of movement are listed, beginning with that "in which the irritation that produces the motion is at a distance from the muscles which perform it" and proceeding "by degrees to those in which the active organ is directly stimulated." The following examples are given.

(1) The contraction of the iris in proportion to the intensity of the light.

(2) The movements of the ear when stimulated by a sudden sound together with the simultaneous movements of the internal muscles of the ear.

(3) The sneezing, vomiting, coughing, and contractions of the "containing parts of the abdomen" which result from irritating the nose, throat or stomach, membrane of the lungs and rectum or gravid uterus respectively.

(4) Respiration as "promoted" by the motion of the blood in the lungs and "a proper change of air."

(5) The discharge of semen and the action of the uterine tubes in laying "hold of the ovaria" as a result of the irritation of the external organs of generation.

(6) The discharge of urine as a result of pressure on the bladder "by the contraction of the diaphragm and abdominal muscles" and later by the "steady and uniform contraction of its own muscular coat."

(7) The "elegant and complex" motions of the stomach and intestinal tube when food is ingested.

(8) The anti-peristaltic motion of the stomach resulting in vomiting when "hurtful" substances are swallowed.

(9) The sudden contraction of the auricle or ventricle of the heart when irritated by blood.

These motions are not produced by the mechanical structure of the bodies of animals and are not dependent upon the connection which the different nerves have with each other either "by being inclosed in the same sheaths of the *dura* and *pia mater*, or by being joined in the ganglia;" this in spite of the support that "men of genius and knowledge" have given to the contrary doctrine. The mechanistic interpretation of these "sympathies" is abandoned chiefly because the motions described show indications of purpose. Monro generalized as follows:

Upon the whole, it appears, 1st, That the actions above mentioned cannot be accounted for on the yet known principles of mechanism.

2dly, We observe, that the muscular fibre varies its operation according to the purpose to be served. That, for instance, when a muscular fibre is punctured, it vibrates, which is the fittest means of throwing off the offending cause; that the alimentary canal, acted on gently by the food, performs a very complex peristaltic motion; that the abdominal muscles act slowly and steadily in expelling the contents of the rectum, but suddenly and convulsively in vomiting; that the bladder of urine, from which there is a small outlet, performs a slow and uniform contraction in discharging its contents; whilst the heart contracts with a jerk.

3dly, The more we consider the various spontaneous operations, the more fully we shall be convinced that they are the best calculated for the preservation and well-being of the animal. (p. 101.)

Monro finally concluded that these spontaneous motions were "directed and conducted by a wise agent, intimately acquainted with the structure, and with all the effects it is capable of producing." He stated that he disagreed both with that "class of philosophers who have supposed that our mind, intimately acquainted with the texture of the body, reasons upon, and thereafter performs the several actions," and with those who "suppose the mind to be the agent, yet deny that she understands the texture of the body; and, therefore, make a conclusion, not very intelligible, that the mind is *necessitated* to act in certain ways." In the first group Monro included Stahl and his followers, and in the second, Whytt. In rejecting both the point of view of Stahl and Whytt, Monro is forced to fall back upon the "wise agent" to which reference has already been made. In a later passage he stated that "the Power which created all things, which gave life to animals and motion to the heavenly bodies, continues to act upon, and to maintain all." This conclusion is not scientifically intelligible, and, it must be admitted, places Monro much closer to the position of Stahl than he apparently was willing to acknowledge.

SUMMARY OF CONTRIBUTIONS IN THE 18TH CENTURY

The concept of reflex action as referring to a type of neuro-muscular response with certain specific objective characteristics, may be said to have been formulated and developed in the 18th century, although the neural structures at the basis of this phenomenon were not understood until the next century. In order to reach the state of development in which we find it at the end of this century, certain necessary steps must have been taken preliminary to the formation of such a concept. Some of the more important of these are, briefly: (1) The distinction between two qualitatively different kinds of animal motion—voluntary and involuntary, (2) the establishment of the physiological sequence of events in the involuntary action, *i.e.*, the establishment of the relationship between the point or area at which a stimulus is applied, the processes occurring in the incoming and outgoing portions of the arc, and the response, (3) the establishment of the *invariability of the relationship* between the elements in the foregoing events, (4) the determination of the center presiding over this series of events, *i.e.*, the point at which the incoming processes are changed into outgoing processes, and (5) the demonstration of the anatomical structures involved. During the 17th and 18th centuries all of these steps but the last were taken. The first step—the distinction between two kinds of animal motion—was suggested by investigators in previous epochs. The second, third, and fourth were the preeminent contributions of the 18th century. All the elements in the fifth step were not experimentally established, but their existence was suggested by the work of Unzer and Prochaska.

Of the investigators whose attention was turned towards the problems of neuro-muscular physiology, Haller, Whytt, Unzer, Prochaska, and Blane made the outstanding contributions. Of these Whytt is the preeminent leader. His contributions (tabulated elsewhere) are important in connection with the definition of the psychological characteristics of voluntary and involuntary motion, the emphasis on the necessity of the relationship between stimulus and response in the case of involuntary motion, and the establishment of the spinal cord as the structure which may independently preside over involuntary functions.

For the most part the investigations which have been described in the present chapter were carried on independently and the investigators made little effort to coordinate results. An important exception to this is to be found in the work of Prochaska and Unzer.

It is impossible to say to what extent the independent investigations and speculations of the men whose work we have reviewed had become a part of the physiological thought of the day. It is remarkable that as late as 1797 Alexander von Humboldt was still endeavoring to explain "sympathy" by anastomoses of the nerves and by the effect of their "sensible atmosphere" on each other,[5] and that such men as Porterfield and the Monros retained

---

[5] *Cf.* Hodge (232), p. 167.

the vague ideas of a nervous fluid.   However, the results of the investigations of the 18th century became the indispensable basis of the doctrines
of the 19th century with regard to neuro-muscular physiology.

The more important advances made during the century with relation to
these topics may be summarized as follows:

(1) The concept of a type of action which is independent of mind or
"will" received a special impetus.   This is the "vital" or "involuntary"
motion which is the subject of Whytt's monograph.   This kind of action,
of course, had been described by Descartes.   In the 18th century, however,
we find it becoming the subject of specific research, as a consequence of
which, its characteristics were accurately defined.   The characteristics
established at this period are among those which still serve to define and
delimit reflex action.   Among the important attributes referred to are:
(a) *Unlearnedness.*   Both Haller and Blane made specific reference to this
attribute.   The latter especially emphasized the fact that experience is not
necessary in the case of certain sorts of animal responses.   Haller cited the
fact that animals newly born can perform "compound" motions without
any previous attempt.   (b) *Innateness.*   Both Haller and Blane observed
that certain responses must be due to a law established "by the Creator"
(Haller) or by "nature" (Blane).   The idea of hereditary patterns is, of
course, only implied, but the notion is certainly present of a type of pre-
formation which determines action independently of acquired experience.
(c) Blane and Whytt also referred to the fact that the involuntary motion
follows as a *necessary consequence of a stimulus.*   This represents an advance
over the conception that tissue itself possesses a mysterious power which
may spontaneously cause motion.   (d) *Involuntary movements connected
with special senses.*   This is the forerunner of the modern conception that
the physiological receptors are essential to the release of reflexes.   Hartley
listed involuntary motions associated with the five "senses" which were
known to his generation.   (e) *Rapidity of involuntary motions* as compared
with voluntary.   Whytt pointed out that the former must be involuntary
since they take place too rapidly for "reason" to be a factor in the process.[6]
(f) Involuntary motions not simple muscular contractions but *coordinated*
movements which are relatively complex.   Blane especially noted this
characteristic.   (g) *The protective or adaptive function of involuntary
movements.*   Whytt and Blane gave particular attention to this point.
(h) *Anatomical center* of involuntary action.   The experiments of Preston
and DuVerny in the 17th century had made it clear that animal motion

---

[6] We have referred to Boerhaave's statement regarding the "celerity" of involuntary
actions, *cf. infra,* p. 63.

could take place in the absence of the cerebrum, and Whytt established the fact that only a section of the cord was necessary for coordinated movement. As Neuburger has pointed out,[7] the result of the investigations of Whytt and the generalizations of Unzer is the demonstration that both sensibility and irritability depend on the central nervous system. Unzer further distinguished between voluntary and involuntary motion on the basis of the portion of the nervous system involved, *i.e.*, involuntary motions do not involve the brain, whereas conscious actions do.

(2) The mechanistic physiology, of which Descartes was a progenitor, became increasingly acceptable to those interested in the sciences of life. La Mettrie's conception of the body as a machine epitomized in popular form this point of view. The decline of the animistic physiology of Stahl, Van Helmont, and Perrault was due to a constellation of causes in which, however, the rise of a theory of reflex action played a major rôle. The reaction against the attempt to explain animal behavior in terms of mechanism is found in the writings of Porterfield, Farr, and the Monros. That this reaction was not effective is demonstrated by the subsequent history of physiology and psychology. Porterfield, Monro, and the rest did not deny the phenomena of involuntary action; they merely offered an interpretation which did not restrict itself to material factors.

(3) In the 18th century the phenomena of habit became a subject for physiological and psychological observation. This especially applied to those highly mechanized motor processes known to modern psychology as automatisms. The "obscure perceptions" of Haller and the "diminutive sensations" of Hartley seem to anticipate the modern idea of subliminal impressions. In addition Haller and Hartley believed that these impressions were capable of releasing motor responses. Whytt and Hartley noticed the similarity between the phenomena of acquired motor habit and "true" involuntary action; a similarity which is recognized by certain modern physiologists and psychologists under the terms "cortical reflex," "acquired reflex," "psychic reflex" and the like. In these similarities, which seem to have attracted the attention for the first time of those interested in the scientific study of human and animal behavior, we have evidence which seemed to justify the extension of the mechanistic hypothesis to all types of human and animal action. These developments were paralleled by the development of a mechanistic psychology at the hands of the Associationists, *e.g.*, Locke, Hartley, and Hume.[8] If all the complex processes of mind were to be explained by the mere association of ideas,

[7] *Op. cit.*, p. 177.
[8] *Cf.* McDougall (347), p. 110 *ff.*

and if these associations were made possible by virtue of a nervous substrate, the chief characteristic of which was a tendency to take on and retain habits, we have the basis for a mechanical explanation of both objective behavior and subjective experience. That is to say, we have here an historical basis for the hypothesis that the phenomena of "involuntary action," "automatisms," and "habits" have psychological and perhaps physiological resemblances which warranted their being included under a single explanatory principle.

(4) The notion that a stimulus, defined in more or less definite physico-chemical terms, as a necessary agent in releasing involuntary action, seems to have been emphasized in the 18th century. In this connection the conception of Swammerdam in the previous century must not be forgotten. His "object" which serves "to put the will in motion" bears a recognizable resemblance to the modern idea of the stimulus as a releasing agency.[9] Astruc and Prochaska pointed out, however, that not only was a stimulus essential, but the strength of the resultant action was dependent on the intensity of the stimulus. The conception of the necessity of a stimulus marks an advance since it indicates a tendency to escape from mysterious powers and forces which control the bodily mechanism. It, also, serves to mechanize further the concept of involuntary action, reducing it to the Cartesian conception of a purely physical event.

(5) The theories of the nature of nervous energy were clarified and delimited during the 18th century. It is a far cry from the crude conceptions of "animal spirits" and "vital spirits" of an earlier time to the more precise, although still unverified, conception of the *vis nervosa* of Unzer and Prochaska. Whytt rejected the idea of hypothetical "fluids" and "spirits" as explanatory principles, and declared for the phrase "influence or power of the nerves," which contained no unverified assumptions as to the physical constitution of the nervous energy. Prochaska's discussion in this connection was particularly notable. He pointed out that the *vis nervosa* is potential or latent energy to be released by the stimulus, as the spark is released by the friction on flint or steel. This was a conception of the nervous impulse which modern physiology was to verify.

It cannot be said, however, that more or less obscure ideas of "spirits," "inflating auras," "nervous fluids" were definitely banished by the end of the century. Their final elimination was to be a task of experimental psychology in the 19th Century.

[9] *Cf. supra*, Chapter III, p. 50.

CHAPTER VIII

THE 19TH CENTURY. THE DISCOVERY OF BELL

"So deeply impressed is the mind, however, with the idea of our motions in walking being altogether voluntary, that it is almost impossible to conceive how the mere circumstance of the foot coming in contact with the ground, can cause the muscles of the lower extremities to produce all the complicated actions which are necessary to take another step; and yet it is certain that these motions are regularly affected, when the mind is entirely abstracted from all thoughts of the actions that are required: so that at these times, which are so extremely frequent, the movements of progression become automatic. It is often said, indeed, that under such circumstances, the muscles contract from habit; but such a vague explanation becomes quite insufficient when it is recollected how invariably every natural phenomenon is preceded by a definite cause."—R. D. GRAINGER, *Observations on the Structure and Functions of the Spinal Cord*, 1837.

We have seen that by the end of the 18th century the concept of reflex action was complete insofar as it referred to a specific type of response; the essential functional attributes ascribed to it by modern physiology had been defined with some degree of precision. This result was not achieved as a consequence of a single line of attack, but was the outcome, rather, of many diverse types of investigation and divergent points of view. We may distinguish several different but not mutually exclusive modes of approach to the problem of neuro-muscular control of animal movements which had been used up to this time.

For Descartes and his followers the domain of the mind, soul, consciousness or will—if we may use these words, for the moment, synonymously—was strictly limited. A large proportion of the animal's activities represented the functioning of an intricate machine. The responses which modern psychology designates as automatisms merely indicated the wholly mechanical nature of the animal body. Closely allied with this point of view was that presented by La Mettrie in his tract, "Man a Machine." It was La Mettrie's argument that if Descartes was correct in insisting that all organisms below man were automata, then man is also a machine, because it can be shown that the brutes display all the evidences of "thinking," "feeling" and "intelligence" which are supposed to be the unique characteristics of an organism possessing a soul. In other words, for La

111

Mettrie, man is a machine as well as the brutes; he acts by virtue of necessity, that is to say because of his organization. It was the essence of this point of view that the peculiar arrangement of the physical elements which constituted the animal body was a self-contained machine, and the interrelationship of the parts, and therefore the functioning of the whole, was intelligible *only* in terms of physics and mechanics. "Since all the faculties of the soul depend to such a degree on the proper organization of the brain and of the whole body, that apparently they are but this organization itself, the soul is clearly an enlightened machine."[1] Supporting this view with varying degrees of assurance were Willis, Boyle, Swammerdam and the iatro-physicists in the 17th century and Whytt, Haller, Prochaska, and Unzer in the 18th century. It was a point of view which might claim a legitimate descent from the rise of physical science during the 16th and 17th centuries. In biological science William Harvey and Vesalius as well as Descartes were its progenitors.

At the opposite pole from the foregoing point of view was the conception that all the activities of the living organism were administered by the soul itself. This was the position of Stahl and his followers, Van Helmont, and the iatro-chemists in the 17th century and, to some extent at least, that of the younger Monro in the 18th century.

Between these two extremes we find the position of those who constituted, perhaps, the majority of the contributors to neuro-muscular physiology of the 17th and 18th centuries. The fact of involuntary action or automatism was recognized, but not all animal action was included in this category. The element of necessity or invariability which was characteristic of these involuntary acts was believed to be present either because of the inherited structural organization of the animal or because of the fact that they had become automatized through habit. In the latter case the soul or will was released from the necessity of over-seeing the various processes and responses necessary for the survival of the animal, and could devoted itself to meeting those situations for which there were no established responses. It was further characteristic of this point of view that these automatized processes had been in the first place conscious and voluntary. Adhering more or less closely to the first-mentioned position were the iatro-physicists, Swammerdam, Boerhaave, and Willis in the 17th century and La Mettrie, Unzer, Prochaska and Whytt in the 18th century. Those who may be identified with the second position were Perrault in the 17th century and Porterfield, Hartley, and the elder Monro in the 18th century.

[1] LaMettrie, *op. cit.*, p. 128.

SIR CHARLES BELL

The distinction between these two points of view was not at all times clear and distinct; the possibility of forming automatized habits was not excluded by those who supported a theory of inherited mechanism, nor was the possibility of inherited mechanism eliminated by all of those who regarded involuntary action in the main as an acquired response. It is clear that those who viewed the involuntary aspect of certain responses as an acquired characteristic also saw in those responses a sort of degenerated will. This is a position which is not incompatible with the animism of Stahl. On the other hand, that view which insisted more rigidly on involuntary action as an inherited type of response approaches more closely to the mechanistic interpretation of Descartes and La Mettrie.

A final channel through which the conception of reflex action developed during the course of the 19th century, was that which concerned itself chiefly with the location of the segment of the nervous system which controlled both voluntary and involuntary action. The mode of attack was experimental for the most part and includes some of the most brilliant and decisive investigations of reflex action during the period which closes with the end of the 18th century. In the 17th century the studies of DuVerny, Willis, Perrault, Redi, Chirac, and Boyle should be mentioned. All of these studies had in common the technique of the experimental destruction in the living animal of some part of the central nervous system for the purpose of determining the effects on animal movement. In the 18th century this type of investigation made its most important contribution to the development of the reflex action concept in the hands of Whytt and Blane.

There were certain *lacunae* in this theory of reflex action, as we find it at the end of the 18th century. The theoretical discussions of function of such able systematists as Haller, Prochaska, and Unzer outstripped their store of experimentally attested facts, especially insofar as these facts were related to the structure of the nervous system. This was not true, of course, of Whytt, whose theories in the main were based, if not on controlled experiment, at least upon exceedingly shrewd observation. Although the theoretical formulations of Unzer and Prochaska regarding the functional aspects of reflex action were substantiated, for the most part, by later experimentation, in at least two important particulars they and the other systematists of the period failed to make a complete statement of reflex theory as we know it today.

At the beginning of the 19th century there was (1) no adequate knowledge of the finer anatomy of the nervous system, and (2) very little comprehension of the significance of the function of reflex action or the nervous system in integrated behavior. The first was a development which was to wait on the advancement of knowledge in certain necessary technical fields, *e.g.*, microscopic technique, and the second was to be the especial contribution of the 20th century.

Johnston (263) has pointed out that the growth of knowledge of the animal organism usually proceeds through three states: (1) identification of the gross anatomical details, (2) detailed study of structure and function, and (3) a concrete statement of the correlation of structure and function. He is inclined to assume that the study of the nervous system in the 19th century was in the second stage. Johnston would probably not insist on a rigid demarcation of the three stages; but even so, there would seem to be some reason for questioning the application of the formula to the case of the development of knowledge of reflex action. During the 18th century the study of the functions of the nervous system developed to a level where a fairly adequate statement of the principles of reflex action could be made. Prochaska, Unzer, Whytt, and Blane had a very workable knowledge of reflex action as a *functioning* mechanism. Indeed, it may be said that the most essential facts regarding the functioning of the reflex mechanisms were known by the end of the 18th century, while the knowledge of the underlying structures was about where it had been at the beginning of the century. The belief was still current that the same nerves transmitted both sensory and motor impulses. The most primitive notions prevailed regarding the structure of the nerve, and the nature of the events which took place during conduction.

With regard to the failure to appreciate the significance of involuntary action with relation to the total behavior of the organism, it should be pointed out that the interest in the study of nervous function in the 17th and 18th centuries was in part the result of the endeavor to find the mechanism or agency through which the "soul" operates in the body. This was explicitly stated by Prochaska (416) in the introductory paragraphs of the "Dissertation."

The nervous system . . . . is of all organs of the animal economy the most important. It is the seat of the rational soul, and the link by which it is united to the body; it is the instrument by which the soul, so long as it is united to the body, produces its own actions, termed animal, and by which it acts on the rest of the body, and the body in turn acts upon it. But, however great may be the importance of the nervous system in these respects, it is of further importance, because it possesses in addition the singular faculty of exciting in the human body various movements without the consciousness or assistance of the soul; nay, plainly against its will it can and does excite them without intermission throughout the whole of life. (Introduction, p. 363.)

Prochaska proceeded to point out that the nervous system "also influences other functions of the human body" such as digestion, nutrition, and secretion. It is true, as we have already indicated, that in Blane, Whytt, and others we find some notion of the protective function of involuntary action. Prochaska pointed out that the reflexion of "sensorial impressions into motorial"[2] maintained the "conservation of the body." These ideas fall short, however, of the comprehension of the *integrative* function of the nervous system by means of "reflex" mechanisms. For the investigators of the 17th and 18th centuries the nervous system was the agency which "controlled" the body through the operation of the "soul;" in the 19th and 20th centuries it came to be an integrative and adaptive mechanism for biological survival.

THE GROWTH OF KNOWLEDGE REGARDING THE STRUCTURE OF THE NERVOUS SYSTEM.[3] THE BELL-MAGENDIE DISCOVERY

The Greek and Roman physicians distinguished between sensory and motor functions of the nerves, and it was known by the time of Vesalius that the nerves were essential to animal motion. As a consequence of the discovery of the compound microscope in the early part, and the microtome in the latter part of the 19th century, rapid advance was made in the knowledge of the histology of the nervous system. The development of the cell-theory by the botanists Schleiden, (1804–1881), and Schwann (1810–1882) was a necessary precedent to the development of the neurone theory at the hands of Waller, Golgi, His, Ramón y Cajal, and others in the latter half of the century.

Without the elaborate physiological and histological techniques of these investigators certain advances in the knowledge of the finer anatomy of the nervous system would have been impossible. Leeuwenhoek and Fontana described in 1787 the "nerve tubes," and Valentin in 1836 stated that these "tubes" were continuous from the periphery to the central nervous system.[4] Johannes Evangelista Purkinje (1787–1869), who made important contributions (417) in many fields of biological science, in 1838 pointed out that the nerve tube contained an inner strand which he believed to be the elemental nerve fibre. This strand we now know as the axis cylinder. Purkinje also described nerve cells in the brain.

In 1836 Valentin described the variable form of central nerve cells, and in 1837 Robert Remak (1815–1865) recognized their processes. In 1838

---

[2] *Op. cit.*, Chapter IV, sec. 1, p. 431.

[3] We have presented only a brief outline history of the morphological studies of the nervous system.

[4] *Cf.* Johnston, *op. cit.*, p. 5 *ff.*

Remak further discovered the non-medullated nerve fibres and Schwann in 1839 made known the cellular character of the membrane surrounding the nerve tubes (neurolemma).

It should be remembered that all this work of the early 19th century preceded the use of the special histological techniques developed by Waller, Golgi, and others.

The correlation of the results of these early investigators of the finer anatomy of the nervous system with the known facts of reflex action made possible the final elimination of such anatomical myths as peripheral nerve anastomoses. The nervous action, however, was still far from being on a secure structural basis. Simple reflexes were thought to take place over a structurally *continuous* pathway extending from the periphery to the central nervous system and back to the muscle.

The scheme presented in Wagner's *Handwörterbuch* (509) in 1844 placed the nerve cell in the spinal ganglion with the two processes extending to the periphery and to the central organ. The scheme of Gerlach provided for a meshwork of cells in the gray matter of the cord.[5] Johnston points out that the conception of Gerlach seemed to provide for the uniformity of response following peripheral stimulation, but it was inadequate to explain certain later discoveries.

[This scheme] did not offer the means of explaining the spreading of the reflex influence to a larger number of muscles, to those of the opposite side and eventually to nearly the whole body. Such spread of the reflex was observed to take place with increased intensity of the stimulus or with prolonged stimulation with failure of the reflexes to remove the cause of irritation (Pflüger 1853 and others). If the gradual and regular spread of reflexes might be explained on the basis of Gerlach's reticulum, the exceptions to such regular spreading were fatal to the conception of structure; namely, the jumping of a reflex from one segment to a distant one on the same or opposite side (Owsjannikow 1874, Gergens 1876, Luschsinger 1878, Langendorff 1880). (pp. 71–2)

The anatomical structures necessary to satisfactorily explain these facts of neural function were to be the discoveries which finally culminated in the neurone theory.

It should be remembered that the investigators of the early part of the 19th century demonstrated these facts of structure by means of a teasing needle, razor, and low-power microscope. They afforded, however, a structural interpretation of reflex action which was an immeasurable advance over the relatively crude anatomical conceptions of Prochaska and other physiologists of the preceding century.

[5] *Cf.* Nagel (382), IV, p. 283 *ff.*, and Johnston, *op. cit.*, p. 71 *ff.* for diagrammatic representations of the earlier schemes of the neuro-muscular relationships.

Although the discoveries regarding the minute anatomy of the nervous system made possible a more accurate conception of neural function by the middle of the 19th century, they were preceded by an advance in the knowledge of the function of the spinal nerve roots which was of fundamental importance to reflex theory. The so-called Bell-Magendie law is as significant to the development of the knowledge of neural action as the discovery of circulation was to the physiology of the blood.

Sir Charles Bell (1774–1842), the leading British anatomist of his period, made numerous discoveries of importance to physiology and anatomy. Although primarily an anatomist, his observations of the physiology of the senses were exceedingly acute. He pointed out (29, 30) that every nerve gives rise to its own peculiar sensation.

Whatever may be the nature of the impulse communicated to a nerve, pressure, vibration, heat, electricity, the perception excited in the mind will have reference to the organ exercised, not to the impression made upon it. Fire will not give the sensation of heat to any nerve but that appropriated to the surface. However delicate the retina be, it does not feel like the skin.

The paper containing this observation was read before the Royal Society in June, 1823, and it seems to anticipate the idea of Müller's law of specific energies.

Bell was severe in his criticisms of the phrenological theories of Gall.

It is sufficient to say, that without comprehending the grand divisions of the nervous system, without a notion of the distinct properties of the individual nerves, or having made any distinction of the columns of the spinal marrow, without even having ascertained the difference of cerebrum and cerebellum, Gall proceeded to describe the brain as composed of many particular and independent organs, and to assign to each the residence of some special faculty.

He studied the movements of the eye, noting one movement especially which "from its rapidity" had escaped observation, namely, the upward movement of the eyeball when the lids are closed, He noted the presence of a third eyelid—the nictitating membrane—in certain animals and especially marked its development in birds.

In 1811, Bell published a brief monograph (28) in which he embodied the results of his investigations of the spinal nerve roots and for which his name is famous. This paper contained the following sentence,

On laying bare the roots of the spinal nerves, I found that I could cut across the posterior portion of the spinal marrow without convulsing the muscles of the back, but that, on touching the anterior fasciculus with the point of the knife, the muscles of the back were immediately convulsed.[6]

This is the first experimental reference to the functions of the spinal nerve roots in the literature. Haller and the other physiologists of the preceeding century had believed that the same nerves transmitted both sensory and motor impulses. Bell in a later work (29) complained of the "extraordinary confusion" in which he found the subject of the nerves, especially in connection with the "mystery of sensation, and voluntary and involuntary motion, performed by a single nerve." In this same work he reviewed his experiments.

I therefore struck a rabbit behind the ear, so as to deprive it of its sensibility by the concussion, and then exposed the spinal marrow. On irritating the posterior roots of the nerve, I could perceive no motion consequent, on any part of the muscular frame; but on irritating the anterior roots of the nerve, at each touch of the forceps there was a corresponding motion of the muscles to which the nerve was distributed. These experiments satisfied me that the different roots and different columns from whence those roots arise, were devoted to distinct offices, and that the notions drawn from the anatomy were correct. (p. 16.)

Later in this same work he referred to the "satisfaction of all Europe" in connection with these experiments and indicated clearly his comprehension of the sensory and motor functions of the spinal nerve roots.

It has been acknowledged that the anterior roots of the spinal nerves bestow the power of muscular motion; and the posterior roots sensibility. When the anterior roots of the nerves of the leg are cut in experiment, the animal loses all power over the leg, although the limb still continues sensible. But if, on the other hand, the posterior roots are cut, the power of motion continues, although the sensibility is destroyed. When the posterior column of the spinal marrow is irritated the animal evinces sensibility to pain; but no apparent effect is produced when the anterior column is touched. (p. 21.)

In Bell's publication of 1811, he may be said to have demonstrated the functions of the anterior roots only. In the quotation just made, however, it seems clear that he understood also the function of the posterior roots. Magendie (1783–1855), who was Bell's most important contemporary in the investigation of these problems,[7] gave in 1822 further experimental

---

[6] Bell quotes this passage from the earlier work in the Preface (p. 8) to his treatise on the nervous system published in 1833 (30).

[7] Neuburger (384), pp. 305–6, points out that Bell's aversion to vivisection and his failure to publish his results made possible conflicting claims for the credit of these discoveries. Neuburger states, however, that Magendie "can scarcely be excused" for his failure to know of Bell's work since John Show, a pupil of Bell's, demonstrated the latter's

proof of the functions of both the posterior and anterior roots. In 1823 he reported his conclusions (324).

Ces faits connus, depuis qu'il y a des maladies, ont été l'objet des recherches des médecins de toutes les époques: on en a conclu avec raison qu'il devait y avoir dans le système nerveux des nerfs pour le sentiment et d'autres pour le mouvement.

Mais ni l'anatomie la plus minutieuse, ni les lésions observées après la mort, ni les expériences sur les animaux vivans, n'avaient pu faire distinguer les nèrfs du sentiment de ceux du mouvement.

J'ai été conduit dernièrement a établir cette distinction; et ce qui avait paru jusqu'ici une difficulte insurmontable, se trouve être un des phénomènes les plus simples des fonctions du système nerveux.

Pour comprendre ce resultat, il faut se rappeler que tous les nerfs du corps et des membres ont leur origine à la moelle épinière; mais la manière dont ils sortent de ce tronc doit être remarquée avec soin. Ils ont deux ordres de racines: les unes sont attachées à la partie anterieure de la moelle, et les autres, au contraire, sont fixées à la partie postérieure. . . .

J'ai constate, par des experiences dire etcs, que ces racines distinctes ont aussi des fonctions tout-à-fait distinctes: les antérieures sont destinées au mouvement, les postérieures au sentiment. Si l'on coupe les premières, l'animal perd tout mouvement, mais il conserve intacte sensibilité, et *vice verse:* si l'on coupes les secondes la sensibilité est perdue, mais l'animal a conservé ses mouvemens. (p. 432–3)

That Bell conceived of a principle which closely approximated the modern principle of reflex action is clear from his discussion of respiration, and his idea of the "nervous circle." In a paper read before the Royal Society in 1822 (30) he presented his theory of the neural basis of respiration, and, after pointing out that the animal may continue to breathe after the removal of both the cerebrum and cerebellum, he stated that "it is familiarly known that if the medulla oblongata be crushed, all actions connected with breathing cease in the instant." The problem of the relation of volition to this type of action is discussed as follows:

It will be objected to these conclusions, that the brain has a certain influence over the action of respiration. I must confess that this subject is obscure or difficult; but even in

---

experiment in Paris in 1821 and Burbach and v. Baer repeated the Bell experiments in 1818, while Magendie did not publish his discoveries until 1822. Bell himself, in "An Exposition of the Natural System of the Nerves" says: "In France, where an attempt has been made to deprive me of the originality of these discoveries, experiments without number and without mercy have been made on living animals, not under the direction of anatomical knowledge, or the guidance of just induction, but conducted with cruelty and indifference, in hope to catch at some of the accidental facts of a system, which, it is evident, the experimenters did not fully understand." *Cf.* also the monograph of Flourens (148) published in 1858 on the Bell-Magendie controversy. Magendie's claims have been recognized by certain writers by referring to the Bell-Magendie Law.

regard to the voluntary motions of the body, they are not directly from the brain, although the brain has power over them. In the same manner these relations of muscles, which are necessary to the act of breathing, are established in the medulla oblongata, and nervous cords connected with it; although the brain receives the impressions through the medulla oblongata of the condition of the respiratory organs, and the will exercises a certain control over them.

If the nerves of a limb which is separated from the body be excited, the muscles will not all become immediately rigid; there will be *an action* of the limb—the hind leg of the horse will seem to kick. This arises from the association of the muscles in the limb through the nerves, and from their being combined in classes. . . . Here then, we perceive, first, that there is a combination between the muscles formed in the body, and independent of the brain; and, secondly, we perceive that there is a peculiarity in the nature of the power exercised upon the muscles, according as they are muscles of volition or muscles of respiration. (p. 86.)

In the above discussion it is reasonable to assume that Bell intended to express the idea that there is some unconscious principle which governs muscular motion and which is exercised independently of the brain. In a paper read before the Royal Society in 1826 (30) the problem of the relation of consciousness to the "governance of the muscular frame" was discussed. In this paper Bell pointed out that, in addition to the motor nerves, there are attached to the muscle sensory nerves, the function of which is to convey a "sense of the condition of the muscles" to the brain. The presence of this sense he regarded as being essential to the regulation of muscular action. This was the basis of the theory of the nervous circle which was presented in the following words.

Now it appears the muscle has a nerve in addition to the motor nerve, which being necessary to its perfect function, equally deserves the name of muscular. This nerve, however, has no direct power over the muscle, but circuitously through the brain, and, by exciting sensation, it may become a cause of action.

Between the brain and the muscles there is a circle of nerves; one nerve conveys the influence from the brain to the muscle, another gives the sense of the condition of the muscle to the brain. If the circle be broken by the division of the motor nerve, motion ceases; if it be broken by the division of the other nerve, there is no longer a sense of the condition of the muscle, and therefore no regulation of its activity. (p. 129.)

In an anonymous review of Bell's "The Nervous System and the Human Body" published in 1843 (31) the relationship of the "circle of nerves" to the principle of reflex action was discussed. In this review it is shown that Bell probably came closer to the theory of reflex function than the paper on the "circle of nerves" would indicate, since his friends had difficulty in getting him to "re-consider what he had once thrown off," the connection between the two theories was considered as follows.

Let the reader bear in mind that the difference between the two theories of the "nervous circle" and the "reflex function" is this;—In the former, the irritation is conveyed to the brain—in the latter to the spine; in the former a conscious—in the latter an unconscious principle determines the subsequent muscular movement. It is curious that Bell had, prior to 1826, stated that an unconscious principle might also be the centre of the nervous circle, though he does not appear to have traced it to the spine.

Though Bell did not, apparently, make a specific and definite reference to reflex action, he comes closer than any of his predecessors to an adequate conception of the neural structures which must serve as a basis for the reflex. Succeeding physiologists elaborated Bell's conclusions by the use of the neuro-histological methods of investigation associated with the names of Waller, Golgi, and others; but the analyses of the reflex process by the later investigators of the 19th century was possible only in the light of the distinction between the function of the posterior and anterior spinal nerve roots. Neuburger refers to Bell's discovery as having awakened the physiology of the spinal cord from a "thousand years' slumber."[8] This is high praise especially in view of the work of Whytt, but there can be no doubt that the modern concept of spinal function is in a large measure dependent on Bell's discovery.

[8] Carmichael (78) has published an excellent review of Bell's contribution to physiological psychology.

CHAPTER IX

MARSHALL HALL

"I believe that my investigations have not only confirmed the opinion stated in my former Memoir—that the phenomena in question do not depend upon sensation,—but have demonstrated that they depend upon a distinct principle of nervous action, long partially known to physiologists, but altogether unapplied to the explanation of the phenomena of life. This principle is that termed *vis nervosa* by Haller, *motorische Kraft* or *vis motoria* by Professor Müller, and *excitabilité* by M. Flourens."—MARSHALL HALL, *Memoirs on the Nervous System*, 1837.

Aside from the advances made in the knowledge of the minute anatomy of the nervous system to which we have already referred, the outstanding advance of the first quarter of the 19th century from the point of view of physiological psychology is the discovery by Bell of the differential function of the spinal nerve roots. Whytt, Unzer, and others had distinguished the sensory and motor portions of the involuntary actions; the contribution of Bell furnished the exact anatomical element which had been wanting previously.

The growing interest in neurological problems stimulated by the work of Bell and Magendie was indicated by the large number of neurophysiological treatises which appeared about this time. A review of these works reveals little that is absolutely new so far as reflex action is concerned; we look in vain for the report of an investigation of the merit of that of Whytt or his great successor, Bell. They are of some interest, however, indicating as they do the status of the physiology of the nervous system at this time. They thus form a background against which we may project the work of Marshall Hall whose work is the most conspicuous feature, next to that of Bell, of the first part of the 19th century.

Francois Longet (1811–1871), a French physician, was the author in 1842 of one of the most ambitious works on the anatomy and function of the nervous system (314) written up to his time. It is remarkable, however, that this author does not mention the contributions of Glisson, Astruc, Unzer, and Blane in his two volumes, and Whytt is mentioned but once. In the rather extensive treatment of the anatomy and function of the spinal cord, the topic of reflex action is treated and the writings of Prochaska in this connection are extensively quoted.

MARSHALL HALL

Julian Jean Cesar Legallois (1770–1814) was a French physiologist whose chief contribution was a confirmation of Whytt's findings regarding the function of the spinal cord in reflex action. In his "Experiments on the Principle of Life" (297) he makes an interesting resume of the facts known at the time.

Tels sont, en résumé, les principaux faits que je fis connaître en 1809: il en résultait que l'entretien de la vie dans une partie quelconque d'un animal dépendait essentiellement de deux conditions, l'une l'integrite de la portion de moelle épinière correspondante, et de ses communications nerveuses; l'autre la circulation du sang artériel dans cette partie, et par conséquent, qu'il était possible de faire vivre telle partie que l'on voudrait d'un animal aussi long-temps que l'on pourrait faire subsister ces deux conditions; par exemple, que l'on pourrait faire vivre toutes seules les parties postérieures du corps d'un animal, après avoir frappé de mort des antérieures par la destruction de la moelle épinière correspondante à ces dernières; ou bien les antérieures, après avoir de meme frappé de mort les postérieures, ou bien enfin les parties moyennes, après avoir détruit les parties antérieures et postérieures de la moelle. (p. 71.)

Direct experiment took the form of destroying certain portions of the spinal cord and noting the effects. He found that sensation and movement disappeared in those parts, the attached spinal segments of which had been destroyed. Legallois seems not to have been aware of the findings of Bell; in fact his knowledge of the work of his predecessors in the field of neurology seems in general to have been deficient.[1] Bell referred to Legallois' experiments as being of the "rudest kind possible." Bell, perhaps because of his dislike of vivisection, seems to have been somewhat impatient with physiological experiments; and to have prided himself on reasoning from anatomy without recourse to experiment.

Legallois attempted to localize the respiratory center which he placed in the medulla, and he believed, that the cord contained centers both of movement and sensation.

Si, au lieu de détruire la moelle on y fait des sections transversales, les parties correspondantes à chaque segment de la moelle joissent du sentiment et du mouvement volontaire, mais sans aucune harmonie et d'une manière aussi indépendante entre elles que si on eut coupé transversalement tout le corps de l'animal aux mêmes endroits; en un mot il y a dans ce cas autant de centres de sensations, bien distincts, qu'on fait de segmens de la moelle. (p. 134.)

We have here apparently a reference to a kind of spinal cord consciousness—a subject about which an important debate was later to take place.

[1] Eckhard, *op. cit.*, noted this deficiency especially with reference to the work of Whytt, whose findings, in fact, Legallois merely verified. *Vide* Eckhard, p. 51.

Claude Francois Lallemand (1790–1853) who was Professor of Clinical Surgery at Montepellier, emphasized the importance of the spinal cord as opposed to the brain as a source of nervous energy. He (279) also referred to the influence exerted by the brain on the activities under the control of the cord, pointing out, however, that this influence is not equal on all portions of the cord. He believed with Legallois that the brain was not the source of all movement, but that it could coordinate movement. Lallemand referred to his observations on acephalous infants in support of his conclusions regarding the importance of the cord.[2]

Herbert Mayo (1796–1852), an English physiologist and anatomist who was another unsuccessful claimant for Bell's honor of having discovered the functions of the spinal nerve roots, attempted to find an experimental basis for the distinction between voluntary and involuntary muscles. Voluntary muscles he designated (343) as those which respond when their divided nerves are mechanically stimulated. Such muscles were those of the trunk, head, limbs, tongue, soft palate, larynx, pharynx, oesophagus and "lower outlet of the pelvis." In the involuntary group were the muscles of the heart, stomach, intestines and the bladder. The muscles which act when a nerve "distributed through them is mechanically irritated" (voluntary muscles) have the following characteristics:

1. They admit of being thrown into action by an effort of the will.
2. With sufficient attention and resolution, their action may be restrained from.
3. Their action is attended with a conscious effort, and is guided by sensation.
4. If divided, the separate parts retract instantaneously to a certain distance, and subsequently undergo no further permanent shortening.
5. When mechanically irritated, a single momentary action alone ensues.
6. They remain relaxed, unless excited by special impressions, both in the living body and before the loss of irritability after death.
7. Their action in the living body habitually results from an influence transmitted from the brain or spinal chord through the nerves. (p. 49.)

These characteristics stated negatively are the attributes of involuntary muscular action. Mayo noted that there were exceptions to both classes so far as the characteristics of individual muscle groups are concerned. Experiments on spinal cord function are referred to:

If in a rabbit the spinal chord be divided both at the foramen magnum and in the middle of the back, on touching the surface of the eye the eyelids are instantly closed; upon pinching the hind foot, the hind leg shrinks from the injury. If the head of a pigeon is cut off, and the upper part of the cranium be instantly removed with a sharp instrument, and the

---

[2] *Cf.* Cayrade, *op. cit.*, p. 25.

cerebrum be removed with a sharp instrument, and the cerebrum be removed by a horizontal section at the level of the tubercles, and the cerebellum and medulla oblongata, by a vertical section at the posterior margin of the tubercles, and the second and fourth nerves be divided,—leaving a segment of the brain connecting with the eyeball by the third nerve only,—on irritating the end of the optic nerve attached to the segment of the brain, the pupil is suddenly contracted. These instances would lead us to infer that each segment of the spinal chord and medulla oblongata, with the nerves derived from it, contains the physical organization requisite for sensation and instinctive action. We observe that in the experiments narrated an impression being made upon an organ of sense, some effect is produced upon the insulated portion of the central organ of the nervous system, which is followed by the transmission of an irritation to voluntary muscles. (p. 282)

It should be noted that Mayo referred to sensation in connection with the functioning of the isolated segments of the spinal cord. This implies some type of psychic function in connection with the cord. As in the case of Legallois we seem to have vague anticipation of the spinal cord "soul" which formed the subject of the Pflüger-Lotze controversy later in the same century.

Further it should be noted that Mayo thought it possible that the action of the iris in response to light was a volitional action which had become involuntary. He pointed out that voluntary actions are not necessarily conscious.

But there are many voluntary actions, which leave no recollection the instant afterwards of an act of the will. I allude to those, which from frequent repetition have become habits. Philosophers are generally agreed, that such actions continue to be voluntary, even when the influence of the will is so faint as to wholly escape detection. We are therefore not authorized to conclude that instinctive actions are not voluntary, merely because we are not conscious of willing their performance. (p. 262)

Mayo noted further the phenomena of muscular tonus, but apparently considered them voluntary rather than involuntary.

It seems probable that the habitual degree of contraction, which is remarked in certain muscles, and has been termed their tone, results from an act of volition; when all the branches of nerves passing to the lips of an ass are divided on either side of its face, the lips are observed to hang flaccid, disclosing the teeth of the animal: in a similar way, when in human beings one side of the face is paralyzed, its expression is lost, the features of that side being partly drawn towards the opposite side, and partly dropping from the mere weight of the integuments. (p. 14)

Michel Fodera (1793–1848) endeavored to distinguish between sensation and "sympathy," pointing out (149) that the first might take place with or without perception.

Si une personne reçoit une impression sur la main, par exemple, elle est ordinairement aperçue par le cerveau; mais si la personne dort ou est préoccupée, la main se retire, quoique le cerveau ne l'aperçoive pas.   Un semblable phénomène a lieu dans les animaux décapités, et meme dans toute autre partie dètacheé du corps.   Dans le premier cas, il y a asensation avec conscience ou perception; dans le second, il y a sensation sans conscience, ou, pour mieux dire, simple sensation. . . .   La difference entre la sensation et la sympathie, consiste donc en ce que, dans la première, l'impression s'arrête sur le lieu affecté, ou elle arrive tout au plus, au cerveau; dans la seconde, l'irritation s'étend au-delà de ces limites, et le reste de l'organisation souffre de son influence.   (p. 9.)

Seemingly his conception was that a kind of simple sensation might take place which closely resembled involuntary action or "sympathy."   It is interesting that he did not believe that the nervous system was always necessary for the production of the "sympathies."

Juste Louis Calmeil (1798–1895), a French physician, followed in the steps of Legallois and Fodera.   He did not assume that the cord was the seat of sensation (77), nor that it originated voluntary motion, however, when it was separated from the brain it was capable "of being excited by mechanical irritations."[3]   These movements were automatic.   He raised the question as to the seat of sensation, and pointed out that in the intact animal perception can take place only in the brain; the spinal cord in this case and in the case of volition merely serving as a conducting medium. Apparently he granted that the cord was capable of taking over certain functions in the event of the removal of the brain.

Marie Jean Pierre Flourens (1794–1867), perhaps the most distinguished French physiologist of his day, in 1824 made his classical studies of the effects of the removal of the cerebrum and cerebellum in pigeons.   The results of these studies together with his studies on the functions of the semi-circular canals have raised him to the rank of the founder of systematic work on the mechanisms of equilibration.[4]   Flourens was interested, however, in all problems which had to do with the functions of the nervous system, in which he recognized a mechanism specialized for the reception of stimulation and the execution of movement.   His paper (147) on the functions of the nervous system in vertebrates published in 1824 attracted the attention of Cuvier and the Academy of Sciences.   In this paper certain problems are proposed in connection with the rôle of the central nervous system in sensation and movement.

Mais la propriété de *sentir* réside-t-elle dans les mêmes parties que la propriété de *mouvoir?*   Mais *sentir* et *mouvoir* ne sont-ils qu'une seule propriété? sont-ils deux propriétés diverses? les organes de l'une de ces propriétés sont-ils distincts des *organes* de l'autre?

---

[3] Calmeil, *op. cit.*, p. 86.   *Cf.* Longet, *op. cit.*, I, p. 314 *ff.*
[4] *Cf.* Griffith (189), p. 12.

. . . Mes experiences montrent, de la manière la plus formelle, qu'il y a deux propriétés essentiellement diverses dans le système nerveux, l'une de *sentir*, l'autre de mouvoir; que ces deux propriétés different de siege comme d'effect; et qu'une limite precise separe les organes de l'une des organes de l'autre. (Introduction)

He then proceeded to classify the properties of the nervous system in three groups: (1) the property of sensing, willing and perceiving, (2) the property of excitability, (3) the property of coördination. The capacity for volition and sensibility resided in the brain and the capacity for coördination of muscular movement resided primarily in the cerebellum. Flourens' discussion of movement is interesting.

Je l'appelle *mouvement coordonné* tout mouvement qui résulte du concours, de l'enchainement, du *groupement*, si l'on peut ainsi dire, de plusieurs autres mouvemens, tous distincts, tous isolés les une des autres, et qui, groupes autrement, eussent donné un autre resultat total.

Ainsi, le saut, la marche, la course, la station, le nagement, le vol, sont des mouvemens coordonnés; des mouvemens resultans du concours de plusieurs parties distinctes, séparées, isolées; dont chacune peut agir seule et séparement, réunie à une, à deux, à trois, à toutes les autres; et produit divers effets selon ces diverses combinaisons.

Pareillement, le mouvement de l'inspiration, et tous les derives de lui; le cri, le baillement, certaines dejections, certaines attitudes, etc., sont encore des mouvemens coordonnes. . . .

Et j'appelle ces derniers mouvemens, *mouvemens de conservation*, par opposition aux premiers qui désignent si bien les mots de *mouvemens de locomotion et de préhension*. . . .

Il reste à parler des mouvemens du coeur et des intestins, communement confondus avec ceux de la respiration, du cri, du baillement, etc., sous les noms vagues et indefinis de *mouvemens involontaires*. (p. 185.)

The emphasis on the coördinating functions of the nervous system is a significant development and is, perhaps, a preliminary concept to that of integration.

We may note two significant developments in the contributions just reviewed: (1) the beginning of the discussion of the possibility of a *sensory* function of the spinal cord, and (2) the emphasis on the *coördinating* capacities of the nervous system. The first, heralds the Pflüger-Lotze controversy in regard to the psychic accompaniments of spinal cord function, and the second anticipates the 20th century emphasis on the integrative aspects of the nervous system. In addition an increasing interest was manifested in the particular sensory, neural, and motor structures at the basis of specific involuntary acts. Among studies[5] of this type may be noted (1) the nervous basis of respiration (Bell, Legallois), (2) the nervous basis of the heart

[5] *Cf*. Longet, *op. cit.*, I, p. 279 *ff*. for a contemporary summary, also von Kempen (267).

action (Haller, Legallois, Wilson Phillip,[6] Flourens, Ollivier[7]), (3) the nervous basis of equilibration, especially in connection with the functions of the semi-circular canals and the cerebellum (Flourens, Purkinje[8]), and (4) the studies of eye-movements (Bell). In the main these studies were based on sound experimentation and resulted in contributions of permanent value.

JOHANNES MÜLLER AND MARSHALL HALL

Marshall Hall (1790–1857), the distinguished English physician and physiologist, is regarded with Descartes, Whytt, and Bell, as one of the foremost contributors to our knowledge of reflex action. He devoted the major portion of his professional life to the study of involuntary motor phenomena in man and in animals. Hodge (232) regards him as the first "to elaborate a mechanical theory of reflex action,"[9] and Garrison, whose estimate is no less high, states that Hall's memoir, read before the Royal Society in 1833 on "The Reflex Function of the Medulla Oblongata and Medulla Spinalis," established the "difference between volitional action and unconscious reflexes."[10] These estimates are in need of a critical revision in the light of the contributions to reflex theory in the 17th and 18th centuries, but there can be little doubt that Hall played an important rôle in giving the subject of reflex action a secure place in medicine and physiology.

Hall was born a hundred and forty years after Descartes' death and twenty-four years after the death of Whytt. He entered the University of Edinburgh in 1809, receiving the M.D. degree in 1812, and was elected to the Royal Society in 1832. The scientific subjects to which he made contributions indicated great versatility as well as industry. In addition to his researches on the circulation of the blood, respiration, and physiology of the nervous system, he published papers on the signs used in algebra and the higher powers of numbers. His papers on reflex action were cordially received by the great German physiologist, Johannes Müller, who, coincident with Hall, made contributions in the same field, and his major works on physiology were translated into French, German, Dutch and Italian.

---

[6] Phillip (406) studied the relation of the heart action to the nervous system and agreed with Haller that the heart was independent of the nervous system.

[7] Ollivier (390) believed that the cord controlled circulation and respiration.

[8] Purkinje was the first (1820) to observe ocular nystagmus after rotation of the body, although he did not connect it with the semi-circular canals. *Cf.* Griffith, *op. cit.*, p. 9.

[9] P. 351.

[10] *Op. cit.*, p. 412.

Hall's interests were not confined to scientific subjects; he was concerned with economic and social problems as well. He was, for example, much interested in the slavery problem in the United States and advocated a system of gradual emancipation of the slaves. The latter years of his life found him engaged in an exceedingly bitter controversy, of which we shall speak later, regarding his claims to priority in connection with his contributions to the physiology of reflex action.

In the Royal Society Memoir (196) of 1833 referred to above,[11] Hall comments on the divergencies of opinion among physiologists as to the function of the spinal cord and medulla oblongata. He proceeds in his study by attempting a classification of animal motions.

There are, in the animal economy, four modes of muscular action, of muscular contraction. The *first* is that designated voluntary: volition, originating in the cerebrum, and spontaneous in its acts, extends its influence along the spinal marrow and the motor nerves, in a *direct line*, to the voluntary muscles. The *second* is that of the *respiration:* like volition, the motive influence in respiration passes in a direct line from one point in the nervous system to certain muscles; but as voluntary motion seems to originate in the cerebrum, so the respiratory motions originate in the medulla oblongata: like the voluntary motions, the motions of respiration are spontaneous; they continue, at least, after the eighth pair of nerves has been divided. The *third* kind of muscular action in the animal economy is that termed *involuntary:* it depends upon the principle of irritability, and requires the immediate application of a stimulus to the neuro-muscular fibre itself. These three kinds of muscular motion are well known to physiologists; and I believe they are all which have been hitherto pointed out. There is, however, a *fourth* which subsists, in part, after the voluntary and respiratory motions have ceased, by the removal of the cerebrum and medulla oblongata, and which is attached to the medulla spinalis, ceasing itself when this is removed, and leaving the irritability undiminished. In this kind of muscular motion, the motive influence does not originate in any central part of the nervous system, but at a distance from that centre: it is neither spontaneous in its action, nor direct in its course; it is, on the contrary, *excited* by the application of appropriate stimuli, which are not, however, applied immediately to the muscular or nervo-muscular fibre, but to certain membranous parts, whence the impression is carried to the medulla, *reflected*, and reconducted to the part impressed, or conducted to a part remote from it, in which muscular contraction is effected. (p. 638)

It is the fourth group of muscular actions which Hall regarded as his own particular discovery.

The first three modes of muscular action are known only by actual movements or muscular contractions. But the reflex function exists as a continuous muscular action, as a power presiding over organs not actually in a state of motion, preserving in some as the glottis, an open, in others, as the sphincters, a closed form, and in the limbs, a due

---

[11] This memoir was preceded by a paper (195a) on the same subject read before the Zoological Society in 1832.

degree of equilibrium, or balanced muscular action,—a function, not, I think, hitherto recognized by physiologists. . . . But the reflex function is peculiar in being excitable into modes of action not previously subsisting in the animal economy, as in the cases of sneezing, coughing, vomiting, etc. (p. 638)

In Hall's Memoir of 1837 (197) he made this reflex function dependent on the action of a special system of nerves—the excito-motory nerves. This system Hall referred to as the "true spinal system" as distinct from the cerebral system. The latter is the seat of sensation and volition *exclusively*. The cerebral system always involves consciousness, it functions during the waking hours, and is the seat of the intellect. The spinal system is unaccompanied by psychical activity, never sleeps, and on it the preservation of the species depends. Hall in the 1833 paper made (196) clear his conception of the anatomical and functional relations of the various kinds of animal motion.

The principles of the movements in the animal economy, viewed in an anatomical and functional point of light, may now be enumerated thus:
1. The cerebrum, or source of the voluntary motions.
2. The medulla oblongata, or the source of the respiratory motions.
3. The medulla spinalis generally, the middle arc of the reflex function.
4. The muscular fibre, or the seat of the irritability.
5. The sympathetic, or the source of nutrition, of the secretions, etc. . .
The reflex function of the different portions of the medulla presides over their corresponding organs: that of the medulla oblongata presides over the larynx and the pharynx; that of the lumbar and sacral portion of the medulla spinalis presides over the sphincter ani, the cervix vesicae; the intervening portions of the medulla give tone and equilibrium to the corresponding portions of the muscular system, and what Legallois has so vaguely designated "life," to the corresponding regions of the body. But the operation of the reflex function is by no means confined to parts corresponding to distinct portions of the medulla. The irritation of a given part may, on the contrary, induce contraction in a part very remote; the irritation of teething may induce spasmodic action or relaxation of the sphincters; the irritation of the nostrils, in the case of a young hedgehog, when so languid that voluntary motion and respiration had ceased, induced as energetic contraction of the most distant part of the panniculus carnosus and of the muscles of the posterior extremities, as irritation of the posterior extremities or tail themselves.

With death the muscular functions enumerated above disappear in order; the voluntary, the respiratory motions, the reflex, the irritability of the muscular fibres themselves, and finally the sympathetic functions. This order is inverted when the functions and organs gradually come into existence in the foetal states. The movements of the foetus in utero are essentially reflex in nature.

The conceptions of Hall regarding nervous action were based on numerous experiments on turtles, hedgehogs, frogs, lizards, and eels. He described an early experiment in the paper of 1833.

methæmatous blood-channels, or more briefly, *methæmata*, would be the most appropriate. The veins, heart, and arteries are mere *machinery* or conveying the blood to and from these methæmata, in which, in reality, *all* the *purposes* and *objects* of the circulation are effected.

7. But to return from this digression—It was during the preparation of that paper that I was struck with the occurrence of the phenomenon to which I have adverted, the first of the series which I have since designated 'reflex actions.'

8. My friend, the late Mr. Henry Smith, and myself had, on a memorable day, observed and traced the pneumonic circulation in the *Triton*. We then removed the head, and divided the insensible body of the animal into three portions, anterior extremities, posterior extremities, and tail :

9. *On irritating the separated tail with the point of a probe or the forceps, it was observed to move and become contorted into varied forms !*

Figure 1.

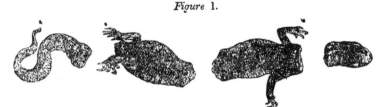

" Marshall Hall *primus tempore* est, qui pronunciavit, in hac hucusque *vasorum capillarium* nomine comprehensa vasorum sanguineorum provincia *distinctionem* faciendam esse : in *arterias minutas, vera vasa capillaria* et *venas minutas* ; nam vera vasa capillaria, vasis arteriosis et venosis parvis, certis et definitis characteribus differunt."

" Josephus Berres ea quæ sequuntur, jam publicaturus, adhuc ignorabat illa, quæ Marshall Hall, in opere supra laudato" "palam fecerat."—C. A. Voigt, *de Systemate Vasorum Intermedio* ; 1840 ; p. 17, 29.

B 2

FROM MARSHALL HALL'S MEMOIRS. IN WHICH IS DESCRIBED HIS ORIGINAL DISCOVERY

This animal [turtle] was decapitated in the manner usual with cooks, by means of a knife, which divided the second and third vertebrae.

The head being placed upon the table for observation, it was first remarked that the mouth opened and shut, and that the submaxillary integuments descended and ascended,

alternately, from time to time, replacing the acts of respiration.   I now touched the eye
or eyelid with a probe.   It was immediately closed: the other eye closed simultaneously.
I then touched the nostril with the probe.   The mouth was immediately opened widely,
and the submaxillary membranes descended.   This effect was especially induced on touching the nasal fringes situated just within the anterior part of the maxilla.   I passed the
probe up the trachea and touched the larynx.   This was immediately followed by a
forcible convulsive contraction of the muscles annexed to it.   Having made and repeated
these observations, I gently withdrew the medulla and brain.   The phenomena ceased
from that moment.   The eye, the nostril, the larynx were stimulated, but no movement
followed.   (p. 644)

In a later paper it was made evident that Hall himself was not unaware
of the importance of the initial experiment, at least as seen in retrospect.
In 1850 he described (201) the event after a lapse of twenty years, and it
is evident that the intervening time had not dimmed the lustre nor de-
tracted from the dramatic quality of that occasion.[12]

My friend, the late Mr. Henry Smith, and myself had, on a memorable day, observed
and traced the pneumonic circulation in the Triton.   We then removed the head, and
divided the insensible body of the animal into three portions, anterior extremities, posterior
extremities, and tail:
   *On irritating the separated tail with the point of a probe or the forceps, it was observed to
move and become contorted into varied forms!*[13]
   On irritating the anterior or posterior extremity in the same manner, these also
moved, being withdrawn and made to approach the adjacent portion of the trunk of the
animal. . . .
   Other similar phenomena were speedily observed; and I was gradually led on to the
development of the spinal or diastaltic system.   (pp. 3–4)

Other experiments are described.

On another occasion, having removed the head of a frog, I divided the spine between
the third and fourth dorsal vertebrae, and separated the upper portion of the animal from

---

[12] In the "Memoirs of Marshall Hall" (193) his widow quotes the following from Hall's
memoranda "dictated twenty-five years afterwards, during his last illness," which also
refers to this event.   "The decapitated triton lay on the table.   I divided it between the
anterior and posterior extremities, and I separated the tail.   I now touched the external
integument with the point of the needle; it moved with energy, assuming various curvi-
linear forms!   What was the nature of this phenomenon?   I had not touched a muscle;
I had not touched a muscular nerve; I had not touched the spinal marrow.   I had touched
a cutaneous nerve.   That the influence of this touch was exerted through the spinal
marrow was demonstrated by the fact that the phenomenon ceased when these nerves
were divided.   And thus we had the most perfect evidence of a reflex, or diastaltic, or
diacentric action.   From that day to this I have not ceased to pursue the subject in all its
phases—physiological, pathological and therapeutic!"   (pp. 85–6.)
   [13] The italics are Hall's as is the exclamatory punctuation.

the lower. There were then the head, the anterior extremities, and the posterior extremities, with their corresponding portions of medulla, as three distinct parts of an animal. Each preserved the reflex function. On touching an eye, it was retracted, and the eyelids close, whilst similar phenomena were observed simultaneously in the other eye. On removing the medulla, these phenomena ceased. On pinching the toe of one of the anterior extremities, the limb and the opposite limb equally moved. On removing the spinal marrow, this phenomenon also ceased. Precisely similar effects were observed in regard to the posterior extremities. (Memoir of 1833)

Hall performed certain experiments which demonstrated the reflex nature of the action of the sphincters.

An interesting experiment demonstrates the powerful influence of the reflex function over the sphincter ani in the turtle. If, after the removal of the tail and the posterior extremities, with the rectum, and of course with a portion of the spinal marrow, water be forced into the intestine, by means of Read's syringe, the cloaca is fully distended before any part of the fluid escapes through the sphincter, which it then does on the use of considerable force only, and by jerks and gushes. The event is very different on withdrawing the spinal marrow; the sphincter being now relaxed, the water flows through it at once in an easy continuous stream, with the application of little force, and without inducing any distention of the cloaca. (Memoir of 1833)

To substantiate his theories, Hall drew on medical literature in connection with infants born without a cerebrum or cerebellum. He pointed out that these infants can swallow when food is brought into contact with the pharnyx, void urine and faeces, and perform other purely reflex functions.

Hall's experiments in connection with the toxic effect of drugs on nervous function were among the earliest contributions in this field. He noted that when a frog is made to swallow a "watery solution of strychnine or opium, the animal soon becomes affected with symptoms perfectly similar to those of tetanus." The reflex function is augmented.

A frog made tetanic by opium was decapitated, and divided just below the third vertebra. The eyes were retracted, and no movement could be detected on irritating the eyelids or skin. Both the anterior and posterior extremities remained susceptible, and tetanic, as before: the limbs were moved in the same spasmodic manner by the same slight impressions. All was changed on removing the medulla oblongata and spinalis. The eyes were no longer retracted. The muscles of the limbs were immoveable under the action of stimuli, and perfectly flaccid, having lost their exalted tone. (Memoir of 1833)

He concluded that the phenomena of strychnine tetany were referrable to the action of the excito-motory system, and, hence, did not depend upon sensation or volition.

Just the opposite effects were observed when a few drops of dilute hydrocyanic acid were placed on the tongue of a frog; the contractions which depend upon reflex functions gradually diminished and finally ceased.

From the point of view of the development of the reflex concept, Hall's generalization regarding the functional relationships within the spinal cord are exceedingly important.   In the memoir of 1850 (201) he says:

> On analysing the facts which have been detailed, I observed that the following anatomical relations are essential:
> 1. A nerve leading *from* the point or part irritated, *to* and *into* the spinal marrow;
> 2. The spinal marrow *itself;* and
> 3. A nerve, or nerves, passing *out of* or *from* the spinal marrow,—*all in essential relation or connection with each other*.   (pp. 4–5)

In the same monograph he made it clear that the three elements referred to in the above quotation were linked together, and constituted a *nervous arc*.   In 1850 Hall applied the term "diastaltic" to the reflex arc which he had described fifteen years before.

> The anatomy of the diastaltic system consists in an esodic nerve, the spinal centre, and an exodic nerve, *essentially linked together*, and constituting a *diastaltic* nervous arc.
> The physiology of this system consists in such an arc or such arcs, in diastaltic action. (p. 36)

This, apparently, was the first use of the term "arc" in connection with the sequence of functions involved in the reflex.

In another interesting section of the Memoir of 1850 Hall discussed the pathology and therapeutics of the "diastaltic" system.   The causes which may act on the system bringing about morbid action are: (1) those which act on the center; emotion, the blood, arachnitis, encephalitis, tumors, (2) those which act on the esodic (afferent) nerves; dental, gastric, enteric, uterine, traumatic, and (3) those which act on the exodic (efferent) nerves; tubercles, tumors, inflammation, wounds, lesions of adjacent tissues.   He proceeded to discuss the therapeutics and pathology of the system in connection with obstetrics, epileptic seizures, paralyses, and other diseases.

It is interesting to note that for Hall emotion as well as volition acts through the cerebral system.   Although the spinal system ("diastaltic") is independent of the cerebral, it is possible for the actions of the former to be modified by the latter.

> The true spinal system is, in a peculiar sense, the seat or nervous agent of the appetites and passions.   Through it the emotions affect, not the expression and the respiration alone, but the pharynx, the larynx, the sphincters, the expulsors, and indeed the whole muscular system of the animal frame.
> The true spinal system is susceptible of *modification* by volition, and, on this account, some of its functions have been denominated *mixed*.   It is also constantly under a certain influence of volition, as is manifest in the difference in respiration, etc., during intense mental attention, sleep, and coma, and ordinary circumstances.   (Memoir, 1837, p. 73)

The exact neurological mechanisms of this modification of reflex action by psychical processes were not made clear, nor did Hall explain the possible extent of such modification.

Hall's position on the problem of muscle sensation is interesting in that he denied the existence of a muscular sense.

The late Sir Charles Bell treated of what he designated a "nervous circle," defining it thus:

'Between the brain and the muscle there is a circle of nerves; one nerve conveys the influence of the brain to the muscle, another gives the sense of the condition of the muscle to the brain.'

I think this view an error. I believe we have no consciousness of the condition of individual muscles, or sets of muscles, as we have no power of acting on such muscles. The sense, sometimes denominated the muscular sense, is, I believe, not in the muscle, nor in any sentient muscular nerve, but in the nerve of touch, or of vision; and volition is not directed to any muscle, or set of muscles, but to the aim, object and purpose of their contraction. We are guided in our voluntary actions, not by muscular sense or nerve, but by the sense of touch or of vision, by the *cutaneous* or the *optic* nerves. (Memoir, 1850, pp. 27-8.)

He noted that patients afflicted with loss of sensation in the fingers will let objects fall unless the eye is directed towards the hand. He, also, noted that patients afflicted with partial paralysis cannot walk in the dark.

If a patient has lost the power of sensation in the feet, he cannot walk in the dark; the eye is essential to the due action of the muscles of the lower extremities. I have a patient afflicted with partial paraplegia, who has no power of *balancing* himself without the aid of the eye.

We have only to consult our own consciousness, to be aware that 'the nervous circle' is not between muscle and muscle, but between one sentient nerve, whether of touch or of sight, and another. The sensation does not ascend from the muscle, nor does volition descend to it; but the former arises from a nerve or sense—of special sense—and the latter is directed to an aim or purpose, in attaining which the former is the *guide*. (Memoir, 1850, p. 28)

In this quotation it is evident that Hall anticipated the observations of Romberg (425) in connection with the so-called "Romberg Sign," although his conclusions in regard to the muscle sense would not be wholly acceptable to modern physiology and psychology.

Hall pointed out that reflex acts frequently resembled volitional acts and noted the evidence of design in the former. This design he attributed to a divine will, and offered it as evidence of the existence of a deity.

Hall was convinced that his observations and conclusions regarding the "diastaltic" system were original—nor was he inclined to underrate them because of that fact. He presented the findings of other workers in the field, although his acquaintance with their experiments seems not to have been detailed.[14]

Regarding Whytt, Hall seems to have failed to appreciate the significance of the former's observations perhaps because of his effort to deny his predecessor's conclusions. Hall also charged Mayo with confounding the nervous agency of sensation and volition with that of reflex action.

Soon after publication of the first two memoirs Hall's views brought him into conflict with certain of his contemporaries. In 1838 John Durance George, one of the Presidents of the Medical Society of University College, London, read before that body a paper on the "History of the Nervous System" (167), which had for its purpose the presentation of material tending to show that Hall had been anticipated in all essential particulars by Prochaska and others. This paper was published in full in three successive numbers of the London Medical Gazette. George introduced his subject as follows:

> This contribution to the history of the nervous system owes its origin to a remark made by Professor Sharpey in lecturing upon the reflex or excito-motory function, 'that of all previous physiologists, Prochaska had approached most nearly in his views to those at present entertained'—a remark which caused some surprise, when I recollected that in Dr. Hall's account of the 'Opinions of Former Physiologists' no such author is mentioned, or even alluded to. I was therefore obliged to seek information as to Prochaska's views from his own writings; and, in pursuing my investigations further, soon found that Dr. Hall's account was very imperfect. . . . (p. 40)

George reviewed the early work on the subject of reflex action, including Redi, Whytt, Blane, Legallois and others, but devoted most of his space to a recapitulation of Prochaska's contribution. Hall's conclusions are compared statement by statement with those of Prochaska and others. George indicates that Hall was anticipated in connection with the following principles:[15] (1) a principle of motion which is distinct from volition and sensation and all cerebral functions, (2) this principle is a function of the spinal marrow, (3) it is called into action by the stimulation of the spinal nerves, (4) the impression is made on the extremity of the nerve, passes to the cord and is reflected back to the muscles, (5) this principle is used to explain sympathetic phenomena, (6) it is applied to the explanation of various convulsive diseases, (7) that it is increased and diminished by the administration of certain poisons—opium, etc., (8) that it is the principle of life in the foetal state. It will be observed that these are the most essential of Hall's doctrines. George's concluding remarks are interesting.

[14] *Cf.* quotation which introduces the present chapter.
[15] George, *op. cit.*, pp. 46–7; 94–5.

I have written it [the paper] because it appears to me that we cannot be too strict in awarding to every individual the credit to which he may be entitled by the facts which his industry has accumulated, or the laws which his ingenuity has inferred from them; whilst, apart from this *suum cuique*, an imperfect history deprives the mind of the pleasure which it feels in tracing each principle from its origin to its end—from the first shadowing forth of the *idea*, to the latest detail added to the system. . . although my present conclusions are not altogether pleasing, for I am convinced that if *more* had been *read*, *less* would have been *discovered*. (pp. 95–6)

That the controversy had become personal and had come to include the charge of deliberate plagiarism of ideas, if not of actual terminology, is indicated by the editorial (313) comment in the Gazette of the same year, under the caption "The Reflex Function, an Old Discovery."

We beg to direct the attention of our readers to the elaborate and interesting paper by Mr. George, in the preceding part of the present number. From this, it is clear that Dr. Marshall Hall was completely anticipated by Prochaska in his views of the reflex function; and the same opinion, we perceive, is expressed by the learned Editors of the British and Foreign Medical Review. It is a very remarkable fact, as stated by Mr. George, that Dr. Hall, though he has published the 'opinions of former physiologists,' makes no mention of the author above named; and certainly this fact will not be regarded as less remarkable, when we inform our readers that there is a copy of Prochaska's work in the library of the Medical and Chirurgical Society, and that, little as the volume was known to others, one member, at least, has shown that he duly appreciated its value, by the fact of his having repeatedly taken it out: that member, need we add, is—Dr. Marshall Hall! (p. 73)

Hall attempted to meet this charge by obtaining a signed statement (199) from the librarian of the Medical and Chirurgical Society to the effect that the works of Prochaska were borrowed during the years 1835, 1837, and 1838, *i.e.*, after the paper announcing the discoveries was read before the Royal Society in 1833.[16] It may be noted, however, that the paper read before the Royal Society in 1833 was republished in 1837, together with a second paper on the excito-motory system neither of which contain reference to Prochaska, although Hall admits having examined his works in 1835. In Hall's memoir of 1850 we find the following statement which may be taken as an answer to the accusations of George and others.

Several similar experiments had been made long ago, by Redi, Whytt, Legallois, Blane, etc. This was fully stated by me in my first publication on the subject. Whytt had even asserted the necessity for the presence of the spinal marrow; and Blane had stated that sensation is excluded. What then? Did those observations lead to any result?—to any detection of the motor Principle involved?—to any application to Anatomy, Physiology, Diagnosis, Pathology, Therapeutics, or Obstetrics? No! Not one tittle of all this was accomplished by any one.

---

[16] George replied to this letter by a scathing communication to the Gazette (168) in which Hall's professional honesty and sincerity are attacked.

In making this assertion, I include Whytt, and Unzer, and Prochaska, of whom so much has been calumniously written in this country.

Whytt speaks of the phenomena in question as dependent on the *soul*. They are in reality *physical*, not *psychical*.

Unzer asserts that the spinal marrow is merely a 'thick chord of nerves,' proceeding, as, he says, all nerves do, from the brain (a view which *excludes* the *idea* even of a really reflex or diastaltic action absolutely) and he may be fairly supposed to speak through his pupil, Prochaska. Now the latter author describes diastaltic actions as 'impressionum *sensoriarum* in motorias reflectio;' and, so far from even entertaining the idea of a diastaltic action of the *vis nervosa*, or of a diastaltic *function* or *system*, confounds effects of volition and emotion, and the action of the heart, stomach, and intestines, with actions really and truly diastaltic. (pp. 8–9)

Hall proceeded to deplore the fact that truth has been "imolated" on the altar of misrepresentation for nearly twenty years. Hall's widow in her "Memoirs of Marshall Hall" (193) published in 1861, dealt with this controversy in a chapter entitled "Discovery and Opposition." She described the reception of the first paper on the reflex function which was read before the Royal Society in 1833. In 1837 a second paper was submitted to the Society and rejected. Hall then addressed the following note to the members of the Council:

I beg, Gentlemen, that you will do me the favour to appoint a commission to witness my experiments, to examine my plain deductions from them, and to look over my paper with care, before you finally condemn my labours. . . . Having quoted from Whytt an experiment of Redi, on the movements of the tortoise when deprived of its head, some one has written—"Will they live after they are made soup of?" Such an observation needs no remark from *me*. It is rather an indignity put on the Royal Society itself. (pp. 88–9)

This entreaty was passed in "contemptuous silence" according to Mrs. Hall. She then proceeds to describe the bitterness of the medical press.

The greater portion of the medical press waged furious war against the discovery. One number of a quarterly periodical contained no fewer than four separate articles against it. . . . Attacks were so perseveringly continued in one journal that, I believe, not a single number of it was published during a series of years which did not contain some adverse article. (p. 89)

An adequate estimate of Hall's work is made difficult by his tendency to exaggerate the importance of his own contributions. He regarded, apparently, his discovery of the "excito-motory" system, *i.e.*, a neuro-muscular system structurally and functionally independent of the system subserving volition and sensation, as his major contribution to neurology. This system, the "diastaltic," as he characterized it, is not taken seriously at the present day. His work in connection with decapitated animals and his observations on the response of parts of the body served by segments of the spinal cord was not new, since Blane, Whytt, and others had performed similar experiments. In the same category are to be placed his observations in connection with a class of animal movements taking place independently of volition and sensation and independently of the cerebrum.

Without attempting to evaluate all the charges which grew out of the bitter controversy of 1838, it is nevertheless difficult to understand how Hall could have been unaware of the work of his predecessors in the same field. Eckhard (125) says that a comparison of the work of Hall with that of earlier workers forces the conclusion that the significance of Hall's contribution to the study of reflex phenomena "has been greatly exaggerated," although he grants that Hall "kindled anew" interest in the study of reflex phenomena. In addition, however, Eckhard believes that Hall made certain real advances in the field. These are (1) the observation that reflex movements are depressed or augmented by hydrocyanic acid and opium or strychnine, (2) the release of certain reflex movements through the brain (eyeball movements in head removed from body), (3) reflexes are released more easily from nerve endings than from the nerve roots themselves, and (4) the observation on the sphincter tonus and its dependency on the spinal cord. Hall (198) summarized his own point of view as follows:

1. I view the reflex function as the *distinct* and *peculiar or proper* function of the medulla spinalis, equally independent of the brain, the sympathetic, and of the anastomoses and the mere origins of the nerves;

2. I regard this function as residing in the medulla, as the *axis* of a *distinct* system of *excitor* and *motor*, and excito-motory nerves;

3. I consider this function and its system of nerves as presiding over the *orifices* and the *exits* or *sphincters* of the animal frame, and over *ingestion* and *egestion;*

4. The brain is the central organ of sensation and volition, the organ of *mental* relation with the external world; the spinal marrow, on the contrary, is the central organ of excito-motory phenomena, and of the *physical* appropriation of certain external objects;

5. *Volition* may *modify* the acts of the reflex function, and these acts may be attended by sensation; but this function is, otherwise, independent of both volition and sensation, of their organ the brain, and of the mind or soul;

6. Respiration even is a part of this peculiar function: it is *excited* on ordinary, and on extraordinary occasions, through appropriate excitor nerves, especially the pneumogastric, but also the fifth and spinal nerves;

7. The *passions*, in an especial manner, demonstrate themselves through the medium of the true spinal marrow; and thus *pain* may induce surprise or fear, and appear to occasion an excito-motory act;

8. The brain *sleeps;* but the spinal marrow *never sleeps;*

9. Finally, the excito-motory system of nerves is the peculiar seat of action of certain *diseases*, and of certain *causes* and *remedies* of disease. (p. 192)

Sherrington is quoted by Stirling (472) in regard to Hall as follows:

As to new facts he noted—(1) that eyeball movements are got from ablated reptilian head, and cease on destruction of brain; (2) that opium increases reflexes though sedative to mind, *i.e.*, distinguished diastaltic from conscious channels; (3) that anencephalous foetus moves to stimulation; (4) that strychnin picks out movements of 'diastaltic' order; (5) that reflexes can be excited easier from nerve-ends than from nerve trunks (he does not seem to have caught the significance of this); (6) that a tonus is exhibited by skeletal muscle which is maintained by diastaltic arc, and that sphincter tonus is of this nature. (His experiments give no *proof* that the tonus is in either case 'reflex' rather than 'automatic;' and his position was remote from to-day's, since he expressly denied Bell's muscular sense and existence of Bell's nerve-circuit, also existence of sensory nerves in muscle, and now, I suppose, most of us regard reflex tonus as maintained by muscular afferents acting on muscular efferents. And in regard to sphincter tonus, I suppose, Goltz's work makes rectal sphincter a 'myogenic' tonus.)

Hall was of much service in boldly illustrating his physiological theories and observations by clinical examples. Also his bold treatment of the cerebro-spinal axis as *functionally* a segmental series helped greatly, I imagine, to establish that—most useful—point of view; but it was not original with him, *e.g.*, Legallois and Grainger. I fancy, too, that Hall was the first to speak at all clearly of the 'spinal shock' phenomenon, and to begin to distinguish between it and 'collapse' vascular.[17]

In his own estimation his chief advance lay in the doctrine of separateness in the central nervous system of the great sub-system for unconscious reflex action, and another great sub-system for sensation and volition. The two were, according to him, absolutely separate, at least if I read him aright. It seems never to have occurred to him that a peripheral nerve-fibre might, on entering a central nervous system, embouch into channels which led, on the one hand, into his one system, on the other hand into his other. Also he missed the important point that the two are so intermingled that many physiological processes pass from one to the other; also that, psychologically, there are a number of reactions that lie intermediate between his extreme types, 'unconscious reflex' and 'willed action.' This narrowness of view was the more notable, because Grainger (1837) distinctly contended that the peripheral nerve led to both kinds of channels. But, altogether, I could not see any real difference between his (Marshall Hall's) view of movements of headless animals, etc., and those of many of his predecessors, Hales, Whytt, Prochaska, and even Descartes. (p. 86)

Also, it must not be forgotten that Hall was among the first to make a broad application of the reflex concept in medical therapy and diagnosis. On the basis of his experimental findings, he was able to give a diagnostic interpretation to the various involuntary responses.

There is some justification in denominating Hall the founder of the me-

---

[17] *Cf.* also Luciani (320), III, p. 312.   Hall's use of the term is very definite: "If we take a frog and divide the spinal marrow near the cranium, the animal is affected by *shock*; the diastaltic force is suspended, there are no diastalic actions, or only such as are very feeble. In a few minutes the diastaltic power and phenomena are restored, the effect of shock having passed away." (Memoir, 1850, p. 70.)

chanical theory of reflex action, in that he seems to have been among the first to insist on a *necessary connection in the central nervous system* between the incoming and outgoing pathways. He thus furnished the basis for that conception of the reflex as a neural arc which functions independently of the brain. From the point of view of the development of the reflex theory, this is Hall's most important contribution. At one stroke he made possible the concept of a mechanized reflex arc, and introduced it to clinical medicine and neurology. The finer details of nervous structure, at the base of the connection between the arms of the arc, the existence of which Hall assumed on functional grounds, were not known until long after his death.

At the same time that Hall was publishing his first papers on the excito-motory system, the distinguished German physiologist, Johannes Müller, (1801–1858) was experimenting in the same field and his observations and conclusions with regard to reflex action closely resembled those of the English investigator. Müller may be regarded as the intellectual successor of Haller and the latter's *Elements* was superseded as a text-book by Müller's *Handbuch*. Müller's appointment to the Professorship of Physiology at Berlin in 1833 marks the recognition of physiology as a duly accredited science, and his contributions and those of his students to the fields of sensory and neural physiology made him the leading experimental physiologist of his day. His contribution to and theory of reflex action in many ways closely parallels that of Hall. The latter had made a preliminary report of his experiments before the Zoological Society in 1832[18] and therefore had the priority—a fact which Müller acknowledges in the *Handbuch*[19] (372).

⌐Allgemeiner wurde das Princip der Reflexion von den sensoriellen Nerven auf motorische durch Vermittelung der Centraltheile zur Erklärung aller Bewegungen, welche auf Empfindungen folgen, in der neuesten Zeit durch die Untersuchungen von Marshall Hall und mir, welche beide im Jahre 1833 veröffentlicht wurden, aufgefasst und durch neue Thatsachen als Erklärungsgrund für eine grosse Anzahl von bekannten, aber falsch erklärten Erscheinungen bewiesen. (I, p. 609.)

Müller in the *Handbuch* devotes a special section to the discussion *Von der Reflexion in den Bewegungen nach Empfindungen*, in which are presented in some detail the views of Marshall Hall. He notes that wherever "general

[18] *Vide* Hall's paper in the London and Edinburgh Philosophical Magazine (198) which contains a translation of Müller's discussion in the *Handbuch*. This is a translation of an earlier edition of the section on *Der Mechanik des Nervenprincips*. Müller made but few changes in the *Handbuch* of 1844; *cf.* Bd. I, p. 580, footnote. Hall's translation is quoted in the present work.

[19] *Op. cit.*, I, p. 610, footnote.

twitchings" originate from "local sensation" this takes place through the spinal cord. These twitchings may not be general but local.

The simplest is this case, in which the local sensorial stimulation, propagated to the spinal marrow or brain, excites merely local movements, and these in the parts lying in the neighborhood, whose motor fibres proceed from the spinal marrow near the sensorial. To these belong the spasms and tremblings of the limbs which are severely burnt, etc. Certain very excitable parts of the organism, as the iris, contract extremely easily, when only slight stimuli excite other sensorial nerves, and the excitement of the latter is propagated to the brain, and from it through the oculo-motor nerves, to the short root of the ciliary ganglion, the ciliary nerves, and the iris. (Handbuch, I, pp. 612–13, Hall's translation.)

In other cases, Müller believes that, although the "sensorial excitement" is local, the response is much more general, i.e., involves larger muscle groups in coughing, sneezing, vomiting, etc. In still other cases the response may be even more diffuse, finally involving the entire trunk. The principle of this spreading or diffusion of response is found, for Müller, in the spatial relations of the cord, i.e., those motor fibres nearest the sensorial fibres which are excited, respond first. It should be noted that Müller uses the term "sensation" and perception, and it is on this point that he takes issue with Hall.

Dr. Marshall Hall shows very beautifully the relation of the voluntary, respiratory, and reflected motions, when he endeavors to prove, that the reflected motions which take place after loss of the brain are not dependent on true sensation, but only on the centripetal nervous actions which take place in sensations. Sensation, will, motion, are the three links of the chain, when a motion is induced by pain; but if the middle link be destroyed, the connection between the first and second with consciousness ceases. We believe also that the reflected motions on stimuli of the skin, which take place after the removal of the brain, do not contain any proof that the stimulus excited true sensation in the spinal marrow; it is rather the centripetal conduction of the nervous principle which commonly takes place in sensations, but which here is no longer sensation, because it is no longer conducted to the brain, the organ of consciousness. During health also numerous reflected motions result from stimuli of the skin, which do not come as true sensation to the consciousness, but still may excite violent impressions on the spinal marrow; as, for instance, the permanent contraction of the sphincters from the stimulus of the excrement and of the urine. But Dr. Marshall Hall goes too far, when he supposes that in health every motion on true sensation is induced by the will, and that all excitation of sensitive parts in the reflected motions are without sensation. For the reflected motions of sneezing, coughing, and many others follow actual sensations. (I, p. 617)

This statement is important; in the first place it seems to indicate an early reaction against the mechanical theory of reflex action associated with Hall's name, and in the second place it emphasizes the elements of the reflex act, *viz.*, the sensory, control, and motor segments. Hall responded to Müller's criticism by indicating that sneezing, coughing, etc., were acts of the excito-motory system which were *attended* by sensation, but not dependent upon it.

Müller, however, agreed with Hall in regarding the spinal cord as the most important agent in the conversion of the sensory into the motor impulse.

The phenomena which we have now described, first from our own observations and then from those of Dr. Marshall Hall, have all this in common with one another, that the spinal marrow is the connecting link between a sensorial and a motorial motion of the nervous principle, though still the course which the conduction in the reflected motions from the sensitive to the motor nerves in the spinal marrow takes may be more definitely pointed out. . . . . More correctly expressed, and translated into physiological language, this means, that in violent excitation of the motor property of the spinal marrow through a sensitive nerve, that part only of the spinal nerve is first excited, and then excites movements, which gives origin to the sensitive nerve; and that the excitation of other parts of the spinal marrow, and the motor nerves arising therefrom, decreases in proportion as they are more removed from the spot excited by the sensitive nerve. (I, p. 619)

In the foregoing passage Müller again has emphasized the cord as the connecting link between the centripetal and centrifugal segments of the reflex arc. Although Hall welcomed the support afforded him by his great German contemporary,[20] he took exception to certain of Müller's conclusions. Hall had confined the reflex function exclusively to the medulla and cord; Müller points out that certain cerebral nerves show reflex phenomena, especially the optic and auditory. A loud sound or brilliant light will cause a "reflected" excitation of the facial nerve, and "thereby closure and winking of the eyelids."

Müller described certain phenomena under the terms *Mitempfindung* and *Mitbewegung* which today would probably be explained as reflex. He, however, discussed these phenomena in separate sections and regarded them as being independent of reflex action. By the term *Mitempfindung* Müller referred to the irradiation of sensation or the association of one sensation with another, *e.g.*, such synaesthetic phenomena as the tickling experienced in the nose when one is in bright light, or the peculiar sensation which accompanies certain tones. By *Mitbewegung* Müller referred to any movement which is called forth by or associated with another movement, *e.g.*, in endeavoring to move the ear, one also moves a portion of the facial musculature.

[20] *Cf.* Hall's discussion of Müller (198), p. 51.

Die Dammuskeln, Musc. sphincter ani, levator ani, transversus perinaei, bulbo-caver-
nosus, ischio-cavernosus, pubo-urethralis werden fast immer zusammen bewegt, wenn der
Willie auch nur einen einzigen intendirt.

Am aufallendsten zeigt sich diese Association bei der Bewegung der Iris. Wir sind
nämlich nicht im Stande, die Augen durch den Musc. rect. Int. nach Innen zu kehren,
ohne zugleich die Iris mitzubewegen und zusammenzuziehen. (I. p. 587)

The movements of the iris in the two eyes simultaneously is another
example of *Mitbewegung*.

In the case of *Mitbewegung* Müller regards all the nerve fibres as collected
together in the brain. Here they are presented to be played upon by the
will as one would play upon the keys of a piano. Necessarily in a given
"willed" movement neighboring parts may be affected since their nerve
fibres must lie close together in the center—hence there will be associated
movements. The difficulty in limiting the action of the will to one fibre is
illustrated in the case of learning any motor performance; it improves with
practice.

Diese Fähigkeit der Isolation wird aber durch Uebung erlangt, das heisst, je öfter
eine gewisse Zahl Primitivfasern der Intention des Willens ausgesetzt wird, um so
mehr erhalten sie die Neigung, der Intention allein, die nebenliegenden Primitivfasern, zu gehorchen, um so mehr bilden sich gewisse Wege der leichtern Leitung aus. Wir
sehen in gewissen Künsten diese Fähigkeit der Isolation auf den höchsten Grad der Aus-
bildung gebracht, wie beim Spielen musikalischer Instrumente, besonders beim Clavier-
spielen. (I, pp. 589–90)

In the case of *Mitempfindung* Müller suggests the possibility of irradiation
in the brain or cord of sensory impressions to neighboring sensory fibres
which in turn cause a sensation.

The exact nature of the connection in the cord was not made clear by
either Müller or Hall. The latter referred to the occurrences in the cord
as "mystery!" Müller, as we have indicated, seemed to think that the
incoming impulses excited only that part of the cord at which they were
received, the excitations decreasing "in proportion as they are more removed
from the spot excited by the sensitive nerve." This interpretation, of
course, is not satisfactory for certain types of reflexes, but represented a
marked advance over the concepts of Prochaska, Unzer, Mayo, and others.

Müller's contributions to the advancement of knowledge of reflex ac-
tion were somewhat overshadowed in this field by those of his contemporary,
Hall. Eckhard lists among others the following points as important in
Müller's consideration of reflex movement: (1) the theory of *Mitempfin-
dungen* and *Mitbewegungen,* (2) Müller experimented in the same field as
Hall, *i.e.,* he was familiar with spinal animal experiments, knew the effect

of opium, but did not believe that a single segment of the cord could serve as the reflex center, and he did not appreciate the importance of the nerve endings as releasing mechanisms in the reflex, (3) many movements which Hall without question classified as reflex, Müller associated with sensation and was uncertain as to their reflex classification, (4) Müller believed that reflexes were elicited through the brain, (5) he raised the question as to the possibility of the ganglia being reflex centers, (6) he did not accept Hall's special excito-motory fibre system.

Both Müller and Hall stressed the sensory, central, and motor segments as the salient elements of the reflex arc. Müller was somewhat less dogmatic than Hall regarding the mechanical aspects of the reflex act, and he seems to have recognized the possibility of psychical activity as a modifying factor in reflex action. In his sharp delimitation of the reflex (unconscious) function from the voluntary (conscious) function, Hall failed to recognize many important types of response which intervene between these two extremes. The study of these intervening types, together with their integrative function in terms of cerebro-spinal paths, is a major contribution of late 19th century and contemporary physiological psychology. After the work of Hall and Müller, however, the status of reflex action as an explanatory principle in the interpretation of human and animal behavior was established. This was achieved, not as a result of the original factual contributions of these investigators, but as a result of the systematic exposition and analysis of the known facts in terms of scientific physiology and medicine rather than in terms of the relation of the soul to the body. There was, as we shall see, a recrudescence of this latter type of metaphysical problem in the later years of the century, but the supremacy of the reflex arc concept has not been seriously questioned by the majority of physiologists since the middle of the 19th century.

CHAPTER X

THE FUNCTION OF THE SPINAL CORD

"Another element has lately been added to the confusion already existing, by the discussion which has arisen respecting the reflex function of the spinal cord; one party maintaining that the phenomena observed are the result of sensation and volition, whilst the other, more justly as I conceive, contend that the excito-motory acts are totally independent of feeling and the will."—R. D. GRAINGER, *Observations on the Structure and Functions of the Spinal Cord*, 1837.

The Professorship of Physiology at the University of Berlin, to which Johannes Müller was appointed in 1833, was the first chair of its kind in a European or English university; this event was but an indication of the growing importance of physiology in the eyes of the world of science. To Müller and his two famous students, Du Bois Reymond, and Helmholtz, we owe the chief advances in physiology during the 19th century, and if we add the names of certain distinguished contemporaries—Weber, Lotze, Fechner, and Wundt—we complete a group which laid the foundations of modern physiological psychology. Through the contributions of all of these individuals there runs a thread of interest in the functioning of the nervous system and sense organs. Many of the numerous problems in sensory and neural physiology raised by the genius of Müller had to await solution until the beginning of the 20th century.

So far as the problems of reflex function were concerned, we find that, in spite of the apparent finality of the work of Marshall Hall and Müller, the dogma of a wholly mechanical response, functioning through the spinal cord and independent of consciousness or volition did not find unanimous acceptance. The experiments with decerebrated animals demonstrated too much. The reflex responses were clearly dependent upon the intact spinal cord; they were independent of the cerebrum, but they were still coordinated and apparently purposive. This seemed to imply some kind of psychical activity or extra-mechanical source of control. The controversy which arose over the interpretation of the functions of the spinal cord lasted until the beginning of the 20th century, and it is the purpose of the present chapter to trace the beginnings of that debate.

An interest which may be termed psychological may be noted in all the

neuro-physiological writing and speculation of the period just following
the contributions of Hall and Bell. R. D. Grainger (1801–1865), the
English anatomist and physiologist, writing in 1837 (181), for example,
states it as his purpose to obtain some definite "information respecting a
subject of the highest physiological import,—the true seat of sensation."

The interest in those aspects of spinal cord function which had to do with
the relation of the cerebral processes to the spinal processes had, in part,
grown out of Hall's dogmatic separation of the two functions. Grainger,
in the work referred to, discusses the conflicting nature of the evidence and
theories in this connection.

A question which has particularly engaged the attention of physiologists, concerns the
properties of the spinal cord, on which subject, however, we possess nothing but the most
conflicting evidence; for, whilst the phenomena presented by those anencephalous foetuses
which have for a time survived their birth, and the results obtained from vivisections
made on different parts of the brain, seem to establish the fact that sensation and volition
are properties of the spinal cord, including under that term the medulla oblongata; the
observation of the effect of accident and disease in the human body, which in such a question is so much more worthy of confidence, distinctly proves, that in no instance whatever
does an organ deprived of its connection with the brain, retain its sensation, or capacity
for voluntary motion. (p. 2)

The relation of volition to the reflex, and the associated problem of the
sensory aspects of spinal cord functioning, mark the beginning of a long
controversy, and foreshadow some of the present day problems in connection
with reflex action.[1]

Grainger expressed his conviction that the brain was the sole organ of
sensation and volition, and that the spinal cord serves, in part, as a conducting medium "of the volitions of the cerebrum." In addition to the voluntary motions under the control of the cerebrum, Grainger believed that the
voluntary muscles may act independently of the volition, being excited by
"the impressions of physical agents on the associated surfaces of the skin
and mucous membranes." This puts him in general agreement with Marshall Hall, whom he (Grainger) regards as having proved the necessity of
the existence of "an independent division of the nervous system, equally
distinct from the great sympathetic and the true cerebral system."

Grainger extends the field of involuntary action to include *all* muscular
action.

An eminent physiologist, indeed, has distinctly stated that all muscular actions, are,
in the first instance involuntary; that some continue so during life; but that there are some

---

[1] *Cf.* Sherrington (441) p. 388, Herrick (223, 224), and Child (88).

over which we gradually acquire a voluntary power, and among these, deglutition is enumerated. The two first statements are correct; but with respect to the third position, although it is true that the mind, as it becomes developed, does acquire a control over the muscles, which are called voluntary; it is only in performance of action which is *strictly* voluntary in their character; the excited actions of those muscles remain throughout life as involuntary as in the first moment of existence. (p. 112)

There is some ambiguity in the meaning of the last phrases in the above quotation, but it seems clear that Grainger supported the position of the "eminent physiologist" that all muscular actions are at the beginning involuntary. Grainger discussed such acts as the flying of pigeons and the walking of man from the point of view of their regularity, apparent purposiveness, and relative freedom from conscious control. He stated that, although the movements of progression, for example, are involuntary, they are under the control of the will, as are, indeed, nearly all involuntary motions. The volition is effective in these motions, however, in more or less inverse proportion to the importance to bodily economy of the function served by the motion. That is, those motions which perform a definite preservative function are almost immune from volitional interference, whereas such motions as those serving progression may be completely under voluntary control. Intensity of the stimulus is also a factor in determining the degree of voluntary control operating in connection with any particular muscle group. When the stimulus is very intense, if "the incident nerves are stimulated to excess, as in burns or tetanus," then the individual can exercise but little voluntary control over the resulting muscular contractions.

Regarding the location in the cord of the centers for reflex action, and the nature of the neural structures which serve volition *via* the spinal cord, Grainger made important contributions. He showed that the cord was the sole seat of spinal reflexes and that fibres from the afferent roots which were involved in reflex action went directly into the grey matter. In addition, he showed that from the afferent roots certain fibres also proceed upward in the white matter to the brain, thus serving sensation.[2]

Grainger summarized his conclusions as follows:

. . . . the following axioms appear to be susceptible of satisfactory proof.

1. That the source of all power, in the nervous system, is the grey matter.

2. That the white fibres are merely conductors.

3. That there exists, in the nervous system, two great divisions, (a) the true cerebral; consisting of the hemispheres of the cerebrum, and the lobes of the cerebellum; of the true sensiferous, and the true volitional fibres of the cranio-spinal nerves. (b) The true spinal;

---

[2] *Cf.* Schäfer (432), II, p. 787.

comprising the grey matter of the spinal cord and the incident and reflex fibres of the cranio-spinal nerves.

4. That there is no special order of respiratory nerves.

5. That there is but one kind of sensibility possessed by animals; that, namely, which is perceived by the mind.

6. That this sensibility is, in the higher animals, the invariable and inseparable property of the cerebral hemispheres, inclusive of the lobes of the cerebellum; and, in the lower animals, of that part of the nervous system which can be shown to be, in office, the true analogue of the brain.

7. That volition is the inseparable attribute of the cerebral hemispheres, and lobes of the cerebellum.

8. That the spinal cord, in every class of the animal kingdom in which it exists; and the analogous part, in those animals in which, in consequence of variety of shape or other circumstances, this cord cannot be detected in the usual form, is the inherent seat of a property, totally distinct from sensation and volition, called the reflex power.

9. That the reflex power is never exercised, without the excitement caused by the application of a physical agent to the external and internal surfaces of the body.

10. That contractility is the special property of the muscular fibre.

11. That contractility has no necessary connexion with sensibility.

12. That contractility cannot be exercised without the application of a stimulus.

13. That this stimulus consists of, a) volition; b) the reflex power of the spinal cord; and, *perhaps*, c) of a direct application of a physical agent to the muscular fibre itself.

Alfred Wilhelm Volkmann (1800–1877), Professor of Physiology at Halle, investigated the sympathetic nervous system and was concerned with the functioning of the spinal cord. He wrote the section on nervous physiology in Wagner's *Handwörterbuch* (507) which contains an excellent discussion of the status of reflex action theory at that time. He introduced his discussion of reflex action with a definition.

Reflectorische Bewegungen nennt man gegenwärtig solche, bei welchen der excitirende Reiz weder ein contractiles Gebilde noch einen motorischen Nerven unmittelbar trifft, sondern einen Nerven, welcher seinen Erregungszustand einem Centralorgane mittheilt, worauf durch Vermittlung des letztern der Reiz auf motorische Nerven überspringt, und nun erst durch Muskelbewegungen sich geltend macht. Der Gang des Reizes beschreibt also einen Bogen, indem die Leitung anfänglich nach innen vorsich geht und erst später in die centrifugale Richtung überschlägt. (II, p. 542)

This definition does not present any new elements; the influence of Hall and Müller is evident, but it is to be noted that the term "arc" has become established in the technical vocabulary of neuro-physiology.

Volkmann considered the problem of the psychic functions of the spinal cord and concluded that it was probably an insoluble one. Hodge (232) quotes from Volkmann's article in Wagner's *Handwörterbuch* on *Gehirn* in this connection.

Strictly considered, however, such experiments prove only that that part of the body furnished with the brain, does not feel the irritation of that part which has been severed from its connection with the brain. But whether the isolated cord does not have sensations of its own, obscure though they be, is not manifest. In lower animals the sensitive principle is unquestionably divisible; whether anything analogous can be assumed for higher animals, can scarcely be decided. All through the history of psychic development, sensation necessarily precedes volition, so that a sensitive organism without voluntary motion is easily conceivable. Yet an observer of another organism can infer the existence of sensation only from the play of voluntary motion. Hence although the latter ceases with decapitation, sensation itself is not necessarily lost; its demonstrability becomes impossible. Impossible as it is to prove that decapitated vertebrates are insensible, still we are unable to assume for them the power of sensation. At any rate we have no occasion to conceive consciousness as divisible in the higher animals, and, as above explained, we can assume the power of sensation to exist only where the perceptions of nerves of sense become the possession of consciousness. (pp. 355–6)

Although Volkmann accepted reflex action as a functional system, he denied Hall's assumption of a special spinal excito-motory system of fibres. The problem of the exact nature of the connection between the afferent and efferent portions of the arc was still unsolved. The principle of "reflexion" did not offer any detail as to the structural basis, underlying the transfer of the impulse from the incoming fibres to the outgoing fibres. Volkmann believed that the transmission of the irritation took place from one fibre to a neighboring fibre in the central nervous system. The transmission of the impulse from one nerve to another in the central nervous system (*Querleitung*) opposed the law of isolated conduction which held for the peripheral nerves.[3] Hodge says of this generalization of Volkmann's:

Not only is reflex action thus explained, but all sympathetic movements and sensations and even *delirium traumaticum*, where a painful wound causes delirium without fever. Even indistinct vision and a defective musical ear are perhaps due to the transition of the irritation from the nerve previously affected to the others which lie near it; and we learn to distinguish fine motions and tones probably by learning to isolate the actions of nerves. In fatigues which are painful the state of the motor nerves springs over to the sensory, and in this way the normal association of movement may sometimes be explained. . . . . Nerve activities which are naturally isolated may become combined by habit and training and may be re-isolated by disuse. (p. 357)

Volkmann performed experiments in an effort to learn whether or not the spinal cord could initiate spontaneous motions. He placed the hind limb of a spinal frog in a posture of extension during the period of spinal shock and noted that after the recovery from shock, the limb was drawn up to the sitting posture. This, he regarded as evidence for the capacity of the cord

[3] Wagner's *Handwörterbuch* (509), II, pp. 5–8.

to initiate spontaneous movement. As Sherrington points out[4] this cannot be regarded as adequate evidence, since the possibility of external stimuli from the organs of muscle sense had not been ruled out.

These and other experiments are discussed in Volkmann's earlier paper on reflex action, published in 1838 (506). This paper contains an analysis of reflex action which marks Volkmann as one of the earliest critics of Marshall Hall. In this analysis Volkmann devotes considerable space to the consideration of the behavior of the beheaded frog. Many of the objections which he raises as a result of that study to the dogma of Marshall Hall anticipate the position later to be assumed by Pflüger.

Volkmann denied the assertion of Hall that the headless frog shows no spontaneous movement. He pointed out that the movements in response to stimuli are purposive and specific.

Wenn man eine geköpfte Amphibie reizt, so sind die nachfolgenden Bewegungen nicht nur im älolgemeinen zweckmässig, in so fern die während des Lebens associirten Muskeln gleichzeitig die Antagonisten dagegen in bestimmter Folge in Thätigkeit kommen, sondern sic sind auch in specie zweckmässig, dass heisst, die Reaction der Bewegung bezieht sich auf die besondere Art des Reizes. (p. 22)

He noted that the responses of the beheaded frog were dependent upon the strength of the stimulus, and also that as a result of the stimulation of a single sensory fibre, not only one, but many muscles responded. This would imply the existence of an immense number of communicating fibres in the cord, and Volkmann believed that there was no evidence for the existence of such a situation.

Volkmann pointed out that there was evidence for the existence of psychical processes in reflex action. He noted that if a man who is lost in thought be pricked with a pin he will cry out, and throw into action a large number of muscles. The same type of phenomena may appear in the case of reflex movement and the problem is to determine the basis in the spinal cord for the distribution of impulses in the two cases. Volkmann believed that responses which in the normal state would have been inhibited by the action of the brain, are released by stimuli in the case of the beheaded animal. He pointed out that during sleep a man will respond to stimuli which during the waking state would be dependent on the will. Attention and will are the important psychical processes in inhibition.

The problem then becomes—how can it be explained that attention is capable of causing the failure of a sensory impulse to excite a motor response?

[4] Schäfer, op. cit., II, p. 818.

Diese würde sich erklären lassen, wenn die Aufmerksamkeit das Leitungsvermögen der sensitiven Fasern steigerte.   Es ist allgemein bekannt, dass Lebhaftigkeit und Schärfe der Empfindungen durch Aufmerksamkeit vermehrt wird.   Dies erklärt man offenbar nur hypothetisch durch eine Steigerung der percipirenden Seelenkraft; mit gleichem Rechte könnte man dieser Hypothese eine andere substituiren, die nämlich, dass die Aufmerksamkeit das Leitungsvermögen der centripetal wirkenden Fasern steigerte.   Eine solche Steigerung müsste ebenfalls lebhaftere Empfindungen zur Folge haben, denn es ist klar, dass die Wirkung des centripetal agirenden Nervenprincips stärker sein müsste, wenn es durch bestimmte Fasern ausschliesslich einem bestimmten Punkt des Sensoriums zugeführt wird, als wenn ein Theil dieses Princips auf Nebenwegen abgeleitet würde. . . . Würde die Faser, welche das Nervenprincip leiten soll, durch den Einfluss einer organischen Thätigkeit, welche wir Aufmerksamkeit nennen, zu einem bessern Leiter erhoben, als die umliegenden Fasern, so müsste das Nervenprincip ausschliesslich durch diese Faser seinen Weg nehmen, gerade so, wie der Blitz seinen Weg durch den Blitzableiter nimmt, weil dieser ein besserer Leiter ist, als das Holz und die Steine des Gebäudes, mit welchem er verbunden ist.   (pp. 33–4)

Volkmann concluded that whatever hypothesis might be adopted as to the mode of influence, there could be no doubt that "through the influence of psychical power reflex movements can be inhibited."   Removal of the brain facilitates the transition of the impulses from the sensory to the motor fibres in the cord; however, other factors as yet unknown appear to be operating here.

The interest in the segmental functioning of the nervous system was not confined to the lower animals as the grotesque and somewhat gruesome experiments of Theodor Ludwig Wilhelm Bischoff (1807–1882) attest.   The head and body of a freshly decapitated criminal were placed at his disposal for scientific investigation.   In his report (47) Bischoff states that he was especially concerned with the question of the persistence of consciousness in the head segment.   The experiments were performed during the first minute after decapitation.   The results were wholly negative.   The fingers of the experimenters were thrust towards the eyes of the decapitated head, the word "pardon" was called into the ears, tincture of asafoetida was held to the nose, all with negative results.   Stimulation of the end of the severed spine did not result in movement.

Hall and Grainger had attempted to establish a doctrine of spinal cord function which was divested of all psychical attributes.   Some of their contemporaries, as we have seen in the case of Volkmann, had difficulty in interpreting in non-psychical terms the behavior of the spinal animal. This behavior bore the external ear-marks of volition and sensation; it was purposive and apparently spontaneous.   They asked the questions: has the spinal cord any psychical capacities?   Is the exclusive seat of consciousness in the cerebrum?

George Paton in 1846 published a paper in the Edinburgh Medical and Surgical Journal entitled "On the Perceptive Power of the Spinal Cord, as manifested by cold-blooded animals" (396), which is probably representative of the growing disposition to be critical of the mechanistic interpretations of Hall, Grainger and others. Both Müller and Volkmann had considered the problems of the relation of consciousness to reflex action and spinal cord function. The tenor of Paton's paper is indicated by his use of the word "perception" in the title.

Paton began by defining sensation and perception, which he regarded as intimately connected but "perfectly distinct." By every irritation applied to the body (a) a sensation is produced and (b) there is perception of its cause, recognition of its external existence. It is only by movement in the case of animals that we may know that they perceive.

> When we, therefore, witness design and adaptation of means to ends in movements performed by this class of muscles, (voluntary muscles) as when an animal, on the application of a stimulus, raises its foot to the part of its body that is irritated, and endeavors to push away the instrument, it clearly indicates perception, or that the animal takes distinct cognizance of the stimulus. (p. 254)

In the case of "involuntary" movements such as respiration, deglutition, sneezing, coughing, contraction of the iris, etc., however, there is no evidence of design on the part of the animal; such apparent design as exists is due to the inherent structure of the part. Thus we see that Paton was distinguishing between two types of animal movement. Paton proceeded to perform experiments on frogs and salamanders in which the cord was transected at various levels and varying portions of the brain removed. After the operation the animals were stimulated in various ways such as being placed on their backs, pinched, etc. The animals righted themselves and reacted specifically and purposively to the other stimuli. Paton concluded that the animals possess perception in the sense that "they could perform distinct perceptive movements, or evince cognisance of the stimulus applied to their body."

> Hence it appears that the function of the spinal cord in cold-blooded animals is not confined to the involuntary or reflex movements of respiration, deglutition, etc. But that we are to attribute to it an inherent power over the voluntary muscles of the body, in regulating and directing them to the attainment of a definite object, or performing distinct perceptive movements on the application of a stimulus. (pp. 260–61)

He stated that if the movements evidenced by the experimental animals are not perceptive, the word must be redefined.

And if these movements be not of a perceptive character then there is no meaning in language, and we must give a new definition to the term perception. For it is of no avail to urge against these facts, the frequently repeated objection, that many movements of adaptation depend on reflex action, and that these may be of an analogous nature. As well may it be asserted that the perceptive movements performed by an animal before division of the chord are of a reflex character, as that these belong to that category. (p. 268)

The last statement in the foregoing is interesting in the light of modern interpretations; the movements of the intact animal were to be regarded as reflex in character.

The views of William B. Carpenter (1813–1885), the English physiologist and naturalist, were in interesting contrast to those of Paton. Carpenter's first paper (80) appeared in 1837, nine years before that of Paton, and was published in the same journal. Carpenter was continuously interested in the subject of reflex function, and in his well-known "Mental Physiology" which appeared many years later (1877) he re-stated the conclusions of the earlier paper.

It was Carpenter's object in his first paper to trace a kind of biological continuity from the simple adaptive movements of plants, through the simplest reflex movements of animals, and more complicated instinctive action, to the volitional acts of man. Carpenter pointed out that in the higher animals there is a nervous and muscular mechanism which has for its purpose the carrying out of adaptive movements. These movements, however, as in those of plants, do not involve any mental processes; "this system acts only by its respondence to stimuli expressly adapted to itself, and by the immediate transmission of the excitation produced by these stimuli to distant parts of the organism." He affirmed that it was very difficult if not impossible to draw a boundary line between the various levels of complexity as regards function.

It appears to me, however, that there has been too much anxiety to draw a definite boundary line; and that without having recourse to the third or intermediate kingdom, proposed by some continental naturalists, we may consider the transition from one division to the other to be of the same gradual character, as is apparent between all great natural groups, when none of the connecting links have ceased to exist. It has, I think, been too much the custom to attribute the motions of the lower animals to the same spontaneous powers of whose existence in the higher classes we can have no doubt; without sufficiently attending to the fact, that in the former, there is no trace of the presence of those parts of the nervous system which in the latter correspond (to say the least) with their manifestation. (p. 27)

Carpenter proceeded to distinguish three levels of function as regards psychical and structural complexity. These three levels form a continuum and are represented by different species of animals, and in the same animal by various levels of neuro-muscular function. The simplest level involves merely impression and "stimulation." By "stimulation" Carpenter meant response—the word stimulation referring to the excitation applied to the muscle by the motor nerve. The movements of some of the simplest animals, and, in the higher animals, respiration, are included in this grouping. No psychical processes of any kind are involved at this level. At the next level the sequence is impression, sensation, motive action, stimulation. By sensation Carpenter meant the "passive reception by the mind of the impression made upon the organ of sense." By motive action, Carpenter did not mean volition, but merely the disturbance which is propagated along the nerve to the muscle. In this second group, Carpenter included the the instinctive acts of the lower animals and the purposive excito-motory functions (in Hall's sense) and sensori-motor functions in which sensation plays a larger part. Finally at the third level we have the sequence impression, sensation, perception, mental acts, volition, motive action, and stimulation. This is the highest type and is, apparently, confined to man, and the higher vertebrates.

Carpenter did not agree with Whytt and Legallois that sensation remains in the spinal cord after decapitation.

This assertion arises solely from the desire of preserving an apparent uniformity in the effects of impressions on the muscular system; and while laying great stress on the constancy of the accompanying sensations while the brain is entire, they have overlooked the fact, that *perception* will follow as well as sensation, if the attention be awake and not directed to other objects. The same argument then which is used to invalidate their dependence upon perception, will also hold good against their being the result of sensation; for, except the continuance of these motions, we have no reason to believe that senation can exist when the brain has been removed; and to say that sensation remains because these motions result from the application of stimuli; and that the motions follow the stimuli because sensation remains, is obviously arguing in a circle. (p. 33)

Carpenter's second group of animal movements is psychologically interesting, since it is in this group that he would place not only those systems which the animal possesses that are already prepared for action, but also those motions which have been acquired by practice. When the practice has been sufficient, the motions occur without the intervention of consciousness, although "an effort of volition was at first necessary to each."

In 1877, forty years after the publication of the paper which we have just reviewed, Carpenter in his "Mental Physiology" (82) reaffirms his position with regard to nervous and psychical action.

From the confidence with which what are asserted to be the inevitable conclusions of Physiological Science, are now advanced in proof of the doctrine of Human Automatism, it might be supposed that some new facts of peculiar importance had been discovered. . . . But after an attentive re-examination of the whole question, I find nothing in the results of more recent researches to shake the conviction at which I arrived nearly forty years ago, of the existence of a fundamental distinction, not only between the Rational actions of sentient beings guided by experience, and the Automatic movements of creatures whose whole life is obviously but the working of a mechanism,—but also between those actions (common to Man and intelligent brutes) which are determined by a preponderating attraction towards an object present to the consciousness, and those (peculiar, I believe, to Man) in which there is, at one stage or another, that distinct purposive intervention of the self-conscious Ego which we designate Will, whereby the direction of activity is modified.

What modern research seems to me to have done, is to elucidate the mechanism of Automatic action; to define with greater precision the share it takes in the diversified phenomena of Animal life, psychical as well as physical; and to introduce a more scientific mode of thought into the Physiological part of the inquiry.   (Preface, ix)

This summary of "modern" work is interesting in view of the work which had taken place during the forty years to which Carpenter referred.   These investigations (which we shall shortly review) included those of Pflüger, Lewes, and the work of Goltz on decerebrated animals.

In the later work, Carpenter amplified to some extent his position with regard to his classification of neuro-muscular mechanisms.   He enlarged the conception of the neuro-muscular functions which are acquired by practice, and included them in the second grouping of excito-motor and sensori-motor responses.   He noted the essential identity between these acquired motor habits (automatisms) and reflexes.

It seems not improbable, however, that some of these reflex movements,—such as are performed by the legs of a Frog as if with the purpose of removing a source of irritation,— were not *originally* automatic, but have *become* so by habit; these *secondarily* automatic actions (as Hartley well designated them) coming to be performed with the same absence of Will and Intention, as the *originally* or *primarily* automatic.   Such is pretty certainly the character we are to assign to the ordinary Locomotive actions of Man. . . .   Now in all these forms of *secondarily* automatic activity, it seems reasonable to infer that the same kind of connection between the excitor and the motor nerves comes to be formed by a process of *gradual development*, as *originally* exists in the Nervous systems of those animals whose movements are primarily automatic; this portion of the Nervous mechanism of Man being so constituted, as to *grow-to* the mode in which it is habitually called into play. (pp. 74–5)

Carpenter also extended the limits of his classification of functions to include ideo-motor reflexion which he localized in the cerebrum.   Here he referred to states of reverie, dreaming, somnambulism, and persistent ideas which bring about bodily action. The scheme as amended is as follows:

1. Excito-motor—center, spinal cord
2. Sensori-motor—center, sensory ganglia
3. Ideo-motor—center, cerebrum
4. Volitional—center, cerebrum

There is a rough distinction between the first two and last two groupings; the first two have to do with the outer life of the individual, and psychical processes are of minimum importance, the last two groupings have to do with the inner life, and the psychical aspect is of primary importance.

The views of Carpenter are significant in the history of reflex theory, since he gives an extended consideration of neuro-muscular problems from the psychological point of view. Although his psychology is frequently of the arm-chair variety, and the data on which his generalizations are based are largely anecdotal, nevertheless, there is evidence of shrewd observation and penetrating analysis. Especially notable is Carpenter's discussion of automatisms which he elaborates under the somewhat crude term of "unconscious cerebration."[5] He points out the identity in many essential respects between these phenomena and reflex action.

Johann Wilhelm Arnold's monograph (11), *Die Lehre von der Reflexfunction für Physiologen und Aerzte* (1842), written five years after Carpenter's first paper, contains an interesting summary of the facts of reflex action. That the spinal cord possesses some type of psychical capacity seems to be the assumption underlying a portion of Arnold's theory which he recapitulates as follows:

(1) Ein Vermögen, äussere Reize inne zu werden, hat in dem Rückenmarke, in gewisser Beziehung unabhängig vom Gehirne und verlängerten Marke, seine Sitz, *Perceptionsvermögen des Rückenmarks*.

(2) Diese Vermögen in Rückenmarke betrifft nicht bles den Reiz überhaupt, sondern auch die Art, den Grad und die Oertlichkeit desselben. Es geht ihm aber die Eigenschaft der mit Bewusstsein verbundenen Wahrnehmungen ab.

(3) Mit dem Perceptionsvermögen (dem Vermögen zu erfühlen) steht in nächster Beziehung das Vermögen des Rückenmarks, den durch die Eindrücke gesetzten Erregungen entsprechend zu reagiren und in Folge dessen zweckmässige, zusammengesetzte und unter sich übereinstimmende Bewegungen zu bewirken, *Reactionsvermögen des Rückenmarks*.

---

[5] Another term, a product of the same period, was "ideogenic tissue." Brett *op. cit.*, III, p. 216, quotes Dr. Ireland: "Cerebration—what a name for thought! When the liver secretes bile, one does not say that it hepatates, or when a man breathes, we do not say that he pulmonates."

(4) Diese Bewegungen sind zwar zweckmässig und harmonisch, es fehlt ihnen aber der Character der Freiheit.   Sie sind nicht die Aeusserungen eines Willens.

(5) Das Rückenmark besitzt nur im geringen Grad das Vermögen, spontane Bewegungen zu vollführen.   Erfolgen bei gekopften Thieren selbständige Bewegungen, so sind sie meist und hauptsächlich die Folge einer Stimmung oder Erregung, welche das Rückenmark vor der Köpfung vom Gehirne oder verlängerten Marke erhalten hat.

(6) Der Grad des Perceptionsvermögens des Rückenmarks hängt von einer besondern Stimmung dieses Organs, welche in demselben vorzüglich vom verlängerten Marke aus bewirkt wird, nur zum geringeren Theile in ihm ohne jenes gesetzt werden kann, ab.   Dies ist auch der Fall mit der Schnelligkeit und Heftigkeit der auf äussere Reize erfolgenden Bewegungen.

(7) Die im Rückenmarke auf diese Weise gesetzte Stimmung dauert einige Zeit in ihm, wenn es auch vom Gehirne und verlängerten Marke getrennt worden ist, und selbst in einzelnen Theilen desselben fort.

(8) Der Vorgang im Rückenmarke beim Innewerden äusserer Einflüsse und darauf folgender Bestimmung von Bewegungen ist dem, welcher im Gehirn bei bewussten Empfindungen und willkürlichen Bewegungen statt hat, analog, nur dass ihm klares Bewusstsein und Freiheit des Willens mangelt, während ihm im höchsten Grade der Charakter der Zweckmässigkeit und der harmonischen Uebereinstimmung zukommt.

(9) Die Eindrücke, welche die Centralorgane durch Nerven erhalten, verursachen verzüglich eine ihrer Qualität entsprechende verschiedene Stimmung, je nach der Natur des Eindrucks und nach dem Nerven, durch welchen er aufgenommen und den Centralorganen des Nervensystems zugeleitet wird, worauf dann diese entsprechend reagiren.

(10) Eine blose Uebertragung des Nervenprincips von den Empfindungs—auf die Bewegungsfasern findet im Rückenmarke nicht statt, Der Ausdruck "Reflex-Function" bezeichnet den Vorgang in diesem Organe bei den durch äussere Reize veranlassten Bewegungen nicht.

(11) Was das Leitungsvermögen des Rückenmarks anbelangt, so sprechen alle Beobachtungen dafür, dass es die Stimmung, in die es einerseits vom Gehirn und verlängerten Marke, und andererseits von den Nerven aus gesetzt wird, in seiner Totalität mittheilt. Man kann nach meinen oben zum Theil benutzten Versuchen nicht annehmen, dass die Fasern des Rückenmarks die Eindrücke, gleich wie die Nervenfasern, isolirt weiter leiten.

(12) Nicht die Zahl der Muskeln, welche bewegt werden, bestimmt das Centralorgan, sondern den Zweck, der erreicht werden soll.   Eine Claviertheorie, wie sie wieder in der neuren Zeit aufgestellt wurde, hat keine Thatsache für, viele aber gegen sich, wie aus dem Obigen erhellt.   (p. 86)

It is notable that Arnold referred to the fact that the reflex depends on the quality, intensity and location of the stimulus.   This represents an advance in the scientific demarcation and delimitation of reflex theory. Regarding the psychical function of the cord, it is clear that Arnold, in his fifth paragraph, admitted the possibility of some degree of spontaneous movement.   Regarding "perception" his statement is not definite; perception is apparently defined as ability to effect a reaction that is specific and purposive.

In 1855 there appeared Herbert Spencer's "Principles of Psychology" (459) which formed a part of a series on "synthetic philosophy."   Brett has said of Spencer that "he was wholly concerned with the problem of finding a place for everything and putting everything in its place."[6] He conceived everything in the world as related to everything else. In psychology he was concerned primarily with the problem of the relation between the simple and complex forms of response. His life extended from the time of Bell to the first years of the 20th century (1820–1903)—a period which embraces some of the most significant discoveries on which modern physiology and psychology are based. He was an evolutionist before Darwin and his interpretations of the response phenomena in the human and animal organisms are determined largely from that point of view.

After pointing out that reflex movements are "foreshadowed" in the lower organisms, he stated that reflex action proper was found only in those animals which possess nerves and muscles.

In such creatures, the response is effected not through the agency of the one uniform tissue constituting the body, which is at once irritable and contractile; but the irritability is confined to one specialized structure, while the contractility is confined to another specialized structure; and the two structures are placed in such relation that irritation of one is followed by contraction of the other. Some impression is made on the peripheral termination of a nerve; the molecular motion it sets up is propagated along the nerve until it reaches a ganglion; the large quantity of molecular motion there disengaged, discharges itself along another nerve proceeding from the ganglion to a muscle; and thus the stimulus carried through an afferent nerve to some *libero-motor* centre, is thence *reflected* in multiplied amount through an efferent nerve to the contractile agent. (I, p. 427).

In some respects this is the most complete definition of reflex action we have considered. It indicates (1) that the path of the nervous impulse is clearly marked, (2) that reflexes are found only in organisms possessing a differentiated nervous system, and (3) that the reflex is always initiated in a group of cells especially modified for the reception of stimuli, *i.e.*, a sensory mechanism.

Spencer regarded the reflex as belonging to the "order of vital changes which, in their higher complications, we dignify as psychical." That is to say, its position is transitional between the purely physical manifestations of life and the psychical manifestations; a nascent psychical life is indicated by its presence.

In connection with the problem as to whether a degree of conscious foresight is to be ascribed to the decerebrated animal, Spencer took the position that these actions do not involve consciousness.

The vivisections of Longet, Vulpian, and others, show that mammals continue to feel and retain certain of their locomotive powers, when both cerebrum and cerebellum have

---

[6] *Op. cit.*, III, p. 223.

been removed; and that birds similarly deprived of these great cephalic ganglia can still walk about, fly, and even pick up food. Nay, there are cases on record of infants that have for days continued to breathe, cry, suck, and go through various movements, although born without either cerebrum or cerebellum. Apart from evidence of this kind, the personal experiences of every adult demonstrate to him that there are many actions belonging to the psychical division, which either may or may not enter into the mental current. (I, p. 398)

Spencer was dealing here with the question which formed the basis of that vigorous controversy, sometimes called after the names of its principals, the Pflüger-Lotze controversy. The details of this debate regarding the extent of consciousness, and its effect on reflex action is the subject of the succeeding chapter.

CHAPTER XI

THE PFLÜGER-LOTZE CONTROVERSY

"What modern research seems to me to have done, is to elucidate the mechanism of Automatic action; to define with greater precision the share it takes in the diversified phenomena of Animal life, psychical as well as physical; and to introduce a more scientific mode of thought into the Physiological part of the enquiry. But in so far as those who profess to be its expositors ignore the fundamental facts of Consciousness on which Descartes himself built up his philosophical fabric, dwelling exclusively on Physical action as the only thing with which Science has to do, and repudiating the doctrine (based on the universal experience of mankind) that the Mental states which we call Volitions and Emotions have a causative relation to Bodily changes they appear to me to grasp only one half of the problem, to see only one side of the shield."—WILLIAM B. CARPENTER, *Principles of Mental Physiology* (Preface to the fourth edition, 1874).

One of the most striking characteristics of the movements of decapitated animals is their apparent purposiveness. This behavior had been the subject of the earliest observations on involuntary organic motion, and the problem of interpreting these apparently purposive actions of the "spinal" animal made in response to external stimuli, now became the subject of a controversy which at one time or another occupied the attention of almost all physiologists who lived during the second half of the 19th century.

Whytt had assumed that a "sentient principle" operated in the body through the agency of the brain and nerves; this principle existed in the cord, and in the case of the lower animals, appeared to be co-extensive with a kind of simple sensation. For Whytt, the functions involved in reflex action were not necessarily in clear consciousness, although they were not wholly mechanical. Both Legallois and Mayo believed that sensation was retained in the segments of the spinal cord isolated from the brain. Paton interpreted the experiments on spinal frogs as indicating the existence of a perceptive capacity residing in the cord. Volkmann recognized the importance of the problem, but doubted if a solution were possible.

On the other hand there had always been those who found no difficulty in interpreting the behavior of decapitated animals. Calmeil, Flourens, Blane, Carpenter, and Grainger did not find evidence for the possession of psychical capacities in the spinal animal. Unzer pointed out that appearances of volition and consciousness in the spinal animal were due to the inference of the observer,—an inference which he believed was erroneous. The most thorough-going statement of the mechanical interpretation of spinal action before the middle of the 19th century was that of Marshall Hall. It was the fact that in the absence of the brain, animals were still able to perform complicated acts, which Hall offered as important evidence that reflex action was mechanical and dependent on a special system of nerves.

These divergent points of view resulted finally in the controversy between Eduard Pflüger (1829–1910) and Rudolph Heinrich Lotze (1817–1881) as to the psychical powers of the spinal cord. Pflüger had studied at Berlin and in 1859 became Professor of Physiology and Director of the Physiological Institute at Bonn. In 1868 he founded the *Archiv für gesamte Physiologie des Menschen und der Tiere* in which appeared many of the important contributions to physiology of the latter half of the 19th century. Lotze made numerous contributions to physiology, philosophy, and medicine. After studying at Leipzig he succeeded Herbart in the chair of philosophy at Göttingen.

Garrison points out that Pflüger believed that the best interests of science were promoted by vigorous controversy, and he seems in this matter to have given his belief full expression, for the controversy, on the part of Pflüger, was marked by vigor, not to say violence.

In a monograph, published in 1853, on the sensory function of the spinal cord (404) Pflüger initiated his attack on Marshall Hall by pointing out that such truth as existed in Hall's work was already known and that portion which was new, was not true. The problem, for Pflüger, hinged on the question of whether or not the brain was the exclusive organ of consciousness, or, stated more broadly, whether or not consciousness was co-extensive with the nervous system. He believed that consciousness was motion, and existed wherever nervous substance was found.

It follows, of course, that the "soul" (consciousness) is divisible, *i.e.*, it may exist in segments of the nervous system, and consequently exists in the spinal cord when the latter is independent of the brain.

Bis jetzt wissen wir bereits, dass die 'Seele' der niederen Thiere ein theilbares Individuum ist, das mit dem Schnitte in so viele Individuen zerfällt, als Körperstucke vorhanden sind. Ich werde zeigen, dass die Theilbarkeit des Sensoriums nicht allein für die niedersten Thiere, sondern für die ganze Thierwelt gilt. Ich werde zeigen, dass ein Kätzchen, dessen Dorsalmark durchschnitten ist, zwei 'Seelen' bekommen hat. Denn das verdere Stück äussert noch spontane Acte der Willkür: schreit, läuft, beisst und kratzt, das hintere emfindet, will und bewegt sich ebenso willkürlich. Obgleich beide Theile vollständig unabhängig voneinander ihre Nervenfunctionen ausüben, sind doch in beiden die Vernunftprincipien speciell vorhanden, weil diese eben nichts Anderes als Markfunction sind, und die Marktheile die ihnen innewohnende Function fortsetzen.   Die noch vorhandene sensorische Thätigkeit erscheint allerdings fast nur auf äussere Reize und bleibt sonst in Ruhe, wie ein aus dem Körper ausgeschnittener Muskel.   Wirkt aber eine Bewegungsursache auf diesen oder jenen Mechanismus, so zuckt hier der Muskel, so entsteht dort sensorische Function.   (Introduction, p. x)

Pflüger proceeds to discuss the following problems: (1) is the soul a single, indivisible whole?   (2) do decapitated animals show any movements except those initiated by external stimuli?   (3) how may the purposive movements of the spinal animals be explained?

Pflüger defines reflex action as follows:

Reflex oder Reflexion nennt man aber den jenigen Mechanismus in der Nervenphysik, vermoge dessen die durch irgend welche Ursache erregte peripherische Empfindungsfaser unter Vermittelung des Cerebrospinalmarkes den gewöhnlichen Erregungszustand bestimmte Motorennerven ändert.   Die Bestimmte Veränderung des Empfindungsnerven bedingt eine Veränderung des Motors wird.   (p. 62)

The reflex action is distinguished from irradiation or *Mitempfindungen* whereby strong nervous impulses may affect neighboring fibres.   As a result of his study of reflexes in man, he formulated the well-known "laws" of reflex action.   These may be briefly stated as follows:

1. The law of unilateral reflexes.   If the peripheral stimulus causes contraction in only one half of the body, the contraction always occurs on the same side as the stimulus.

2. The law of reflex symmetry.   If the effects of stimulation of a sensory nerve spread to the other side of the cord, it affects only those muscles which are symmetrical with the ones already excited.

3. The law of unequal contraction on the two sides.   If a reflex action is elicited which involves both sides of the body and the action is unequal on the two sides, the side of the stronger contraction is the part in which the stimulation occurred.

4. The law of reflex irradiation.   The spread of reflexes takes place more easily in the direction of the head as indicated by muscular contractions.

Fifty years later Sherrington pointed out that these "laws" had been "so generally accepted as to obtain a doctrinal eminence which they hardly merited."[1]

Pflüger's experiments with spinal animals were of the usual sort.   In them he thought he found evidence of the action of a spinal cord consciousness in the control of movement.   If the tail of a spinal salamander was stimulated by a flame, it should by the first "law" be drawn into the flame.

Vide Sherrington (441), p. 164 ff.

He found that it was not, except when the animal was under the influence of strychnine, in which case its tail went into the flame, thus furnishing proof for the "law."   The brain, Pflüger believed was a reservoir of motor forces and by means of it, sensations could be compared and verbally expressed.   The cord had only the power of bringing about movement.

In contrast with the somewhat bitter style of Pflüger, Lotze's exposition is calm and judicial.   He pointed out that activities once performed by the intact animal left behind traces in the nervous system which made it possible for the same stimulus to elicit the same response, although the brain might have been removed.

The origin of certain movements of beheaded animals we seek not in an intelligence yet living, but in one which exists only in its after-effects.   We believe that an animal-body whose soul has had no experiences, or which has not worked out some experience into the life of ideas, would not be in a condition to perform those movements after the excision of its brain; we consider it not as a mechanism of the first construction, but as one of practice. When, under the influence of the soul life an association has once been formed between a mere physical impression of a stimulus and a movement which is not united with that stimulus by the mere relation of structure and function, and when that association has been firmly established, this mechanism can continue the activity without requiring the actual assistance of intelligence.[2]

Lotze noted that many voluntary movements become habitual and take on the appearance of reflexes; they finally become ineradicably rooted. In his article on "Instinct" in Wagner's *Handwörterbuch* (316) he discussed the behavior of the beheaded animal and pointed out that the complex purposive movements avail but little in protecting the animal in those situations in which the conditions are complicated.

Der geköpfte Frosch, den man kneipt, bewegt seine Pfote abwehrend und zurückstossend nach der Stelle des Reizes, wo das vollständige Thier sein Heil in der Flucht gesucht hätte, wohl wissend, dass jene Bewegungen zwar an sich selbst zweckmässig, aber den Verwicklungen der Umstände nicht gewachsen waren.   Der Gebrauch der Glieder also, insofern er überhaupt in einer localen Direction derselben besteht, ist keine unabhängig Alles selbst vollziehende That der Willkür, sondern nur eine Benutzung des vorhandenen Mechanismus, dessen Ablauf die Seele nur wollen oder nich wollen, keineswegs aber selbst erst in seinen Einzelheiten einrichten kann.   (II, p. 195)

For Lotze the actions of the spinal animal were not due to intelligence and sensation but to traces in the plastic nervous system of intelligence and sensation which had survived decapitation.   These channels, stamped into the nervous system, are competent in effecting purposive movement when the animal is placed in a situation which presents stimuli similar to

[2] Quoted by Gault, *op. cit.*, p. 528 from the *Gelehrte Anzeiger*, 1853.

the original stimulus combination; a new combination of stimuli, however, finds the animal helpless.

It would be interesting, but inappropriate for present purposes, to trace all the ramifications and implications of the Pflüger-Lotze controversy, since for at least fifty years, the issues involved in this debate were a center of interest for philosophy, psychology, and physiology. The immediate contributions of Pflüger and Lotze are insignificant compared to the experimentation and theoretical discussion which their debate excited. From this mass of material we can select only those contributions which seem to be pertinent to reflex theory.

The issues around which the conflict raged were clear cut. The two important problems may be stated in the form of a question: Does the behavior of the spinal animal (a) give evidence of the existence of consciousness, and (b) show the marks of "purposiveness"? In connection with the first part of the question, the debate centered around (1) the metaphysical problem of whether or not consciousness or the "soul" was divisible, i.e., was exclusively associated with the cerebral hemispheres, and (2) the physiological problem of whether or not any of the movements of the spinal animal were spontaneous, i.e., took place in the absence of any external stimulation as a result, presumably, of an independent act of volition. In connection with the second part of the question the argument centered about the evidence for "design" offered by the coördinated movements of the decapitated animal.

The relation of these problems to reflex action becomes clear when it is remembered that the behavior of decapitated animals furnished the most important proof, in the view of Marshall Hall and many of his predecessors, for a "mechanical" theory of reflex function. Not only are the problems of spinal cord function which have just been stated related in an historical sense to reflex theory, but a pressing psycho-biological problem at present faces the physiologist and psychologist in connection with the effect of cortical action on the spinal centers, or to state it in psychological terms, the effect of concomitant psychical processes on reflex action.[3]

A result of the Pflüger-Lotze controversy which was most significant to physiological and psychological science was the stimulating effect of the debate on experimental investigations. Decapitation experiments seem to have become the rule in the physiological laboratories. One of the first to repeat Pflüger's experiments was Auerbach (12). His conclusions supported those of Pflüger, and he was of the opinion that psychic force might be set free in any part of the brain or spinal cord.

[3] Cf. Sherrington, op. cit., p. 388.

Perhaps the most far-reaching and carefully conducted experiments on spinal function were those of Friedrich Leopold Goltz (1834–1902). His earliest paper on this subject was published in 1869 and had to do with the function of the nervous centers in the spinal frog (175). Goltz placed an intact frog in water which was gradually heated. The frog became restless as the water grew warm, began to struggle and when the water reached 42 degrees C. died. A brainless frog was perfectly quiet in the same situation, gave no evidences of pain and made no effort to escape. At 56 degress C. the animal died. During the time the brainless animal was in the water, acid was placed on its back. The animal immediately responded by bringing its hind foot to the stimulated spot and wiping away the acid. If placed in the bottom of a vessel of water the brainless frog ascends to the surface to breathe. It seizes the female in the sexual embrace—rejecting a male of similar size and shape. When not stimulated, however, the animal sits perfectly quiet "like a mummy." With the exception of the quiet attitude just referred to, the animal responded in most respects as would a normal animal. Goltz was conservative in interpreting his results.[4] He referred to the purposive movements as being due to an "adaptive faculty" (*Anpassungsvermögen*) and the movements themselves as "responsive movements" (*Anwortsbewegungen*). He made this statement which is significant in the light of the controversy:

> So long as the physiologists satisfied themselves that the brain was the sole organ of sensation, it was easy to declare all the actions of the brainless animal to be merely reflex. But now we must ask whether the greater part of these actions are not due to the *power of adaptation* in the central organs, and are therefore to be struck out of the class of simple reflexes? If I bind one leg of a brainless frog and observe that he not only sees an obstacle, but crawls aside from it, I must regard these movements as regulated by his central power of adaptation; but now suppose I unbind the leg and remove the obstacle, then if I prick the frog he hops forward. Must I now declare this hop to have been a simple reflex? Not at all. In both cases the physiological processes have been similar. (Quoted by Lewes, (301) p. 524.)

Other experimenters made similar investigations, among whom Flourens (147), Longet (314), Nothnagel (387), and Vulpian (508) may be mentioned. The results were uniform; the interpretations variable. Fish and birds were the subjects for this type of experiment.

Perhaps the most important experiments on mammals were those of Goltz on dogs in 1876–1892. Of these, one in particular excited wide inter-

---

[4] *Cf.* Schäfer (432), II, p. 698 *ff.*; Ferrier (145), p. 121, and Lange (281), Book 2, p. 126 *ff.* In this connection *cf.* Ziehen's concept of the "deflex" (552, p. 16 *ff.*) and *infra* Chapter XIV, p. 233.

est. In a paper published in 1892 (177) Goltz presented his observation on the behavior of three dogs in which the cerebral hemispheres had been completely removed. One of the animals lived fifty-one days, a second ninety-two days and the third, eight months without a cerebrum. The behavior of the latter was described in some detail. The animal was able to walk in the normal fashion. It required intense stimuli to awaken it from sleep such as violent shaking, the blast of a horn, etc. When awake it reacted to loud sounds by shaking its ears, to a glare of light by shutting its eyes; it reacted to pain, and tactual stimuli by barking and snarling. The animal took no food or drink spontaneously. Food was placed in the back of the mouth which initiated the process of swallowing. It rejected meat which had been rendered bitter by quinine. The animal showed no sign of recognition of those who came in contact with it; it gave no indications of pleasure when stroked. Although the removal from the cage always preceded feeding, the animal invariably resisted such removal.

Although Goltz continued to be exceedingly conservative in the interpretation of his results, it is clear that they were of great significance to the issue involved between Pflüger and Lotze as to psychical functions of the spinal cord.

An investigator who followed the work of Goltz with great interest, and who experimented on his own account was George Henry Lewes (1817–1878). Lewes was a philosopher and literary critic as well as a physiologist. It was not until 1859–60 that he published in the latter field. In 1859 there appeared the "Physiology of Common Life," in 1862 he published "Studies in Animal Life" and in 1874–9 "Problems of Life and Mind." This latter contains a section on the "Physical Basis of Mind" which was published in 1877 (301) in which he devoted a large part to an essay on "The Reflex Theory." This essay is largely devoted to substantiating and amplifying Pflüger's position. In 1858 Lewes had read a paper (299) before the Leeds meeting of the British Association for the Advancement of Science on the "Spinal Chord as a Sensational and Volitional Center." This appeared but five years after the publication of Pflüger's essay on the sensory function of the spinal cord and may be taken as the most important presentation in English up to that time of the Pflüger position.

In the paper just referred to, Lewes presented the results of a repetition of the Pflüger experiments with decapitated animals as well as new experiments of the same general nature. His conclusions are as follows:

I will not occupy the attention of this Meeting with the recital of other experiments. These already cited suffice to indicate the nature of the evidence on which I found my positions. And indeed I might rest on one simple fact as proof that the spinal chord is a sensational centre, namely, the fact that whenever sensibility is destroyed all actions cease to be coördinated. Every one knows how greatly our muscular sensibility aids us in the performance of actions; but it has apparently been forgotten, that if sensibility be destroyed in a limb, by section of the posterior roots which supply that limb, the power of *movement* will be retained so long as the anterior roots are intact; but the power of coördinated movement will be altogether destroyed. With diminishing sensibility we see diminishing power of coördination, the movements become less and less orderly; and with the destruction of sensibility the movements cease to have their coördinated harmony. (pp. 137–8)

This coördination is present in the decapitated animal, since it can perform complex movements; hence, sensibility must be present as this is necessary for such coördination.

The whole case may be summed up thus: (1) Positive evidence proves that in decapitated animals the actions are truly sensorial. (2) Positive evidence, on the other hand, seems to show that in human beings with injured spines the actions are not sensorial, but reflex. (3) But as the whole science of physiology presupposes that between vertebrate animals there is such a general concordance, that whatever is demonstrable of the organs in one animal will be true of similar organs in another—and inasmuch as it is barely conceivable, that the spinal chord of a frog, a pigeon, and a rabbit should have a sensorial function, while that of man has none—we must conclude that the seeming contradiction afforded by human pathology admits of reconcilement. No fact really invalidates any other fact. If the animal is such an organized machine that an external impression will produce the same action as would have been produced by sensation and volition, we have absolutely no ground for believing in the sensibility of animals at all, and we may as well at once accept the bold hypothesis of Descartes that they are mere automata. If the frog is so organized, that when he cannot defend himself in one way, the internal mechanism will set going several other ways—if he can perform, unconsciously, all actions which he performs consciously, it is surely superfluous to assign any consciousness at all. His organism may be called a self-adjusting mechanism, in which consciousness finds no more room than in the mechanism of a watch. (p. 138)

In 1873 (300) Lewes discussed Goltz' experiments on decapitated frogs especially in connection with the response of the animal when placed in gradually heated water. He pointed out that the response of brainless frogs is very like that of intact animals when suddenly immersed in hot water. He presented the results of some experiments of his own in which he had removed the skin from the legs of frogs, the nervous centers of which were intact. These animals permitted their legs to be burnt to a cinder without response, although they responded normally when stimulated on patches of skin which the experimenter had allowed to remain.

In the essay on reflex theory published in 1877 (301) to which we have already referred, Lewes summarized the evidence for and against the Pflüger-Lewes position, thus affording an excellent survey of the status of the controversy at that time.   In this essay Lewes made it clear that the data based on the observations of the spinal animal are significant in the development of the concept of reflex action.

The two main positions of the Reflex Theory are, 1) that reflex actions take place without brain coöperation,—as proved by observations of decapitated animals; 2) that they take place without brain coöperation,—as proved by our being unconscious of them.   (p. 504)

In regard to these positions Lewes says:

1) The proof drawn from observation of decapitated animals is defective, because the conditions of the organism are then abnormal—there is disturbance of the mechanism, and a loss of some of its components.   The fact that a reflex occurs in the absence of the brain is no proof that reflexes when the brain is present occur without its participation. 2) The absence of consciousness cannot be accepted as proof of the brain not being in action, because much brain-work is known to pass unconsciously, and there are cerebral reflexes which have the same characters as spinal reflexes.   (p. 505)

Lewes attacks the evidence for the existence of the anatomical structures which are assumed to underlie reflex action.   He points out that it is a case of an "imaginary physiology" resting upon an "imaginary anatomy."

The sensory nerve is not seen to enter the spinal cord at one point, and pass over to a corresponding point of exit; it is seen to enter the gray substance, which is continuous throughout the spinal cord; it is there lost to view, its course being untraceable.   Nor does the physiological process present the aspect demanded by the theory: it is not that of a direct uniform reflexion, such as would result from an impression on one spot transmitted across the spinal cord to a corresponding motor-nerve.   The impression is sometimes followed by one movement, sometimes by another very different movement, each determined by the state of neural tension in the whole central system.   (p. 481)

Lewes rejects the idea of a fixed anatomical mechanism or a pathway as being the basis of reflex action.   The fact that irradiation of reflexes seems fixed to certain paths is not due, in his opinion, to any anatomical condition, but to the "fluctuating physiological disposition" of the centers.

[This] enables us to understand why the reflex action which is at one moment a distinctly conscious or even a volitional action, is at another sub-conscious or unconscious. When an object is placed in the hand of an infant the fingers close over it by a simple reflex.   This having also been observed in the case of an infant born without a brain, one might interpret it as normally taking place without brain coöperation, were there not good grounds for concluding that normally the brain must coöperate.   Thus if the object be placed in the hands of a boy, or a man, the fingers will close, or not close—not according to an anatomical mechanism, but according to a physiological condition: if the attention preoccupy his sensorium elsewhere, his fingers will probably close, probably not; if his sensorium be directed towards the object, either by the urgency of the sensitive impression,

or by some one's pointing to the object, the fingers will close or not close, just as he chooses
—perhaps the hand will be suddenly drawn away.   The center of innervation for the
fingers is in the cord, and from this comes the final discharge of the sensitive stimulation;
but the neural processes which preceded this discharge, and were consequent on the stimulation, were in each case somewhat different.   In each case the impression on the skin
was carried to the cord, and thence irradiated throughout the continuous neural axis,
restricted to certain paths by the resistance it met with, but blending with waves of simultaneous excitations from other sources, the final discharge being the resultant of these
component forces.   (pp. 503–4)

The absence of consciousness cannot be accepted as a differentia of reflex
action, since most reflex actions will be accompanied by consciousness
whenever attention is directed to them.   Lewes points out that all actions
are excited by stimuli, therefore the absence of spontaneity cannot be accepted as a satisfactory criterion.

What are called the spontaneous actions are simply those which are prompted by internal, or by not recognizable stimuli; and could we see the process, we should see a neural
change initiated by some stimulation, whether the change was conscious and volitional,
or unconscious and automatic.   The dog rising from sleep and restlessly moving about,
is acting spontaneously, whether the stimulation which awakens him be a sensation of
hunger, a sensation of sound, the sharp pain of a prick, or a dash of cold water.   If he
wags his tail at the sight of his master, or wags it when dreaming, the stimulation is said
to be spontaneous; but if after his spinal cord has been divided the tail wags when his
abdomen is tickled, the action is called reflex.   In all three cases there has been a process
of excitation and reflexion.   (p. 482)

The brainless animal is believed to give evidence of spontaneity, it does
not always react in precisely the same way.   Hence it is not a mere machine.
The spinal cord, of course, does not react in the special forms of sensation
such as color, taste, sound, etc., since the sense organs which serve these
sense modes are not in communication with the spine.   The cord does,
however, innervate the skin and muscles, and it can combine and coordinate.

It has its memory, and its logic, just as the brain has: both no longer than they are
integral parts of an active living organism: neither when the organism is inactive or
dead.   (p. 495)

The cord, however, does not have the same functions as the brain.   All
that Lewes wished to establish was the common character of cerebral
and spinal processes.

Finally, regarding the function of the cerebrum, Lewes believes that it
has the office of "incitation and regulation" rather than innervation.
Injury to this organ interferes with the regularity and complexity of the
responses.

There is therefore ample evidence to show that what is specially known as Intelligence is very imperfect after the cerebral influence has been abolished; but this does not prove the Cerebrum to be the exclusive seat of Intelligence, it only proves it to be an indispensable factor in a complex of factors. Still less does it prove the Cerebrum to be the exclusive seat of Sensation, Instinct, Volition; for these may be manifested after its removal, although of course even these will be impaired by the loss of one factor. (p. 528)

It becomes evident that for Lewes the concept of reflex action has lost many of the special characteristics which it had for his predecessors, e.g., Marshall Hall. Lewes does not deny the reality of involuntary action, but he denies its mechanical nature.

Many writers seem to think that the involuntary actions belong to the physical mechanical order, because they are not stimulated by cerebral incitations, and cannot be regulated or controlled by such incitations—or as the psychologists would say, because Consciousness in the form of Will is no agent prompting and regulating such actions. But I think this untenable. The Actions cannot belong to the mechanical order so long as they are the actions of a vital mechanism, and so long as we admit the broad distinction between organisms and anorganisms. Whether they have the special character of Consciousness or not, they have the general character of sentient actions, being those of a sentient mechanism. And this becomes the more evident when we consider the gradations of the phenomena. Many, if not all, of those actions which are classed under the involuntary were originally of the voluntary class—either in the individual or his ancestors; but having become permanently organized dispositions—the pathways of stimulation and reaction having been definitely established—they have lost that volitional element (of hesitation and choice) which implies regulation and control. (pp. 416–7)

All actions are due to mechanisms, but are not mechanical.

All actions are reflex, all are the operations of a mechanism, all are sentient, because the mechanism has Sensibility as its vital property. In thus preserving the integrity of the order of vital phenomena, and keeping them classified apart from physical and chemical phenomena, we by no means set aside the useful distinctions expressed in the terms voluntary and involuntary; any more than we set aside the distinction of vertebrate and invertebrate when both are classed under Animal, and separated from Plant, or Planet. (p. 423)

In Lewes we have the ablest summary of the evidence for the non-mechanical interpretation of nervous function up to his time. He represents a culmination of a marked reaction which had been initiated by Pflüger, against the explanation of reflex action as a special mechanism, wholly machine-like in character. The conception of Lewes' is more consistent than that of Pflüger. The latter seems to have accepted reflex action with certain reservations as to the psychical accompaniments, while Lewes, on the other hand, rejected it as a special mechanism, but saw clearly enough the value of the reflex arc concept as an explanatory principle in neuro-muscular action. He pointed out that *all* action is based on a reflex arc and that the cerebrum and spinal cord constitute an axis of reflexion. This axis has the common property of sensibility as well as other psychic capacities. In this extension of the concept Lewes makes an advance over the interpregation of Pflüger.

Among other physiologists who supported Pflüger, Mortiz Schiff (1823–1896), pupil of Magendie and Longet, may be mentioned. In his *Lehrbuch* (433), after a lengthy consideration of the problem of spinal cord function, he summarizes his conclusions as follows:

> Nachdem ich auf diese Weise die Controverse über die Ursache der Reflexthätigkeit im Rückenmark mit derjenigen Ausführlichkeit behandelt, die mir das grosse Interesse der Sache und eine gerade jetzt alle denkenden Physiologen lebhaft beschäftigenden Frage, selbst innerhalb der engen Grenzen dieses Lehrbuches, zu gestatten schien, freue ich mich, mit den Pflügerschen Ansichten in folgenden Kardinalpunkten übereinstimmen zu können.
>
> 1. Es ist durchaus kein beweisender Grund vorhanden, dem Rückenmark eines vor Kurzem enthirnten Thieres die Fähigkeit der Empfindung abzusprechen.
> 2. Es ist vielmehr höchst wahrscheinlich, das wirkliche Empfindungen nach Reizen auch in einem solchen Rückenmarke zu Stande kommen.
> 3. Das Grundprincip, nach welchem sensible Eindrücke in Bewegungen umgesetzt werden, ist im Hirn und Rückenmark nicht verschieden.
> 4. Die *Spinalen* Bewegungen unterscheiden sich von den Cerebralen wesentlich dadurch, dass bei letzteren, wie dies *Cuvier* schon hervorhob, die centralen Sphären der höheren Sinnesorgane (Gesicht, Gehör, vielleicht auch Geruch) als in sich und auf die motorischen Nerven reflectirende Erreger mitwirken. Hingegen haben wir gesehen, wie sehr bedeutend der Einfluss ist, den die Entziehung jener Mitwirkung auf den ganzen Charakter der Bewegung und Empfindung im Rückenmark notwendig haben muss. (I, p. 221)

This is strong support, indeed. Garrison (162) characterizes Schiff's work as showing "almost prophetic insight into many things of present moment."

Another experimenter, Talma (478), investigated the effect of dividing the sensory nerve in a spinal frog. He found that in the leg in which the sensory nerve had been divided, the movements elicited by stimuli were uncoordinated. He interpreted this as giving evidence for the presence of a spinal "soul" since the sensory impulses coming from the muscle under normal conditions furnish to the spinal cord the necessary information for the coordination of movement.

Only the more important discussions of, and contributions to the study of spinal cord function have been reviewed. The subject concerns the present study only as it bears upon the theory of reflex action; this aspect of the subject finds its clearest expression in the discussions of Lewes'. Study in the field leads inevitably to the consideration of the nature and location of consciousness on the one hand, and to the topic of cerebral localization on the other.[5]   The work on cerebral and spinal function, however, in the latter half of the 19th century, exemplified especially in the contributions of Goltz, is from the historical point of view an outcome of the Pflüger-Lotze controversy.   This controversy was concerned with certain aspects of the concept of reflex action, especially as they were related to the theories of Marshall Hall, who in turn consciously or unconsciously, developed ideas which had their origin with Unzer, Whytt, and in the 17th century, Descartes.   We may trace here an historical continuity in connection with the functioning of the nervous system from the beginning of the 17th century to the present.   This continuity parallels the rise of modern physiology.

LATER INTERPRETATIONS OF SPINAL CORD EXPERIMENTS

There was little disagreement as to the facts regarding the behavior of spinal animals as presented by Pflüger, Goltz, Lewes, and others; their theoretical interpretations, however, were more varied.   Sir David Ferrier (1843–) writing in 1886 (145) summarized the difficulties of interpretation of these phenomena.

When we turn from the consideration of the facts themselves to the theory of their explanation, we enter on a *quaestio vexata* of physiology and psychology.

One fundamental fact, however, seems to be conclusively demonstrated by these experiments, *viz.*, that in the absence of the cerebral hemispheres the lower centres, of themselves, are incapable of originating active manifestations of any kind.   An animal with brain intact exhibits a varied spontaneity of action, not at least immediately, conditioned by present impressions on its organs of sense. . . . Hence the phenomena manifested by the different classes of animals after ablation of the hemispheres admit of generalization under the law that the lower ganglia are centres of immediate responsive action only, as contradistinguished from the mediate or self-conditioned activity which the hemispheres alone possess.   (pp. 115–6)

Ferrier pointed out that the faculty of adaptation exhibited by the spinal cord is not proof of consciousness and he found difficulty in proving that consciousness attaches to the cord since consciousness involves language which is a function of the cerebral centers.   Regarding the experiments of Pflüger he wrote:

This experiment proves, at least, that what is termed reflex action is not a rigidly invariable movement like that of the wheels and levers of a machine, which will only go faster or slower according to the strength of the motor, but never vary its character; but

---

[5] For example, the work of Fritsch and Hitzig (160) and later of S. I. Franz (158).

rather a mode of reaction which varies with the intensity of the stimulation and the vital conditions of the organism. G. H. Lewes, however, sees in this selective adaptation or power of fluctuating combination in accordance with external conditions, proof of sensibility or sentience; and he assumes that the activity of the spinal cord, as of all nerve centres, implies feeling or sensation. But if we regard mere adaptation in accordance with external conditions as indicating sensation and volition, we should be logically bound to attribute the same to plants, in which this adaptation is often remarkably conspicuous.

It is certain that the reactions of the spinal cord severed from the brain do not affect the consciousness of the individual. But this, according to Lewes, does not disprove the existence of consciousness in the spinal cord, which may be inferred from the character of its reactions. (pp. 73–4)

Ferrier admits that the activity of all the nervous centers is fundamentally of the same order, but hesitates to apply to the reactions of the cord the same term which connotes consciousness in the individual. He would extend the range of reflex action to the brain rather than apply to the cord terms which denote subjectivity.

But it seems to me that the appearance of deliberation and power of fluctuating combination seen in Pflüger's experiment has been greatly over-estimated. Though the irritation caused by a drop of acid usually at first causes movements only of the same limb, I have not unfrequently, in repeating the experiment, observed both feet simultaneously brought up to the part, with a view to repel the cause of offence. In this we have an instance, among many others, of the association in the cord of the centres of movements of the same kind in both limbs, due either to commisural connections or to physiological association in past experience, or both together.

Such being the case, it is not difficult to conceive that, when the relief offered by scratching at or near the part is not attained when the foot is amputated, the continuance of the irritation brings the other leg into play by associated reflex action. (p. 74)

Regarding the purposive character of the spinal movements Sherrington pointed out in 1900 (432) that the Pflüger-Lotze controversy occurred before the advent of the Darwinian theory. Considered in the light of this theory the movements of the spinal animal must have a certain purposive and adaptive character.[6] In connection with the consciousness of the spinal animal, Sherrington maintained that the criterion should be the existence of associative memory. Judged by this criterion, consciousness is everywhere lacking in spinal cord functioning.

Such a view of the relation of spinal reflexes to consciousness corrects a tendency to see in such reflexes the germs of volitional acts. The mainsprings in the evolution of volition are feeling and perception. From reactions unconscious, and therefore devoid both of feeling and perception, volitions cannot have sprung. On the other hand, our individual experience shows how readily volitional acts by repetition and practice ultimately become

---

[6] *Cf.* also Sherrington (441), p. 235 *ff.*

actions involving neither attention nor even consciousness,—create, in fact, habitual reflexes. The spinal reflexes may be regarded as descended from volitional acts, inherited and therefore instinctive habits of simplest order, testifying to a so-to-say primitive process akin to memory in the spinal cord. (II, p. 860)

If the last assumption were true, it might be expected that the spinal reflexes would be more in evidence in the more elaborate nervous systems. To this Sherrington replies:

As a fact, they are there less obtainable and seem there less active than in simpler systems. This may be due to the greater solidarity of the whole nervous system in its higher than in its lower forms. The greater solidarity renders the more severe the injury wrought by mere isolation of any part from the whole. And this the more so that in higher animals the great projection senses of the cranial region dominate the spinal cord and actuate the motor organ, the skeletal musculature of the whole body, more than in lower forms. (II, p. 860)

Sir Michael Foster deals extensively with the problem of spinal cord reflexes in the "Textbook" (155) published in 1897. At the beginning, his discussion brings up for consideration a factor which had been neglected by his predecessors. He points out that the spinal cord is separate anatomically from the cerebral hemispheres, but in the normal life of the animal the brain works by means of the cord and the cord functions while under the control of the brain.

We . . . must greatly hesitate to take it for granted that the work which we can make the spinal cord or a part of the spinal cord do, when isolated from the brain, is the work which is actually done in the intact body when the brain and spinal cord form an unbroken whole. Moreover this caution becomes increasingly necessary, when in our studies we pass from the simpler nervous system of one animal to the more complex nervous system of another; . . . We need caution when from the results of experiments on dogs or rabbits, we draw conclusions as to the digestion or circulation of man, but we need far greater caution when from the behavior of the isolated spinal cord of one of these animals we infer the behavior of the intact spinal cord of man. (Pt. III, pp. 973–4)

This marks an advance in the history of reflex theory, since it emphasizes the nervous system as a functioning unit. It was indicated in the first chapter that one of the sources of confusion in the interpretation of reflex action, lay in ascribing to the responses of the intact organism, the characteristics of the simple spinal reflexes.

Foster pointed out that "reflexion" implies altogether too simple a process which is supposed to take place in the spinal cord on the arrival of an afferent stimulus. In other words the processes which take place in the cord on the arrival of an afferent impulse are more complex in nature than that of the afferent impulse itself. This is indicated by the fact that in reflex action the movements are coordinated, *i.e.*, more than one muscle is in play and certain relationships are maintained as to duration, amount, and time of occurrence of contraction. The so-called "muscle sense" plays an important part in this connection in both voluntary and reflex action.[7] By means of the afferent impulses at the basis of this sense it is possible for preliminary coordination to take place.

> We are led therefore to the conclusion that in a reflex action carried out by the cord two kinds of afferent impulses are concerned: the ordinary afferent impulses which start the movement, which discharge the nervous mechanism within the cord and so provoke the movement, and the afferent impulses which connect the nervous mechanism with the the muscles about to be called into play, and which take part in the coordination of the movement provoked. (Pt. III, p. 982)

It is important to note in connection with this hypothesis of Foster's, that this same coordinating mechanism involving afferent impulses from the muscles is present in both reflexes and spinal action, and in both it takes place in the cord and is, presumably, without conscious accompaniments. It follows then that in "voluntary" movement there is a large unconscious and, presumably, reflex element.

Regarding consciousness in the spinal animal, Foster is of the opinion that it does not possess consciousness like our own, "because absence of spontaneous movements seems to be irreconcilable with the existence of an active consciousness whose very essence is a series of changes." There may be, however, a certain kind of consciousness.

> We may, on this view, suppose that every nervous action of a certain intensity or character is accompanied by some amount of consciousness, which we may, in a way, compare to the light emitted when a combustion previously giving rise to invisible heat waxes fiercer. We may thus infer that when the brainless frog is stirred by some stimulus to a reflex act, the spinal cord is lit up by a momentary flash of consciousness coming out of the darkness and dying away into darkness again; and we may perhaps further infer that such a passing consciousness is the better developed the larger the portion of the cord involved in the reflex act and the more complex the movement. But such a momentary flash, even if we admit its existence, is something very different from consciousness as ordinarily understood, is far removed from intelligence, and cannot be appealed to as explaining the 'choice' spoken of above. (Pt. III, p. 983)

While denying "intelligence" to the animal, this conception of reflex action makes possible exceedingly nice adjustments and interrelationships between internal and external factors.

---

[7] *Cf.* Talma (478) and Longet (314), I, p. 326. Talma offers experimental evidence in this connection; the coordinating function of the cord which is dependent on the "muscle sense," he regards as part of the "psychical" activity of the cord.

As late as 1913 we find an affirmation of Foster's position in regard to the psychical processes in the spinal cord. Luciani (320) quotes Foster in this connection and then comments:

> Though direct confirmation of Foster's hypothesis on the nature of the spinal psychical functions is wanting, it appears to us to be logical and generally admissible. Those who take the manifestations of perception and memory as the distinguishing signs of consciousness, and absolutely deny the psychical character of coordinated reflexes, do not reflect that the spinal cord is not claimed as the seat of the *higher* intellectual functions, but only as that of a simple *rudimentary* intelligence due to the synthesis of a small group of elementary sensation. The approach of a dog on hearing its own name, the return of a hungry animal to the place where it is accustomed to find food, are conscious acts of perception involving a process of memory. Of course, nothing of the sort can be observed in a "spinal" animal. . . . But from our point of view, these facts—even if they show that the spinal frog exhibits no sign of perception and memory—do not exclude the possibility of its possessing transitory flashes of consciousness, arising from a psychical synthesis of elementary sensations. (III, p. 340)

Thus does an echo of the Pflüger-Lotze controversy persist into the present century. Luciani believed that the idea of an inheritable, instinctive, coordinated act involves also a kind of unconscious spinal memory—which might be denominated, fossil intelligence. How much of this persists in the cord of the higher vertebrates, he deemed a question for the "future to decide."

The conception of the persistence of unconscious memories in organic substance as an explanation of purposive action, is found in Hering's essay on memory (219) first given as a lecture before the Imperial Academy of Sciences at Vienna in 1870. He attributes an unconscious memory to all organized matter. In the essay referred to, he points out how in both the lower animals and man at birth certain mechanisms appear ready for action. These motions are as efficient and skilful the first time they appear as they are later.

> But if animals so easily find the most practical means of attaining their ends the very first time, if their motions are so excellently and perfectly adapted to their purposes, it is due to the inherited disposition of the memory of their nervous substance, which only awaits an occasion to work in full conformity with the situation, and remembers just what is necessary for that occasion. . . . .
>
> Thus the body, it is seen, and what is of greater import, the whole nervous system of a newborn animal, is predetermined and predisposed for intercourse with the world which it enters; it is prepared to respond to irritations and influences in the same way as this was done by its ancestors. . . . .
>
> A far-reaching memory, or reproductive faculty, we must assume, is to be ascribed to the whole body, as well as particularly to the brain of a newborn man. By the help of this memory he is able to acquire the attainments which were developed in his ancestors some

thousands of times and are necessary for his life, much more quickly and easily. What appears as instinct in animals, in man appears in a freer form, as a predisposition. (p. 22 ff.)

Another commentator on the observations of Pflüger was Henry Maudsley. He discussed the problem of spinal cord function at length in his book on "The Physiology and Pathology of the Mind" (337) published in 1867, fourteen years after the publication of Pflüger's study. Maudsley did not agree with Pflüger in attributing consciousness to the cord: the apparent purposiveness in the movements of the spinal frog and the anencephalous infant he ascribed to the innate constitution of the nervous system.

In the constitution of the spinal cord are implanted the capabilities of such coordinate energies; and the degree of the irritation determines the extent of the activity. But this takes place without consciousness; and all the design which there is in the movement is of the same kind as the design which there is in the formation of a crystal, or in the plan of growth of a tree. . . . . The design of an act is nothing else but the correlate in the mind of the observer of the law of the matter in nature; and each observer will see in any event exactly that amount of design which he brings with him the faculty of seeing (p. 65)

Maudsley was of the opinion that the capacities of the spinal cord for apparently purposive movement are, for the most part, not inborn in man, but are the result of practice. With repetition an act becomes easier to perform and requires less conscious attention, and finally becomes automatic. It then closely resembles reflex action.

For while secondary automatic acts are accomplished with comparatively little weariness—in this regard approaching organic movements, or the original reflex movements— the conscious efforts of the will soon produce exhaustion. A spinal cord without memory would simply be an idiotic spinal cord incapable of culture—a degenerate nervous centre in which the organization of special faculties could not take place. (pp. 69–70)

Some of the issues raised in connection with spinal cord function are still subjects for debate. We have referred to Luciani's acceptance of Foster's position with regard to the presence of a spinal cord consciousness. The position of Foster and Luciani in this connection is scarcely in agreement with that of Bayliss, for example, who would regard the introduction of mentalistic terms into physiological explanations as unnecessary. The problem with which we come in contact at this point is not merely that of the existence of consciousness in the spinal animal, but also the much larger problem of the relation of consciousness to reflex action in the intact animal. This ultimately includes the question of the place of consciousness in any type of animal behavior.

In the first chapter the point of view of one group of psychologists and physiologists was outlined which to a large extent excluded consciousness as an essential element in animal behavior; all types of behavior could be accounted for in terms of reflex arcs. The position represented by Watson (527), Bechterew (25), Loeb (307), Bethe (41), Beer, Bethe and Von Uexküll (26), and Pavlov (400) is typical of this point of view. In part, the historical antecedents of this school may be traced in the development of the Pflüger-Lotze controversy in connection with reflex action. Although, in the view of a large and influential school of psychologists, the reflex arc may have taken the place of consciousness as an explanatory principle in animal behavior, it is evident that the matter is not so satisfactorily settled for the neurologist. We find Herrick writing in 1924 (223):

Consciousness, then, is a factor in behavior, a real cause of human conduct, and probably to some extent in that of other animals. We have endeavored to show that it belongs to the general class of individually modifiable action, whose manifestations in some form are coextensive with life itself. This series of activities as viewed objectively forms an unbroken graded series from the lowest to the highest animal species. And since in myself the awareness of the reaction is an integral part of it, I am justified in extending the belief in the participation of consciousness to other men and to brutes in so far as the similarities of their objective behavior justify the inference. . . . . .

The conclusion is that if consciousness, when present, is a real factor in the causative complex resulting in behavior as I believe it to be, obviously this factor cannot be ignored in the scientific analysis of the field of behavior as a whole. (pp. 304–5)

Herrick further points out that to the unprejudiced observer, mind "appears to be as truly a cause of certain bodily actions as muscular contraction is a cause of bodily movement." Hence, it is "bad scientific method" to ignore the investigation of mind by whatever means may be available.

Now, we have no scientific evidence that the physiological functions of the cerebral cortex differ in fundamental nature from the organismic functions of other parts of the nervous system, and the fact that the most interesting and important of these functions can be only very incompletely investigated by the ordinary physiologcal methods now in vogue should not lead us to refuse to observe them by one method that is available, namely, by introspection. (p. 302)

The proposals[8] of Beer, von Uexküll, and Bethe (26) in 1899 in connection with a nomenclature of the physiology of the nervous system, which did not contain psychical terms, represent on the other hand, a reaction against the mentalistic interpretations of neural functioning. Bethe (41) denied psy-

[8] Cf. Washburn (524), p. 20 ff., for a discussion of the implications to psychological theory of the work of Bethe, Beer, and others who represent this point of view. Cf. infra, Chapter XVI, p. 281 ff.

chic life to ants and bees, and believed that in man sensation might not be scientifically studied. Another modern physiologist, Loeb (306), greatly extended the concept of tropistic and reflex action. Regarding the experiments of Pflüger, Loeb wrote in 1903:

> I believe we are now in a position to prove that Pflüger's observations not only allow but demand an entirely different explanation, and that it is wrong to make them a criterion for the existence of consciousness. The experiment with the tail of the eel is a case of a tropism. The eel is positively stereotropic. It is forced to bring every part of its body as far as possible in contact with solid bodies, like Nereis, many insects, the stolons of Hydroids and the roots of many plants. . . . . This is no more a process of consciousness than the boring of a root in the sand. It exists in every segment of the eel, and if touched on one side with the finger positively stereotropic curvations toward the finger ensue. . . . . The whole discussion of the "spinal-cord-soul" was needless, and might have been avoided if Pflüger had realized that those phenomena which the metaphysician calls consciousness are a function of the mechanism of associative memory. (p. 250)

In the case of the spinal animal the phenomena observed were not due, Loeb believed, to associative memory but to inherited mechanisms. The "spinal-cord-soul" was merely another instance, in Loeb's opinion, when biologists have been led astray by "their blind acceptance of metaphysical notions." Loeb thought that the most important problem in the physiology of the central nervous system "is the analysis of the mechanisms which give rise to the so-called psychic phenomena." These are completely described by the term associative memory which he defined as follows:

> By associative memory I mean the two following peculiarities of our central nervous system. First, that processes which occur there leave an impression or trace by which they can be reproduced even under different circumstances than those under which they originated. . . . The second peculiarity is, that two processes which occur simultaneously or in quick succession will leave traces which fuse together, so that if later one of the processes is repeated, the other will necessarily be repeated also. (p. 213)

The physical nature of this mechanism will be eventually analyzed, according to Loeb, into chemical and physical terms.

The conflict in point of view, for example, between Herrick and Bethe, indicates that the problem of consciousness in relation to reflex action which, perhaps, begins with Descartes and bulks large in the work of Hall, Volkmann, Grainger, Carpenter, Pflüger, Lotze, Lewes, and Goltz in the past century, is still an open problem. In this connection reference should also be made to the recent theoretical discussion of Lashley (291),[9] as well as to the experimental contributions of Lashley (287, 294) and Franz (158) in connection with the problem of cerebral functions.

[9] *Cf.* Herrick's discussion of Lashley's point of view (223), p. 303.

In regard to the second aspect of spinal cord function, that is, the "purposiveness" of spinal reflexes, we have already noted that the Pflüger-Lotze controversy took place before the advent of the Darwinian theory. Sherrington has pointed out that every reflex *must* be purposive in a biological sense. The "purpose" of the early investigators, was, of course, a personal, conscious purpose. Sherrington probably presented the consensus of contemporary physiological opinion in this connection when he said in 1906 (441):

> Older writings on reflex action concerned themselves boldly with the purpose of the reflexes they described. The language in which they are couched shows that for them the interest of the phenomena centered in their being regarded as manifestations of an informing spirit resident in the organism, lowly or mutilated though that might be. Progress of knowledge has tended more and more to unseat that anthropomorphic image of the observer himself which he projected into the object of his observations. The teleological speculations accompanying such observations have become proportionately discredited. (p. 236)

Sherrington believes, however, that there is a place in physiology for the study of purpose, and that it is essential that such a study should occupy the physiologist in the near future. In the case of reflex action, he asserts that it can only be intelligible to the physiologist when he knows its aim.

An important result of the Pflüger-Lotze discussion and the experimentation which followed it, was the establishment of the brain as the dominating segment in the nervous system. The Pflüger concept of a spinal soul gave to the spinal cord a prominence which modern neurology does not sanction. The Pflüger point of view also tended to emphasize the segmental independence of the parts of the nervous system, and the reflex was conceived as a relatively independent performance. One of the most important results of the modern interest in the problems of neural function which were set by the Pflüger-Lotze debate, has been the overthrow of the idea of such independent reflex arcs. This contribution may be credited to Sherrington. His concepts of the final common path (1904) and of the internuncial paths have emphasized the integrative aspect of the nervous system and made the so-called "simple reflex" a physiological abstraction.

> Reflex-arcs show, therefore, the general features that the initial neurone of each is a *private* path exclusively belonging to a single receptive point (or small group of points) and that finally the arcs embouch into a path leading to an effector organ; and that their final path is common to all receptive points wheresoever they may lie in the body, so long as they have connection with the effector organ in question. Before finally converging upon the motor neurone the arcs converge to some degree. Their private paths embouch upon *internuncial* paths common in various degrees to groups of private paths. The

terminal path may, to distinguish it from internuncial common paths, be called *the final common path*. The motor nerve to a muscle is a collection of final common paths. (p. 116)

The cardinal function of the synaptic nervous system is "the coordination of the activities of the trunk with requirements of the head." The spinal cord from this point of view is a "mere appendage of the brain."

The integrating power of the nervous system has in fact in the higher animal, more than in the lower, constructed from a mere collection of organs and segments a functional unity, an individual or more perfected solidarity. We see that the distance-receptors integrate the individual not merely because of the wide ramification of their arcs to the effector organs through the lower centres; they integrate especially because of their great connections in the high cerebral centres. Briefly expressed, their special potency is because they integrate the animal through its brain. The cerebrum itself may indeed be regarded as the ganglion of the distance-receptors. (p. 353)

As we have already pointed out, the manner and extent of cerebral influence on reflex action is still in debate. Sherrington has called attention to its importance as a problem of physiology and psychology. The Pflüger-Lotze problem no longer has to do with the spinal cord soul, but has been supplanted in part, at least, by the psycho-biological problems of (1) the extent that a reflex act may be modified by mental processes, and (2) the adequacy of the reflex to account for all the adjustive acts of the organism.

THE NEURONE THEORY

In following the devious course of the Pflüger-Lotze controversy from the time of Marshall Hall until the beginning of the 20th century, it has been necessary to neglect certain important developments in the field of the morphology of the nervous system,—developments which are an intrinsic part of the modern conception of reflex action. An adequate expression of reflex theory such as is found in Sherrington's work was not possible until an accurate knowledge of the structure of the nerve cell was made possible by the discovery of histological techniques in the latter half of the 19th century.

The conception of Gerlach[10] that there existed a continuous pathway through a net work of fibres was not adequate to explain the spreading of reflexes from one segment to a distant segment of the spinal cord. The cell theory had been generally accepted, but the nerve fibres were supposed to be detached formations. Two concepts are necessary to make intelligible the facts of nervous function brought to light during the 19th century: (1) the neurone theory, and (2) the concept of the synapse.

[10] *Cf.* Johnston, (263), p. 70.

As early as 1824, Rolando made cross sections of the spinal cord, and in 1836 Valentin made sections of the cord under water. In 1846 Benedikt Stilling (470) was the first to make consecutive sections of the hardened spinal cord in a systematic way for microscopic study.[11] With the invention of the microtome, about 1860, which made possible exceedingly fine sections of nervous tissue, Johnston dates the beginning of the modern period of neurological study. This instrument permitted the cutting of successive sections of known and uniform thickness. This method of successive sections together with the development of methods of staining tissues made it possible to study the nerve elements and their connections.

In 1850 Augustus Waller (1816–1870) (511) demonstrated that if a nerve is cut, degeneration takes place peripherally, indicating that the fibres receive their nourishment from the nerve cell and are prolongations of it. In 1865 Deiters showed that each nerve cell has an axis-cylinder growing from it, and a number of processes which are dendrites. In 1873 the Italian histologist, Golgi (1844–1926) (172) applied chromic acid salts and silver nitrate to the brain substance and demonstrated the nerve cells and their processes. In 1886 Wilhelm His (1831–1904) showed that the nerve cell develops from a columnar epiblastic cell into a neuroblast. The Spanish histologist, Ramón y Cajal (1852–) extended and improved the method of Golgi (418). The method of Ehrlich (the methylene blue method) stains the nervous tissues in the living state.

These and other histological staining methods made possible the demonstration of the complete nerve cell in its various forms and gave some knowledge of its inner structure. The whole matter was summarized (510) by Wilhelm Waldeyer (1836–1921) in 1891 when he affirmed that the nervous system is made up of cells or neurones, each consisting of a cell body (nucleus) and all its processes, "irrespective of their number, length, complexity, character and position."[12] This cell or neurone forms an isolated unit and is the basis of the functional activity of the nervous system which is composed of a vast number of such cells. This doctrine, after a long controversy, supplanted the continuity theory of nervous conduction and is now universally accepted.[13]

The primary function of the neurones is conduction. The work of Golgi, Ramón y Cajal and others showed that the conduction of the nervous impulse could not be continuous, but that conduction must take place over a

[11] Villager (505), p. 98 ff. Cf., also Johnston, op. cit., and Garrison, op. cit., p. 470.
[12] Cf. Sherrington in Schäfer's "Textbook" (432), II, p. 594.
[13] Harrison (204) demonstrated in 1910 the ameboid outgrowths of the nerve fibres from the cell body of the neurone.

chain of nervous cells.   Not only had the earlier investigators of the functions of the nervous system believed that there was continuous conduction in the nerve cells, but that conduction might be in either direction.   Prochaska (416) may be quoted as illustrating the doctrine which prevailed at the beginning of the 19th century in this regard.

Since the nerves represent cords commencing in the cerebrum, medulla oblongata, and medulla spinalis, and thence extended throughout the whole body, two extremities are noted in each nerve; of these, the one is internal and continuous with the cerebrum, or medulla oblongata, or medulla spinalis, and termed the origin or beginning of the nerve; the other is external where the nerves terminate in various parts of the body, and termed, therefore, the end of the nerve.   It is besides certain, that the nerves have the property of most readily receiving impressions, however great or of whatever kind they may be, and of transmitting them when received with great rapidity along their whole length.   Consequently, if an impression be made at the termination of a nerve, which is termed an external impression, it is very rapidly transmitted along the whole length of the nerve quite to its origin; and vice versa, if the impression be made at the commencement of the nerve, which is termed an internal impression, it is transmitted with the same rapidity to the termination of the nerve.   But if the impression be made midway on the trunk of the nerve, it is rapidly transmitted at the same moment to both its origin and termination.   (Chapter III, sec. 1)

The Bell-Magendie experiments demonstrated that stimulation of the ventral spinal roots resulted in muscular contraction, but evoked no signs of sensation.   Conduction might take place from the dorsal to the ventral root but not conversely.   This was the basis of the "law of forward conduction."[14]   The point of functional contact between neurones acted in a valve like manner, permitting conduction in one direction only.   Foster (155) seems to have been the first to apply the term "synapsis" to this area of functional contact.

The axon if it leaves the spinal cord ends in one or more end-plates or in other terminal organs.   If, as is the case with a large number of cells, the axon continues to run and finally ends in the central nervous system, its mode of termination as well as that of the collaterals to which it may give rise is in the form of an arborescent tuft, which is applied to the body or dendrites of some other cell.   So far as our present knowledge goes we are led to think that the tip of a twig of the arborescence is not continuous with but merely in contact with the substance of the dendrite or cell-body on which it impinges.   Such a special connection of one nerve-cell with another might be called a synapsis.   (Part III, p. 929)

The exact nature of the functional relationship at the synapse has been the subject of much discussion which need not be reviewed in this place.   Whatever the anatomical situation at the synapse, its significance in the function-

[14] *Cf.* Sherrington, *op. cit.*, II, pp. 613, 797 *ff.*

ing of the reflex arc can scarcely be overstated. The degree of resistance at this point of functional contact has been made the basis of explanations of the persistence of habits; delay at this point is regarded as the explanation of the increased time of conduction in reflex arcs; toxic conditions induced by fatigue are thought to affect the synapse more than other parts of the nervous system; these are only a few of the problems which have been explained on the basis of the synapse. Sherrington makes a surface of separation between neurones the most important explanation of the differences between reflex arc conduction and conduction in the nerve trunk.[15]

The concepts of the nerve cell as an isolated conducting unit, and of a particular functional connection between neurones, furnish the final links on the structural side in the development of the reflex theory as it was known at the beginning of the present century.

SUMMARY

The issues raised as a result of the Pflüger-Lotze controversy bulked large in the interests of those concerned with experimental physiology and psychology during the latter half of the 19th century. The problems of the relation of consciousness to structures in the central nervous system, cerebral localization, and the nature and source of "control" of voluntary and involuntary activities were inter-locking problems; the workers of this period brought to bear on them the experimental techniques which had yielded fruitful results in other fields. The issue immediately before Pflüger and Lotze may now be regarded as of small consequence, but the amount of experimental activity which the debate engendered makes the controversy of major importance to the history of physiological psychology in general, and of reflex action in particular.

That the majority of physiological opinion by the close of the century was in favor of the position of Pflüger's opponents seems certain. Mechanistic physiology and psychology was firmly seated in the saddle; the pre-experimental conceptions inherited from Descartes, Willis, Boerhaave, Swammerdam, LaMettrie, Unzer, and Prochaska which had received experimental support from Whytt, Hall, and Müller were not to be easily dislodged. Lange in the "History of Materialism" (281), the second edition (1875), discussed the results of the controversy. His statement may be regarded as the prevailing opinion by the end of the century.

Let us drop personification; let us cease to seek everywhere in the parts of the frog thinking, feeling, acting frogs, and try instead to explain the phenomenon out of simpler

---

[15] *Cf.* Sherrington (441), p. 18.

phenomena, *i.e.*, from reflex movements, not from the whole unexplained soul.   Then we shall easily discover, too, that in these already so complicated sequences of sensation and movement there is afforded the beginning of an explanation of the most complicated psychological activities.   This would be a path to follow up. . . . . What sensation and what consciousness there may or may not be in the spinal centres when separated from the head, we cannot possibly know.   This only we may certainly assume, that this consciousness can do nothing that is not based in the mechanical conditions of the centripetal and centrifugal nerve-conduction and the constitution of that centre. (Second Book, third section, p. 128)

Although the "spinal soul" of Pflüger did not survive the attack of the mechanists, not all of the phenomena presented by the behavior of the "spinal" animal was readily explainable in terms of the simple principles of the spinal reflexes.   The phenomena of inhibition, for example, and certain aspects of the adaptive behavior of the decapitated animal did not conform readily to the interpretations laid down by Hall and his followers. These problems were the particular points of attack for the investigators in the first years of the 20th century.   The work of Volkmann, Lewes, Carpenter, Ferrier, and Goltz introduced certain psychological problems in connection with reflex action which formed the prelude to the contributions of the next century.

CHAPTER XII

THE INHIBITION OF REFLEX ACTION

"Releasing forces acting on the brain from moment to moment shut out from activity whole regions of the nervous system, as they conversely call vast other regions into play. *The resultant singleness of action from moment to moment is a keystone in the construction of the individual whose unity it is the specific office of the nervous system to perfect.* The interference of unlike reflexes and the alliance of like reflexes in their action upon their common paths seem to lie at the very root of the great psychical process of 'attention.'"—SIR CHARLES SHERRINGTON, *The Integrative Action of the Nervous System,* 1906.

After the middle of the 19th century, as a narrative, the story of the development of the concept of reflex action no longer follows a single thread. Rather, the plot becomes so diversified and so enormously complex that it is truer to say that a number of plots appear and develop simultaneously. The problem of the selection of the relevant items from the multitude of contributions in the fields adjacent to that of reflex action becomes exceedingly difficult.

During the latter part of the 19th and the first years of the 20th century there appeared to be an increasing interest in the problem of the modifiability of reflex action. In physiology these problems have become crystalized around the concept of inhibition, and in psychology they relate themselves to the phenomena of attention and the effect of cortical or "voluntary" processes upon concomitant reflex or involuntary activities.

In spite of the enormous amount of work on the problems connected with the effects of inhibition (*Hemmung*) and *Bahnung*[1] on reflex action, the nature of these processes is still shrouded in mystery. Numerous theories are proposed, none of which offer an adequate interpretation of the observed phenomena. A critical review of the current theories in this difficult and highly controversial field would be beyond the purpose of the present volume, but an historical résumé of the theories during the last years of the 19th and the first years of the 20th century throws into relief an important aspect of the development of reflex theory itself.

During this period there appears to be a growing realization that the

---

[1] This term has been variously rendered in English by the words "facilitation," "augmentation," "canalization," "reinforcement," etc.

problems of nervous function were not solved by the analysis of behavior into simple reflexes.   The body functions as a unit; this unity is composed of the simultaneous coöperation of a large number of mechanisms.   Such a unity requires the elimination or restraint of certain processes and the facilitation of others.   These problems were envisaged under the term "integration" during the first decade of the 20th century and they have advanced towards solution as a result of the work of Sherrington; before 1900 they were stated in terms of inhibition and facilitation.

Stated in a simple form, we have, in the case of inhibition, instead of a reaction which is positive, a situation in which the stimulus calls out a *negative response*, that is, brings about the elimination or diminution of the response.   A consideration of the requirements of bodily economy, of course, makes it clear that there must of necessity be a very large number of such negative responses, since it is obvious that in the integrated organism, stimuli could not uniformly call out positive reactions.   In order to effect orderly movement, for example, it is necessary that certain groups of muscles must relax simultaneously with the contraction of other groups. This process involves a simultaneous positive and negative reaction—the latter phase of the phenomena is included under the term "inhibition." The phenomena of inhibition are especially striking in the field of consciousness.   Not all of the contents of consciousness are of equal clearness; certain processes are focal and others marginal.   The increase in clearness is brought about by means of attention in which, necessarily, inhibition or some analogous process plays an important rôle.   Here, as in the case of reflex inhibition referred to above, we know little about the neural or physiological mechanisms at the base of the inhibiting process.   In fact, we know but little about the extent and nature of the inhibiting function of attention itself.   Attention plays an important part in certain, little-studied, abnormal conditions, *e.g.*, the hyperaesthetic phenomena in hysteria and hypnosis are, in part, the result of attentional activities in which inhibition is an essential process.

The Weber brothers—Eduard (1806–1871) and Heinrich (1795–1878)— discovered the inhibitory effect of the vagus nerve on the heart.   The first experiment (1845) made by them consisted in bringing the heart to a standstill by placing one pole of an electromagnetic apparatus in the nostril of a frog, the other on a cross-section of the cord at the level of the fourth vertebra.[2]   "The field of inhibition was then localized to a region between the optic lobes and the *calamus scriptorius*, the *vagi* were found to be the

---

[2] Wagner's *Handwörterbuch*, 1846, (509).

channels of communication, and the results were extended to warm-blooded animals."[3] Other investigators, in 1870, showed that the vagus nerve contained accelerator as well as inhibitory fibres. The discovery of the Webers has been referred to as one of the "great monuments of physiologic discovery."[4] Volkmann had previously (1838) observed the same phenomenon, but had rejected it as being due to an experimental error.[5]

The inhibitory action of a nerve had been suggested at a much earlier date, for Descartes had discussed the problem of simultaneous relaxation and contraction of muscles.[6] Sherrington, noting that Charles Bell had referred to the inhibitory action of the nerves, quotes him (441) as follows:

The nerves have been considered so generally as instruments for stimulating the muscles, without throught of their acting in the opposite capacity, that some additional illustration may be necessary here. Through the nerves is established the connection between the muscles, not only that connection by which muscles combine to one effort but also that relation between classes of muscles by which the one relaxes and the other contracts. I appended a weight to a tendon of an extensor muscle which gently stretched it and drew out the muscle; and I found that the contraction of the opponent flexor was attended with a descent of the weight, which indicated the relaxation of the extensor. (p. 287)

Descartes imagined that the seat of the inhibition was in the muscle itself rather than in the nervous centers. In the *Traité de l'Homme* he makes a drawing of the situation as he conceives it in the muscles of the eyeball[7] in which channels are pictured between the opposing muscles.

Both Descartes and Bell seem to have pictured inhibition as a peripheral phenomenon, *i.e.*, for them it took place in the muscle itself rather than in the nerve centers.

With the discovery by the Webers in 1846 of the inhibitory action of the vagus on the heart, the search began for similar specific mechanisms. The muscle of the intestinal wall was shown to have an inhibitory nerve by Pflüger (405) in 1857, and the ring musculature of the submaxillary artery also was shown to receive an inhibitory nerve by Bernard (36) one year later. In 1885 Pavlov (398) discovered inhibitory nerves for the adductor muscles of the bivalve mollusc *Anodon,* and Biederman (43) in 1886 found an inhibitory nerve for the claw muscles of the arthropod *Astacus.* These researches all showed specific inhibitory nerves for the visceral and circula-

---

[3] *Vide* Garrison, p. 410.
[4] *Ibid.*, p. 410.
[5] Sherrington (441), p. 287.
[6] In the "Passions of the Soul," Article XI.
[7] *Cf.* Sherrington, *op. cit.*, p. 289, for a reproduction of these drawings.

tory muscles of vertebrates. Sherrington in 1913 (444) pointed out that no such inhibitory mechanisms have been discovered for the skeletal muscles of vertebrates; skeletal muscle receives but *one* kind of nerve, namely an excitory motor nerve, while vascular and visceral muscles receive both excitatory and inhibitory nerves. Hence, the inhibitory effects observed in skeletal muscle are always of a reflex nature and are dependent on the motor center which receives two kinds of centripetal nerves, excitatory and inhibitory.

Hering points out (221) that Weber made the distinction between the two varieties of inhibition referred to above, and quotes him in this connection as follows:

> Die Thatsache, dass ein unwillkürlich in Thätigkeit befindliches Muskelorgan durch den Einfluss zu ihm gehender Nerven in seiner Thätigkeit gehemmt werde, ist neu, und würde ganz ohne Beispiel da stehen, wenn wir die Nervi vagi also die eingentlichen zu den Muskelfasern gehenden Herznerven und die Hemmung als die Folge ihrer unmittelbaren Einwirkung auf dieselben betrachten wollten. Wir haben zwar Beispiele von ähnlichen Hemmungen der unwillkürlichen Thätigkeit animalischer Muskeln; aber diese entstehen vielmehr dadurch, dass die Nerven nicht in, sondern ausser Thätigkeit gesetzt werden, nämlich durch Einwirkung auf das Rückenmark, welches ihre Thätigkeit unterhält Hierher gehört das Beispiel der Sphinkteren des Afters und der Blase, welche durch ihre Thätigkeit die Offnungen derselben verschlossen halten und dadurch, dass ihre Thätigkeit suspendiert wird, den Durchgang der Auswurfsstoffe gestatten. Auch die Erfahrung, dass der Wille Krampihafte Zusammenziehungen, wenn sie nicht zu heftig eintreten, beschränken und die Entstehung mancher Reflexbewegungen hemmen könne, welche daher viel leichter entstehen, wenn das Gehirn weggenommen oder betäubt worden ist, als bei gesunden und unverletzten Tieren, beweist, dass vom Gehirne aus hemmend auf die Bewegungen eingewirkt werden könne. So wie aber auf diese animalischen Muskeln der hemmende Einfluss nicht unmittelbar durch ihre motorischen Nerven, sondern zunächst auf das Rückenmark ausgeübt wird, von dem aus ihre Thätigkeit unterhalten wird, so scheint auch der hemmende Einfluss der Nervi vagi auf die Herzbewegungen nicht unmittelbar auf die Muskelfasern sondern zunchst auf diejenigen Nerveneinrichtungen einzuwirken, von denen die Herzbewegungen ausgehen, welche aber hier in der Substanz der Herzens selber befindlich sind. (pp. 510–11)

We note in this quotation that Weber extends the inhibitory concept to cover the increased activity of the spinal reflexes which is observed after the removal of the brain. Volkmann (507), Hall,[8] and others also had observed these phenomena. The notion of the inhibitory action of one part of the nervous system on another part became an "accepted doctrine"[9] with the "center" theory of Setschenow.

---

[8] Whytt and others before Hall had noted the ability of the individual to voluntarily inhibit certain reflexes.

[9] *Cf.* Sherrington in Schäfer (432), II, p. 838.

SETSCHENOW AND THE "CENTER" THEORY OF INHIBITION

Johann Setschenow or Syechenow (1829–1905), Professor of Physiology at Moscow University, was among the first to give extended experimental consideration to the problems of central inhibition. His monograph on the inhibitory mechanisms in the brain for the spinal reflexes of the frog (438) was published in 1863 and marks an epoch in the development of theories of reflex inhibition. Setschenow introduced his monograph with the statement that he was investigating the hypothesis that the brain is responsible for the inhibitory effects observed in the spinal reflexes. The inhibitory mechanisms may be demonstrated in three ways:

(1) Durch Einschnitte in die Hirnmasse an verschiedenen Stellen, (2) durch chemische oder electrische Reizung verschiedener Hirntheile, und (3) durch Erregung des Gehirns auf physiologischem Wege. (p. 3)

Türck (491) had developed a technique which consisted in applying acid stimuli to the extended leg of the frog and noting the time until the animal removed its foot. This gives a numerical expression for the reflex excitability of the spinal cord. Setschenow followed this technique, measuring the time by a metronome beating a hundred times a minute. Using the time as a measure of reflex capacity, in one series of experiments Setschenow sectioned various portions of the brain and medulla to determine the effects of such sectioning on the spinal reflexes. In a second series he applied other chemical stimuli (salt) to the same areas and observed the effects as measured by the reflex times. The results of both series of experiments indicated that the seat of the inhibitory mechanisms, as indicated by a depression or disappearance of reflex excitability, was in the optic thalamus, corpora quadrigemina, and medulla oblongata.

Ich stelle nunmehr alle die Thatsachen zusammen, welche bis jetzt am Frosche erhalten worden waren:

1) Die Hemmungsmechanismen für die Reflexthätigkeit des Rückenmarks haben ihren Sitz beim Frosche in den Seh und Vierhügeln und in dem verlängerten Mark;

2) diese Mechanismen müssen als Nervencentra im weitesten Sinne des Wortes angesehen werden;

3) die sensiblen Nervenfasern bilden einen (wahrscheinlich den einzigen) der physiologischen Wege für die Erregung dieser Hemmungsmechanismen.

Das sind die definitiven Resultate, zu welchen ich durch Versuche am Frosche gekommen bin. (p. 35)

The experiments of Setschenow with human subjects, in which he investigated the inhibiting effect of cutaneous stimulation on certain reflexes, were particularly interesting. His method was to tickle the subject whose hand was placed in a solution of sulphuric acid. He noted that the time until the hand was withdrawn increased with the intensity of the tickling. In other words the sensitivity of the skin as measured by the withdrawal reaction from the acid solution was depressed with increased intensity of the tickle-stimulation.

The anatomical concepts of Setschenow in connection with the results of his experiments are made clear by the accompanying figure (Fig. 3)

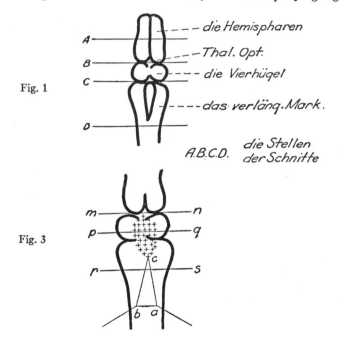

FIGURE 1, AFTER SETSCHENOW, Page 6.   FIGURE 3, AFTER SETSCHENOW, Page 8

which is a copy of the drawing (438) in his monograph. In the normal animal the course of the nervous impulse was thought to be over the route *acb*, hence the reflex time was longer than in the animal in which, by reason of experimental interference, the route was over *ab*. When the centers at *c* were experimentally stimulated they inhibited the appearance of the reflex movement. In the figure *mn*, *pq*, and *rs* are the various locations at which Setschenow experimentally sectioned the nervous system of the frog. The crosses mark the inhibitory area. It should be noted that Setschenow observed an augmentation of reflex activity when a section was made between the *corpora quadrigemina* and the *medulla oblongata*; a similar result was noted when the incision was made at the fourth ventricle.

There was almost immediate objection to the work of Setschenow. Alexandre Herzen (1839–1906) in his monograph published in 1864 on the inhibitory centers of reflex action (225) took exception to Setschenow's results. The experimental work reported in this monograph was done with the aid of the physiologist, Moritz Schiff (1823–1896), "friend and master" of the author.

The most important point made by Herzen and Schiff was that strong irritation of any part of the nervous system, peripheral or central, was accompanied by a depression of reflex activity. The experiments of Setschenow were repeated with somewhat different results, and the interpretations were rather strikingly phrased as follows:

En voilà assez, j'espère, pour prouver que malgré toute leur dignité, les centres moderateurs sont forcés de démenager des quartiers aristocratiques du cerveau, dans les boulevarts plus modestes de la moelle épinière et enfin dans des fauborgs des nerfs periphériques eux-mêmes. Mais, dira-t-on, vous voyez des 'centres moderateurs' partout? Non, mais je crois à la solidarité de tout le systeme nerveux, car chaque irritation qui frappe un point de la matière grise peut se réfléchir de ce point à toutes les autres parties du système nerveux. Les expériences que j'ai exposées me semblent prouver d'une manière irrecusable que l'irritation violente d'une partie assez considerable *quelconque* du système nerveux, *central ou periphérique*, a pour conséquence immédiate une grande dépression de l'action réflexe dans tout l'organisme. Nous ne pouvons donc en aucune facon nous mettre d'accord avec m. Seczenow, quand il dit que ses expèriences *prouvent* que les "centres moderateurs" *existent en effet*, et qu'ils sont situés dans les couches optiques dans les corps quadrijumaux et peut-être dans la moelle allongée. (p. 37)

Herzen and Schiff repeated the work of Matkiewicz, a pupil of Setschenow, who had published a monograph on the effects of alcohol and opium on reflex action, or rather, on the inhibitory centers of reflex action. The objections to the findings of Matkiewicz were similar to the objections made to the work of his master Setschenow, that is, the conclusions of Matkiewicz were based on the assumption of the existence of "centers."

The final conclusions of Herzen are interesting.

La dépression s'explique ainsi: toute l'energie du système nerveux étant préoccupée par une irritation extraordinairement forte (mecanique ou chimique), il ne réagit plus à des irritations faibles. La dépression dure au moins autant que l'irritation qui l'a produite et souvent plus longtemps, car après chaque manifestation functionelle, et surtout après surexcitation, le système nerveux, plus ou moins épuise, a besoin d'un certain temps pour se remettre. L'augmentation s'explique de la manière suivante. L'irritation qui frappe le système nerveux apres que l'on en a separe une partie assez considerable, ne peut plus se répandre sur tout le système nerveux; elle se concentre sur la partie restée entacte et la force à réagir plus violemment.

Les seules parties du cerveau qui aient une influence particulière sur l'action réflexe de tout le reste du système nerveux sont les hemisphères—et nous avons vu que cette influence n'a rien de commun avec une *fonction moderatrice.*   (p. 65)

The conception of nervous energy implied above that action in one part of the nervous system makes use of energy which is "drained" away from other possible activities, bears a resemblance to the so-called "drainage" theory of inhibition of William McDougall (346).

"INTERFERENCE" THEORIES

Goltz in his classic study of the spinal frog (175) in 1869 gave attention to the problem of inhibition, especially cerebral inhibition. It had already been shown by Simonoff (452), Ott (391), and Herzen (225) that what appeared to be inhibitory "centers" existed in various parts of the brain and in the spinal cord itself. These observations together with the anatomical difficulties in assuming the existence of a large number of specific centers which the theory of Setschenow demanded, made that theory untenable. Goltz formulated an hypothesis which is free from many of the objections to the "center" theory of Setschenow, and also embraces a larger number of experimentally attested facts. It was Goltz' view that any reflex center which is functioning, forfeits its functional activity for that particular reflex, if it receives any other afferent impulse. Hering (221) quotes Goltz in connection with this theory as follows:

. . . . dass ein Centrum, welches einen bestimmten Reflexakt vermittelt, an Erregsbarkeit für diesen einbüsst, wenn es gleichzeitig von irgend welchen anderen Nervenbahnen aus, die an jenem Reflexakt nicht beteiligt sind, in Erregung versetzt wird.   (p. 516)

This theory Hering terms the "interference theory."[10] Studies published by V. Cyon (97, 98) in 1870 and 1874 amplified this theory, pointing out that nervous conduction takes the form of a wave motion, hence, interference of impulses may be explained on the basis of interference of waves.

In this connection should be mentioned the theories of Sir Lauder Brunton (1844–1916). In a paper (65) published in 1883 he discussed in some detail the evidence of Herzen and Setschenow for the existence of specific inhibitory centers, and pointed out that an unimaginable number of special centers must be posited. After describing the physical phenomena of interference in light and sound waves, he applies the same mechanism to nervous inhibition.

[10] *Op. cit.*, p. 516.

If we try to explain all those instances of inhibition by the assumption of special inhibitory centres for each action, we must suppose in connexion with every sensory nerve, that centres exist which lessen or abolish the ordinary reflexes produced by stronger or weaker stimulation applied to the nerve. Besides, this we must suppose other centres which inhibit motor actions in other parts of the body; . . . . This complication reminds us of the multitude of inhibitory centres which one must imagine in glass in order to explain the occurrence of Newton's rings by them, but it seems to me that all these cases are readily explained on the hypothesis that the motor and sensory cells concerned in them are so placed with relation to each other that the stimuli passing from them produce interference *under normal or nearly normal conditions of the organism.* (p. 437)

Inhibition may take place both by the process of interference and, also, by diversion.

We have hitherto considered cases in which the inhibition was probably brought about by interference of two stimuli, so that the one counteracts the other in much the same way as two rays of light interfered with one another in Newton's rings. In one case which we have mentioned, the movement of the hand when it is tickled is entirely arrested by a strong effort of the will, and the hand is allowed to remain perfectly passive and limp. Here we suppose the impulse sent down from the motor centres in the brain to interfere with that which has originated in the cord by irritation of the sensory nerves, and to counter-act it so that no muscle whatever is put in action. But very frequently we find that a result apparently similar is produced by a different mechanism, *viz.*, by diversion of the stimulus into other channels. In the former case the arm is felt to be quite limp, but in the latter though it is quite quiet, it is perfectly rigid—all the muscles being intensely on the stretch. Here the stimulus which would usually have excited convulsive movements of the arm and probably of the body, resulting in a convulsive start, have been diverted from the body into other muscles of the same limb. (p. 437)

Brunton explained the actions of drugs on the nervous system in terms of interference.

On the hypothesis of interference, the phenomena produced by atropia and by morphia can be more simply explained. These drugs, acting on the nervous structures, gradually lessen the functional activity both of cells and of fibres; the impulses are retarded, and thus the length of nervous connection between the cells of the spinal cord, which is calculated to keep them in proper relation in the normal animal, just suffices at a certain stage to throw the impulses half a wave length behind the other, and thus to cause complete inhibition and apparent paralysis.

As the action of the drug goes on, the retardation becomes still greater, and then the impulses are thrown very nearly, but not quite, a whole wave-length behind the other, and thus they coincide for a short time, but gradually again interfere, and therefore we get on the application of a stimulus, a tonic convulsion followed by several clonic ones, and then by a period of rest. (p. 485)

The experiments of von Frey (159) in 1876 in connection with the simultaneous stimulation of the vaso-constrictor and vaso-dilator nerves to the

submaxillary gland, showed that the vaso-constrictor impulses obtained victory during the period of stimulation, while the vaso-dilator impulses made their effects felt later.   As Bayliss (21) points out, this result is inconsistent with the existence of a purely physical process of interference, since such a process would necessarily result in a total abolition of the impulses.[11]

The interference theory of Goltz, while not generally accepted today, was less crude, and embraced a wider field of phenomena, than the "center" theories which had held sway previously.

METABOLISM THEORIES

Ewald Hering (1834–1918) published his famous essay on light sensations (217) in 1878, and in 1889 the well known paper on the theory of the processes in living substance (218).   The theories advanced in these papers were used to explain inhibitory phenomena in neuro-muscular action.   The theory of Hering is based on the metabolic state of the nerve and rests on the relationship between assimilation and dissimilation.   Inhibition is assumed to be the assimilative phase of the metabolic cycle.   Excitation, on the other hand, is associated with the dissimilative phase, and occurs with the giving off of energy, while inhibition occurs with the building up or recovery of energy.   During the assimilative phase, however, the system is less sensitive to stimulation.

The theory of Hering, elaborated by Gaskell (164) and Meltzer (351) became a center of scientific attention.   The problem, of course, included more than the immediate question of nervous inhibition, but with these larger aspects we are not here concerned.   The question in debate was whether or not functional quiescence (inhibition) was the product of the assimilative phase of the nutritional cycle in the nerve cell.   Bernard, who discussed the problem in 1879 (37), concluded that function is a phenomenon of dissimilation in living tissue, and that the word nutrition is to be reserved for the phenomenon of assimilation.   Waller (514) in discussing the Hering theory in 1892 quotes Bernard as follows:

D'une manière générale, nous distinguerons donc dans le corps vivant deux grands groupes de phénomènes inverses: les phénomènes *fonctionnels* ou de dépense vitale, et les phénomènes *plastiques*, d'organization ou d'accomulation nutritive.   La vie se manifeste par ces deux ordres d'actes entièrement opposés dans leur nature: la désassimilation, qui consiste dans une oxydation ou une hydration d'une nature particulière et qui use la

---

[11] *Cf.* Bayliss (21), p. 420.   Wundt (544), I, p. 91 *ff.*, points out that the theory of interference is "tempting" but untenable.

matière vivante dans les organes en *fonction;* la synthese assimilatrice ou organisatrice, qui forme des réserves ou re-genere les tissus dans les organes considères en *repos.*

Waller is of the opinion that more data are necessary before the question of inhibition in relation to assimilation and dissimilation can be decided. He summarizes the experimental investigations in connection with inhibition as follows: (1) cardiac inhibition (Weber), (2) vasodilatation (Bernard), (3) the phenomena of color contrast presented in connection with Hering's work on vision, (4) dilatation of the pupil (Grünhagen's experiments in 1875), (5) the excitatory and electrical effects and after-effects of anodic and kathodic influences (Hering), (6) Biedermann's experiments on the claw of the crayfish, (7) the positive electrical effect of vagus excitation on the tortoise auricle (Gaskell) and (8) the failure of response in a frog's muscle when its nerve is excited under certian conditions of strength and frequency of stimulation (Wedensky). Waller says in connection with these experiments:

They have been thus simply enumerated as a memorandum of the chief topics and data to be taken into estimation in forming any opinion with regard to the nervous mechanism of "phenomena of arrest," and the generalization of special "inhibitory" nerves. We may, I think, in the present state of knowledge, hold that the sum of these data goes far to establish the view that anti-motor are hardly less general than motor phenomena; on the other hand, considering the incomplete character of evidence that has been diligently sought for, we should be restrained from prematurely admitting the universal existence of specific inhibitory nerve-fibres analogous with the well-known cardio-inhibitory nerve-fibres. (pp. 61–2)

Verworn attempted to prove the Hering assumption that "increase of the assimilatory processes brought about by stimulation would be associated with a reduction of the specific irritability."[12] In 1913 (503) he reported his failure in this attempt.

These totally negative results of my investigation had awakened strong doubts concerning the assimilation hypothesis of inhibition. Above all, this explanation seemed to me to be impossible for the nervous system. . . . . As I studied the problem in this manner, it became clear to me that all the conditions necessary for the genesis of inhibition are realized in the existence of the refractory period, and that I had already produced inhibition by prolonging the refractory period, by oxygen withdrawal, in the strychninized frog. (pp. 201–2)

The objections[13] of Verworn to the Gaskell-Hering hypothesis of inhibition seem to hinge on the proposition of Hering that inhibition is an ac-

[12] *Vide* Verworn (503), p. 200.

[13] See also the discussion of the difficulties in the Hering hypothesis from the modern point of view by Forbes (150) in 1912, and Bayliss, *op. cit.*, p. 421 *ff.*

companiment of assimilation. It was Verworn's opinion that inhibition was due on the contrary to "dissimilatory depression."[14]

Kronecker and Stirling (273) in 1874 first demonstrated the refractory period in the heart. Marey in 1876 (332) demonstrated the same phenomenon and gave it its present name. He showed that the heart has a period of inexcitability during which it will not respond to stimuli and this period falls during the systole. In 1877 Romanes (424) demonstrated the same phenomenon for the Medusa. In 1899 Zwaardemaker and Lans (554) showed the existence of a refractory phase in the eye-lid reflex, and Dodge (106) in 1910 demonstrated the phenomenon in the knee-jerk. For Marey, as Sherrington points out,[15] the refractory phase meant the time during which the heart was inexcitable to a stimulus; in present usage, the term refers to a conductor which responds intermittently to stimuli. The work of Lucas and Adrian (319) on the conduction of the nervous impulse has thrown light on the phenomena of the refractory phase. They have shown that stimuli may be so timed in the case of the nerve muscle preparation, that after the response to the first stimulus, the subsequent stimulations have no perceptible effect. This is due to the fact that the subsequent stimuli find the nervous conductor in a state of lowered excitability (refractory phase) as a result of the preceding impulse and hence fail to "get through." Lucas has explained this as "conduction with a decrement." Forbes (151) in 1922 has suggested that this phenomenon may be at the basis of inhibition. This is also the view of Dodge (111) who thinks that this phenomenon "may be assumed to be an essential part of the post-stimulation phenomena in all irritable tissue."

The theory that the refractory phase is at the basis of inhibitory phenomena may be termed the Verworn-Lucas theory. Historically, it may be traced back to the assimilation-dissimilation theories of Hering and Gaskell which were fundamentally modified by Verworn. That there is a certain connection between the interference theory of von Cyon and Goltz and the Verworn-Lucas theory was indicated by Sherrington writing in 1913 (444):

This inhibitory process does not amount merely to the subsidence of an excited state in its own nerve; it is more than that, for it is able to suppress excitatory processes started from other sources. A natural surmise seems that it may be of the nature of interference,

---

[14] *Op. cit.*, p. 201.
[15] Sherrington (441), p. 45.

somewhat as waves of sound or light by interference mutually extinguish or reduce each other. This surmise accrues from the knowledge that the nervous impulse, the excited state, is oscillatory or undulatory. Each wave of excitement is accompanied by a refractory state during which a further stimulus fails to evoke further excitement. This may be an outcome of the "all or nothing law" believed by many to hold for the nervous conductor as it does for the heart. The refractory phase, inasmuch as it precludes or lessens response to a stimulus delivered during its persistence, resembles a state of inhibition. Experiments on peripheral nerve-muscle preparations (Keith Lucas) indicate that with certain frequencies of repetition of stimuli the impulses generated and transmitted along the nerve fibre are too weak to be conducted across places of higher resistance in the line of conduction. The synapses of the nervous arc may be such points of higher resistance. Possibly in such phenomena we have the beginning of an explanation of the nature of reflex inhibition.

The history of the experimental development of the Verworn-Lucas theory begins with the observations of Moritz Schiff published in the *Lehrbuch* (433). Schiff noted that if a motor nerve is stimulated with rapidly repeated stimuli the contractions of the muscle gradually grow weaker and finally disappear. If the stimuli are stopped at this point and later renewed, the muscle then responds with a single twitch. Schiff ascribed this phenomenon to fatigue of the nerve. Wedensky in 1885 (532) and later in 1903 (533) studied this phenomenon and showed that it did not depend on fatigue as Schiff thought, since the nerve will conduct during the period of "exhaustion." In his later work, Wedensky showed that the same effect might be obtained in a nerve a portion of which had been experimentally narcotized, there having been no preliminary fatigue induced in the nerve. The phenomena described by Wedensky and Schiff, sometimes known as "apparent inhibition," were investigated by Keith Lucas (319) in connection with his epoch-making investigations on the conduction of the nervous impulse.

It is unnecessary to describe the technique and results of Lucas' experiments which resulted in the "all or none" generalization in regard to nervous conduction. The monograph published by Adrian in 1917 (319) after Lucas' death contains the essence of his work. He regarded the Wedensky phenomenon as a special case of conduction with a decrement; the first impulse "gets through," and the second if properly timed falls within the refractory phase of the first and hence does not effect a contraction. Lucas' interpretation of this effect is as follows:

The interpretation of the fact is simple when we recall the observation in a former section, that an early second impulse resembles one which has passed some way through a region of decrement. The second impulse falls at such a time that its impulse passes down the nerve in this reduced condition. On reaching the junctional tissue it cannot pass through, probably because that tissue conducts with a decrement.   The reduced impulse has, however, passed along the nerve and left there a new state of impaired conduction; consequently the third impulse, if suitably timed, will also be propagated in a reduced condition and fail to pass the decrement.   This state of things can be continued as long as the stimuli fall on the nerve with the appropriate frequency.   (pp. 89–90)

Although the Wedensky phenomenon is produced in isolated nerve muscle preparations, the problem remained as to whether the same situation obtained in the conduction in the reflex arc.   Lucas believed that a process analogous to the Wedensky effect might be considered as a normal event in the central nervous system, although proof was difficult there because of the complex situation.

However, there are several difficulties to be faced.   In the first place, reflex inhibition does not amount to a mere prevention of active contraction in the muscle, but to the abolition of a continued state of tone.   The inhibition of active contraction is easily explained, but we are on more doubtful ground in dealing with the tonic contraction.   We have assumed that it is maintained by a series of impulses which do not differ in kind from those we have studied in isolated nerve, but the phenomena of decerebrate rigidity give some grounds for believing that an entirely different mechanism is at work. . . . .On the other hand, it seems unlikely that the mechanism by which a tonic contraction is inhibited is radically different from that which cuts short an active reflex contraction. When the inhibitory nerve is stimulated it makes no difference whether the muscle is actively contracting in response to reflex excitation or is merely in the state of tone or of decerebrate rigidity; in either case it is thrown into complete relaxation and it would at least make for economy if the process of inhibition were the same for the active contraction as for the tonic, depending in either case on the extinction of excitatory impulses which were formerly able to reach the muscle.   (pp. 97–8)

He proceeds to point out that there may be several distinct forms of inhibition, "one depending on the extinction of impulses and another on a general depression of function in the inhibited tissue, as in the action of the vagus on the heart."

That inhibition plays a rôle in the bodily economy that can scarcely be over-estimated, has been pointed out by Sherrington.   Some type of inhibition is involved in nearly every type of muscular adjustment.   The nicety of this adjustment is especially demonstrated in the coördination of muscles involved in simultaneous adjustment.   Sherrington has referred to this type of inhibition—when there is simultaneous contraction and relaxation—as "reciprocal innervation" (441).   In connection with his study of the function of inhibition in the maintenance of posture in 1913 (444) Sherrington says:

Reflex inhibition in the interest of co-ordination intervenes in the taxis of antagonistic muscles.   In the anatomical arrangement of the musculature, individual muscles are frequently so placed as to exert their pull in diametrically opposed directions. Striking examples of this occur at hinge-joints, such as the elbow and the knee, where extensor and flexor muscles act on the same bony lever in exactly opposite senses. Experiment shows that in reflex flexion of the joint the afferent nerve evokes at one and the same time a reflex contraction of the flexor muscle and a reflex relaxation of the extensor. . . . .

In this co-ordination, as in all here discussed, the inhibition is not peripheral but central —that is, it has its seat not in the muscle nor in the peripheral nerve but in the nervous centre, probably about the starting point of the 'final common path.' (p. 256)

For Sherrington inhibition is always associated with excitation, and serves the biological adjustment of the organism at all levels of integration. In the paper quoted above he further remarks:

. . . . Whether we study it in the more primitive nervous reactions which simply interconnect antagonistic muscles, or in the latest acquired reactions of the highly integrated organism, inhibition does not stand alone but runs always alongside of excitation. In the simple correlation uniting antagonistic muscle-pairs, inhibition of antagonist accompanies excitation of protagonist. In higher integrations where, for instance, a visual signal comes by training to be associated to salivary flow, the key of the acquiring of the reflex and of its maintenance is attention. And that part of attention which psychologists term negative, the counterpart and constant accompaniment to positive attention, seems as surely a sign of nervous inhibition as is the relaxation of an antagonist muscle, the concomitant of the contraction of the protagonist. In the latter case the coordination concerns but a small part of the mechanism of the individual and is spinal and unconscious. In the former case it deals with practically the whole organism, is cortical and conscious. In all cases inhibition is an integrative element in the consolidation of the animal mechanism to a unity. It and excitation together compose a chord in the harmony of the healthy working of the organism. (pp. 307-8)

The importance of this conception of inhibition lies in the fact that it serves the organism as an integrative mechanism in the nervous system and embraces activities at a conscious, as well as physiological, level. Those higher types of adjustment which make possible the acquirement of new response sequences on the part of the organism become physiologically somewhat more intelligible when considered from this point of view. That is to say, certain of those phenomena ordinarily embraced under the term "learning" or "conditioning" may be interpreted in terms of inhibition.

This similarity between learning and inhibition has received attention from psychologists and physiologists. In 1923 Dodge (109), in a study of the nystagmic reflex in response to rotation of the organism, pointed out that the disappearance of this reflex with the repetition of rotation might be explained on the basis of central inhibition. When the number of nystagmic eye movements following each successive rotation are plotted, the curve bears a marked resemblance to the learning curve which the psychologist secures in his laboratory from human and animal subjects.

Leaving aside the question of whether or not this is true "learning," Dodge suggests that it may have elements in common with inhibitory phenomena.

It is possible that the neural conditions in both learning and the development of refractoriness have some fundamental neural factors in common. There is considerable evidence in modern physiology of the nervous system that the nerve action in stimulation, facilitation, and inhibition is not qualitatively different. The apparent antithesis in effect may be due to the peculiarity of the tissues which a given nervous impulse reaches. It is possible that the difference may be referred to the relation between the refractory phase of the tissue affected and the frequency of the stimuli-pulsations. . . . .

If our second supposition is true, that is, if there is some fundamental neural factor which is identical in the learning process and in the disappearance of a reflex by habituation, we are obviously led one step further to the assumption of the essential identity of the neural process in these two cases up to some point of their systematic connections. Students of animal behavior have given currency in our tradition to the concept of trial and error. It is a descriptive expression for the fundamental learning process of animals. In animal life the elementary form of learning seems to be very largely the elimination of useless or inappropriate modes of response from the repertoire of multiple responses to a repeated stimulus. In recognition of the epoch-making researches of Pavlov, the final outcome is commonly called a conditioned reflex. (pp. 32-3)

Pavlov[16] has developed the conception of the inhibitory nature of the conditioned reflex in recent papers (400). Howell in his 1925 review of the subject of inhibition (242) says of Pavlov's conception:

In his explanation of the mode of action of the cortical tissue Pavlov makes constant use of the property of internal inhibition, which is defined as an inhibition that develops gradually or is worked out under a given set of conditions. His general thesis is that when a conditioned reflex does not correspond with reality it is inhibited. Thus, to take a simple example, if a stimulus is applied to the skin and, at the same time, food is given a conditioned reflex is soon established, so that the stimulus to the skin, when used alone, will give the food reflexes (saliva, movements, etc.). When this conditioned reflex is first established it can be obtained also from neighboring regions of the skin, it is not localized to one point. A narrow localization of the reflex can be established, however, if the stimulation of one point is always accompanied by food while that of other points is not. The food reflex from the other points gradually diminishes and disappears, due to the development or working out of a process of internal inhibition, which in cases of this kind is classified as a differential inhibition. (pp. 161-2)

Howell distinguishes this internal inhibition from external inhibition. The latter is innate and is exemplified by the action of the vagus on the heart. Internal inhibition on the other hand is acquired with repetition, and Howell doubts if it may be compared, on the basis of our present knowledge, with external inhibition.

[16] For a more detailed discussion of Pavlov's contribution to the history of reflex action see Chapter XVI. *Cf.* also McDougall's recent discussion of Pavlov's theory in the Jr. of General Psychology, April–July, 1929, p. 231.

THE "DRAINAGE" THEORY OF INHIBITION

The theory that nervous energy flows along the nerve fibre as a liquid might flow through a pipe, that it may be dammed, drained off, or concentrated at particular points, although anticipated by both Obersteiner and Alexander James,[17] found its most complete expression with McDougall in 1903. McDougall in a paper published in that year (346) reviews the current theories of inhibition, pointing out that in the special inhibitory fibres in the visceral and vascular musculature is a more primitive type of nervous control which "has been tried by nature and found wanting." Inhibition is effected, however, in skeletal musculature and the evidence points to its being brought about by some method of simply cutting off or withdrawing the excitatory impulses. The field in which the nature of this withdrawal mechanism may be studied, lies in the higher integrations in the brain, especially in connection with the operation of attention.

The turning of attention (voluntarily or involuntarily) from object a to object b (*e.g.*, from a visual to an auditory presentation, in consequence of a sudden increase of the intensity of the latter) while both continue to affect the sense-organs, means that the excitation-processes initiated by b have suddenly attained a greater range, have penetrated further into the higher levels of the brain, while those initiated by a have as suddenly ceased to penetrate to systems of neurones in the same higher levels, and have become restricted to neurones of the reflex and sensory-reflex levels only.   (p. 168)

McDougall comes to the conclusion that inhibition is always associated with increased excitation.

It appears, in fact, that the inhibition of a mental process is always the result of the setting in of some other mental process, and, if we consider the underlying physiological processes, we see that this means that the inhibition of the excitation of one neural system is always the result of the excitement of some other system, *that inhibition appears always as the negative or complementary result of a process of increased excitation in some other part.*   (p. 169)

In 1902 Mott (369), in a paper read before the British Medico-Psychological Association, had presented somewhat similar views. He had stated that excitation always affected a redistribution of active energy, pointing out that in the redistribution there were both positive and negative elements. For nervous energy, McDougall suggests the word "neurin."[18]

[17] *Cf. infra* p. 209 *ff.*, and also William James (249), p. 579 *ff.* McDougall also presented his hypothesis in a series of articles in Mind, 1902–1906, entitled " The Physiological Factors of the Attention Process."

[18] It is interesting to note that Samuel Solly (1805–1871), a physiologist, in his treatise (455) on the brain, introduces the term "neurine." a "substance in which the peculiar

McDougall presents a neural scheme by which a strongly stimulated neural chain has "drained" into it, by means of collateral neurones, any available neurin from an associated chain, so that the latter chain does not function, with a consequent inhibition of the muscle to which it leads.

The "drainage" theory of McDougall has much to recommend it, especially as an explanatory principle of certain attentional phenomena. Physiologists have been inclined to reject it, however.[19]   It has been pointed out (1) that it did not explain the action of the vagus on the heart, (2) that it was based wholly on analogy, and (3) that it made assumptions regarding the nature of the nervous impulse which the work of Lucas and Adrian have not substantiated.[20]   It must not be forgotten, however, that there may be more than one kind of inhibition, and it is interesting to note that the drainage scheme bears a close resemblance to Descartes' conception of the excitation and inhibition of muscles.

THE OBJECTIONS TO THE "DRAINAGE" THEORY

The most recent critique of the "drainage" theory has been made by Dodge in a series of papers (111, 112) published in 1926.   Dodge prefaces his study by recapitulating the fundamental hypotheses of inhibition. These are: (1) the hypothesis of specific inhibitory nerve centers (Setschenow, Langendorf, Wundt); (2) the hypothesis of wave interference (Cyon and Brunton); (3) the hypothesis of artificially stimulated anabolism, or "the anabolic phase of self-regulated metabolism" (Gaskell, Hering, and Verworn); (4) the hypothesis of drainage of neural energy (A. James, McDougall); (5) the refractory phase hypothesis (Verworn, Lucas, Forbes); (6) the chemical or humoral hypothesis, (Loewi, and, more recently, Sherrington, and Adrian).

"Four theories in the list stand out" according to Dodge, each of which "is supported by sufficient theoretical or experimental evidence to command attention."   These are the theories of specific centers, drainage, refractory phase, and the chemical theory.   In connection with the drainage theory, Dodge objects both to the experimental evidence which McDougall presented, and to the theoretical assumptions which lie behind it.

---

powers of the brain and nerves reside."   This substance, for Solly, acts as a conductor for both nerves of sensation and volition, as well as for the afferent-efferent conduction in the "excito-motory" system in reflex action.

[19] Cf. Bayliss (21), p. 424 ff., and Sherrington op. cit., p. 201 ff.

[20] Cf. Howell (242), p. 169.   McDougall has recently discussed the objections to his hypothesis in a paper entitled "The Bearing of Professor Pavlov's Work on the Problem of Inhibition" in the Jr. of General Psychology, 1929, 2: 231.

The experimental evidence on which McDougall based his drainage theory was derived chiefly from experiments in contrast and in bi-retinal rivalry. . . . . McDougall found under certain conditions that when two fields unequal in size and in illumination are presented one to one eye, and one to the other, the smaller, less brightly illuminated field reinforces the other in that part which falls on the corresponding area of the other retina. That is to say, the bi-retinal bright images reinforce one another. In that part of the field where the image of the larger area is uni-retinal, it is darkened. That is to say, the light area that falls on a part of one retina which corresponds to the dark are of the other retina is darkened. . . . . It seems doubtful if this crucial experiment will stand analysis. The whole field of bi-lateral rivalry is too little known to permit its exploitation as proof of anything except our ignorance. (p. 113)

The basic assumption of McDougall that nervous energy exists in a definite quantum and that it may be distributed into various channels, is, in the opinion of Dodge, out of harmony with modern knowledge of the nature of the neural impulse.

It is doubtful if any other picture of neural action has been as productive of misinterpretation of vertebrate neurology as the hydrodynamic analogy of the flow of liquid in tubes. In the neural physiology of vertebrates there is no evidence whatsoever of a neural flux corresponding to the flow of blood. Yet the discredited hypothesis lives on as a didactic figure. Even in the most favorable case of conduction in nerve fibers, analogy to the flow of liquid through tubes does not hold. Such an analogy implies decrement between the nervous action at the exit of the nerve fiber from the neurone cell and its termination in the end brushes. As a matter of fact decrement is not discoverable under normal circumstances either in the main axone or its collaterals. The progress of neural excitation along the axone without decrement corresponds neither to the passage of a fluid nor a simple electrical current. There is evidence on the contrary that axone conduction consists of an electrochemical process, in which the excitation at each point of the axone becomes the condition for the excitation of the neighboring points. (p. 114)

Dodge attempted to put the "drainage" hypothesis to an experimental test in which he made use of the patellar reflex and the reflex eyelid reaction, with results that, in the small number of cases used, were uniformly negative for the "drainage" hypothesis. He caused his subject in the case of the knee-jerk to respond by a voluntary finger movement to the same stimulus which released the knee kick. His assumption was that the knee-jerks which were accompanied by the simultaneous voluntary reaction would be consistently diminished in extent if the drainage theory held.[21]

[21] The present writer has pointed out (140) certain objections to this type of experiment as a test of the "drainage" hypothesis. These experiments will receive more adequate attention in connection with the discussion of the history of the study of the knee-jerk in Chapter XV.

THE CHEMICAL OR HUMORAL THEORY

A theory of inhibition which has recently been discussed by Sherrington (449) and Adrian (3) is the so-called chemical or humoral theory.[22]   According to Fulton (161) a fundamental assumption of the chemical theory is that there is produced at some point in the reflex arc an inhibitory substance which has the power of neutralizing the excitatory substance which is also produced by the passage of nervous impulses over the arc.   Fulton continues:

> The conception of inhibition as a process involving electrical or chemical "neutralization" of an excitatory substance makes it evident that the two processes must be able to progress concomitantly in the same morphological situations.   Various structural conditions of the central nervous system lead us to suspect that the foci in which these processes co-exist are in or about the perikarya of the neurones.   The common focus might, for example, be localized at the surface membrane of the body of the nerve cell or in the dendritic synapses.   For many reasons, however, the synapse *per se* is unlikely, for such an interface exists in peripheral nerve-muscle preparations, and yet we do not encounter this type of persistent excitation, nor is it evident that the persistent excitatory processes in the retina are dependent upon synaptic connections. . . . . It appears more probable on many grounds that the seat of the excitatory and inhibitory processes is within the perikarya of the nerve cell, itself.   (p. 358)

Adrian points out that the "chemical" and the "refractory phase" theories agree "in assuming that the disturbance which travels along the inhibiting nerve-fibre has no specific properties which would distinguish it from the normal excitatory disturbance."[23]   Inhibition is produced by the "normal type of impulse travelling in the normal type of nerve-fibre and it is only when the myoneural junction or the synaptic region of the central nervous system is encountered that the specific conditions arise which make the impulse give an inhibitory instead of an excitatory effect."

ATTENTION, INHIBITION AND REFLEX ACTION

The relation of attention to inhibition has been a subject of interest since the 4th century B.C., when Hippocrates (230) noted that an intense pain at one point inhibited a lesser pain at another.   In the early years of the 20th century, Heymans (227), after a long and carefully conducted series of experiments on sensory inhibition, deduced a general law of inhibition which stated that the inhibitory power of a stimulus measured by the in-

---

[22] For a discussion of the contemporary work see Fulton (161), Chapter XIV.   A critical discussion of the contemporary theories and investigations of inhibition is beyond the purposes of the present volume.

[23] Adrian, *op. cit.*, p. 400.

tensity of a second stimulus which it can just completely inhibit, is proportional to its intensity. Heyman's experiments seemed to establish the validity of this law for vision, pressure, taste, and sound. Later experiments of this type on animals (460) and man (461, 462) conducted by Spencer, tended to confirm Heyman's generalization.

The relationship between attention, which we know as a conscious phenomenon, and the physiological processes subsumed under facilitation and inhibition is one of the most difficult problems facing physiological psychology. The difficulties of investigation, and the conflicting theories are evidence of the great complexity of the problem even in a simple experimental situation of which physiology makes use, i.e., the isolated nerve-muscle preparation. In the intact animal the experimental difficulties are greatly enhanced. These problems, in the case of man, are associated with the effect of changes in the attentional state of the subject upon simultaneous neuro-muscular action. In other words, what are the reciprocal effects of the concomitant functioning of two neuro-muscular arcs?

The experimental investigations of attention indirectly or directly are related to the problem of inhibition and facilitation, since whether one explains attention in terms of the facilitation theory of G. E. Müller (371), or the inhibition theory of Wundt (546), or the facilitation-inhibition theory of Exner (132), or the motor theory of Ribot (420), some phase of the process of facilitation and inhibition is involved. Pillsbury (409) in 1908 made clear the importance of these processes as the physiological basis of attention.

We are compelled to assume, then, from our present-day knowledge of the nervous action and from the psychological facts, that attention physiologically is due to the reinforcing and inhibiting effect of one group of nerve cells upon another group, which makes the group affected more easily excited by impressions coming in from the external world or from other cells in the cortex. . . . .

We have been assuming throughout that there is both reinforcement and inhibition involved in the attention process, without, however, definitely deciding between the three theories which were mentioned at the beginning of the chapter. As we have seen, it would be perhaps easier to explain the attention process as one of reinforcement alone, but there are facts which make it certain that inhibition plays a part at times. A strong stimulus appealing to one sense tends to decrease the activity of attention in the other senses, and, as Sherrington's experiments show that every motor impulse from the cortex involves both reinforcement and inhibition, it seems necessary to assume that with each increase in the excitability of one set of cells there goes a corresponding impulse to decrease the activity of all other cells whose activity could in any way conflict with the effectiveness of the first. But there is certainly no room for the assumption of Wundt that attention is an inhibitory process alone. (p. 259)

In approaching the problem of attention, it is difficult to escape the point of view of naïve popular psychology. We *seem* to "direct" our attention from one object to another; attention appears to be a controlling force of some sort. This apparent selective activity is, of course, the result of facilitation and inhibition of psychical processes. The exact nature of the facilitating and inhibiting activity, considered either as a psychical process in consciousness or as a mode of action in the neurones, is still, to a large extent, shrouded in uncertainty.

The study of the effects of attention—or perhaps we may say, facilitation and inhibition—on various psycho-motor activities, attracted the interest of the earlier investigators. Whytt noted that "vital motions" under certain conditions might be restrained. Hall, Prochaska, and Blane made similar observations. From the rise of experimental psychology in the 19th century until the present there has been an increasing number of experimental contributions to the subject. A large proportion of these studies have taken the form of the measurement of attention in terms of the effects of attention. Geissler (166) in an interesting historical summary classifies the methods of measurement of attention into six groups: The degrees of attention may express themselves in changes in (1) peripheral vision; (2) muscular strength; (3) liminal and differential sensitivity; (4) reaction time; (5) accuracy of work; and (6) report of the subject as to the degree of attention which has been experimentally induced by a graded distraction.

Important physiological and psychological problems in connection with facilitation and inhibition are involved in the use of any of these methods; the concern of the present section is primarily with the fourth. The study of the effect of attention (considered as a facilitating and inhibiting process) on neuro-muscular performance as exemplified in "reaction time" experiments and reflex-action experiments is an important mode of attack on one of the basic problems in physiological psychology.[24]

One of the first studies of the effect of attention on reaction time was that of Obersteiner (388) in 1879. Obersteiner started with the assumption that the rate of conduction of the nervous impulse to and from the cerebral centers, and the latencies in the receptor and effector mechanisms, are approximately constant. Consequently, variability in the reaction time is due to changes in the cerebrum, which are associated with attention, fatigue, bodily discomfort, etc. He studied the reaction times of subjects

[24] The quotation from Sherrington which appears at the beginning of this chapter is pertinent in this connection.

who were sleepy, fatigued, suffering from headache, and found that these conditions all lengthened the reaction time as compared with the time of the same subject in the normal state. The same result was found when auditory distraction (soft music), visual distraction, and cutaneous irritation (induction current), were introduced. He concludes:

We have thus become acquainted with a series of influences which cause variations in the course of a simple psychical process which we can attribute to a diversion of attention, and it has been possible to measure the amount of this diversion by the degree of retardation of the reaction. (p. 449)

The technique of Obersteiner was crude and his conclusions were based on an insufficient number of cases, but his study is of historical interest since it was one of the first systematic investigations in connection with these problems. Obersteiner makes clear his conception of the rôle of inhibition in the attentive process.

Ideas tend to call up other ideas by association, and naturally along the most easy channels. But we can check the current of ideation along the easiest paths, and divert it into paths which are more difficult. We think attentively, and inhibit continuously. The more powerful this inhibitory working of the attention, the more intense the thought, the more numerous the paths opened up, and the more productive in its consequences. Just as a ball placed on a slope will roll straight down unless sufficient force is exerted to turn it aside, so our ideas tend to take the easiest path of association unless we direct them by exercise of our volition, the power of attention. (p. 443)

Cerebral inhibition was an object of inquiry on the part of other investigators. Alexander James reviews the evidence (248) presented by Langendorff (221), Setschenow (438), Goltz (176, 177) and others for the existence of inhibitory centers, especially in connection with the heightening of reflex activity resulting from the removal of the higher centers (medulla oblongata, optic lobes, and cerebrum) which had been noted by these observers. This increase in reflex activity as indicated by the height to which a weight attached to the leg of a decapitated frog was lifted, was believed by James to be the mechanical effect of the prevention of the passage of nerve force to the optic lobes and cerebrum.

But now an important consideration presents itself. It this increase in the intensity of muscular contraction, which takes place when the higher centres (medulla oblongata, optic lobes, cerebrum) are removed, is brought about by the nerve force which would otherwise have passed to them being directed to the muscles, and if in the normal condition the passage of this nerve impulse to those centres will excite their several functions, it follows that our experiments may be looked upon as affording what may be called a "mechanical equivalent" of their collective functions. It follows, further, that if we in a similar manner test and compare the strength of the reflex contraction before and after the removal of the cerebral lobes only, we may obtain a "mechanical equivalent" of their individual functions.   (pp. 296–7)

This intensification of response is the result, in the opinion of James, of a "concentration" of nerve force which may be brought about in two ways:

. . . first, by preventing overflow of nerve force from the nerve tract involved to other tracts; and, secondly, by preventing interference with the nerve force in the nerve tract involved by overflow into it from other tracts.   (p. 300)

The increased reflex action in the decapitated animal is due to the first method mentioned above, *i.e.*, there is no overflow of energy from the cord into the higher centers; hence, the "concentration" of energy on the movement with the result that it is more vigorous.   The intensification of vision, hearing, muscular energy, etc., in hypnotic states, was believed by James to be the result of the same process of "concentration."   Finally the author saw evidence for concentration in the field of every day life—especially in connection with learning.

But we do not require to look to frogs, hypnotic patients, or paraplegics to assure ourselves of the value of concentration of nerve force.   We all know how the action of stimuli—visual, auditory, cutaneous—interferes with study, and conversely how the working out of a difficult problem renders us for the time incapable of perceiving all ordinary stimuli.   The staggering gait and inco-ordinate, purposeless movements which occur in the child when he is learning to walk may be looked upon as being in part at least, due to a want of concentration, for here the various stimuli necessary for equilibration—cutaneous, muscular, labyrinthine, visual, visceral—are probably carried to other areas, as well as those intended to receive them, and from these areas the motor-nerve impulses are carried to muscles other than those required to contract.   As the result of practice, however, certain definite nerve tracts are channeled out; no useless escape of nerve force takes place, and the function is performed perfectly.   Similarly in learning to read, to play a piece of music; we all know that such actions can be best performed when they are done, as the expression is, "without thinking."   (p. 300)

Thus James is able to extend his concept of concentration of nervous force to include a theory of learning.   The idea expressed by Obersteiner in connection with "the current of ideation" passing more easily along certain paths than others indicates essentially the same point of view.   It is, of course, a conception of the nervous impulse that is crude from the modern point of view, but is significant in the development of theories of reflex action in that it brings such diverse phenomena as hypnosis, learning, and reflex facilitation under a single explanatory principle.   That these phenomena have many features in common cannot be doubted.

REACTION TIME AND INHIBITION

A relationship between attention, and inhibition and facilitation has been suggested; the theory of the connection between these processes and neuro-musuclar performance on the one hand, and sensory processes on the other has been discussed. It now remains to trace its historical development. So far as neuro-muscular performance is concerned, we find in the latter half of the 19th century a marked interest in the problem of the effect of attention (facilitation and inhibition) on (1) voluntary reaction (reaction time experiments) and (2) reflex action.

The time relationship of neuro-muscular phenomena has received attention ever since the measurement of the speed of nervous conduction by Helmholtz (214) in 1845. Haller had made crude attempts to measure neural rates; Müller had regarded the problem as impossible of solution, but his student Helmholtz solved it. In view of the fact that the short interval between the stimulus and the reflex response had been regarded as one of the important *differentiae* of reflex actions, the investigations of the time assumed considerable theoretical importance. The comparison between the time of the reflex and the time of the voluntary reactions to stimuli is especially significant in connection with reflex theory. We have, during the latter half of the 19th century, a long series of painstaking studies of reaction (volitional) times which, to a large extent, occupied the first laboratories of experimental psychology.

The history of reaction time experimentation would merit independent treatment; here it can be given only in the briefest outline. Beginning in the latter part of the 18th century with the investigations of the "personal equation" in connection with certain astronomical observations, through the period of the late 19th century when the interest centered about the measurement of the velocity of the nervous impulse and the duration of mental processes, until the development of interest in the "reaction consciousness" in Wundt's laboratory in the early nineteen hundreds, the story forms an interesting and significant chapter in the history of psychology.[25] In the earlier period, the interest was physiological rather than psychological. The work of Donders (117), Exner (131), and von Kries and Auerbach (272) falls in this period which extends from about 1868 to 1887. Exner substituted the term "reaction time" for the older "physiological time." These investigators gave but little attention to the psychical

[25] *Cf.* Titchener (483), p. 356 *ff.*, and Sanford (431) for historical summaries of the reaction time work. Exner (131) contains an historical summary of the work on the "personal equation" with bibliography.

factors which might influence the times obtained. It is notable, however, that Exner stressed the importance of controlling attention in these experiments.

With the work of Lange in 1888 (282) in Wundt's laboratory, a new period in the study of reaction time may be said to begin. Lange, on the basis of the direction of attention, distinguished two types of reaction, the "muscular" or "shortened" reaction and the "sensory" reaction. In the former type the subject directs his attention to the muscular response and in the latter it is directed to discriminating sharply the stimulus to which he responds. The muscular type of reaction is of much briefer duration; Lange found it to be in the neighborhood of 125 sigma, while the sensorial reaction was approximately 225 sigma. Reaction times were analyzed under more carefully controlled conditions by Martius (334), Alechsieff (6), Bergemann (34) and others. Bergemann obtained muscular reactions as short as one hundred sigma; this type of reaction was called a "brain reflex."[26] With the work of Ach (1, 2) the reaction experiment became a method by means of which the "reaction consciousness" was systematically investigated with a view to determining the nature of volition, action, etc. With that aspect of reaction experimentation we are not directly concerned. For the purposes of the present investigation, the result of the reaction time work in the late 19th and early 20th centuries was the generalization that the temporal course of the process could be modified by changes in the direction of attention. Other experimenters, *e.g.*, Bliss (49), Cattell (84), have demonstrated the effect of attention, although the results have not always been in agreement. The investigation of Obersteiner (388) has already been discussed. Obersteiner showed the effects of the presence or absence of a distraction on the reaction time, while Lange and those who succeeded him in this work, systematically controlled the direction of attention with relation to two variables, the stimulus and the muscular response.

Many investigators had experimentally observed inhibition and facilitation in connection with reflex action. We have already indicated the nature of the extensive literature in this restricted field of investigation. These investigations indicate that the reflex is subject to facilitation and inhibition as a result of a variety of external and internal conditions. Sternberg (468) in his comprehensive monograph on the tendon reflexes, published in 1893, suggested the following as modifying directly or indirectly these reflexes: (1) repetition of stimulation, (2) stimulation of neighboring parts of the spinal cord, (3) intensity of the stimulus, (4) simultaneous

---

[26] *Cf.* Martius (334), p. 168 *ff*

voluntary contraction of the muscles, (5) emotional state of the subject, (6) mental condition of the subject—in connection especially with individuals suffering from mental disorder, (7) drowsiness and sleep, (8) fatigue, (9) diseased conditions in the spinal portion of the arc, (10) hypnotic conditions, (11) alteration of the blood supply of the spinal center, (12) toxic substances in the blood stream, and (13) psychical conditions in the normal subject, e.g., changes in the direction of attention. The items on this list are obviously not mutually exclusive and most of them are general rather than specific.

The fact that modifying processes, such as those listed above, are as effective in the case of voluntary or non-reflex action as in the reflex itself, has led Wiersma to point out the essential identity between the two types of response. In 1921 (540) he indicated that between reflexes and the "willed" action there was a continuity, and that they were governed by the same laws. Wiersma finds evidence for the identity between the two varieties of movement in (1) the comparison of reflex time and reaction time, i.e., there is no sharp break but only a difference in the order of magnitude, (2) the fact that both types of movement are dependent to some extent on the strength of the stimulus, (3) the purposiveness exhibited by both processes, especially in connection with the elimination of dangerous or unpleasant sources of stimulation, (4) the "spreading" of the movement to other muscle groups when the stimulated group is partially or wholly ineffective in carrying out the "purpose" of the movement, (5) the similar effects of attention on both types of movement, and (6) the inhibitory phenomena shown in both varieties of movement. The last two items in Wiersma's list are of especial interest from the point of view of the present discussion. Wiersma finds evidence for the application of Heymans' conclusions in connection with psychical inhibition to reflex phenomena.

Die gegenseitige Hemmung gleichzeitiger Bewusstseinsinhalte ist von grosser psychologischer Bedeutung. Das Sternenlicht wird am Tag nicht gesehen, starke Geräusche hemmen die Wahrnehmung schwächerer, kaum wahrnehmbare Berührungen werden von kräftigen Druck-empfindungen verdrängt. Die Versuche Heymans haben die reziproke Hemmung gleichzeitiger Wahrnehmungen klar ans Licht gestellt, und es hat sich ergeben, dass gleichartige Empfindungen einander am stärksten hemmen. Dementsprechende Hemmungserscheinungen zeigen auch die Reflexe. Im obigen ist schon auf den Einfluss der Praökkupation hingewiesen worden und im folgenden werde ich die gegenseitige Hemmung gleichzeitiger Reflexbewegungen nachzuweisen versuchen. (p. 259)

As an example of the antagonistic effect of competing reflex systems, Wiersma believed that the knee-jerk is in competition with postural reflexes

(*Stellungsreflexe*). That is to say, the constant inflow of impulses in connection with posture are inhibitory to the knee-jerk, and conditions which inhibit the posture reflexes, facilitate the knee-jerk. The postural reflexes are diminished under two conditions as follows:

Erstens kann der Bewusstseinsgrad des zentripetalen Reizes niedriger werden, wodurch der motorische Impuls schwächer wird und zweitens kann der zentrifugale motorische Impuls in seiner Leitung gestört sein. In beiden Fällen wird der hemmende Einfluss auf die Kniereflexe verringert sein. (p. 261)

In consequence, the knee-jerk is normally exaggerated in subjective counting, electrical stimulation, stimulation of cold, simultaneous muscular contraction, and is pathologically exaggerated in anxiety conditions, *e.g.*, in melancholia and hysteria. This exaggeration of the knee reflex occurs because the mind is occupied with the processes listed above, to the exclusion of impulses from the receptors in the muscles which are involved ordinarily in the postural reflexes.

Wiersma applied his theory to other reflex processes in an endeavor to prove his thesis that essentially the same law holds for reflex inhibition that holds for psychical inhibition, that is, that a "weaker" reflex—presumably one which serves a biologically less important purpose—is displaced or reduced in intensity by a "stronger"—that is, biologically more important—reflex. While judgment may be suspended in regard to this theory, it is significant as an effort to bridge a gap between psychical and physiological levels of function.

The relationship between sensori-motor functions occurring simultaneously in the nervous system is a problem that other investigators have taken into account. Dodge (106) in 1910 referred to attention as a "serious and troublesome source of changes in the amplitude of the knee-jerk." He suggested the possibility that there was a relation between changes in attention and the tonus of the muscles. This is a problem of great psychological importance, since it suggest the possibility that tonus is the physiological process at the basis of attention. Tonus is reflexly maintained—*i.e.*, it is dependent on a nervous arc through the spinal cord and according to Sherrington is the reflex basis of posture and attitude. Posture and attitude are among the most marked of the objective evidences of attention, *e.g.*, we speak of the "attitude of attention." The exaggeration of these tonic reflexes observed in decerebrate rigidity, reported by Sherrington in 1898 (439), indicated the effects of the removal of cortical control (attention might be regarded as the psychical expression of this control) on these reflexes.

Inhibition and facilitation phenomena were observed in another field of investigation. After the work of the English physician, James Braid (1795–1861), in 1843, (59) scientific attention was focused on hypnotism. Braid's theory of hypnotism was wholly physiological, *i.e.*, he believed the phenomena exhibited in the hypnotic condition were due to changes in cerebral circulation. Alexander James (248) in 1881 called attention to the enhancement of sensory and motor capacities in the hypnotic state in order to make use of these data to support his "concentration" theory of nervous inhibition. Heidenhain (213) explained the phenomena of hypnosis entirely on the basis of inhibition. He pointed out that there were certain analogies between the behavior of the hypnotized subject and the phenomena observed in decerebrated animals.

In face of all these facts, it appears to me that the hypothesis *that the cause of the phenomena of hypnotism lies in the inhibition of the activity of the ganglion-cells of the cerebral cortex*, is not a too adventurous one; the inhibition being brought about by gentle prolonged stimulation of the sensory nerves of the face, or of the auditory or optic nerve.

These sensory nerves, when in that state of stimulation which has above been fully described, would behave, in regard to certain psychical cells of the cerebral cortex, like the cardiac branches of the vagus in regard to the ganglion cells of the heart, or like the fibres of the superior laryngeal nerve towards those cells of the medulla oblongata which preside over respiration, or like those sensory fibres of internal organs which are concerned in Lewisson's experiment and in hysterical paralysis. (pp. 46–7)

Heidenhain believed the hypnotized person was in all respects an "imitating automaton;" the movements were in response to sensory stimulation and resembled willed action, although in reality they were reflex in nature. There were objections to this theory by Gurney (191), and Moll (363), but it is interesting to note the emphasis on the psychological as well as the reflex aspects of the problem.

It is impossible here to discuss the psychological and physiological theories of hypnotism; we can only touch on the problem in order to indicate the ramifications of reflex and inhibitory phenomena. Comparatively little experimental work has been done in the field of suggestion and hypnotism, although theoretical and practical problems of great importance may be attacked in this field.

The effect of suggestion during the hypnotic state was demonstrated in an interesting experiment by Nicholson (386) in 1920. This experimenter, using the ergographic technique, showed that instantaneous recovery from complete muscular exhaustion was possible in a subject who was thrown into the hypnotic state and given suggestions of strength. This experiment bears an interesting resemblance to the work of Rimathè (423), Patrizi (397) and others who used the same technique in studying the effect of changes of attention on muscular work in normal subjects.

Beaunis (22) in 1887 reported that the reaction time is markedly reduced in the hypnotic state. This investigator also found marked changes in pulse rate, auditory acuity, dynamometric capacity, etc., during the hypnotic condition as compared with the normal state. Brown-Sequard (64) in 1882 discussed the phenomena from the standpoint of inhibition and *dynamogénie* (facilitation) and concluded that they might be explained by the operation of these two processes.

L'acte initial lui-même, à l'aide dequel un individu est jeté dans l'hypnotisme, n'est qu'une irritation periphérique (d'un des sens ou de la peau) ou centrale (par influence d'une idée ou d'une émotion) qui produit une diminution ou une augmentation de puissance dans certains points de l'encephale, de la moelle épinière ou d'autres parties, et le braidisme ou l'hypnotisme n'est rien autre chose que l'état très complexe de perte ou d'augmentation d'énergie dans lequel le système nerveux et d'autres organes sent jetés sous l'influence de l'irritation première periphérique ou centrale. Essentiellement donc l'hypnotisme n'est qu'un effet et un ensemble d'actes d'inhibition et de dynamogénie. (p. 30)

SUMMARY

A recapitulation of the phenomena subsumed under the terms facilitation and inhibition would be exceedingly difficult. Their complexity and variety are an indication of the difficulties in constructing an adequate theory to explain them. The experimental study of these phenomena is one of the particular contributions of the latter part of the 19th century to the development of reflex theory. Sherrington has pointed out that reflexes seldom if ever occur in isolation; they occur in orderly combination. In so occurring they are inter-related and mutually modified; facilitation and inhibition are at the base of this integration. It is perhaps no exaggeration to say that none of the theories so far presented adequately explain all the experimentally attested facts.

In the first years of the present century an increasing amount of evidence has accrued—the current investigations of Fulton (161), Sherrington and Liddell (450, 451), Golla and Hetwer (173), Dodge (114) and others offer still further support—to substantiate the position that the reflex may be regarded no longer as a "simple" response involving only the spinal cord. The study of the widely diversified processes which have been regarded as inhibitory, has contributed not a little to this result.

An important development from the point of view of physiological psychology is that the similarity between certain varieties of psychical phenomena—especially in hypnosis and attention—and inhibition as exhibited in reflex action, has been stressed by numerous observers from Alexander James to Sherrington and Wiersma. That the inhibitory phenomena observed in the spinal animal, *e.g.*, the inhibition of the response to pinching of the toe in the frog by a simultaneous stimulation of the other leg, the phenomena of reciprocal innervation, the inhibitory processes observed in the hypnotic state, the elimination of unnecessary actions in learning, the inhibitory effects observed in simultaneous stimulation under the "double task" methods, the effects of directing the attention as observed in Heymans' psychical inhibition, and the effects of attention on reaction time, have some common denominator must be apparent.

Dodge (111) has recently pointed out the responsibility which psychology has in investigating these problems. He states that whatever may be one's definition of psychology, there can be no doubt that its province lies in part, at least, in the examination of the behavior of the animal with an intact nervous system. It is in such a nervous system that the problems of inhibition and facilitation are peculiarly apparent. The psychologist, however, is especially dependent upon the studies made by the physiologist on experimentally isolated nervous segments, but he (the psychologist) must take the scientific responsibility of extending the results obtained from the functionally simple physiological systems to the complex conditions of "human behavior, experience and personality." Dodge continues:

Both his [the psychologist's] limitations and his responsibility impose special obligations to scientific caution. While it is often regarded as unfortunate that nerve fibers, nerve muscle preparations, and reflexes cannot be functionally isolated in the intact human on demand, it may not be forgotten that it is exactly in the mutual interrelationships of the various neural strata in human behavior and the integration which is called consciousness that there lies a group of problems of the utmost practical importance. (p. 3)

CHAPTER XIII

The Reflex Maintenance of Posture

"There still remains to be mentioned, that important property of living muscular fibres, which consists in a perpetual state of tension taking place at all times, in a greater or less degree, independent of any temporary stimulus. . . . . A certain degree of this tention is necessary for the performance of the natural motions of the muscles, whether voluntary or involuntary, and the vigour with which the several actions are performed, depends on the fibres possessing a due degree of this constant tone giving scope to motion."—Sir Gilbert Blane, *Select Dissertations on several subjects of medical science. Dissertation VIII. On muscular motion*, 1788.

The nervous mechanisms by means of which the muscle maintains a permanent state of contraction have attracted the attention of investigators since the end of the 17th century. The functions of that "obscure organ,"[1] the cerebellum, and of those non-acoustic structures in the inner ear which are involved in the maintenance of posture, although they became the objects of scientific inquiry within the first two decades of the 19th century, still remain uncertain. The extraordinary complexity of the results of investigation in these fields make an intelligible summary a difficult undertaking. It is the purpose of the present chapter to outline these studies only insofar as they are related to the history of reflex action. The numerous and important contemporary investigations in these fields[2] can be presented in brief summary only.

Sherrington has pointed out that the organism is subject not only to environmental influences which play upon receptor cells at the surface, but is affected also by stimuli within the organism itself. The name "proprioceptors" is given by Sherrington to these receptor mechanisms which lie embedded within the deeper tissues, particularly in the muscles, tendons, and joints. These mechanisms may be distinguished from the "exteroceptors" which lie near the surface of the body, as, for example, the eye, ear, and skin, and are affected by environmental stimuli. It had been contended that the muscle did not contain receptors, but Ruffini and Sherrington demonstrated in 1892 and 1893 the sensory nature of the

[1] *Cf.* Fulton (161), p. 515.
[2] For a critical exposition of contemporary studies see Fulton, *op. cit.*, p. 491 *ff*. *Cf.* also Hoff and Schilder (233), Delmas-Marsalet (100), Fearing (136), and Ranson (418a).

"muscle spindles" which are located in the muscle, although these structures had been observed as early as 1851 by Hassal and in 1862 by Kölliker.[3]

The demonstration of the sensory nature of the muscle spindle is fundamental to the understanding of the nature of the mechanism of bodily posture and its relation to tendon and muscle tonus phenomena. Cobb (91) has recently pointed out that the significance of the contribution of Sherrington and Ruffini lies in the fact that it afforded proof that the "muscles are amply supplied with sense organs, from one-half to one-third of the bulk of a so-called 'motor' nerve to a muscle being made up of sensory fibres arising from cells in the dorsal root ganglia." These observations furnish a structural basis for the afferent side of the proprioceptive reflex arc, and it is this arc which functions in the maintenance of posture and also, according to recent interpretations, in the tendon reflexes and in the maintenance of muscle tonus.

The subject of muscle tonus has a long and interesting history in experimental physiology which cannot be given detailed attention here.[4] Fulton notes that Galen used the word "tonus" with reference to the static contraction of the muscle. Fifteen hundred years later Whytt noted the "natural" contraction of the muscles arising from the constant and "equable action of the nervous power on their fibres." This constant state of slight tension is due, according to Whytt, to nervous influence which is action "in a very gentle manner."

Hartley, a contemporary of Whytt's, noted the "moderate degree of contraction, or tendency thereto, which is observable in all the muscles . . . . during vigilance." It was, however, in 1788 in a Croonian Lecture (48) that Blane gave the more accurate description which is quoted at the beginning of the present chapter. Especially noteworthy is Blane's observation that a certain tonus is necessary for the performance of muscular action either voluntary or involuntary. Humboldt (244) used the term *tonus* in 1797. Müller gave the topic somewhat extended treatment in the *Handbuch*, using the term tonus in referring to the steady tension normally present in skeletal muscle when not engaged in a specific act.

Müller's contemporary, Marshall Hall, refers to the tonic contraction of

<hr />

[3] *Cf.* Schäfer (432), II, p. 1007 ff. *Cf.*, also Bell's reference in 1826 (30) to the "circle of nerves" which convey the nervous influence of the brain to the muscle, and the sense of the condition of the muscle to the brain; *vide supra*, Chapter VIII, p. 119 *ff.*

[4] An historical summary of the topic may be found in Sherrington's paper (446) in 1919, and in Spiegel's monograph (463) in 1927. Heidenhain (212) also has an excellent presentation of the history of tonus.

the sphincters as a reflex act, although he does not attempt to analyze the stimuli which bring about such contraction. It was not until a later period in the 19th century that experimental study of tonus was first attempted, and the early investigations seem to have given divergent results. Sherrington in 1915 (445) says of these experiments:

> Their plan of observation was to look for a slight elongation of the muscle (frog) after severance of the muscle's nerve. Heidenhain, Auerbach, Schwalbe, and Pflüger were among those who failed to get clear evidence of any such lengthening. In the fifties of the last century the existence of "tonus" of skeletal muscle seems to have become doubted by many physiologists. (p. 195)

It has already been noted that Herbert Mayo, writing in 1822 (343), made a reference to experimental observations on tonus.

Brondgeest (63) in 1860 contributed the fundamental experiment. He was able to show that in the frog, the limb in which the afferent spinal roots had been severed, was less flexed, when the frog was held vertically, than was the corresponding sound limb. Other investigators confirmed the observations of Brondgeest and definitely established the reflex nature of tonus.

DECEREBRATE RIGIDITY AND TONUS

Sherrington in 1898 (439) described the muscular phenomena which follow the experimental removal of cerebral hemispheres. If in the monkey or cat, transection is performed in or below the lower half of the bulb, a condition of complete relaxation of the muscles of the neck, tail, and limbs results; when the hemispheres are removed the musculature of the animal presents a wholly different appearance. This condition is described by Sherrington as follows:

> To this condition of flaccid paralysis supervening upon transection in the lower half of the bulb the condition ensuing on removal of the cerebral hemispheres (mesencephalic transection) offers a great contrast. In the latter case, the animal, on being suspended just in the same manner as after the former operation, hangs with its fore-limbs thrust backward, with retraction at shoulder-joint, straightened elbow, and some flexion at wrist. The hand of the monkey is turned with its palmar face somewhat inward. The hind-limbs are similarly kept straightened and thrust backward; the hip is extended, the knee very stiffly extended, and the ankle somewhat extended. The tail, in spite of its own weight . . . . is kept either straight and horizontal or often stiffly curved upward. . . . . When the limbs or tail are pushed from the pose they have assumed, considerable resistance to the movement is felt, and, unlike the condition after bulbar section, on being released they spring back at once to their former position and remain there for a time even more stiffly than before.

Of this "decerebrate preparation," Sherrington, in 1915 (445), says:

Removal of the brain from the posterior colliculi forwards in the cat provides an excellent tonic preparation of the extensor muscle of the knee. This tonus is still retained by the muscle to the full after severance of all the skin nerves of both hind limbs. Further, the muscle still retains its full tonus after severance of *all* nerves of both limbs excepting only the nerve of the tonic muscle itself. (pp. 195–6)

Decerebrate rigidity is a case of exaggerated muscle tonus; it involves those muscles which maintain posture. This is made clear by Sherrington in the following quotation taken from the study quoted above:

Evidently, therefore, the distribution of this reflex tonicity embraces just those muscles whose contraction tends in the erect position of the animal to counteract the effect of gravity on the various several regions, the muscles which prevent those parts, and the animal as a whole, from sinking to the ground. And from the muscles antagonistic to those, the reflex tonicity is absent. In other words, the reflex tonus obtains in, and is confined to, those muscles which maintain the animal in an erect attitude. . . . . *Reflex tonus is postural contraction. Decerebrate rigidity is simply reflex standing.* (p. 197)

The maintenance of posture, then, is a reflex function; it is identical with muscular tonus and its receptors lie within the muscles themselves. The problem of the "purpose" of muscle tonus is solved; so far as skeletal muscle is concerned, it serves to keep the body in an upright position, that is, it is a reflex of attitude as distinct from a reflex of movement.

Sherrington describes six characteristics of the reflex postural contraction of muscle: (1) its low degree of tension, (2) its low degree of fatiguability, (3) the difficulty in obtaining the postural contraction by artificial, *e.g.*, electrical, stimulation, (4) the relative ease with which reflex inhibition interrupts the postural contraction, (5) the "lengthening" and (6) the "shortening" reactions obtainable from muscles exhibiting postural contraction. The two latter features are demonstrated by the ability of the contracting muscle to take up a new postural length when an observer forcibly bends or extends the limb although the tension ("tensive pull") remains unaltered. Regarding the "lengthening" and "shortening" reactions, Sherrington says:

In the above examples of lengthening and shortening reactions of skeletal muscle, the alterations in posture, to which the limb was subjected in showing its power of adjustment, were alterations imposed by passive movement. The observer moved the limb into the new attitude which the reflex postural contraction then took up and lightly fixed. But the reflex adaptation to the new posture occurs just as well or better, when the changed position of the joint is brought about by active reflex movement excited, for instance, by faradizing an afferent nerve trunk. Thus in the postural reflex preparation when a reflex extension movement of the knee has been provoked, the shortening reaction appends itself to the reflex contraction, and on discontinuing the stimulus which caused the extension movement the extensor muscle still remains shortened, and the knee still continues in the extended position. This lends to the reflexes of the decerebrate preparation a character recalling some features of catalepsy. The limb brought by active or passive movement into a new posture when released remains in that new posture.

In the same paper Sherrington has defined posture as "those reactions in which the configuration of the body and of its parts is, in spite of forces tending to disturb them, preserved by the activity of contractile tissues, these tissues then functioning statically." He proceeds to emphasize the fact that tonically contracted muscles maintain posture as well as execute movement.

Disturbance of the individual's ability to maintain an erect bodily posture are of clinical significance as indicative of the functional integrity of the proprioceptive system. Marshall Hall had noted that patients afflicted with a partial paralysis could not walk in the dark. Hall did not believe that this was due to a loss of "muscle sensation;" he believed that there was no direct consciousness of the action or position of the body musculature. In his view the so-called muscle sense was only a combination of cutaneous and visual sensations. This opinion was in opposition to that of Charles Bell, Hall's famous contemporary, who believed that a "nervous circle" existed between the brain and the muscles, by means of which the knowledge of the condition of the muscle was conveyed to the brain and the influence of the brain was conveyed to the muscle.

Hall's observation that a patient afflicted with partial paraplegia had "no power of balancing himself without the aid of the eye" is historically significant, since it anticipated the important clinical observation of Romberg (1795–1873) that patients suffering from *tabes dorsalis* are unable to stand erect with the eyes closed. In 1853 (425) Romberg described this "pathognomic sign" as follows:

If he [the patient] is ordered to close his eyes while in the erect posture, he at once commences to totter and swing from side to side; the insecurity of his gait also exhibits itself more in the dark. It is now ten years since I pointed out this pathognomic sign, and it is a symptom which I have not observed in other paralyses. . . . . Since then I have found it in a considerable number of patients, from far and near, who have applied for my advice; in no case have I found it wanting.

The testing for ability to maintain balance has since become one of the routine procedures in neurological examinations.[5]

---

[5] *Cf.* Maloney's monograph on locomotor ataxia (330) for an excellent discussion of posture from the point of view of the clinician.

EARLY STUDIES OF POSTURE

The function of the maintenance of posture has been variously described by such phrases as "static sense" (Külpe, 274), "sensations of orientation" (Mach, 321), "ampullar," and "vestibular sense" (Titchener, 482), "labyrinthine sensation" (Myers, 376, Starling, 464), "sense of equilibrium," "spatial sense," etc. These terms all have to do with the knowledge of the position of the body in space, or more specifically with the maintenance of balance.

The early investigators were interested in the problem of static equilibrium from the point of view of the mechanics of the body and the location of the center of gravity. It is perhaps significant of the change of emphasis in physiology that the modern texts and systematic treatises (*e.g.*, Starling, Bayliss, and Howell) contain no chapters on the *mechanics* of the body but their discussion of equilibration is confined to the topics of semi-circular and vestibular *functions*.

This interest in static equilibrium is illustrated by the work of the Weber brothers (531), and Borelli (54), who were interested in determining the location of the center of gravity as a problem in bodily mechanics. Braune and Fischer (60), Vierordt (504), Leitersdorffer (298)[6] and others endeavored to define the normal erect posture (*normal stellung*) from the point of view of the "attention position" in military hygiene. Luciani (320) says of Vierordt's findings:

He [Vierordt] found that the anterior-posterior and lateral oscillations are considerably greater in the symmetrical military posture than when the weight was thrown upon the one leg (assymetrical). The latter posture is accordingly the most natural, and preference is given to it in sculpture and painting. (III, p. 113)

Vierordt is credited by Luciani with being the first investigator to make use of graphic registration in the study of posture. Hinsdale (228), working in Wier Mitchell's clinic in 1887, seems to have made the first formal experimental study of static equilibrium. Mitchell and Lewis (362) in a paper on the knee-jerk had discussed sway incidentally, and it was at Mitchell's suggestion that Hinsdale's study was made. Mitchell already had made equilibrium data objective and quantitative. He says (in connection with station in locomotor ataxia):

For this we select station, the relative power to stand steady, with eyes upon or shut. This symptom can be made numerically accurate by standing the patient in front of a bar marked in inches, and placed on a level with the ears. The extent of lateral sway of the head may thus be easily observed; a like observation records the anterior tendency.

---

[6] The work of Leitersdorffer is briefly discussed by Zuntz and Loewy (553).

The first is rarely over half an inch in health, the second does not usually exceed an inch, even with closed eyes.   Any large increase is suspicious.   (p. 370)

Hinsdale studied the sway of adults and children. His method of graphically recording sway is described as follows:

. . . . attaching to the top of the man's head a flat piece of cardboard, upon which was stretched some smoked paper. The subject was then placed under an index which was free to move up and down in a fixed line, and which traced curves on the paper as the subject who stood beneath swayed in any direction.

Hinsdale noted that no one was found who could stand absolutely still, "the body swayed forward and backward, and from side to side, in every instance." His important conclusions were as follows: (1) normal sway is "about one inch in the forward and back line, and three quarters of an inch laterally," (2) children sway more than adults, (3) closing the eyes increases sway about fifty per cent, (4) ether exaggerates sway, (5) the "law of rhythmical motion" governs sway in man.

In 1890 Hinsdale published a second paper (229) in which station was studied with reference to respiration. He found no observable relation.

Bullard and Brackett (67) in 1888 studied the static equilibrium of 181 men, using the graphic method of recording their data. They note that the anterior-posterior is greater than the lateral sway.

The studies of Hinsdale, Mitchell and Lewis, Bullard and Brackett, emphasized the clinical aspects of posture. The psychological aspects of the problem involved in the perception of changes in equilibrium and the accuracy of the individual's adjustment thereto, and the introspective analysis of the sensational components in sway, with a view to determing whether or not there exists a separate sense quality which may be assigned to the receptors in the non-acoustic portion of the ear, has received attention from modern investigators, e.g., Burtt (70) and Garten (163).

Titchener (482) stated the difficulties from the point of view of introspective analysis as follows:

The study of the semi-circular canals and the vestibule presents a curious difficulty to psychology, a difficulty the reverse of that which we have just met in our discussion of the sensitivity of muscle, tendon and joint.   There we had a tangled complex of sensation, and the problem was to distribute them among the available end-organs.   Here, we have highly developed end-organs, but no very obvious group of sensations to refer to them. (p. 174)

Warren (520) and Griffith (187, 188) have studied the problem in connection with the experience of rotation; Griffith in his study of dizziness found no evidence for a separate sensory quality.

LATER STUDIES OF POSTURE

Static equilibrium as an index of neuro-muscular efficiency has been a subject of numerous psychological investigations. Hancock (204) used sway as a means of studying the motor ability of children; Bolton (52) and Wallin (516) used it in connection with the intelligence of children and mental defectives. Perhaps the most extensive use of posture as an index of neuro-muscular function has been made by Miles, who described (356) an apparatus for measuring the amount of sway which he called an "ataxia-meter."[7] Regarding the factors which influence station Miles mentions height, weight, position of the feet, type of footwear, sex and age. He points out the importance of the visual factor in the maintenance of equilibrium and finds that in the case of one subject there was a reduction of approximately 45 per cent in the amount of sway with the eyes open. Regarding the relative effect of the kinesthetic (muscle sense) and purely labyrinthine elements in equilibration the following is a pertinent quotation:

We shall not be able, figuratively, to close the eyes of the "kinetic-static" sense. These impressions from the labyrinth are bound to function along with the great mass of kinesthetic sensations. Their relative prominence and importance in the test are of interest that we may have a clearer idea of what is being measured in station. In the first place, it is instructive to notice the experience of the young aviator who is practically helpless if he has to fly in the dark or in a cloud and cannot use his vision by which to correct the position of his plane with the horizon. . . . . Ideally the labyrinth should be able to take care of just such conditions, but practically any impressions from it are not sufficiently strong to be a sure basis for orientation. Similarly in *tabes dorsalis* kinesthetic sensations are reduced or arrested. The tabetic can stand with some stability while he can see, but in the dark or with eyes closed the impressions from the labyrinth are too vague or weak to suffice. (p. 324)

Miles' apparatus was used by Fearing in a series of three studies on sway (134, 135, 137) of which one is of some interest in connection with the effects of attention on postural responses. In this study (137) the effect of controlled and uncontrolled attention upon sway was investigated. In the early studies there had been some suggestion that the total sway score was affected when the subject directed his attention to the sway situation or gave it to matters extraneous to the situation during the test periods. To quote from this paper:

The distinction between "controlled" and "uncontrolled" attention is expressed in the difference between the situation in which the reagent has a task, which, in popular

---

[7] The "Cephalograph," an apparatus for recording the amount of sway, is described by Maloney and Knauer (331) in 1914.

language, definitely "occupies" his attention during the critical periods, and the situation in which no task is set. (p. 1)

In terms of the experimental situation the difference between controlled and uncontrolled attention was determined by the introduction of a systematic auditory distraction in one experimental series. This distraction took the form of a series of taps, sounded at irregular intervals during the sway period, which the subject was instructed to count, and report the total. In the second series of experiments no distraction was introduced and no instructions were given regarding the direction of the subject's attention. One hundred and twenty subjects, sixty in the distraction series and sixty in the control series, were used. There was a reduction in the amount of sway in both series of experiments, but in the series in which a distraction was introduced the reduction was much greater. In other words, the control of attention, by systematically directing it towards some object extraneous to the sway situation, reduced very appreciably the amount of sway.

The distinction must be made, in the discussion of the general subject of equilibration, between the ability of the individual to maintain his body erect (static equilibrium, posture) and the bodily phenomena which accompany the stimulation of the vestibular labyrinth. The modern interest in the experimental study of equilibration has in part been concerned with the latter phase, especially in connection with the effects of rotation of the organism—a phase of the problem which received its initial impulse in the testing and training of aviation recruits during the recent war. The characteristic accompaniments of rotation—nystagmic eye movements, vertigo, etc.—are usually associated with the functioning of the non-acoustic labyrinth, and a vast literature has accumulated[8] in the study of these reflexes. The history of these investigations has been adequately presented elsewhere (189); we need only mention the outstanding figures in the long list of contributors, whose work, beginning in 1828 with Flourens, has paralleled the non-labyrinthine studies of posture. Others whose contributions in this field are important are Goltz (1870), Breuer (1872), von Cyon (1873), Crum Brown (1874), Mach (1874–76), James (1882), Kreidl (1892), and Ewald (1887–89, 1892–96). Among the contemporary contributors are Maxwell (341), Magnus (326, 327, 328), Dodge (109), Holsopple (236, 237), Griffith (186) and Fearing (139).

Sherrington gives some attention to the important problem of the

---

[8] Griffith (189) in his comprehensive history of vestibular equilibration lists 1700 titles during the period 1500–1922.

structural basis of the postural reflexes.   Are the afferent nerves in the skeletal muscles the sole channels through which impulses cause postural adjustment?   Ewald (130) and others had demonstrated the importance of the labyrinth in connection with muscle tonus.   Sherrington has shown, however, that for the "crude maintenance of the act of standing" in the cat and dog the fore-brain, mid-brain back to and inclusive of the posterior colliculi, the labyrinths, and the cerebellum are unessential.   Such crude equilibration probably does not include such postural adjustments as the intact organism exhibits.

There has developed a controversy regarding the part which the non-medullated fibers from the sympathetic nervous system play in the maintenance of tonus.   The investigations of Dusser de Barenne (123), Hunter (246), and others have demonstrated the existence of these fibers, and these investigators have maintained that the autonomic nervous system inner-vates the skeletal muscles in reflex postural tonus.   Fulton summarizes the evidence for and against this assumption and concludes that the proposition is as yet unproven.

Maintenance of posture in the intact organism may be considered as (1) a reflex response initiated by nervous impulses arising in the non-acoustic labyrinth, (2) a consicous response dependent upon kinesthetic, cutaneous, visual and auditory cues, and (3) a response in part dependent upon reflex connections with receptors in the ampullae and vestibule and in part depend-ent upon voluntary responses to the sensory cues outlined in (2), (4) a reflex response initiated in the muscles and joints and passing via the posterior column to the cerebellum.   The part which consciousness plays in the postural adjustments is of some theoretical interest.   The following quota-tion from Head (211) indicates that the intervention of consciousness is not essential.

> The afferent stream from deep structures, passing up the posterior column of the spinal cord, can effect two terminal centres.   One of these is the cortex, with consequent recogni-tion of posture and movement; the other, the cerebellar system, regulates and controls the postural and tonic aspects of muscular activity without in any way exciting consciousness directly.   We know that some part of our body has assumed a certain position, or that a definite movement is taking place under the influence of the will; but the preliminary co-ordination of muscle-groups and shifting of tonic innervation, necessary for such changes, are carried on, without the accompaniment of any conscious process.

Morat (367), Obersteiner (389), Cleghorn (90) and others have pointed out that the maintenance of posture is the result of the cooperation of several senses.[9]

---

[9] *Cf.* Fearing (136) for a discussion of the neural paths underlying the equilibratory response.

Magnus and Kleijn in a series of papers, beginning in 1909 (see Magnus 326), have studied the postural reflexes in relation to the functioning of the labyrinth. They were able to show that the labyrinth affected the tonus of the extensors of the limbs. While working with decerebrate preparations these investigators observed that movements of the head and body markedly modified the tone of the limbs. The otolith organs of the labyrinths (not the semi-circular canals) and the nerve endings in the muscles, tendons, and joints were the sources of these postural changes. Stimulation of the semi-circular canals resulted in compensatory eye movements. One of the results of the observations of Magnus and Kleijn was a scheme of classification of the postural, semi-circular canal, and tonic reflexes. These reflexes are divided into two large groups: (1) the *statische Reflexe*, *i.e.*, the reflexes involved in lying, standing and sitting, and (2) the *statokinetische Reflexe*, *i.e.*, the compensatory reactions, the stimuli for which are acceleration or retardation of movement (*e.g.*, rotation of the body).

The *statische Reflexe* are true postural reflexes. They are divided into "standing" reflexes (*Stehreflexe*) and "righting" reflexes (*Stellreflexe*). The former group are concerned in the maintenance of passive posture, while the latter are concerned with the ability of the organism to change from an abnormal position to a normal posture. The "standing" reflexes may be studied in the decerebrate animal and indicate the position of the head in determining the posture of the body. They involve tonic reflexes, the neck reflexes and labyrinthine (otolith organs) reflexes. These reflexes combine in various ways, thus rendering analysis difficult; the two most important receptor fields are in the neck muscles and labyrinth. The animal when under the sole dominance of these reflexes can stand, but it cannot *change* its posture, hence it is obvious that in the intact animal other than postural mechanisms must be involved.

These mechanisms are included in the "righting" (*Stellreflexe*) reflexes which may be demonstrated in the "midbrain" animal. In the decerebrate animal, as used by Magnus and Kleijn, the brain stem is transected in the region of the tentorium; in the "midbrain" animal the transection severs the cerebral hemispheres including the thalami. The "midbrain" animal rights itself when placed in an abnormal position; in whatever position it is placed, the head is always held upright, and since the position of the head reflexly controls the posture of the trunk and limbs, the animal has control over all postures. These postural responses persist after the removal of the brain and may be regarded as a kind of geotropic reflex. Sherrington referred to these results in 1924 (448) in the following terms:

Plant-growth orientates itself in regard to the line of gravity, geotropism; and so in the rabbit, cat, and monkey, stalking, walking, running with their element in common, the erect attitude, are shown by Magnus and de Kleyn to be, shortly said, refined geotropic reflexes. Any position other than the erect one excites in the reflex animal restoration of its erectness. The head, for instance, is righted by an act having its unconscious source in the pull and pressure of two microscopic stones in a special pair of tiny gravity organs bedded in the skull. With righting of the head goes rotation of the eyeballs in the opposite sense, keeping the vertical meridian of each retina in correspondence with the actual vertical. Appropriate reflexes bring the whole animal from any other position into the symmetrical right-side-up one. The well known manoeuvre which enables the cat, when inverted and falling from a short height, to right itself in the air during its fall, alighting squarely on its feet, is shown by Magnus and his colleagues to be executed perfectly by reflex action, after removal of the entire higher brain. Detailed analysis proves this whole reaction to be a chain of reflexes again essentially geotropic. (pp. 262–3)

Sherrington then points out that these responses are not represented in consciousness by any sensory quality. The "right-side-upness" of the world is an "innate unargued datum" and part of the elementary reflex equipment of the organism.

TENDON REFLEXES AND POSTURE; THE "STRETCH" REFLEX

It had been noted by the earliest observers that a certain degree of tension was essential for the appearance of the knee-jerk. Hoffman had suggested that the tendon reflex was a special case of a proprioceptive reflex. Langelaan (283) in 1916 stressed the identity of the tonic and tendon reflex.

Shortly summarizing, we may say that the term 'tonus' designates the state of the muscle when continually subjected to the influence of weak stimuli, emanating from its own proprioceptors. By the term 'tendon reflex' we indicate the sudden variation of the tonus, evoked reflexly by a brief but vigorous stimulus of the proprioceptors of the muscle and the tendon. Hence *tonus and tendon reflex as to their intimate nature are identical*, and the tendon reflex may therefore serve as a touchstone for the tonic state of the muscle. (pp. 326–7)

The recent (1924) papers of Sherrington and Liddell (450, 451) have presented generalizations which mark a very important advance in the history of the postural reflexes. The experiments of these observers show that a gradual stretch applied to a muscle evokes a contraction. This response is dependent upon the proprioceptive arc and seems to be graded by the degree of stretch. The muscles which are most sensitive to the stretch stimulus are the anti-gravity muscles. The passively stretched muscle of the decerebrate preparation acts in response to the stimulus of the stretch itself; the maintained contraction, which is tonus, furnishes its own stimulus.   Following Gowers' use of the term "myotatic," the authors suggest this term in place of the more awkward "stretch" reflex.   Sherrington andLiddell summarize the specific fidings in their first paper (450):

> In the knee-extensor (decerebrate preparation) a stretch applied to the muscle evokes contraction in it.   This is reflex and purely proprioceptive, its receptors lying in the fleshy region of the muscle.   A stretch less in extent than .8 per cent of the total muscle-length suffices to evoke the reflex.   Slow stretches, *e.g.*, of 6 mm., performed in 6 sec., evoke the reflex as well as do quick.   The latency of the reflex is short, *e.g.*, less than 20 sigma, but the lower limit of latency we have not determined.
>
> Within limits, so long as the stretch increases, the reflex continues to increase.   When augmentation of the stretch ceases, augmentation of the stretch contraction also ceases and the reflex usually declines, merging into long-lasting plateau-like contraction, which is maintained by the stretched-posture, consequent from the precurrent stretch-movement. Withdrawal of the stretch causes immediate cessation of this postural stretch contraction. The stretch-reflex, unlike the ordinary contralateral extensor reflexes, therefore, exhibits little or no after-discharge, *i.e.*, the reflex is relatively dead-beat.   (p. 241)

Sherrington and Liddell make it clear that the maintenance of posture is the function of the myotatic reflex.

> In other words, the stretch-reflex of the antigravity muscles is a fundamental element in the reflex posture of standing.   Evidencing this rôle played by the postural stretch-reflex of the knee-extensor.   After transcollicular decerebration, reflex standing, in the above mentioned sense, and the knee-extensor's postural stretch-reflex are markedly evident.   On the other hand, spinal transection at once, for the time being, practically annuls both.   (p. 235)

The knee-jerk and the patellar clonus are regarded as "fractional examples of the more comprehensive stretch-reflex."   In other words the knee-jerk is produced by a very slight stretch of extremely brief duration.   A stretch of less than one-twentieth mm. lasting less than one-twentieth of a second is sufficient to produce the jerk.   Patellar clonus may be regarded as a rhythmic series of knee-jerks.

The myotatic reflexes in reflex standing are a composite of many single stretch reflexes.   In the Linacre Lecture in 1924 (447), Sherrington emphasizes this aspect.

> A peculiarity which distinguishes the stretch-reflex from other reflexes is that, whereas in other reflexes the reflex contraction excited from source implicates whole groups of the limb muscles, the stretch-reflex excites in the limb just the one muscle stretched.   The reflex standing of the limb is a harmonious *congeries* of stretch-reflexes, each component reflex being the self-operating reaction of an individual extensor muscle.   This mode of production of the reflex posture allows it latitude in detail.   The standing pose is still maintained though the observer shift in detail, within limits, the position of the feet. Thus a foot may be advanced or set backward, and the shift alters the position in detail,

but the reflex animal still stands.   The altered incidence of gravity involved by the shift compensates itself, and greater and lesser stretch wherever they occur excite, as we have seen, a correspondingly greater or lesser stretch contraction which antagonises further yield and compensates the altered stretch.   (pp. 929–30)

SUMMARY

The work of Sherrington and Liddell brings under a single explanatory principle, phenomena which have hitherto appeared to be widely divergent. Posture, tonus, and tendon phenomena have been the subjects of prolonged controversy.   An exhaustive account of the discussions of these topics has not been attempted, but it is clear that the conception of the myotatic reflex while not closing this particular chapter of physiology, marks a highly significant advance in the knowledge of neuro-muscular adjustment.

The intimate relationship between posture and tonus, and the connection between the latter and the psychical process of attention, seem to indicate the possibility of renewed attack on the problem of attention.   All the facts seem to point to an intimate connection between attention and the tonic state of skeletal muscle; it has been suggested that tonus *is* attention expressed in neuro-muscular terms.   The study of posture—static equilibrium—offers an opportunity to experimentally analyze the relationship between attention and neuro-muscular functioning.

CHAPTER XIV

MOTOR AUTOMATISMS AND REFLEX ACTION

"But, the objection against the mind's being concerned in the vital and other involuntary motions, drawn from our not being conscious of its interposing for this end, is quite overturned, by considering that a great variety even of the voluntary motions are many times performed, when we are insensible of the power of the will exerted in their production. Thus, while in walking we either meditate by ourselves, or converse with others, we move muscles of our legs and thighs, without attending to, or knowing anything of the matter."—ROBERT WHYTT, *An Essay on the Vital and Other Involuntary Motions of Animals*, 1751.

The character of purposiveness which seems to adhere to the movements of the decapitated animals and to certain types of unconscious acts in man, was the occasion, as we have seen, for a prolonged controversy in the latter half of he 19th century. Although this controversy resulted in a general victory for the principles of mechanistic physiology, there still remained certain phenomena of behavior which did not appear to be wholly consistent with those principles. The interpretation of these phenomena has been one of the major tasks of present day physiology and psychology. For example, the understanding of those exceedingly complex cortical processes associated with the so-called higher thought processes, and the interpretation of the relationship between the cortical processes and the neuro-muscular phenomena over which the spinal cord presides, have been accomplished in part, at least. Although the physiology of learning is still to a large extent obscure, it too, has yielded in a measure to the physiological and psychological experimentation of the first twenty-five years of the 20th century. The fiction of the "simple" reflex, apparently so firmly established during the first decades of the 19th century, has vanished together with the sharp dichotomy between voluntary and reflex action.

AUTOMATIC ACTS AND ZIEHEN'S CONCEPT OF THE "DEFLEX"

The sharp distinction between voluntary and reflex action had the merit of being logically and verbally simple. There were, however, certain borderline phenomena which could not readily be classified in one or the other of these categories. Ziehen, in his work on physiological psychology, the English translation of which appeared in 1892 (549), and in his more recent

232

Leitfaden der Physiologischen Psychologie (552) has dealt comprehensively with those types of animal adjustments which lie between the reflex on the one hand and the complex voluntary act on the other. Since Ziehen's treatment of these phenomena is both comprehensive and original, a consideration of his interpetations will give an adequate presentation of the problem.

After defining a reflex action in its simplest form as the situation in which "a stimulus acting upon the nerve-end reaches a ganglion-cell, and is transmitted by the latter along a new nerve-path to contractile masses, so as to impart motion,"[1] Ziehen points out that the "fitness," *i.e.*, apparent purposiveness, of the reflex act is not a basis for inferring psychical correlates for spinal cord action. That is to say, there is no justification for the "spinal soul" of Pflüger. Ziehen then proceeds to examine more closely the behavior of the frog in which the cerebrum, exclusive of the optic thalamus, has been removed.

> All reflex action is retained. A prick on its foot easily causes it to leap off. If we place an obstacle in the path of its retreat, it avoids the obstruction, or, in rare cases, clears it with a well estimated bound. The mere act of leaping away may possibly, in case of necessity, be regarded as a complicated reflex act; but the fact that the frog avoids the obstacle while retreating shows at once that quite another process is concerned. (p. 13)

The avoidance of the obstruction, Ziehen regards as a response to an "intercurrent" stimulus in the form of an irritation at the terminations of the optic nerve, which is of a wholly different character from that of the reflex. This intercurrent visual stimulus *modifies the reflex action* and the animal avoids the obstruction. He continues:

> Those motor reactions that are not the invariable result of a definite stimulus, as are the reflex acts, but that are modified while in progress by the action of new intercurrent stimuli, we shall call *automatic acts* or *reactions*, in the more restricted sense of the words. (pp. 13–14)

In the *Leitfaden*, published in 1924, Ziehen substituted for the term "automatic acts," the term "deflexes." In other words, the term "deflex" is coordinate with the term "reflex" as descriptive of a phenomenologically distinct type of neuro-muscular response. The deflex shares with the reflex

[1] *Vide* page 7 in the English translation of 1892 (549). Unless otherwise noted the quotations will be taken from this work. With one important exception which will be noted later, careful comparison between the text of this work and that of the *Leitfaden* (552) has failed to show any important changes insofar as the discussion of reflex action and motor automatisms is concerned.

the characteristic absence of concomitant psychical or conscious processes. In comparing the deflex with the reflex Ziehen says:

> While the reflex acts are essentially constant, the automatic acts (*i.e.*, the deflex) are characterized by great diversities. The motions executed in deviating from a definite course vary according to the character and position of the intercurrent stimulus that causes the deviation. By reason of this infinitely greater variability, the automatic acts or reactions resemble the conscious or voluntary acts. On the other hand the automatic acts are quite like the reflex acts in that they have no psychical concomitant. (p. 18)

The deflex appears in the animal series at the level of the *echinodermata*. The starfish is observed to avoid obstacles—a capacity which is lost when one of the rays is severed from the central disk. The severed ray is still capable of locomotion, but the motions are aimless. Certain reflexes still persist in the severed ray, *e.g.*, it rights itself, as does the decerebrated frog. The deflex appears, according to Ziehen, to have developed from the reflex through the agency of natural selection.

There is another type of deflex which appears in the ontogenetic development of the individual. This class of responses are termed "automatic acts" in the volume of 1924 on physiological psychology, and they represent acts which were originally voluntary, but which have become, by a process of retrogressive development, automatic. Ziehen says of them:

> Call to mind once more the above-cited example of the pianist, who plays a well-practised piece while his thoughts, his consciousness, wander elsewhere. We designate this playing as automatic, although it was not automatic originally. Before the piece can be executed automatically, the player must practise it for hours with the application of all his energy and attention, and many such voluntary acts must take place. Hence automatic action may be acquired by *practice*, *i.e.*, by the frequent repetition of the so-called voluntary acts. These acts, executed at first *with* the constant co-operation of mental images, gradually lose their psychical concomitant and become automatic. For this reason, transitions from one stage to the other, also, characterize this form of the development of automatic action. (pp. 16–7)

This latter group of automatic acts are specific in character and are not inheritable, and, like the deflex, they do not have psychical concomitants.

We have, then, two types of response both of which are distinct from the reflex. There is on the one hand, the deflex which has developed phylogenetically from the reflex and represents a general but non-psychical capacity of the animal to adapt itself to novel features of its environment, and on the other those automatic acts which appear ontogenetically, are specific rather than general, and have become unconscious through repetition.

This conception of certain types of response which resemble the reflex in some degree, although discussed by Ziehen in 1892, was not wholly new at that time. Even before the 18th century vague ideas of automatisms as distinguished from reflexes seem to have attracted the attention of various investigators of involuntary action. Swammerdam, as we have noted in a previous chapter,[2] had observed that in walking we may "salute a person we meet, merely because another in our company takes off his hat, or because we are affected by such external habit, though we do not know who the person is we have saluted, nor so much as think of saluting him."

William Porterfield in 1759 (411) referred to those motions which "through use and custom" have become unconscious. Haller (202) noticed the lack of consciousness in the "obscure perceptions" in walking, winking, and like movements. He concluded that it "is evidently false that all motions arise from the mind."

Robert Whytt in 1763 (537) in his monograph in involuntary motion discussed the hypothesis that the mind may control motions which are outside the field of consciousness. He noted that while walking we may carry on conversation without attending to the movements of the legs. This lack of conscious accompaniment seems to be characteristic of a variety of voluntary motions which "are many times performed."

We . . . . acquire, through custom and habit, *a faculty of performing certain motions with greater ease than we were wont to do them,*[3] but also, in proportion as this facility is increased, we become less sensible of any share or concern the mind has in them.   Thus a young player upon the harpsichord or a dancer, is, at first, very thoughtful and solicitous about every motion of his fingers, or every step he makes, while the proficients or masters of these arts perform the very same motions, not only more dexterously, and with greater agility, but almost without any reflexion or attention to what they are about.   (p. 334)

This is a very early reference to the automatization of motor habit, and it is significant that Whytt recognized a resemblance between these actions and the motor performances with which his monograph is primarily concerned, *i.e.*, reflexes.

In 1749 David Hartley published his "Observations on Man" (209). In this book he distinguished between automatic acts and secondarily automatic acts. The former depend upon sensations (as opposed to voluntary motions which depend upon ideas), and the latter depend upon the "most diminutive sensation, ideas and motions, such as the mind scarce regards." Repetition of motion tends to eliminate the action of the will and make the act automatic.

[2] *Vide supra,* p. 50 ff.
[3] Italics not in the original.

George Prochaska in the "Dissertation" (416) published in 1784 considered the movements of the heart, oesophagus, stomach, and intestinal canal as being completely automatic throughout life. In the case of voluntary muscles, he noted that under certain abnormal conditions the control of the mind is renounced "as is seen in hysterical, epileptic, or infantile convulsions, or in those affected with St. Vitus's dance; and these movements, although performed by muscles designated voluntary, can only be termed automatic."

> The raising of the hand and the application of it to the head in apoplexy belong also to the class of automatic movements, also the turning of the body in sleep, and partly even somnambulism itself, which, however, it would seem is partly also to be ascribed to obscure sensations and volitions which the mind instantly forgets. (Chapter V, Sec. IV)

Sir Gilbert Blane in the Croonian Lectures of 1788 (48) distinguished between habit and unlearned automatisms. Of the former, he said:

> It is the nature of a voluntary muscle to perform any motion with greater ease, the more frequently it is repeated, and to act most readily with those muscles, or in company with those sensations with which it has been used to combine its action either at once or in succession. This is the foundation of habit, and is the principle by which all the practical attainments of man acquire facility and perfection. (p. 263)

At the beginning of the 19th century, as has been previously indicated, interest in involuntary phenomena was tremendously accelerated by the discoveries of Bell and Magendie in connection with the function of spinal nerves, and by the work of Marshall Hall on reflex action. The work of the latter, like that of Whytt of the preceding century, may be regarded as one of the guide posts in the history of involuntary action. Hall was concerned primarily, however, with the establishment of a physiological concept of reflex action and in his work it is possible to find but little reference to anything corresponding to automatisms in the modern sense. He regarded the action of the sphincters as being "automatic," and discussed the involuntary motor phenomena in epilepsy. Hall did much to establish the concept of a mechanical functioning reflex arc, but seems to have been but little concerned with acquired motor automatisms.

Johannes Müller in the *Handbuch* (372) made reference to a variety of movements which he termed *Mitbewegungen* that possess certain characteristics of automatisms. In this class of movements, Müller referred to any movement which is called forth or associated with another movement. In endeavoring to move the ear, for example, one also moves the facial musculature. The ability to eliminate these accessory movements improves with practice. The piano player learns to limit movement to certain muscles.

The rigid distinction of Hall, Müller, and other physiologists of the early 19th century, between voluntary action on the one hand, and involuntary (reflex) action on the other, met with opposition on the part of Griesinger (183) in 1843 and Laycock (295) in 1845. These investigators, working independently, suggested the possibility of reflex action taking place through the brain, *i.e.*, a "psychical reflex." According to Griesinger the psychical reflex includes the action of the brain in connection with "ideas of effort" (*Vorstellungen in Strebungen*) which may be either conscious or unconscious. Laycock extended the "laws of reflex action" to the brain, and attempted to find in the cerebral nerves a basis for action which is strictly analogous to the reflex action taking place through the spinal nerves. In the case of hydrophobia, Laycock finds an example.

I have stated that the idea of water, whether obtained through the eye or ear, will excite the hydrophobic gasp and convulsions; it will also excite a conservative act, the patient, when water is presented to him, is horrified, and immediately attempts to remove it. This movement is strictly involuntary, and not the result of sensation; the water is repelled from the lips with a violent spasmodic jerk, and often in spite of the urgent volitional attempts of the patient to the contrary, just as the hand is snatched away from a spark of fire, or the headless frog leaps from the needle. (p. 302)

Some years later the idea of psychical reflex action was elaborated by Carpenter (82) under the term "unconscious cerebration." He says:

This "Unconscious Cerebration," . . . . is the precise parallel, in the higher sphere of Cerebral or Mental activity, to the movements of our limbs, and to the direction of those movements through our visual sense, which we *put in train* volitionally when we set out on some habitually-repeated walk, but which then proceed not only *automatically*, but *unconsciously*, so long as our attention continues to be uninterruptedly diverted from them. (p. 515)

This process Carpenter also calls "ideo-motor" action, a principle which is extended to cover the acts of the somnambulist, the hypnotized subject, the phenomena obtained with the use of the planchette or ouija board, the solving of problems during sleep, and the like.

Richet developed a theory of "psychical reflexes" in a paper published in 1888 (421). The essential elements according to his definition of reflex action were: (1) its involuntary character, (2) its immediacy, and (3) the necessity of peripheral excitation. Richet distinguished between *conscience* and *connaissance*, the latter term being applied to the mental experience which accompanies the psychical reflex. This experience is vague, fleeting, indefinite, and is characteristic of the psychical reflex but not of the simple reflex. In the simple reflex it is the amount of stimulus rather than the quality of the stimulus which determines the motor response as in the case of the psychical reflex. When there is some appreciation of the exciting stimulus—as in the case of the ability to partially inhibit the reflex wink when a pretended blow is aimed at the eye—Richet terms it a psychical reflex. Psychical reflexes may be innate or acquired. The latter include habits and account in a large measure for the differences in response between individuals, *i.e.*, it is the individual's particular body of acquired psychical reflexes which differentiates him from others with the same hereditary equipment.

Reflex action was the principle used in the explanation of hypnotic phenomena offered by Heidenhain (213) in 1880. Heidenhain regards the hypnotised person as behaving like an "imitating automaton." The movements in such a subject are described as "imitation automatisms," "speech automatisms" and "command automatisms"—the latter being actions carried out at the command of the operator. These automatisms for Heidenhain are merely reflex acts the stimuli for which are the movements (visual stimuli) or commands (auditory stimuli) of the hypnotist. Consciousness and will are not involved; the hypnotized subject, in fact, might be regarded as a spinal animal.

This point of view was in opposition to that of Janet as indicated in the classic work of 1889 (251), in which the automatisms of the subconscious states were regarded as giving evidence of the existence of a secondary consciousness.

Janet in this work made clear what he meant by unconscious action: it is an action which has all the psychical accompaniments except that it is wholly ignored by the person who executes it. Actions which are immediately forgotten are not included under this definition.

Further consideration of the theories of automatic action in connection with abnormal states would lead to an analysis of the phenomena of hysteria, somnambulism, hypnotism, suggestion, etc., as they are related to theories of the unconscious action. These are topics beyond the limit of the present chapter. Reference to the work of Moll (363), Bernheim (39), Gurney (191), Despine (104), Binet, (44), Binet and Férè (45, 46), F. Myers (377, 379) and others indicates the extent of this field as well as its controversial nature.

The French physiologists and psychologists were primarily concerned with automatisms as they appeared in various abnormal states. In contrast, the interest in the subject indicated by the work of the English investigators—Whytt, Hartley, Blane, and especially Carpenter—emphasized the relation of automatic action to certain phases of motor habit. This is evident in the systematic work of Sully (475), Maudsley (337, 338), Bain (16), and the American psychologist, Baldwin (17). Sully noted the mechanical nature of habitual action and, following Hartley, he called it "secondarily automatic." Movements of this type are unconscious and closely resemble reflex action. Maudsley stated that learned acts may become "secondarily automatic" and take place without consciousness; walking, for example, is an act of this type. Bain, following Marshall Hall, divided reflexes into excito-motor and sensori-motor. The latter may involve consciousness, but do not include movements of "emotional diffusion." These movements accompany the expression of emotion, and are involuntary but not unconscious. Baldwin, under the caption "Motor Value of the Subconscious," discussed those "motor phenomena which fall below the threshold of conscious reaction." Action during "absent mindedness," post-hypnotic suggestion, etc., were discussed under this heading. Baldwin noted that a "nervous man will arrange his necktie or stroke his mustache fifty times a day without 'knowing it,' and all of us have our little motor habits, which we are conscious of but do not observe."

The experimental attack on the problems of motor automatisms seems to have been undertaken first in the latter part of the 19th century. Jastrow (256) in 1892 devised the automatograph for the laboratory study of involuntary movements. This instrument consists of a writing pen attached to a glass frame which is supported by steel balls. The hands of the subject rest on the glass which responds to very slight movements. Jastrow noted that involuntary movements tended to follow the direction of attention; the hand tended to follow the direction of the eye. In a later study (254) Jastrow registered the sway of the body by a writing needle attached to the head. He found that the head tended to follow the direction of attention.

In 1895 Lindley (304) studied the automatic motor phenomena of mental effort, using the questionnaire method. He classified the automatisms into (1) those due to sympathy and imitation, (2) excitatory automatisms, i.e., those which seem to facilitate brain work provided they do not distract attention, (3) those automatisms which precede concentrated attention, and (4) automatisms of posture.

Newhold (385) in 1895 discussed the problem of processes which take place in the brain without being represented in consciousness. He especially referred to the phenomena of crystal gazing and hallucinations on the sensory side, and to automatic writing on the motor. His experiments were in connection with crystal gazing (sensory automatism) and automatic writing. Newhold did not believe in the hypothesis of a submerged personality, but explained the automatic phenomena as ideas obtaining motor expression.

The experiments of Solomons and Stein (457) in 1896 approached the problem of normal motor automatisms. The object of their experiments was to investigate the limits of motor automatisms in the normal individual, and to determine if possible whether or not the performances of the hysteric and "split" personalities were allied to the automatic acts of the normal individual. They listed four elements in the unconscious movements of secondary personalities: "(1) general tendency to movement without conscious motor impulse, (2) tendency of an idea in the mind to go over into a movement involuntarily and unconsciously, (3) tendency of a sensory current to pass over into a motor reaction subconsciously, (4) unconscious exercise of memory and invention." The investigators attacked the first problem by the use of the planchette—a form of Jastrow's automatograph—which the subject operated while reading a novel. The subject performed various movements under these conditions. Under (2) the subject was given a pencil which he kept continuously moving while engaged in reading a novel. The writing soon became automatic, and frequently words were written which the subject had just read. In the third group of experiments, the subject was required to write from dictation while engaged in reading. Whenever the attention was sufficiently distracted in this experiment, "real" automatisms appeared, that is, the writing from dictation went on below the level of consciousness. In these cases the subject was unable to recall a single word written. The experimenters discuss the problem of consciousness without memory vs. "real" unconsciousness in this connection.

The consciousness without memory seems to *approach as its limit,* simply a condition in which the subject has not the faintest inkling of what he has written, but feels quite sure that he has been writing.   (p. 501)

This is a state of "real" unconsciousness and closely resembles the phenomenon of hysteria. A similar type of experiment was performed in connection with automatic reading, in which the subject reads aloud while being read to. The subject gave his attention to the material read to him, and after practice, he was able to continue his own reading in an entirely automatic fashion. Unconscious invention (4) was experimented on by means of automatic writing.

The experimenters concluded that a large number of acts ordinarily called intelligent, such as reading, writing, etc., are in reality automatisms. In regard to the problem of whether or not there was an analogy between these normal automatisms and the phenomena of secondary personalities, the experimenters make the following comment:

It will be remembered that these phenomena occurred in us whenever the *attention* was removed from certain classes of sensations. Our problem was to get sufficient control of the attention to effect this removal of attention. In hysteria this removal of attention is affected by the anaesthesias of the subject. We *would* not, the hystèrique *can* not, attend to these sensations. Whatever else hysteria may be then, this, at least, seems most probable. It is a *disease* of the *attention*. An hysterical anaesthesia or paralysis is simply an inability to attend to sensations from this part. (pp. 510–11)

Stein (465) in a later series of experiments was able to "teach" a normal subject certain automatic movements when his attention was distracted. The movements "taught" were figure eights, m's, curves, etc.

Solomons (456) in 1899 continued the study of motor automatisms using the reaction method. In these experiments, the subjects were required to react to auditory stimuli while reading entertaining literature. The usual chronoscopic technique was employed. Most of the subjects were able after practice to react automatically. The reaction times ranged from over 200 sigma to less than 100 sigma. The experimenter divided the reactions into four groups. (1) Reactions above 290 sigma which contain an element of will. (2) In reactions below 290 sigma nothing is "left of the motor impulse except the feeling of personal activity." These correspond to the "sensory" reaction type. (3) These are reactions from 175 to about 225 sigma and are characterized by a prominence of the "reaction feeling." The fourth group may be "extra-cortical," although the author points out that lack of knowledge of the finer anatomy of the sensori-motor paths makes generalizations in this field difficult.

Work, similar to that of Solomons and Stein, was carried out by Tucker (489) at Stanford University in 1896. A large number of subjects were used by this investigator and the automatograph of Jastrow was employed. The conclusions were (1) there is a physiological tendency for the hands to move inward toward the "median plane of the body," (2) ideas of motion tend to cause involuntary movements, (3) involuntary muscular movements tend to imitate moving stimuli.

D'Allonnes (8) in 1905 devised apparatus with which the subject graphically recorded involuntary movements while letters and digits were presented to him. Involuntary movements were also recorded while words, phrases, and arithmetical operations were presented for his consideration.

The results of this experiment were of the usual sort and seem to be in general agreement with those of Solomons and Stein.

Curiously enough, there has been but little attention given to the experimental phases of the subject of motor automatisms since the group of experiments which have just been reported. This in spite of the enthusiasm of Myers (379) for experimental data on the problem of the subconscious expressed in his review of the paper of Solomons and Stein. Experiments on automatic writing are described by Myers (377) in connection with the phenomena of the seance room, and in the papers of Downey and Anderson (118, 119).

The results of the experiments of Lashley (288) in 1921 on cerebral functions bear directly on the problem of automatisms. He was concerned with the functional location or cortical representation of automatized habits in rats. The habit established was the discrimination between light and dark alleys in the Yerkes discrimination box. Lashley notes that no data are available as to the amount of practice necessary to thoroughly automatize a habit in man. Thirteen hundred repetitions were used in the case of the rats. The visual area of the cortex was destroyed and the animals tested for retention, with the following results:

> The functional activity of the visual cortex is still necessary to the performance of the habit and there is no indication that subcortical nuclei have taken over any part of the reaction, even sufficient to facilitate relearning. The cerebral area functional in learning seems to retain the same function after prolonged training. (p. 465)

That is, destruction of the visual cortex resulted in a loss of the visual-motor automatism. This seems to answer the question as to whether "lower centers" take over the functions of the higher centers when a habit becomes automatized.[4] Lashley comments as follows:

> If long practiced habits are not reduced to subcortical levels what is the neurological basis of automatization? The musician may not speak when first learning a difficult movement but later his verbal reactions are dissociated from the manual co-ordinations so that the two processes may go on simultaneously. It is this capacity to function without exciting reaction systems other than those directly concerned with its performance that characterizes the automatic habit. Such a condition might be brought about by blocking cerebral associative connections, and this seems to be the only alternative to reduction to subcortical levels. An analogous situation is presented by the differentiation of the conditioned reflex to a specific stimulus. Whether the confining of impulses to a single path is the result merely of repetition or of some active inhibitory or blocking process cannot be decided from existing evidence. (pp. 467–8)

---

[4] Cf. Pike (408) who notes that the underlying nervous mechanism does not change with habit formation. Cf. also Herrick (224), Chapter IX.

Lashley suggests that the mechanisms of conflict and repression in the Freudian sense may have something in common with the processes of automatization.

Maxwell (340) had attempted in 1916 to work out a neurological schema which would serve as a basis for automatic writing. He noted that these movements are combined and coordinated, and that they express coordinated thought. His neurological schema was based on a hierarchical arrangement of centers in an attempt to account for the observed levels of complexity.

Although but little has been done in the last fifteen years in the way of experimental work, the theoretical interest in the phenomena of the subconscious and unconscious has resulted in a large literature. It is not the present purpose to review this material, but reference may be made to certain papers which bear more or less directly on automatisms. The paper of Hart (208) contains an excellent review of the theories of the subconscious, especially in connection with the problem of the existence of a subconscious personality. With reference to this problem Münsterberg (374) pointed out that there were three types of theories: (1) the subconscious is regarded as a complete psychical system—a personality. This is the theory of the layman; (2) the subconscious is psychical in nature but not a system—merely split off material. This is the medical view; (3) the subconscious is not psychical, but is merely brain process. This is the orthodox psychological view. The view of Prince (414) which regards the evidence as indicating an existence of psychical activity, is expressed in the same symposium of which the paper of Münsterberg is a part.

From time to time there have appeared in the psychiatric and spiritistic literature descriptions of particular types of motor automatisms. Typical of these reports is that of James (250) and Cory (93) in connection with automatic drawing, and that of Salmon (430) and Bancroft (19) in connection with clinical observations. The automatic phenomena in epilepsy and sleep walking (ambulatory automatisms) are presented by Singer (453), McCarthy (345) and Courtney (94). The definition of these ambulatory acts as given by McCarthy is interesting.

It is that condition in which an individual consciously or unconsciously performs more or less complex ambulatory acts over which he has no control. These occur in hysteria, epilepsy and neurasthenia.

Recently an interesting clinical application of the technique of automatic writing has been made by Mühl (370) who used it as a means of obtaining information regarding the subconscious factors underlying personality.

Mühl included in this article a discussion of the levels of consciousness. These are (1) focus of attention, (2) consciousness, (3) fringe of awareness, (4) paraconscious, (5) personal unconscious, (6) genetic unconscious. These levels are dissociated in abnormal states, and the material obtained by means of automatic writing is from the paraconscious and unconscious.

The importance of automatisms in the phenomena of the seance room and in connection with the states of trance, "possession," thought transference, etc., have been attested by Myers and others. Coover (92), in his monograph on psychical research stresses its importance as an explanatory principle in interpreting subjective experiences and muscular manifestations, which are, in reality, hallucinations and motor automatisms.[5]

RECENT CONCEPTIONS OF MOTOR AUTOMATISMS AND REFLEX ACTION

A considerable degree of terminological confusion has been introduced into the discussion of reflex and involuntary action by the phenomena of automatisms—a confusion which doubtless reflects the difficulties in the way of interpretation of the phenomena themselves. The terms "reflex," "involuntary," "automatic," "automatism," "spontaneous," and "vital" have been used interchangeably since the beginning of the 17th century in referring to a type of action which may be very broadly characterized by the absence of or a low degree of "central" control. Certain characteristics of the reflex, however, have received general acceptance, as for example, its brief time, its relative independence of consciousness and volition, its predictability, *i.e.*, the certainty of appearance when a particular stimulus is presented to the receptor, and its purposiveness in the sense that it serves some protective or adaptive end. Many of these characteristics, as Ziehen has noted, may be applied, also, to the automatism. Actions of this character are "automatic" in the sense that they are relatively free from central control.

The term "automatic," on the other hand, has been applied frequently to responses, the stimulation of which are internal rather than peripheral; this is the usage of Bayliss (21) Tigerstedt (480), and Foster (155). Tigerstedt includes the "products of decomposition and internal secretion" present in the blood and lymph as sources of automatic excitation to the nerve cells. Foster calls attention to the "spontaneous" movements of pigeons in the absence of the cerebral hemispheres, and suggests that the term "mechanical spontaneity" may be applied to these movements.

[5] *Op. cit.*, pp. 143, 152.

And we may here perhaps remark that all these facts seem to point to the conclusion that what may be called mechanical spontaneity, sometimes spoken of as 'automatism,' differs from the spontaneity of the 'will' in degree rather than kind. Looking at the matter from a purely physiological point of view (the only one which has a right to be employed in these pages), the real difference between an automatic act and a voluntary act is that the chain of physiological events between the act and its physiological cause is in the one case short and simple, in the other long and complex. (p. 1078)

We have already noted Ziehen's observations of the movements of the decapitated frog in avoiding an obstruction.

Bayliss discussed the question of whether or not the constant activity exhibited by the respiratory and vasomotor centers is "actually automatic," or whether it is the result of afferent impulses from the periphery. Such impulses are able to modify the state of these centers, but he states that it "seems possible" that a state of automatic activity may exist, although it is difficult to differentiate it from excitation which is the result of "stimulating substances in the blood."

As distinct from these usages, the term "automatism" is applied in psychology to those motor phenomena which are not conditioned by consciousness. Tuke in his "Dictionary" (490) defines automatism as follows:

A state in which a series of actions are performed without cerebral action or conscious will, as during reverie or in certain morbid conditions.

Baldwin's Dictionary (18) gives the following definition:

The performance of actions apparently involving some degree of psychological determination, without consciousness of the personal subject.

The same authority defines automatic action "in psychology" as

A succession of acts in response to repeated or continuous excitation, proceeding in more or less complete independence of attention.

The adjective automatic, however, is applied

To those functions of the living organism which are independent of external stimuli, finding their stimulus in the conditions of the organism itself.

Richet in the *Dictionaire* (422) gives a somewhat more restricted definition. He divides movements into four classes: (1) reflex; determined by exterior stimuli, (2) automatisms; determined by interior stimuli which are voluntary, (3) machine-like (*machinaux*); determined by the will, but continue without the intervention of the will, (4) volitions; determined and continued by the will. The interior stimulus necessary for the automatism is not the will, although it is psychical in nature; it is a "volition accompanied by complete amnesia." He points out that such movements are rare in the normal individual, but are found in somnambulistic states, delirious states, intoxication, mediumistic phenomena (table tipping, automatic writing, etc.), and hypnotism. Richet sees some resemblance between the movements of the automatic writer and those of the pianist who is able to converse while playing the piano. This application of the term "automatism" to certain phases of motor habits indicates an extension of the concept to cover a type of involuntary action which is not abnormal and which is not reflex in the usually accepted physiological sense. A brief survey of the standard physiological texts indicates that the physiologists are not inclined to differentiate sharply the two kinds of involuntary action, namely reflexes and automatized habits.

Howell (241) sees in the reflex an expression of the automatic activity of a mechanism. "Repeated experiences" of the individual as well as inheritance may account for the existence of neural paths of least resistance. Mitchell (360) regards habits as "developed reflexes." Habits begin as volitions and after sufficient repetition take on the character of reflexes. Sherrington (441) points out that volitional acts may become involuntary and, conversely, involuntary reflexes may be brought within the range of consciousness.

Familiar instances of individual acquisition of motor co-ordination are furnished by the cases in which short, simple movements, whether reflex or not, are by practice under volition combined into new sequences and become in time habitual in the sense that though able to be directed they no longer require concentration of attention upon them for their execution. (p. 389)

Luciani (320) discusses reflex action from the point of view of its genetic development and states that many "fully unconscious coördinated reflexes" were at the outset voluntary. He refers especially to such acts as walking, reading, piano playing, etc.

These statements are typical of the point of view held by a group of representative physiologists in which involuntary action established through learning is denominated an "acquired reflex." This view receives, perhaps, its most definite expression in the following quotation from Sherrington (in Schäfer's "Textbook," (432)):

On the other hand, our individual experience shows how readily volitional acts by repetition and practice ultimately become actions involving neither attention nor even consciousness,—create, in fact, habitual reflexes. The spinal reflexes may be regarded as descended from volitional acts, inherited and therefore instinctive habits of simplest order, testifying to a so-to-say primitive process akin to memory in the spinal cord.   (II, p. 860)

Turning from the physiologists we find that the attitude which regards involuntary movement as a kind of degenerated volition receives a complete expression in Wundt (545, 546) and, as we have noted at the beginning of the chapter, in Ziehen.   The steps in this process are volitional acts, impulsive acts, automatic acts, and reflexes.   The automatic act is the result of habituation, and is characterized by a decrease in the conscious accompaniments.   The "purposive" aspect of reflexes is the result of the fact that they were the voluntary acts of previous generations.   Others who have concerned themselves with the relationship between volition and automatic acts are Meynert (354) who derived voluntary acts from automatic responses of Ziehen's "deflex" type, and Münsterberg (374) who derived automatic acts from volitional acts.

The automatizing process in connection with motor learning is stressed by other psychologists of whom James, Bentley, and Pillsbury are examples. Habit, for James (249), is "mechanically nothing but a reflex discharge." Pillsbury (410) indicates that in an act which has become habitual by repetition, attention is required only at the beginning; with the process of habituation the conscious accompaniments are gradually lost, finally, in the case of certain acts, even the initiating stimulus may be unnoticed. In discussing the effect of repetition on action, Bentley (33) stresses the shrinkage and disappearance of certain processes in consciousness; the action becomes automatized, that is, "the original perception is dropping out; that a single determination is holding together the entire complete act and that it is almost entirely without mental factors."   Eventually, according to Bentley, a state is reached in which the act becomes an "acquired reflex."

From the systematic texts and treatises, both in psychology and physiology, further examples might be cited, describing the characteristic features of the development of a variety of involuntary actions which may be regarded as being distinct from the reflex, yet carrying many features in common.

In addition to learning, the topics of attention and emotion in systematic psychology seem to have contributed discussions which are pertinent to the development of a concept of automatic action in the field of normal psychology.

In connection with attention Pillsbury points out (409) that the movements which adapt the organism for the reception of the stimulus attended to, as, for example, turning the head, turning the eyes, etc., are involuntary in nature. IIe refers to them as "reflexes of the attention." Külpe (275) and Ribot (420) make similar references. Stout (473) stresses the division of attention in the case of the skilled piano player.

The expressive movements of the face and body associated with emotional states are referred to as involuntary by Wundt (546) and Titchener (482). The classical work of Darwin on the expression of the emotions stresses the involuntary character of the muscular accompaniments.

These references, selected more or less at random, indicate the ramifications of the problem of involuntary action insofar as it applies to the particular type of movement usually designated by the term "motor automatism." In this brief survey we have limited ourselves to the field of normal psychology, and to such material as might be found in the standard textbooks.

The most striking fact in connection with the examination of these texts is the paucity of material which bears directly on the subject of involuntary action, especially in connection with automatisms. In the foregoing paragraphs the material was obtained from discussions which bear only indirectly on the subject in hand. With few exceptions the current textbooks in psychology contain no theoretical discussion or experimental data on antomatisms as such.

Under the heading "automatic reactions" Dunlap (122) refers to action which are characterized by a low degree of consciousness. These reactions, which were originally conscious, cover a wide variety of movements.

The class of automatic reactions is, however, a large and varied one, ranging from the type in which ideational reactions have been reduced to the perceptual level with only occasional ideational movements, down to the type from which all consciousness has been eliminated completely—a type seldom realized. (p. 197)

These reactions, according to Dunlap, are not to be confused with reflex actions which they resemble—the important distinction being that the automatic action may at any moment revert to the conscious type.

Warren (523) refers to sensori-motor activities which are automatic and involuntary. Angell (9) discusses the tendency of ideas to produce motor changes, i.e., slight involuntary movements, which are called "ideo-motor." Ideas or objects which "at once" touch off movement are discussed by both Titchener (482) and Külpe (274) as "ideo-motor" or "sensori-motor" action. The following quotation from Ladd and Woodworth (277) seems to adequately characterize this point of view.

Certain ideas lead to certain definite movements, with which they have become associated by past experience. They may do so either with or without the full consent of the subject. When an idea leads to its appropriate movement with the full consent of the subject, we call it voluntary movement; but when the idea leads to movement, as it always tends to, while the subject's attention and intention are elsewhere directed, the movement is often named *ideomotor*. Examples of the last are seen in involuntary whispering of what one reads or thinks, in involuntary gestures, and often, in rather an amusing way, in the movements of spectators at an athletic game or an acrobatic show, when they are much absorbed in the movements about to be executed by the performers, and unwittingly execute such movements themselves. (p. 535)

A recent criticism of the theory that every idea of movement tends to realize itself in action is found in the work of Moore (366), who restricts the application of the theory. He sums up his position as follows:

The theory of ideomotor action as propounded by James involves two distinct elements. One, that a kinaesthetic image must be the cause of voluntary movement. For this we found no evidence whatsoever. The second element is that the idea of a movement tends to realize itself in action. That this is universally true, is not demonstrated. It would, however, offer a satisfactory explanation of certain pathological phenomena if it were true. There is, moreover, strong evidence to show that some ideas have typical movements of *expression*, involuntary and unconscious, and common to a number of subjects.

If, therefore, the ideomotor theory of ideas be limited to the statement that some ideas have characteristic motor expressions, and some and perhaps all ideas of movement have a definite tendency to flow over into action, it may be looked upon as the expression of the facts as now known to psychology. (p. 330)

AUTOMATISMS IN ABNORMAL MENTAL STATES

The foregoing is a brief survey of the part played by the automatism in systematic psychology, at least so far as it concerns the normally functioning individual. It is, however, in connection with abnormal mental states, that the chief interest in automatisms has developed. A survey of contemporary theory with reference to this field leads to a consideration of the phenomena of hysteria, multiple personality, hypnosis, somnambulism, dissociation, and the various abnormal transient states known as "fugues," "episodes," etc.

One of the striking aspects of involuntary motion in abnormal states which is frequently noted, is the fact of dissociation. A movement or group of movements is dissociated from the normal waking consciousness. McDougall (350) in a recent text in abnormal psychology introduces the chapter on "Automatisms" as follows:

When a dissociated system manifests itself in bodily movements during the persistence of waking consciousness and normal control of the rest of the organism, it is usual to speak of the movements as automatisms. (p. 253)

These dissociated movements range all the way from muscle twitches to movements which produce intelligible vocal and written utterances, and McDougall regards them as expressing mental activity, *i.e.*, they are not the expression of purely mechanical activity which is analogous to the normal consciousness. McDougall believes that the automatisms of the waking state, *i.e.*, automatic writing, are of exactly the same kind as those in which the normal personality seems to be asleep, as for example, trance states, somnambulism, hypnosis, etc. In all these states there is a "subsidiary stream of conscious mental activity" which may be described by Prince's term "conscious activity."

Miss Washburn in a discussion of dissociation suggests (525) a series of situations in which associative dispositions fail to be established between simultaneous movement systems. She attempts to answer the question: what are the conditions under which the normal associative tendencies are disrupted? Four situations are suggested as bringing about the dissociation: (1) general disturbance or shock to the organism, (2) disagreeableness of an experience, (3) concentrated attention may be responsible for the dissociation, and (4) the conditions of hypnotic trance. Under (1) is included the forgetfulness for movements which take place just preceding a strong emotional shock. In (2) she refers to the dissociation which occurs in connection with unpleasant experiences—the "complex" of Freudian psychology. In (3) we have the phenomena of automatic writing. In regard to the hypnotic state, Miss Washburn expresses the opinion that in certain individuals there exists some peculiarity of cortical organization which predisposes them to dissociation as exhibited not only in hypnosis, but in other types of dissociation.

Jastrow (255) finds two "functional modes" of accomplishing dissociation: (1) conscious direction is displaced, and (2) part of the muscular apparatus ordinarily under conscious direction is "wrenched away" and placed under subconscious control. Hypnotism is an example of the first, and automatic writing of the second.

Another feature of automatic motor performance in dissociated states is their purposiveness and close resemblance to the movements in the normal state. The consideration of the history of reflex action in the 19th century indicates that the "purposiveness" of the reflexes of the spinal animal was the subject of a protracted debate. That discussion centered around the problem of whether or not the movements of the spinal animal, *e.g.*, in withdrawing the leg from noxious stimuli, gave evidence of the existence of a guiding intelligence, or conscious sensation. A similar problem has existed in connection with the motor automatisms appearing in dissociated states. Are these movements "mechanical reflexes" in the physiological sense? Janet (252) wrote, in this connection:

> The first characteristic to be noted in all these actions is that they are not simple, mechanical reflexes; they are *intelligent acts*, which can be understood only if we admit, as present in the mind of the subject, sensations, remembrances, and even more complicated reflections. The simple cataleptic attitudes of the anesthetic arm depended, as we have demonstrated, on the existence and persistence of certain very delicate muscular sensations; the adaptation of movements, however, to the nature of an object put into the hand, the obedience to verbal suggestions, cannot be understood if there are no tactile or auditive sensations. (p. 254)

This is, of course, a restatement of his position in the earlier classical work *L'automatisme Psychologique* (251).

Prince (415) is of the same opinion in regard to these phenomena, pointing out that the evidence for the existence of a "coconscious" is as valid as the evidence for the existence of consciousness in any other individual but one's self.

Bernheim (40) points out that the phenomena of somnambulism, dreams, hypnosis, etc., always occur in a state of partial consciousness. Automatisms "sont ceux qui se realisent par un mecanisme organique, sans que l'action cérébrale psychique, volonté et intelligence consciente, intervienne dans cette réalisation." Reflexes, certain habitual acts, ideo-motor phenomena belong to this category. Bernheim raises the question of whether or not the phenomena of somnambulism, hypnosis, suggestion, etc., may be explained by the doctrine of unconscious psychical action. Is it possible, for example, for one to sustain a conversation by unconscious psychical action? In such a situation automatic action plays an important part, but, in the opinion of Bernheim, it does not completely account for the behavior of the individual.

> Pour répondre à une question et parler, il faut entendre la question, il faut que cette question entendue actionne le psychisme et soit comprise, il faut que ce psychisme actionne évoque l'idée de la response, il faut que cette idée évoque les images acoustiques corrélatives, c'est-à-dire se traduise en parole intérieure, il faut que cette parole intérieure soit transmise par la volonté au centre bulbaire qui la réalise. Sans doute dans ces opérations complexes, comme dans toutes les opérations psychiques, nous l'avons vu, l'automatisme intervient pour une part. Mais que tout ce mécanisme se fasse machinalement par le seul automatisme intelligent des centres corticaux sensoriels et moteurs associés en polygone, sans collaboration de la conscience et de la volonté, même quand il y a élaboration d'idées, c'est ce que je ne puis admettre, ni comprendre. (p. 20)

In the opinion of Bernheim, the organism is so constructed that certain types of movement can take place independently of conscious control—

these are automatisms—between these activities and those of the completely conscious organism exist a series of transitions rather than sharply separated categories of action.

Baudin (20), in a recent textbook, has divided the automatic phenomena into normal and abnormal, classifying under the former heading motor phenomena of reverie, ideo-motor action, impulsive action, motor phenomena during distraction of attention, habit, etc. Under abnormal automatisms, he includes motor phenomena of somnambulism, hypnosis, epilepsy, and hysteria.

SUMMARY

It appears that, historically considered, the conceptions of automatic action developed from those of reflex action. The division of all animal movements into two categories—voluntary and reflex or involuntary—was an heritage from the Cartesian dualism. That it was not an adequate division, seems to have been vaguely recognized by the end of the 18th century, but it was not until the latter part of the 19th century that any attempt was made to formulate systematically the problems which were revealed as a result of the more careful analyses of the adjustmental responses of the animal. The vast amount of experimentation and speculation which resulted from the Pflüger-Lotze controversy contributed not a little to the understanding of these responses.

The phenomena of motor automatisms, automatic action, impulsive action, etc., include a wide range of responses. In view of their importance, there is a stimulus for speculation as to the reasons for the strikingly small amount of attention given them in current treatises on animal behavior. In the field of normal psychology they appear in connection with attention, habit formation and ideo-motor activity. In the field of abnormal psychology these phenomena appear, in one form or another, in practically every type of atypical state or function. They are involved, for example, in such problems as the nature of the so-called subconscious, hypnotism and multiple personality. There seems to be an essential identity between automatisms as found in normal life, *i.e.*, automatized habits, or unconscious, non-reflex adjustments, and the responses observed in the various abnormal states.

Motor automatisms bear an important relationship to the theory of reflex action. Historically this is evidenced by the early concern with "cerebral reflexes," "psychical reflexes" and the particularly useful conception of the "deflex" as developed by Zeihen. The common characteristics of involuntariness, lack of cortical control,[6] and low degree of conscious accompaniments seem to be more than mere surface resemblances. Our understanding of these relationships is still uncertain and awaits intensive investigation at the hands of experimental psychology. Our lack of knowledge in this field illustrates that the classification of behavior in categories, the limits of which are rigidly fixed, together with the adoption of a specific terminology, frequently serves to check scientific advance, unless the categories are regarded merely as temporary and convenient devices for purposes of scientific discussion. The terms "reflex," "involuntary," "voluntary" and "automatic" are more than classificatory designations; they have come to carry a burden of implications, philosophical, physiological and psychological, as to the nature of nervous function. *It is essential that they be used with caution, and that the hypothetical implications which they have acquired during the 17th and 18th centuries be regarded as provisional only.*

[6] The results of Lashley's experiments (288), of course, do not support this assumption.

CHAPTER XV

THE TENDON REFLEXES

"In general, then it may be said that the knee-jerk is increased and diminished by whatever increases and diminishes the activity of the central nervous system as a whole, and that it is even more noticeably altered by temporary changes in the activity of certain mechanisms of the spinal cord and brain."—WARREN PLYMPTON LOMBARD, *The Variations of the Normal Knee-jerk and their Relations to the Activity of the Central Nervous System*, 1888.

One of the most striking manifestations of the widespread scientific interest in the functions and processes of the nervous system which characterized experimental physiology in the 19th century, was the intensive experimental work which resulted in the demonstration in rapid succession of a multiplicity of reflex responses. The reflexes associated with the functioning of the non-acoustic labyrinth, the skin reflexes, the coordinating reflexes of the eye-muscles, the psycho-galvanic reflexes, to name only a few, were established as functional entities.

Perhaps no other reflex presents so variegated a history as does the knee-jerk.[1] Because of the ease with which it may be elicited, the objective definiteness of the response, the relative simplicity of the neural mechanisms involved, and its usefulness to clinical neurology, it has been almost a constant object of clinical and experimental investigation since its discovery in 1875. The extent of these investigations is indicated by the comprehensive monograph of Sternberg (468), published in 1893, in which over 500 titles are listed. The history of these investigations and those of the succeeding twenty-five years is of especial interest to students of neuro-muscular phenomena, since it parallels and illustrates certain major technical developments in the study of these phenomena, and offers data pertinent to their fundamental problems. These developments are concerned especially with methods of registration of muscular response, particularly as they relate to the technique of the study of reflex temporal relationships, and to the problems of inhibition and facilitation. The investigations which

---

[1] In general, the purpose of the present chapter is to discuss only those phases in the history of the study of this reflex which seem to be of particular interest to physiological psychology. The knee-jerk is, of course, only one example of the so-called tendon reflexes. As Hoffmann (234, p. 3) has pointed out, the term 'tendon' reflex is a misnomer since the tendon is not essential to the response.

are of particular significance to the history of physiological psychology are those which study the reflex as a functional part of the intact nervous system, and not as an artificially isolated and simplified unit. It is primarily from this point of view that the historical survey of the knee-jerk will be undertaken.

Wilhelm Heinrich Erb (1840–1921) and Carl Friedrich Otto Westphal (1833–1890) independently described, in 1875, the phenomena which occur when the patellar tendon is stimulated. In Erb's paper (127) the phenomenon is referred to as the *Patellarsehnenreflex*, while in the paper of Westphal (535) it is designated as the *Unterschenkelphänomen*. The original observations of Erb and Westphal were made in connection with clinical work. The growing clinical interest in specific reflex performances and the comparative ease with which the phenomenon may be elicited, resulted in a literature which by the end of the 19th century had run into hundreds of titles.[2] Grainger (182) and Gowers (179, 180) appear to have been among the first of the English neurologists, and Charcot (86) and his students among the first French neurologists to investigate the phenomenon. In addition to the designations of Erb and Westphal, the following are some of the terms used in referring to this reflex: "tendon phenomena," "tendon reflex," "knee reflex," "knee-jerk," "tendon jerk," "patellar reflex," and "knee phenomenon."

A division of opinion regarding the essential nature of the tendon phenomena appeared in the original papers of Erb and Westphal. The former regarded the muscular contraction in response to the stroke on the patellar tendon as a "true" reflex. In opposition to this Westphal regarded the response as being the direct mechanical twitch of the muscle to the stroke on its tendon. He believed, however, that a state of tonus in the muscle is a necessary condition of the response.

Schultze and Furbringer (435), Senator (437), Tschirjew (488) and others almost immediately demonstrated that the tendon phenomenon was dependent on a reflex spinal arc. Schultz and Furbringer abolished the knee-jerk by cutting the n. cruralis in rabbits, while Tschirjew and Senator extinguished the jerk by cutting the spinal cord between the fifth and sixth lumbar vertebrae. These results tended to support the "reflex" theory of Erb, although they did not eliminate tonus as an explanation.

Erb's theory as to the reflex nature of the knee-jerk was supported by Burckhardt (68), Buzzard (72, 74), and Prevost (413). Opposing this group were Eulenburg (129), Ziehen (550), de Watteville (528), Beevor (27), Ferrier (145), Horsley (239), and Waller (513).

---

[2] *Cf.* Sternberg (468), Netter (383), Zeizing (548), and others.

It was urged against the reflex theory (1) that the time of the knee-jerk (*i.e.*, the time between the stroke on the tendon and the beginning of the muscular contraction) was too brief to allow for conduction to and from the spinal cord, (2) that the knee-jerk did not show the characteristic of "purposiveness" as did reflexes, (3) that the knee-jerk was not inhibited, but only affected through the action of antagonists, and (4) the knee-jerk was not affected by narcotic agencies.

EXPERIMENTAL TECHNIQUES IN THE STUDY OF TENDON PHENOMENA

The experimental techniques in connection with the study of the tendon responses have undergone an interesting metamorphosis. The method of Erb and Westphal—and the method used today in the neurological clinic—was simple; the subject was required either to sit with the leg swinging freely, or with the legs crossed, and the operator struck the patellar tendon a smart blow either with the side of the hand or with a percussion hammer. The height and rapidity of the resulting upward kick of the leg was noted by the operator. In the experimental studies instrumental aids became necessary in recording the contraction, and in standardizing the stimulus to be applied to the tendon.

Perhaps the first systematic analysis of the technique for eliciting and recording the knee-jerk was that of Dodge (106). In recording the knee-jerk, three indicators—to use the phrase of Dodge—may be listed in the order of their historical development: (1) thickening of the muscles in the stimulated leg, (2) movement of the leg directly recorded, and (3) registration of the action current in the muscles by the galvanometric technique. Brissaud (62) in 1880, ter Meulen (352) in 1882, Jarisch and Schiff (253) in 1882, and others used the registration of the thickening of the muscle as the indicator of the response. Bowditch and Warren (57), Lombard (309) and others recorded directly the movement of the leg. Among the first to make use of registration of the action current in the stimulated muscle by means of the galvanometric technique in the study of the knee-jerk was Dodge (106). Jolly and Snyder in 1910, Hoffman, and Golla and Hetwer in 1922 are among those who have used the string galvanometer. By action current is meant the electrical response which appears in excitable tissue (muscle and nerve) when a propagated disturbance passes over it. Its registration by means of the string galvanometer has made possible the exact determination of the time relationships in muscle and nerve.[3] The

---

[3] *Cf.* Fulton (161), p. 56 *ff.*

invention in 1922 by Erlanger and Gasser (128) of the cathode ray oscillograph, which is an inertialess recording mechanism, has made possible the observation of action currents in an undistorted form.

The direct registration of the movement of the leg may be accomplished by a system of levers and pulleys, which actuate electrical or pneumographic time markers. Dodge, in his monograph, found this method the least satisfactory. It is notable, however, that Bowditch and Warren made use of this technique in a study the results of which are quoted in nearly every modern physiological text. The method of recording the thickening of the muscle has been adopted in many of the recent investigations, *e.g.*, those of Dodge (112), Miles (357), Dodge and Benedict (115), and Schlosberg (434). It is interesting to note, however, that Tuttle (492) in a series of investigations in 1924 recorded the excursion of the leg by means of a lever system. In recording directly the thickening of the muscle, it is possible to obtain a record of the moment of stimulation of the tendon, since the blow of the stimulating instrument causes a slight mechanical twitch in the muscle; this precedes the reflex proper, and is recorded on the kymographic records. This feature is an important advantage of this method.

The registration of the response has for its object the demonstration of one or more of the following aspects of the jerk: (1) the time between the stimulus and the beginning of the contraction—the reflex time, (2) the height of the muscle contraction curve, (3) the duration of the contraction, (4) the form of the contraction, and (5) the steepness of the ascent. The various methods of registration described emphasize one or more of these factors.

It is essential that the form of stimulation be standardized. A percussion hammer is usually used and may either be actuated by a coiled spring or electrically released from above the knee and actuated by gravity. It is probable that the latter method secures the most satisfactory mechanical control.

TEMPORAL RELATIONSHIPS IN THE TENDON PHENOMENA

In 1875, the discussion regarding the reflex nature of the newly discovered tendon phenomenon chiefly centered about the time relationships. It was asserted by those who adhered to the Westphal point of view that the jerk was not a true reflex, *i.e.*, did not involve neural conduction to the spinal cord and back, because the time was too brief to permit such a transit. Foster (155) writing some twenty years after the discovery of Erb and Westphal gave perhaps the best statement of this view.

If the time which elapses between the blow on the tendon and the beginning of the movement be measured this is found to be very short, .02 sec., far shorter than that of any known reflex act; and indeed if the measurement be made between the tap and the very beginning of the contraction of the muscular fibres themselves (as may be done by a special arrangement), the interval is actually less than that which occurs when the contraction is brought about by stimulating the motor nerve at some distance from the muscle. It seems impossible, in view of this fact, to regard the act as a reflex act; and we are led to the conclusion that the contraction is idio-muscular, is brought about by the vibrations started in tendon running up to the muscle and directly stimulating the muscular fibres, and not by nervous impulses making the reflex circuit through the spinal cord. (Pt. III, p. 999)

Foster proceeded to state, however, that the irritability of the muscle and its readiness to respond to direct stimulation was dependent upon the spinal cord, *i.e.*, the muscle was in a state of tonus which was maintained by a nervous arc involving the cord.

Sherrington, however, writing in 1893 on the knee-jerk, reported that it could be inhibited centrally like other spinal reflexes. He said:

It would thus seem clear that the exaggeration of the knee-jerk produced by severance of the branches given from the great sciatic nerve to the hamstring muscles is not due to the fact that the resulting relaxation of those muscles simply leaves the joint mechanically more free to move. The exaggeration would seem due rather to the severance of the nerves in question interrupting a stream of centripetal impulses that passes up from the hamstring muscles and enters the spinal cord by certain afferent roots, and in the cord exerts a depressing or restraining influence on the jerk. . . . . Further, it would seem that at the knee joint excitation of the afferent fibres coming from one set of the antagonistic muscles induces reflex tonic contraction of the opposing set with extreme facility, despite the fact that the opponent muscles are not innervated from the same spinal segments. . . . . Thus the degree of tension in one muscle of an antagonistic couple intimately affects the degree of "tonus" in its opponent, not only mechanically, but also reflexly, through afferent-efferent channels and the spinal cord. (p. 563)

This was strong evidence in favor of the reflex nature of the jerk.

In the period from 1875 until 1895 a number of investigators measured the time of the tendon phenomenon, that is, the time elapsing between a blow on the patellar tendon and the beginning of the muscular contraction. The following table summarizes these findings.[4]

[4] *Cf.* Nagel (382), IV, p. 265, Sternberg *op. cit.*, p. 29 *ff.*, Zeizing *op. cit.*, p. 15 *ff.*, Netter *op. cit.*, p. 8 *ff.*, and Rosenheim (427), p. 184 *ff.*

INVESTIGATOR	YEAR	TIME (IN SIGMA)
Tschirjew	1879	58–61
Gowers	1879	15–90
Brissaud	1880	50
Waller	1880	30–40
James	1880	25
ter Meulen	1882	35–90
Eulenberg	1882	32
De Watteville	1882	20
Rosenheim	1884	31–33
Jendrassik	1894	23

Exner (131) in 1873 had measured the time of the wink reflex in response to an electrical stimulus, obtaining values between 57 and 66 sigma. From these times Exner substracted the conduction time in the nerve and the time of the muscle latency. He thus obtained the "reduced reflex time" of between 47 and 55 sigma.

Although there were great differences in the times obtained by Tschirjew, Gowers and others in measuring the tendon response—due in part, of course, to differences in methods used—it is clear that these times are of an order of magnitude in general much below that obtained by Exner in measuring a "true" reflex. Waller, in discussing the times obtained by himself (513), stated in 1890 that in man any reflex movement of the leg must take "at least" 100 sigma. Exner's are less than this, but Waller says:

Moreover it may be urged that we do know that Exner's reflex, viz. the closure of eyelids consequent upon stimulation of the conjunctiva, which is the nearest approach we know of on man to a pure reflex, is only .05 second. This item does not however seem to me to incline the balance in either direction; it is the shortest known "reflex time," and it is the reaction of a very mobile muscle of small bulk, via very short channels of innervation. Admitting the measurement (and I have verified it) I do not think that it weighs either way; it is longer than the "direct" intervals quoted above, but not sufficiently so to contrast with them; it is probably shorter than a true reflex time of the leg or thigh but not sufficiently short to allow us to admit a rectus femoris reflex time of only .03 second. In sum it cannot be used as evidence in either sense. (pp. 387–8)

Waller believed, then, that the tendon phenomenon was not a true reflex, but that the integrity of the reflex arc was its *sine qua non* condition. Data obtained from experimentation on rabbits confirmed these results. Waller found that the times for the tendon phenomenon in the rabbit were about 8 sigma, while "true" reflex contractions obtained by stimulating the skin of the same animal were found to take place in about 33 sigma.

Accurate timing of reflex phenomena was difficult with the techniques used by these investigators. After pointing out the need of more accurate timing methods Sternberg (468) indicated that positive experimental proof of the nature of the tendon phenomenon was not available, since too much weight was not to be attached to the short latencies.

Es ist daher dem Argumente der zu kurzen Reflexzeit nur ein geringes Gewicht beizu-messen. Man muss sich sagen, dass wir uns eben mit der Thatsache befreunden müssen, dass so einfache Reflexe, wie die Sehnenreflexe, bei denen keine Coordination von Muskeln in bestimmter Reihenfolge nöthig ist, wie das etwa beim Zurückziehen eines Beines der Fall ist, in ganz kurzer Zeit verlaufen können. Auch ist eine so kurze Reflexzeit für den wahrscheinlichen Zweck der Sehnenreflexe erforderlich.

Wiewohl also ein exacter experimenteller Beweis nicht gegeben ist und höchstwahr-scheinlich überhaupt nicht gegeben werden kann, spricht die weitaus grössere Wahr-scheinlichkeit dafür, dass das Muskelphänomen beim sogenannten Sehnenreflexe in gleicher Weise wie das Knochenphänomen als ein Reflexvorgangaufzufassenist. (p. 56)

With the use of the galvanometric technique with photographic record of the thread deflections by Jolly (264, 265) and Snyder (454) in 1910 and 1911, the fact was demonstrated that the time between stimulus and response in the case of the knee-jerk was theoretically long enough to allow for conduction to and from the spinal cord. Dodge had already (106) (1910) demonstrated that the time of the responses of the muscle to direct stimulation was shorter than the times obtained for the knee-jerk by the earlier investigators. He was able to obtain times in the neighborhood of 15 sigma in the case of the extirpated frog's muscle. Jolly in 1911 using the galvanometric technique obtained times in the neighborhood of 6 sigma for the knee-jerk in the spinal cat. In the case of man the same observer found the average of fourteen observations on each of three subjects to be 20.5 sigma, 22.7 sigma, and 20.7 sigma respectively. Snyder found an average time of 11.3 sigma in man. Jolly points out that "it is, therefore, necessary to reconsider the question as to whether the latent period of the knee jerk is long enough to include the various times occupied in reflex action."

These "times" are (1) latency of the afferent endings, (2) time of conduction from the vastus internus and part of the crureus division of the quadriceps to the cord by the anterior crural nerve and back by the same nerve trunk to the muscle, (3) latent period of the electrical change in the muscle, and (4) time occupied at the synapse.

Analyzed on this basis, the total time of the response in the spinal cat yields the following according to Jolly.

Total latency of jerk...		6.6
Latency of afferent ending...................................	0.97	
Nerve conduction..	1.45	
Latency of motor ending.....................................	2.38	
	4.8	4.8
Synapse time..		1.8

It is notable that the times found for man by Jolly were very similar to those offered by Waller as proof that the tendon phenomenon was not a true reflex. It must be confessed, however, that the evidence on the temporal side offered by Jolly and Snyder is scarcely to be regarded as final, since it is based on certain assumptions with regard to the speed of nerve conduction, and motor and sensory latencies which are not yet finally established.

In 1921, Jolly (266) studied the times for homonymous and heteronymous reflexes in the frog, with the view of finding the difference between the two types and thus "to obtain a measure of the delay in transmission of the reflex impulses in the spinal cord, or 'synapse time.' " Spinal and decerebrate animals were used and the time measurements were by means of the Einthoven string galvanometer. The average time for 41 cases of the heteronymous reflex was 15.7 sigma, while the average for 40 cases, homonymous reflex was 14.3 sigma. Regarding the difference Jolly wrore:

I do not think that the above experiments taken by themselves would justify us in assuming that in the spinal frog at the temperature employed, and with the frogs in good condition, the intraspinal path of the heteronymous reflex involves a larger number of synapses than that of the homonymous reflex. . . . . It would rather appear that we are dealing with mechanisms involving the same number of neurones on the two sides. . . . . The fact that the homonymous time is usually slightly the shorter may possibly be due to the motor neurons responding rather more readily to stimuli reaching them through afferent nerves from the same side of the body. (p. 35)

Jolly analyzed the total time as follows:

If we select a reflex time recorded at a room temperature of 23 degrees C. from a frog in good condition, first response, thirty-five days after operation, we find an interval of 11.4 sigma for the total reflex time. The length of nerve from toes to cord and from cord to thigh was found post mortem in this frog to be 16 cm. The rate of conduction in the nerve of Zenopus at 23 degrees C. was determined in the usual manner by electrical stimulation at two points, with the electrical change in the muscle as indicator, and was found to be 37 M. a second. The latency of the muscular response to stimulation close to the muscle was found to be 2.4 sigma. If we allow 1 sigma for the latency of sensory nerve endings we may suggest the following analysis:

Total reflex time.......................................   11.4
Nerve conduction................................... 4.3
Muscle latency....................................... 2.4
Latency of sensory endings........................... 1.0
                                                     ―――   ―――
                                                     7.7   7.7
    Synapse time.......................................   ―――
                                                                  3.7 (p. 37)

The same type of temporal analysis is exemplified in the work of Hoffmann (234) who studied the tendon reflexes—which he terms *Eigenreflexe*—and who characterized these temporal elements as follows:

> L = the conduction time in the nerve (*Leitungszeit*)
> l = the length of the nerve
> N = the rate of conduction (*Leitungsgeschwindigkeit*)
> M = the latency of the muscle
> S = the latency of the end organ
> R = the "true" reflex time

The total reflex time ("Z") then is equal to R + M + L + S. Hoffmann emphasizes the importance of determining the value of N (the rate of conduction). This value varies, *i.e.*, it is dependent upon the *length of nerve*. The relationship is one in which the rate is decreased as the length of the nerve increases. Hoffmann arrives at this conclusion by dividing the length of nerve expressed in centimeters by the total reflex time (l/Z).

Je grösser der Nervenweg ist, der beim Reflex durchlaufen werden muss, um geringer ist die Brutto-geschwindigkeit des Prozesses l/Z. Mit anderen Worten, wenn man von Muskellatenz, Latenz der sensiblen Endorgane, und reiner Reflexzeit ganz absieht, so ist Leitungsgeschwindigkeit um so langsamer, je grösser die Nervenstrecke ist, die durchlaufen werden muss. Dies gilt für alle Möglichkeiten, den Eigenreflex zu messen, mit Ausnahme des Masseterreflexes. Hier ist die Nervenleitung so kurz, dass die Muskellatenz und die reine Reflexzeit schon entscheidend ins Gewicht fallen. (p. 47)

In comparing the gross velocities (l/Z) in five cases with a short reflex arc (170 cm.) with those having a long reflex arc (190 cm.), he finds the velocity in the first to be 56.7 M. per second and in the second 49.3 M. per second. Hoffmann found that the length of the reflex arc (Achilles tendon reflex) increased in direct ratio to the length of the body.

The total time, according to Hoffmann, for any reflex remains relatively constant in the normal individual; in the diseased individual this time is lengthened. The rate of conduction in the case of disease is slower than in the case of health. The following table indicates the values of l/Z for the Achilles tendon reflex in certain diseased conditions.

m. per sec.

In internal disease (*inneren Krankheiten*)..............................50.1
Organic disease of the central nervous system........................51.5
Other neuroses...49.6
Functional nervous diseases...59.9

Hoffmann regards the tendon reflex as occupying a peculiar position in that there is only one synapse involved in the spinal cord. The time occupied in the cord is estimated to be in the neighborhood of one sigma.

The recent investigation by Tuttle, Travis, and Hunter (499) of the time of the knee-jerk and Achilles tendon jerk has shown that the reduced knee-jerk time for eight subjects averaged 19 sigma with a range of 10 to 32 sigma. By "reduced" was meant the time elapsing between the delivery of the stimulus at the patella ligament and the beginning of the electrical change in the muscle. The authors interpret these results as indicating that the jerk is a true reflex.

The later investigators of the time relations of the knee-jerk—Jolly, Snyder, Dodge, Hoffmann, and others—seem to be agreed that so far as time is concerned the knee-jerk may be a true reflex, that is, it is dependent on a neural transit from the muscle to the spinal cord and return. Hoffmann makes the rate of conduction the most important element in the determination of the reflex time. It should be noted that Hoffmann regards the synapse time, and the muscle and sensory latencies as relatively constant for any given reflex.

Waller (513) summarized the evidence bearing on the reflex nature of the tendon phenomenon under seven heads. These are: (1) lost time of the tendon phenomenon as compared with the lost time of direct and of reflex muscular contractions, (2) lost time of tendon the phenomenon in muscles at different distances from the cord, (3) clinical observations, (4) experimental section of nerves and nerve roots, (5) destruction of the spinal cord, (6) muscular tonus, (7) crossed tendon reflexes. The evidence from all of these fields of investigation except (1) and (2) indicate that a reflex arc is essential for the knee-jerk. In the opinion of Waller, the evidence from the measurement of the time relations tended to indicate that the time was too brief for a reflex to take place, and hence the phenomena were not reflex, but were dependent on the reflexly maintained muscular tonus. The data which have been presented indicate that this objection of Waller's has yielded before improved methods of temporal measurement in physiology and psychology.

Dodge (106) presents evidence which tends to further establish the reflex nature of the tendon jerk. This evidence may be summarized: (1) He finds that the course of the wave of contraction proceeds from the central end of the muscle rather than from the distal end as might be expected if the contraction were the result of direct mechanical stimulation. (2) The length of the reflex arc involved increases the total time occupied by the reflex, *e.g.*, the latent time of the knee-jerk is shorter than that of the Achilles tendon by from 11 sigma to 16 sigma. (3) The knee-jerk may only take place as a result of coordination of flexor and extensor muscles; a nerve center is essential to such coordination, and hence a reflex arc is implied.

More recently Hoffmann (234) had discussed the proofs that the tendon response is reflex in nature. He points out that it disappears when the spinal cord is destroyed, it disappears after extirpation of either the anterior or posterior nerve roots, it disappears in deep narcosis or if the motor or sensory nerve endings are paralyzed with novocain, and that the time of the knee-jerk bears a clear relationship to the length of the neural arc.

VARIABILITY IN TENDON REFLEXES

The enormous variability of the tendon reflexes has been a subject of comment for practically every investigator of these phenomena. The result has been a large amount of experimentation which has greatly modified the general theory of reflex action. The possibility that the course of the reflex was modified by simultaneously activated neuro-muscular mechanisms suggested itself as an explanation of the observed variability. The study of inhibition and facilitation had antedated the discovery of the knee-jerk, and it is not surprising that this reflex should have been considered in the light of those investigations.

Jendrassik (1829–1891) in 1885 (259) noted the differences in the percentages of failure to elicit the knee-jerk as reported by the different investigators. Berger (35) had reported 1.56 per cent failure, Eulenburg (129), 4.8 per cent, Bloch (50) .72 per cent, Pelizaeus (402), .04 per cent. Jendrassik suggested that these differences might be due to the techniques used by the investigators, and further suggested that if some other muscle group were thrown into contraction simultaneously with the knee-jerk, the latter would be exaggerated.

Zu diesem Zweck benutzte ich meine Erfahrung, nach welcher die Sehnenreflexe, besonders aber das Kniephänomen sich bedeutend steigern, wenn wir mit den übrigen Muskeln unseres Körpers grosse Kraft erzeugen. So z.B. fällt das Kniephänomen viel starker aus, wenn wir die Muskeln der Arme stark anspannen. Ich setze das betreffende Individuum welches mit der gewöhnlichen Methode kein Kniephänomen hatte, auf den Rand eines Tisches mit möglichst erschlafften Beinen, und während ich auf seine Patellarsehne klopfe, fordere ich es auf, die gebeugten Finger derrechten und linken Hände in einander auszuhängen und sie bei nach vorne ausgestrecken Armen so stark als möglich auseinander zu ziehen.   (p. 413)

The *Jendrassik Handgriff* became a clinical device which was widely used. In 1886, Mitchell and Lewis (361), making a study of the circumstances which increase or decrease the knee-jerk, noted that a reinforcement of the jerk occurred with simultaneous voluntary action, upon painful stimulation of the skin and simultaneous visual stimulation.

In 1887 Lombard (311) studied the variability of the normal knee-jerk. He studied the effects of fatigue, hunger, music, voluntary movement, etc., on the extent of the jerk.   He summarized his conclusions as follows:

> The causes of these variations of the knee-jerk are not only alterations in the muscles and nerves involved in the process, but, to a still greater degree, changes in the activity of the central nervous system, either as a whole or in part.   Thus fatigue, hunger, enervating weather, and sleep, conditions which decrease the activity of the whole central nervous system, decrease the average knee-jerk, while rest, nourishment, invigorating weather, and wakefulness, influences which increase the activity of the central nervous system, increase the average knee-jerk. . . . . Thus voluntary movements and strong emotions, when synchronous with the blow, are found to increase the movement, and this is noticed even during sleep when the dreams are vivid.   Similarly, sensory irritations, even when not strong enough to produce visible reflex actions, markedly reinforce the knee-jerk, but whether on account of their effect upon the brain, or upon the spinal cord, must be proved by future experiments.   (p. 68)

THE INVESTIGATION OF BOWDITCH AND WARREN

The experiments of Bowditch and Warren (57) published in 1890 mark the most ambitious attack on the problem of facilitation and inhibition of the knee-jerk undertaken up to that time.   The present importance of this investigation is evidenced by the fact that the conclusions are quoted as definitive by most of the modern workers in this field.   They are represented in such texts as those of Howell (241), Luciani (320), Ladd and Woodworth (277), Schäfer (432) and Sherrington (441).   The universal acceptance of the Bowditch and Warren results as well as their theoretical importance warrants a re-examination of the data and conclusions.

Mitchell and Lewis (361) had noted that "the muscular action or circuit closing, must precede the tap (on the knee), in order to reinforce it, by a period which is, as yet, undetermined."   This suggested to Bowditch and Warren the importance of making a study of the effect of varying the interval between the reinforcing act or stimulus and the stimulation of the patellar tendon.   The reinforcing act consisted not only of a voluntary muscular contraction, but also of sensory stimulation,—visual, auditory, and cutaneous. The muscular reinforcing act consisted of a voluntary clenching of the hand in response to a bell stimulus. In the case of vision, the reinforcing stimulus was a flash of light caused by the sudden opening and closing of a stop-cock in a gas pipe supplying a burner in a lantern; the auditory stimulus was produced by dropping a large paper torpedo "near the head of the individual experimented on;" and the cutaneous stimulus consisted of blasts of air directed on the conjunctiva, the mucous membrane of the nose, and the skin of the neck.

The subject was placed on his side, and the patellar stimulus hammer attached to the leg. The movement of the leg during the kick was recorded on a smoked surface by means of a system of levers attached to the foot. The apparatus was so arranged that the experimenter was able to control electrically the time between the reinforcing stimulus and the tap on the tendon. The reinforcing stimulus *always* preceded the tap.

The time sequence may be represented schematically by the following figure.

```
: ----------------r---------------:           :           :
:                                 :           :           :
Bell                         Hand            P          K
:                                 :           :           :
_____
:                                             :           :
:                                             :           :
: ---------------------------i-----------------------------:
```

The series in which a voluntary muscular contraction was the reinforcing stimulus contributed the major part of the data. In this series the subject was instructed to clench the right hand on a piece of wood in response to a tap of a bell. The experimenter, by means of the apparatus, controlled the time elapsing between the bell and the tap on the knee (P); this time was designated as i. The subject reacted to the sound of the bell by clenching the hand; this was a voluntary reaction time designated as r. The object of the experiment, then, was to determine the effect on the extent (amplitude) of the knee-jerk by varying the interval i. Each series of experiments lasted about an hour during which varying intervals of i were used interspersed by experiments in which there was no reinforcing act. These were called "normal" and the differences between the extent of the knee jerks in the normal and reinforced series gave a measure of the reinforcing effect.

Tabulation of these differences according to the value of the interval i showed "clearly that if the blow (on the knee) follows the signal (bell) at an interval not greater than 0.4 second the reinforcing act increases the extent of the knee-jerk. If the interval exceeds this amount a diminution of the knee-jerk results." If the interval i was prolonged to 1.7 seconds the reinforcing act was without effect. From this the authors concluded:

. . . . when by a brief act of volition the muscles of the forearm are innervated, the spinal cord is thrown into such a condition, that that portion of it which is concerned in the production of the knee-jerk is for a short time in a state of exalted activity, which is succeeded by a period of depression and then by a slow return to the normal state. (p. 38)

The authors state that the value r is "always subject to considerable variation" and proceed to study the data when they are tabulated on the basis of $i - r$, i.e., the interval of time between the *beginning* of the muscular reinforcing act and the blow on the knee.

The authors note that the value of $i - r$ may be a minus quantity "in certain cases," i.e., that the blow on the knee fell *before* the subject had reacted to the bell stimulus. "In certain cases" seems a scarcely adequate characterization since this situation is found in nearly half of the observations. The time sequence in these cases may be represented schematically as follows:

Inspection of the published data indicates that the tap on the knee, 'P,' may take place, in the cases where "the individual failed to react promptly to the signal," as much as 160 sigma before the clenching of the hand; since the time of the knee-jerk, 'P – K,' as measured by this technique cannot have been more than 70 sigma, it is clear that the knee-jerk was frequently completed *before the act which the experimenters had intended to reinforce it.* In these cases the greatest amount of facilitation, as indicated by the extent of the knee-jerk, occurs.

The assumption of the investigators seems to have been that the occurrence of a voluntary act in response to an auditory stimulus adequately controlled all the factors which might affect the amplitude of the co-incident knee-jerk. They found that in certain cases the subject failed to react promptly to the bell signal; in such cases the greatest degree of facilitation occurred. In other words, unusually long reaction times resulted in facilitated knee-jerks. That some other factor was present than the auxiliary muscular or other reinforcing act, seems probable. The process of attention suggests itself; in any case the attentional state of the subject does not seem to have been under adequate experimental control.

However, our lack of exact knowledge of the specific effects of attention in connection with co-incident, neuro-muscular processes does not warrant interpretation of the Bowditch and Warren results in terms of attentional effects. Since the experiments of Bowditch and Warren are in a field which may be expected to yield much that is of major importance to both physiology and psychology, and since their conclusions are widely quoted in contemporary texts, it may be pertinent to suggest the following critical generalizations regarding their investigation.[5]

(1) The assumption was made that the presence of a voluntary muscular action at some point in the experimental sequence sufficiently controlled the factor of "simultaneous activity of the other portions of the nervous system." In the experiments reported the auxiliary muscular reaction took the form of a voluntary response to an auditory stimulus; this reaction was repeated many times and, doubtless, became highly automatized, a condition which is not conducive to controlled attention. That is, opportunity would seem to have been offered under these conditions for the subject to "give" attention to the knee-jerk, and this, conceivably, would modify the amplitude of the jerk.

(2) The events which occurred between the bell signal and the muscular response are of great importance, since analysis of the data indicate that it was *during this time that a large proportion of the knee-jerks occurred.* The knee-jerk was "always augmented" when it occurred before the voluntary reaction by which it was supposed to be reinforced. The assumption seems warranted that the augmentation was not due to the "reinforcing" muscular act, but to some factor appearing before that act, *e.g.,* the accompaniments of the attention process.[6]

Sternberg (468) pointed out in 1893 that simultaneous voluntary muscular action exaggerates the knee-jerk since it serves to direct the attention of the subject away from the knee; when the attention is directed towards the knee there is a tendency towards voluntary contraction of the same

[5] A more extended critique may be found in the paper by Fearing (140). *Cf.,* also Bowditch's paper of 1888 (56).

[6] The attention process, whether defined in terms of behavioristic psychology as a form of sensory adjustment which increases the effectiveness of stimulating conditions, or in terms of structural psychology as an increase in sensory clearness, may be expected to bring about nervous and muscular changes which would modify a co-incident reflex, *e.g.,* the knee-jerk.

muscle which is involved in the reflex. This, according to Sternberg, inhibits the reflex contraction.

Twitmyer (500) in 1902 noted the influence of extraneous and, comparatively speaking, uncontrolled factors on the extent of the knee-jerk. His comments are as follows:

When the patella tendons are struck at exactly the same place with blows of constant force and at regular intervals, no two of the resulting knee-jerks are of the same extent. This variation is usually referred to some accidental stimulus acting upon the subjects, e.g., a loud or distracting sound or to an idea to which the subject directs his attention, an emotional state of greater or less intensity, any one of which conditions may produce a variation in the extent of the jerk, or in a general way to a change in the activity of the central nervous system. From the very nature of the case such sources of variation are not wholly avoidable. However secure the subject may be kept from accidental sensory stimuli, the stream of consciousness is never altogether within control of the experimenter and the organic processes of digestion, circulation, etc., are constantly producing some slight or more profound modification in the equilibrium of the nervous system. (pp. 8–9)

Twitmyer's paper is of especial significance to the history of the knee-jerk since it was one of the earliest attempts to study the variability of the "unaugmented or normal knee-jerk" in human subjects. Twitmyer found a wide range of individual differences in the amplitude of the kick (0–165 mm.). He noted that subsequent to the kick there are swings of the leg which are not to be ascribed to the pendular swings of the leg coming to rest. These after-kicks frequently exceed the knee-jerk itself in amplitude and tend to increase in extent as the knee-jerks are repeated. Twitmyer suggested the following hypothesis which is significant as a contribution to the theories of knee-jerk variability.

Let us assume that the repeated transmission of reflex excitation along a reflex arc, including the spinal segment, an afferent and efferent conduction path or from a given segment in the cord to a segment somewhat removed, develops a pathway offering increasingly less resistance. . . . . . A blow of constant force on the tendons will then result in a more and more intense stimulation of both the quadriceps and its antagonist. This increase will be relatively constant, consequently the extent of the initial kick is still checked by the simultaneous stimulation of the hamstring muscles. The actual extent of the kick, however, tends to increase somewhat with the continuation of experimentation. With the increased intensity of the reflex influence, the flexors are thrown into more violent contraction, which contraction now becomes an adequate stimulus to the sensory fibers terminating in the flexors and as a result there is a vigorous excitation to the cord and ultimately to the quadriceps. This excitation therefore contributes its quota to the second outward excursion of the leg and frequently is sufficiently vigorous to produce a kick larger than the initial kick. This view is fully corroborated by Sherrington's experiment in which he succeeded in greatly augmenting the extent of the knee-jerk by merely compressing the hamstring muscle when it is completely dissected away from its attachments, while the nerves were still intact. (p. 24)

Twitmyer's study is especially interesting since it contains one of the first recorded observations on the phenomenon later included under the term "conditioning." He found that there appeared a decided kick of both legs following "a tap of the signal bell occurring without the usual blow of the hammer on the tendons."

Hoffmann (234) in his monograph on the *Eigenreflexe* objected to the conclusion of Sternberg that voluntary contraction of a muscle precludes its simultaneous reflex contraction, *i.e.*, inhibits the reflex. Using the galvanometric technique and registering the action currents in the muscle, Hoffmann showed that a simultaneous voluntary contraction of the extensors (*Agonisten*) facilitates the reflex, while a simultaneous contraction of the flexors (*Antagonisten*) inhibits the reflex. Hoffmann pointed out that there are many points of similarity between voluntary contraction of a muscle and the contraction due to stimulation of the tendon (Hoffmann's *Eigenreflexe*). He suggests that tonus may also be related to voluntary contraction.

RECENT EXPERIMENTS USING THE BOWDITCH AND WARREN TECHNIQUE

Tuttle in a paper in 1924 (495) presents the results of a study of the effects of mental activity on the knee-jerk. The technique[7] was in many respects similar to that used in the Bowditch and Warren study. A gravity hammer was used and the apparatus was so arranged that successive blows were automatically delivered at the tendon. The height of the kick was recorded on a kymograph drum, and served as a measure of the reflex movement.

In view of the paucity of quantitative data on this subject it was decided to measure the knee-jerk under active and passive conditions of highly socialized forms of peripheral stimulation. We did not feel free to hazard a definition of what psychologists have generally agreed to included under the term 'attention' or 'mental activity' but preferred to assign to the subject a problem which we felt reasonably sure would release the type of response which most psychologists would agree required 'attention' or was performed under 'attentive attitudes'. The terms *passive* and *active* which we have chosen in place of *non-attentive* and *attentive* are not meant to carry theoretical implications as to their psychological character beyond those which the reader himself wishes to interpret from the nature of the problems that were assigned to the subjects. (p. 401)

The general method of attack was to obtain records of tendon responses to uniform blows administered at a regular rate while the subject was in a passive condition as regards attention, alternated with periods of mental work. The mental work consisted of mental arithmetic (addition, extract-

---

[7] The apparatus is described by Tuttle in a separate paper (492).

ing of square root, etc.), conversation, mental tests, and in the case of one subject, consideration of a problem in electrical wiring. The average amplitudes measured in millimeters of the passive and active periods were compared. The conclusions of the investigator may be stated in his own words.

The records from all subjects studied show that mental activity as defined in this paper increases muscle tonus as exhibited by the knee-jerk. . . . .

If mental activity of the problem type as used in this experiment involves the psychological factors of attention, then the conclusion seems justified that muscle tonus as measured by the knee-jerk is either (a) one of the factors in the attentive process, (b) a function of the attentive process or (c) the process of attention itself. (pp. 418–9)

Tuttle and Burtt (71) using Tuttle's technique for eliciting and recording the knee-jerk, studied the effect of emotional conditions on this reflex. Pleasant, unpleasant, and affectively indifferent words were visually presented to the subject who was required to react by giving an associated word, in an effort to determine the effect on the amplitude of the knee-jerk of the various types of words presented. The conclusions of the investigators were stated as follows:

There is a depression of the reflex on the average for unpleasant stimulus words amounting to 16 per cent. There are slight and less consistent indications of a similar depression for pleasant stimulus words. All the unpleasant categories used were effective in some instances in producing depression.

. . . . The correlations between the extent of a reflex and the association reaction time for the stimulus word presented in connection with it are small, but all those that are of possible statistical significance are negative. This result suggests that the depression of the reflex and the slowing of the association time involve the same aspect of the stimuli, presumably the affective tone. (p. 561)

In these experiments the subject had reacted in every case *before* the knee was stimulated. The assumption was, presumably, that the subject's attention during the interval between the vocal response and the tap on the knee, was occupied with the word or with his response. However, there was no guarantee that this assumption was justified. In any event this period was critical so far as the knee-jerk is concerned. In spite of these objections these experiments present significant results. The conclusion cannot be avoided that mental processes, or the neuro-muscular accompaniment of such processes included under the term "attention" significantly modify the knee-jerk.

The extent to which these co-incident processes are taken into account or controlled, is not always clear from the descriptions of the experimental investigations. So far as the existence of the fundamental fact of variability is concerned, however, all investigators are agreed. In certain of the recent investigations of the time of the knee-jerk, the amount of variability of the measures has received the attention of the experimenters. Tuttle, Travis, and Hunter, for example, in their recent study of the time of the knee-jerk and Achilles-tendon reflexes (499) found, for the former, a range of times from ten to thirty-two sigma in eight subjects. For the Achilles-tendon reflex the range was from twenty-five to thirty-eight sigma. Rounds (428) in 1928 studied the time of the Achilles-tendon reflex and found a range of from thirty-two to ninety-seven sigma in eighty subjects.

Tuttle, Travis and Hunter suggested in the above-mentioned paper, as an explanation of this variability, that the knee-jerk and Achilles-tendon jerk involve "a spinal reflex arc but may include a pathway much more complex, which would furnish an adequate basis for the variations in range." From this point of view the variability in the speed of the reflex is but an expression of the individual differences in a fundamental neural capacity, viz., rate of conduction of the nervous impulse. Some support is given this hypothesis by the findings of Travis and Hunter (486) in another investigation in which the coefficients of correlation were obtained between the knee-jerk times and various "tests" of intelligence. In a group of forty-four subjects the correlations were positive and uniformly high, ranging from .71 to .87. The authors conclude that "the rate of transmission of the nerve impulse was thought to be important in intelligent responses because the more of the nervous system (especially in the higher centers) that is active within a given interval of time the more likely is there to be an adequate response to a complex situation."

In the study, similar in some respects to the foregoing, made by Rounds (428), the coefficients of correlation between the Achilles-tendon reflex and various measures of speed in mental reactions are relatively high, ranging from .28 to .51.

These results are of interest, but, in view of the uncertainty as to what the "intelligence" tests measure, careful verification will be necessary before certain conclusions may be drawn regarding the nature of the "higher" neural or psychical process involved in the knee-jerk.

In his extensive study of the conditions of human variability, Dodge (114) made use of the knee-jerk. It was his purpose to study "quantitatively the changes that occur in human reactions at different levels of the nervous system in response to the repetition of identical stimuli." The knee-jerk, lid reflex and rotation nystagmus represented the neuro-muscular processes at the reflex level. Dodge concludes that the "most nearly general and probably the most important of the conditions of human variability . . . . is the refractory phase." He continues:

The data justify us in regarding refractory phase as an important and probably universal condition of human variability. It limits the frequency of responses when the repetition of stimuli is more rapid than a certain critical interval. It probably operates to modify the pattern of response to repeated stimuli in humans as well as in animals. It facilitates the consolidation of isolated conscious events into series. One may reasonably expect that those factors will eventually dominate the consciousness of recurrent events which have, or come to have, relatively low refractory phases. (p. 104)

A consideration of these problems leads, of course, to the larger problem of inhibition as it involves all neuro-muscular performances. In the previous discussion of inhibition[8] the major theories have been reviewed. The knee-jerk has been a favorite reflex in the experimental investigations of these various theories. The refractory phase as an aspect of inhibition has been demonstrated in the knee-jerk by Dodge (106). This investigator, also, used the knee-jerk in testing the "drainage" hypothesis of McDougall. McDougall's hypothesis as stated (346) in 1903, assumed that "inhibition of the excitation of one neural system is always the result of the excitement of some other system, that inhibition appears always as the negative or complementary result of a process of increased excitation in some other part." Dodge states (112) the question to which the experiment, designed to test this hypothesis, should give a specific answer:

Is it or is it not a fact that decrement of a reflex regularly occurs as a correlate of increased spread of neural excitation? Is it or is it not a fact that spread of excitation so as to involve the cortex or the initiation of a cortical reaction actually inhibits a related reflex?. . . . If the inhibition of a reflex by drainage actually follows the spread of excitation in the cortex, then it ought to be possible to inhibit a reflex by voluntary reaction to the same stimulus that normally excites it. (p. 118)

Assuming that the knee-jerks which were accompanied by a simultaneous voluntary reaction would be consistently diminished in extent if the "drainage" theory held, Dodge caused his subject to respond by a voluntary finger movement to the same stimulus which released the knee-jerk. In no case was there any noticeable effect on the jerk. That is to say, the results were negative for the "drainage" theory insofar as Dodge's experiment presented a situation for adequately testing that hypothesis. That there is a certain degree of similarity between this type of experimentation and that of Bowditch and Warren (57) is evident. In the discussion of

[8] *Vide supra* Chapter XII.

the latter experiments certain objections were indicated, objections which make it appear that the "drainage" hypothesis has not yet been wholly annihilated.[9] In any case additional experimentation is undoubtedly necessary to further test the implication of this hypothesis insofar as it applies to responses of the intact organism. The paper of Wiersma (540) is pertinent in this connection. This author has pointed out that simultaneously fluctuating systems, e.g., the postural reflexes, may be expected to modify the knee-jerk; that is, those conditions which inhibit the postural reflexes facilitate the knee-jerk.

Golla and Hetwer (173) are among the contemporary investigators who have noted the variability in the magnitude of the knee-jerk. They believe that the greatest factor contributing to this variability in the intact human nervous system, is cortical activity. This may be rendered negligible by taking "suitable precautions" during the experimental procedures. If the process of attention may be included under the term "cortical activities," the experimental control of this process would seem to be essential in all knee-jerk experimentation. These investigators in another study (174) have compared the time relations in reflex and voluntary responses by the use of the galvanometric technique. The results are stated as follows:

> The time relations of the co-ordination of various muscles in certain voluntary move ments is the same as when a similar movement is elicited as a spinal reflex response. Electromyograms of the patellar and the Achilles reflexes were obtained, recording the contraction of the antagonistic muscles concerned. It was found that in the patellar reflex the contraction of the flexor muscles of the knee follows that of the quadriceps extensor at an interval of 7 to 10 sigma. If a voluntary kick in imitation of a knee-jerk be made, it will be seen that the flexor contraction follows the extensor in 10 sigma, that is in about the same time. (p. 66)

In this connection it is worthwhile to note the suggestion of Fulton (161) that voluntary activity is little more than a "release" phenomenon; "that is, myotatic reflexes are constantly being set up, especially in antigravity muscles, and voluntary activity is conditioned by the degree of cerebral inhibition, which determines how great shall be the response to any given myotatic stimulus."[10]

Other factors which have a modifying influence on the knee-jerk have been investigated, e.g., sleep, alcohol, drugs, temperature, etc. Using the

---

[9] Vide Fearing's article op. cit., and supra Chapter XII, p. 204 ff.

[10] Cf. Fulton, p. 489 ff. and Chapter XXI. Cf. also the paper of Travis, Tuttle, and Hunter (499) on the nature of the action currents in the quadriceps during the knee-jerk as compared with those obtained during a voluntary jerk.

Tuttle technique (492), Emery (126) studied the effect of temperature on muscle tonus as indicated by the knee-jerk. It was found that a decrease in the temperature was accompanied by an increase in tonus, that is, an increase in the amplitude of the knee-jerk.

The knee-jerk, on the other hand, was found by Tuttle (496) to be depressed or absent during sleep. This confirms the results of Rosenbach (426), Bowditch and Warren (57) and Lombard (311) in the previous century, and Lee and Kleitman (296) in 1923.

Alcohol also seems to act as a depressant. Dodge and Benedict (115), Miles (357) and Tuttle (494) have studied the effects of the ingestion of alcohol on the knee-jerk. Dodge reported that the alcohol tends regularly to depress the patellar reflex, that is, "it lengthens the latent time in five out of six of the subjects by an average of 9.6 per cent and decreases the height of the contraction by an average of 48.9 per cent." Miles in the 1924 monograph on the effects of alcohol found:

(1) The amplitudes of the patellar reflex vary widely for different subjects . . . . any consideration of the alcoholic effect must take this into account. (2) The ingestion of a liter of liquid at 18 to 19 degrees C. is accompanied by a large increase in the amplitude of the patellar reflex. This increase is less when the liquid contains alcohol. (3) Following alcohol the amplitude of the patellar reflex decreases to a level considerably below that shown following the control mixture and below that exhibited in the preliminary for the day. Thus the alcohol effect is pronounced, amounting at its maximum . . . . to 38 per cent. (p. 238)

Tuttle finds that alcohol may have either an excitatory or depressant effect on the knee-jerk. Twelve cases were investigated, nine of which showed augmentation and two depression of the knee-jerk. One case showed no effect. The two subjects who showed depressant effects were accustomed to drink alcohol daily.

It is impossible to state to what extent the variation in the results reported by these investigators may have been due to differences in technique. The experiments of Miles were carefully controlled and involved the Dodge technique of direct registration of the thickening of the quadriceps muscle. Tuttle made use of the height of the kick as a measure of the reflex and does not seem to have introduced experimental controls. The factor of attention enters into the experimental situation here, as it must in any experimental attack on tendon reflex problems. To what extent it was controlled in these experiments is uncertain.

Although the results do not bear directly on the problems which are discussed in the foregoing paragraphs, the recent papers of Sherrington and Liddell (450, 451) mark an important advance in knee-jerk research. These investigations, which have been referred to in greater detail in Chapter XIII, have shown that a gradual stretch applied to a muscle (especially the anti-gravity muscles) evokes a contraction. The knee-jerk and the patellar clonus are regarded as "fractional examples of the more comprehensive stretch reflex." A stretch of less than 1/20 mm., lasting less than 1/20 second is sufficient to produce the response. The term "myotatic" is applied to these reflexes.

SUMMARY

In the preceding pages no attempt has been made to exhaustively analyze the vast literature on the subject. Such an analysis would be scarcely profitable. Only those phases in the development of the knowledge of tendon reflexes (as exemplified by the knee-jerk) have been considered which seem to bear especially upon reflex theory.

The most striking feature of the tendon reflex is its variability. This is evidenced even in experiments where every effort is directed toward controlling all the known variables. Perhaps the most systematic attempts to investigate this variability are the experiments of Lombard (311), Bowditch and Warren (57), and the recent study of Dodge (114). The Bowditch and Warren study yielded significant results, but during the immediately succeeding decades there seems to have been a curious lapse of scientific curiosity in this particular field.

The knee-jerk would seem to offer an excellent means of studying some of the "urgent" problems of physiology and psychology to which Sherrington has referred.[11] The ease with which the knee-jerk may be elicited has made it the subject of a vast number of minor investigations, i.e., investigations of the type which yield specific categorical answers to problems of practical significance to the clinician. It has been used relatively infrequently in investigations directed towards the solving of the more fundamental psycho-neurological problems. The relation of a concomitant mental process, or, stated in neural terms, the relation of the "higher" and "lower" physiological systems, is such a problem. The great variability of the knee-jerk may indicate that it is an exceedingly sensitive, indicator of the functioning of such systems. Such investigations as those typified by Bowditch and Warren, Lombard, and more recently Dodge and Tuttle, are steps in the direction of solving problems of great theoretical significance to neurology and psychology.

[11] *Cf.* Sherrington (441), p. 388.

Whatever may be the final solution of the host of problems raised by the numerous investigations which have been briefly surveyed in the present chapter, it is clear that the myth of the knee-jerk as a simple spinal reflex is shattered. Beginning with the important investigation of Dodge in 1910 the data have been accumulating that the knee-jerk, and perhaps all other "simple" reflexes, *cannot be regarded as isolated units of function in the intact nervous system.*

CHAPTER XVI

MODERN CONCEPTS

"Our picture of human adjustment is not a mosaic of reënforcing or conflicting reflexes, instincts, habits, and voluntary acts or a succession of discrete responses under these various categories, but a dynamic continuum, a sort of spiral process with a relatively simple front at any given moment and a highly complex background. Adequate experimental analysis should disclose that the front is really a succession of beginning reactions and elaborated adjustments. The beginning reactions are evoked by current stimuli superposed on the remains of consummated responses to past stimuli by which they are inhibited, reënforced, or qualitatively modified."
—RAYMOND DODGE, *Protopraxic and Epicritic Stratification of Human Adjustments*, in the *Washburn Commemorative Volume*, 1927.

It is stated by McDougall (347) that "it was not until the middle of the nineteenth century that the nature of reflex action was clearly understood."[1] This statement must be revised in the light of the contributions of Whytt, Unzer, Blane, Prochaska, and others in the 18th century, together with the fairly definite conceptions of Willis in the preceding century. The important functional characteristics of the reflex were well established by the end of the 18th century, but it remained for the physiological science of the next century to demonstrate the structural elements of the reflex arc in a form which bears a recognizable resemblance to the modern conception.

A completely adequate statement of the accomplishments of the 19th century with regard to the development of the theory of reflex action is difficult because of the exceedingly diversified physiological activities which are directly or indirectly related to the topic of neuro-muscular integration. It is the century which saw the appointment of the first Professor of Physiology, the first adequate measurement of the speed of the nervous impulse, and the establishment of the first laboratory of experimental psychology. The phrase "physiological psychology" itself seems to have been used for the first time in 1831 by Chardels (87).[2] These are but indications of the changing emphasis so far as research in the field of animal behavior was concerned. We may, however, characterize some of the more important developments in connection with reflex theory during this century.

[1] p. 105.
[2] *Cf.* Ziehen (549), p. 3 *ff.*

(1) The conception of reflex action changed during this period from that of a simple, invariable, and relatively isolated neuro-muscular phenomenon to that of a complex, highly adaptive response. The theory of the reflex as an integrative mechanism in animal behavior seems to have been the peculiar contribution of the century. This point of view received its most important statement in the publication of Sherrington in 1906 (441). But the shift in emphasis is apparent in such studies as those of Lombard (310, 311) and Bowditch and Warren (57).

(2) The introduction to clinical medicine of the concepts of neuro-muscular functioning as exemplified in the reflex arc was made during this period. This was one of the major contributions of Marshall Hall. In the latter half of the century we note a further extension of this field in the application of the newly acquired knowledge of specific reflexes, *e.g.*, the knee-jerk, vasomotor mechanisms, equilibrium reflexes, and others, to the interpretation and diagnosis of mental and nervous diseases.

(3) Perhaps the most significant advance of the century was the increased knowledge of the structural mechanisms at the basis of the reflex arc. Without this knowledge, of course, the modern concept of the reflex would be impossible. The most important of these investigations led to the Bell-Magendie discovery of the functions of the posterior and anterior spinal nerve roots, and to the series of brilliant experiments which culminated in the neurone theory and the concept of the synapse.

(4) The Pflüger-Lotze controversy was far-reaching in its effect on our conceptions of neuro-muscular control. The issue immediately before Pflüger and Lotze is at present of small consequence, but it has served as an effective stimulus to further experimentation in the field of reflex action. The controversy may be said to have been initiated with the work of Marshall Hall in 1838, who emphasized the machine-like nature of involuntary action. The experimental contributions of Goltz and the theoretical discussions of Lewes, Carpenter, Ziehen, and others made reflex action a center of physiological and psychological interest. The results of their work form the setting of some of the more important problems in the field at the present time. The work of Volkmann, Müller, Lewes, Carpenter, Ferrier, and others focussed attention on certain psychological aspects of reflex action and formed a necessary prelude to modern problems in this field.

(5) The increasing curiosity regarding reflex action, which developed after the work of Marshall Hall, resulted in the discovery of a vast number of specific reflexes. It is only necessary to refer to the postural reflexes, vestibular reflexes, ocular reflexes, tendon reflexes, and skin reflexes,

all of which were the subjects of specialized experimental investigation during the century, to indicate the growth and range of interest in this field.

The Expansion of Mechanistic Physiology

As indicated elsewhere, the conceptions of mechanistic physiology played an increasingly important rôle in the biological theorizing of the 19th century. So far as these conceptions applied to neural physiology, they were the result in part, at least, of the Pflüger-Lotze controversy. A thorough-going application of the mechanistic principles to animal behavior was made by Jacques Loeb (1859–1924), whose work on the comparative physiology of the brain (306) published at the turn of the century, marks an important development in the history of physiological psychology.

Loeb's work has a peculiarly intimate connection with the issues in the Pflüger-Lotze discussion. While at Strassburg, Loeb studied under Goltz when the latter was experimenting on the effects of extirpating portions of the nervous systems of animals, investigations which played so important a rôle in the above-mentioned controversy.[3]

It was Loeb's purpose to explain all behavior in mechanistic terms, *i.e.*, according to physico-chemical principles. He defined a reflex as follows:

A reflex is a reaction which is caused by an external stimulus, and which results in a coördinated movement, the closing of the eyelid, for example, when the conjunctiva is touched by a foreign body, or the narrowing of the pupil under the influence of light. In each of these cases, changes in the sensory nerve-endings are produced which bring about a change of condition in the nerves. This change travels to the central nervous system, passes from there to the motor nerves, and terminates in the muscle-fibres, producing there a contraction. This passage from the stimulated part to the central nervous system, and back again to the peripheral muscles, is called a reflex. (pp. 1–2)

In interpreting this series of events, Loeb rejected the figure of speech which makes the spinal cord analogous to a mirror which reflects light. The same principles operating in the tropistic responses of plants, operate in the reflex responses of animals; that is to say, it is essential only that there be a protoplasmic bridge between the irritable tissue and the responding mechanism. No specific qualities in the central nervous system are necessary. In other words, conductibility and irritability are the necessary conditions of the reflex response.

[3] For details of Loeb's life see Flexner (146), and the interesting article by Palmer (392).

A study, then, of comparative physiology brings out the fact that irritability and conductibility are the only qualities essential to reflexes, and these are both common qualities of all protoplasm. The irritable structures at the surface of the body, and the arrangement of the muscles, determine the character of the reflex act. The assumption that the central nervous system or the ganglion-cells are the bearers of reflex mechanisms cannot hold. But have we now to conclude that the nerves are superfluous and a waste? Certainly not. Their value lies in the fact that they are quicker and more sensitive conductors than undifferentiated protoplasm. (p. 7)

Because the animal possesses nerves, it is better able to adapt itself' presumably because of increased sensitivity, to changing conditions. The so-called psychic life is explained by the principle of "associative memory," which he defined in the following passage:

The most important problem in the physiology of the central nervous system is the analysis of the mechanisms which give rise to the so-called psychic phenomena. The latter appear, invariably, as a function of an elementary process, namely the activity of the associative memory. By associative memory I mean the two following peculiarities of our central nervous system: First, that processes which occur there leave an impression or trace by which they can be reproduced even under different circumstances than those under which they originated. This peculiarity can be imitated by machines like the phonograph. Of course, we have no right to assume that the traces of processes in the central nervous system are analogous to those in the phonograph. The second peculiarity is, that two processes which occur simulataneously or in quick succession will leave traces which fuse together, so that if later one of the processes is repeated, the other will necessarily be repeated also . . . . By associative memory we mean, therefore, that mechanism by means of which a stimulus produces not only the effects which correspond to its nature and the specific structure of the stimulated organ, but which produces, in addition, such effects of other causes as at some former time may have attacked the organism almost or quite simultaneously with the given stimulus. (pp. 213-4)

We may expect to find in physico-chemical processes the explanation of the ultimate nature of the associative memory. The investigation of these processes, Loeb regarded as the proper sphere of research of all those who are interested in the problems of integrated behavior.

Shortly before the publication in 1903 of Loeb's book, two papers appeared, one by Bethe (41) the other by Beer, Bethe, and von Uexküll (26) in which a position similar to that of Loeb was supported. In these papers the authors pointed out that there is no scientific justification for assuming that animals have any psychic life. This appears to be a reformulation of the Cartesian doctrine of animal automatism, which explained all animal behavior in terms of reflexes unaccompanied by consciousness. In the paper by Beer, Bethe, and von Uexküll, a neurological nomenclature was proposed which did not carry any implications as to psychical processes in animal responses.[4]

---

[4] *Cf*. Meyer (353), p. 556, and Jennings (260), p. 330 *f*.

The first years of the 19th century witnessed the inception of another line of investigation which was destined to be of enormous influence in connection with the development of a mechanistic theory of physiology and psychology.   Ivan Petrovitch Pavlov (1849–   ), with his collaborators, about 1900 began a series of experiments on the salivary reflex in the dog which they have continued to the present time.[5]   The results of these researches had not been available to English students in a complete form until the publication, in 1927 (400), of an English translation of the author's lectures, and in 1928 (401) of an English translation of a collection of articles, reports, lectures, and addresses delivered by Pavlov during the preceding twenty-five years.

The elements of Pavlov's theory are relatively simple.   Proceeding from the assumption that the individual organism begins as an aggregate of inborn reflexes, he shows that these mechanisms alone are inadequate to account for all the precise relations between the organism and environment which the adjustments of complex existence demand.   The types of response which demonstrate the existence of a more exact rapport between organism and environment are found in situations where the animal responds not only to stimuli which bring immediate benefit or harm, but to other agencies which signal the approach of these potentially harmful or beneficial stimuli.

The instrument through which these important types of adjustment function is the cerebral hemispheres, that is, these responses disappear in decorticated animals leaving only the simple undifferentiated reflexes. The most important distinction between these signalling responses and inborn reflexes is that the latter are present from birth, while the former are built up gradually during the course of the animal's individual existence. For example, although food, through its chemical and physical properties, when placed in the mouth evokes the flow of saliva—this is the primary inborn reflex—at the same time the sight, or odor of food may release the same response.   It is to these signallizing reflexes that Pavlov has given the name "conditioned reflexes," to distinguish them from the inherited or "unconditioned reflexes."

[5] Pavlov records in a note preceding the "Bibliography" in the 1927 English translation of his lectures (400) that the first paper on the so-called "psychic reflexes" was published in 1899 by Dr. Wolfson in the form of a thesis entitled "Observations upon Salivary Secretion."   The term "conditioned reflex" was used in print for the first time by Pavlov's collaborator, Dr. Tolochinov in 1903.   Whytt's reference to the conditioned salivary reflex is an interesting anticipation of Pavlov, *vide supra* Chapter V, p. 80.   Others also have anticipated Pavlov in describing the chief phenomena of conditioning; *cf.*, Cason (83a)

I. P. Pavlov

After referring to Descartes' formulation of the reflex theory as a "genuine scientific conception," Pavlov defines the reflex as follows:

> An external or internal stimulus falls on some one or other nervous receptor and gives rise to a nervous impulse; this nervous impulse is transmitted along nerve fibres to the central nervous system, and here, on account of existing nervous connections, it gives rise to a fresh impulse which passes along outgoing nerve fibres to the active organ, where it excites a special activity of the cellular structures. Thus a stimulus appears to be connected of necessity with a definite response, as cause with effect. It seems obvious that the whole activity of the organism should conform to definite laws. If the animal were not in exact correspondence with its environment it would, sooner or later, cease to exist. (400, p. 7)

Reflexes are "machine-like, inevitable reactions" and serve as "elemental units in the mechanism of perpetual equilibration."

The salivary reflex has been used almost exclusively in Pavlov's investigations. By means of a simple operation it was possible to transplant the opening of the salivary duct from the inside of the mouth to the outside skin. The amount and rate of salivary secretion thus could be measured and recorded readily. In order to study the conditioning process experimentally, accessory stimuli of various types—auditory, visual, thermal, olfactory—were presented to the animal at the same time that food (unconditioned stimulus) was presented. After several repetitions, it was observed that the secretion of saliva occurred when the accessory (conditioned) stimulus was presented without the presentation of the primary or unconditioned stimulus. This is the basic experimental situation, the investigation of which has consumed the major energies of Pavlov and his students for many years.

The conditioned reflex is not an unmodifiable type of response, but is subject to a variety of external and internal influences both during and after its establishment. External inhibition of the conditioned reflex ensues when some other excitatory process occurs in the central nervous system, e.g., a disturbing stimulus unrelated to the experimental situation. To exclude these disturbing factors, it was necessary to build a special laboratory in which the experimental rooms are insulated from each other. The dogs are isolated from the experimenter, who mechanically controls the course of the experiment from another room.

When the conditioned stimulus is presented several times without reinforcement, i.e., without at the same time giving the usual unconditioned stimulus, it becomes ineffective and is an example of internal inhibition. These inhibitory effects may irradiate over the entire cerebral cortex and even the lower centers.

The work of Pavlov and his co-workers is characterized by a rigid exclusion of all explanatory concepts and terms which imply the existence of any subjective factors. The organism is regarded as an aggregate of reflexes which may be released by inter-changeable stimuli.[6] Both the conditioned and unconditioned responses are mechanical and based upon a necessary connection between stimulus and response. The "higher" activities of the organism, for example, those dependent upon the functioning of the cerebral hemispheres, are summed up in the single principle of conditioning, and the only path to scientific righteousness from this point of view, seems to lie in the use of the "physiological" or "objective" method embodied in the conditioned reflex technique.

Pavlov is convinced of the "futility of subjective methods of inquiry," and questions the significance and scientific status of those methods of modern psychology which are neither "physiological" or "objective" in the Pavlovian sense. In support of this conviction he refers to the statement of William James that psychology was not a science but the hope of a science, and to the opposition of Wundt (before 1913) to the separation of the chairs of psychology and philosophy, on the ground that it would be impossible for the professors of the new science to agree on a common examination schedule! With the advances of experimental psychology of the last fifteen or twenty years before him, the modern psychologist can view with equanimity this testimony, and even wonder ar the naïveté which proposes it as evidence that psychology cannot claim to be a science.

There can be no doubt but that the investigations of Pavlov and his collaborators during the past twenty-five years have furnished not only an experimental method which has become standard in physiological and psychological laboratories, but on the side of theory they have presented a body of explanatory principles which have contributed not a little to the offensive and defensive armament of the Behaviorist, Social Psychologist, Psycho-sociologist, Criminologist, and Psychiatrist. The mechanistic conceptions of neuro-muscular functions as embodied, for example, in the doctrines of the Behaviorists, have, in particular, benefited from the principle of reflex conditioning. Those conceptions which first appeared in modern form with the work of Harvey and Descartes in the 17th century, have come, as a result of the application of the technique of conditioning to the study of the more complex forms of behavior, to include within their

---

[6] By the application of this principle, complex behavior is made verbally simple, at least. Restless movements of the dog when confined are regarded as a manifestation of the "Freedom reflex;" inquisitive behavior is denominated the "What-is-it?" reflex, etc., cf., Pavlov op. cit., p. 11–12.

scope every type of animal response. There are, however, indications that, as a result of the investigations of the *Gestalt* school of psychologists, the mechanistic interpretation of behavior has been challenged with a certain measure of success.

In this connection it is interesting to note that there is a recent recrudescence of the 18th century effort to create a mechanism which would duplicate the activities of a living man. In the present instance the attempt is made to construct a mechanism which will show the phenomena of the conditioned reflex. The authors, Hull and Baernstein (243), point out that,

The belief of the reflexologists and the behaviorists that the mental life is essentially a function of various complex organizations of conditioned reflexes offers a challenge to the attempt at a synthetic verification. Logically, if it were possible to construct non-living devices—perhaps even of inorganic material—which would perform the essential functions of the conditioned reflex, we should be able to organize these units into systems which would show true trial-and-error learning with intelligent selection on the elimination of errors, as well as other behavior ordinarily classed as psychic. Thus emerges in a perfectly natural manner a direct implication of the mechanistic tendency of modern psychology. (pp. 14–5)

Descartes was interested in this problem, and in the 18th century Vaucanson and others constructed such mechanisms. A hundred years later, Lange in his "History of Materialism" (281) commented on these attempts as follows:

The first intoxication of great physical and mathematical discoveries is over; and as the world, with each fresh deciphering of a secret, offered yet new riddles, and as it were visibly grew great and wider, so there revealed themselves, too, in organic life abysses of unexplored connexions which as yet had been hardly thought of. An age that could quite seriously believe that in the mechanical masterpieces of Droz and Vaucanson it had come upon the traces of the secrets of life, was hardly capable of measuring the difficulties which have accumulated in the mechanical explanation of psychical phenomena only the higher as we have gone on. (III, p. 111)

The question may be raised if the intervening years since Vaucanson worked, or Lange wrote, have seen any simplification of organic processes which would serve as a basis for greater optimism for the success of such a project in the 20th century, than was apparent in the 18th or 19th centuries.[7]

The conditioned reflex has been demonstrated not only in the case of the salivary reflex in the dog but in man and other animals as well. Among these investigations that of Cason (83, 83a), Twitmeyer (500), Krasnogorski

---

[7] *Cf.* Meyer (353), Harvey (210), and Russell (429) for attempts of a similar nature. *Cf.*, also *supra*, Chapter VI, p. 87.

(271), Mateer (336), Lashley (286), Morgulis (368), and Bechterev (25) may be mentioned. Recently Schlosberg (434) has studied the conditioned knee-jerk. He was able to condition the knee-jerk to a bell, click, buzz, and tactual pressure in forty-four out of forty-nine subjects, although he found that the conditioned knee-jerks were "very unstable, varying considerably in both height and frequency of appearance, even within one experimental period." The study of Hamel (203) of the temporal aspects of the voluntary and conditioned finger reaction showed that the times of the conditioned reflex were of the same order of magnitude as those of the voluntary reaction; this is evidence which is inconsistent with the assumptions of the Behaviorists, e.g., Watson (526) as to the nature of the conditioning process.[8]

CURRENT USAGES OF THE TERM "REFLEX"

The problem of the classification of animal action is not a simple one, although some sort of systematization is demanded for the purposes of clear discussion. Descartes and his successors were able to make but the simple distinction between voluntary and involuntary action; the latter being entirely mechanical and reflexive in nature. With the vast increase in psychological and physiological knowledge since the middle of the 19th century, so simple a division is inadequate. It has become necessary to establish criteria on which the more adequate categories must rest.

In the case of reflex action this is by no means easy. The broad distinction between voluntary and involuntary is somewhat uncertain in view of the difficulty in defining the term voluntary. "Automatic" actions are not easy to classify; for the physiologist the term is frequently used with reference only to those actions which are wholly unconscious, such as the beating of the heart, and glandular activity. On the other hand the highly learned actions such as playing the piano, typewriting, etc, are called "automatic" by the psychologist. The issues are still further confused by the tendency of modern physiologists and psychologists, especially the latter, to apply the term "reflex" to *all* types of nervous action which involve a receptor mechanism, an afferent conductor, central elaboration, an efferent conductor, and an effector mechanism. The Cartesian idea and the concept of the earlier physiologists of the reflex as a specific kind of response distinct from all other types of action is then completely elimi-

---

[8] Cason (83a) has criticized this investigation. For the more general application of the principle of conditioning in psychology, education, and hygiene, the reader is referred to Burnham (69), Watson (526), Humphrey (245), Yerkes and Morgulis (547), Cason (83a), and Mateer (336).

nated; unless, of course, *all* nervous action is presumed to be involuntary, machine-like and invariable.

Objections to this latter position have not been wanting among physiologists. Hough (240) points out the advantages from the point of view of instruction of the diagrammatic simplicity of the reflex mechanism as usually presented. He questions, however, the success which attended the attempt to explain everything in cerebral physiology in terms of reflex action.

One has only to read the text-books to find out. Some things, especially localization, are dwelt upon at length; the possibilities of excessively complex coördinations are suggested by the anatomical structure; but we miss entirely the satisfaction of seeing the cerebral functions clearly pictured in terms of neurone structure. We trace the "way in" and the "way out;" we see that the connection between the afferent and efferent nerve fibers is in the cortex; but what takes place in the cortex? Is it objectively nothing more than our typical reflex raised to the *nth* power of complexity? Perhaps it is; but does any one feel reasonably sure of it? For one, I confess I do not . . . . We know that there are nervous actions which are not reflexes at all; furthermore, there are nervous actions which usually pass as reflexes, although they present striking and perhaps fundamental points of difference from the typical reflex arc of our neurone theory . . . . My present purpose and indeed the purpose of this paper is to challenge the wisdom of making the reflex arc the type of all nervous action either in our own thinking or in the presentation of the subject to students . . . . (p. 408)

Hough proceeds to distinguish the following classes of nervous action: (1) automatic, (2) axon reflex, (3) unconditioned reflex, (4) conditioned reflex, and (5) volitional. He points out the dangers of assuming that one kind of nervous action underlies the various responses which have been called "reflex."

We have seen that accurate knowledge of the "way in" and "way out" of the nervous impulse was not available until the discoveries in the early part of the 19th century. At present we can scarcely claim to have exact knowledge of processes which occur in the central portion of the reflex arc. The situation is baffling and for two centuries has successfully resisted the assaults of the experimentalists. The fact that the animal responds, that is to say, reacts, under one set of conditions which are loosely termed "involuntary," and under another set of conditions which are loosely termed "voluntary" has presented a problem which has engaged the attention of investigators in the field of neuro-muscular adjustment for the past two hundred years. A survey of the terms which have been applied to the agencies which effect these responses reveals the uncertainty and mystery in which the whole question is involved. Among the terms which have been used in this connection, are the following: "sentient principle," "animal spirits," "soul," "sympathy," "vis insita," "vis nervosa," "will," "sensorium commune," "archaeus," "rational mind," "blas," "sensitve soul," "conceptive force," "sentient impression," and "associative memory." These terms are variously defined and do not refer to identical processes, but they all represent attempts to characterize the processes or agencies connecting the incoming with the out-going nervous impulses.

It is not to be regarded as extraordinary, then, that phenomena apparently simple as those referred to by the term "reflex," should be so difficult of interpretation. A source of confusion has been that physiology and especially psychology have taken for granted a simplicity of function because of an assumed simplicity of neural structure. The reflex arc is easily diagrammed in the textobook; such a diagram readily forms the basis for a discussion of simple stimulus-response relationships, which is misleading even in connection with the simpler animal responses, and positively inapplicable to the more complex organic responses.

PHYSIOLOGICAL INTERPRETATIONS

The simplest view of reflex action is perhaps the one which may be termed the "specific" theory. From this point of view the reflex is regarded as a type of action qualitatively distinguishable from all other types of animal response, that is, it has characteristics which separate it from "willed" reactions, or "learned" reactions, or automatic reactions.

Typical of this point of view are the statements of Howell (241) with reference to reflex action.

By a reflex action we mean the involuntary production of activity in some peripheral tissue in consequence of a stimulation of afferent nerve fibers. The conversion of the sensory or afferent impulse into a motor or efferent impulse is effected in the nerve centers, and may be totally unconscious as well as involuntary . . . . (p. 139)

The impression of purposefulness in the reflex action—at least so far as the purposefulness is the result of conscious choice—is without basis in fact. The reflex is mechanical and automatic.

Most physiologists, however, are content to see in these reactions only an expression of the automatic activity of a mechanism. It is assumed that the sensory impulses from any part of the skin find, on reaching the cord, that the paths to a certain group of motor neurons are more direct and offer less resistance than any others. It is along these paths that the reflex will take place, and we may further assume that these paths of least resistance, as they have been called, are in part preformed and in part are laid down by the repeated experiences of the individual . . . . and we may imagine, therefore, a system of reflex apparatuses or mechanisms which when properly stimulated will react always in the same way. (p. 143)

The production of the reflex is due to a fixed mechanical arrangement, and consciousness is not necessary to explain the reaction. Apparently "repeated" experience may form a reflex path. We may assume this to be the basis of an automatism, although Howell does not discuss that class of action specifically. Howell points out that reflexes may occur in the brain. These actions, however, are not to be included among true reflexes because the latter are involuntary. So far as the nervous mechanism is concerned, they are identical with true reflexes. Regarding the added psychical factor in the case of the brain reactions Howell says:

The added feature of a psychical factor, a reaction in consciousness, enables us to draw a line of distinction between these activities and those of so-called pure reflexes; but the distinction is perhaps one of convenience only, for, although the extremes may be far enough apart to suit the definition, many intermediate instances may be found which are difficult to classify. All skilled movements, for instance, such as walking, singing, dancing, bicycle riding, and the like,—although in the beginning obviously effected by voluntary coördination, nevertheless in the end, in proportion to the skill obtained, become more or less entirely reflex,—that is, involuntary. In learning such movements one must, as the saying goes, establish his reflexes, and the result can hardly be understood otherwise than by supposing that the continual adjustment of certain sensory impulses to certain coördinated movements results in the formation of a more or less complex reflex arc, a set of paths of least resistance. (p. 149)

It thus becomes clear that automatisms are to be regarded as reflex in nature. Although Howell refers (p. 148) to reactions occurring through the brain as "reflexes," he denies this name to those actions which are not involuntary, at the same time pointing out that neurologically they are identical with reflexes. The characteristic of reflex function is involuntariness; the characteristic of reflex mechanism is afferent-efferent conduction. Learned action becomes involuntary, therefore reflex. The criteria of involuntariness are not made clear; presumably they have to do with the diminution of conscious accompaniment and control. Langendorff in Nagel's *Handbuch* (382), and Tigerstedt (480) present similar views.

THE "GENETIC" GROUP

A second avenue of approach to the problem of classification may be termed "genetic." In this group we have placed those individuals who assign certain specific characteristics to reflexes, but emphasize the continuity of the series from the reflex to the "willed" action. It is typical of this point of view that there is no sharply drawn line of demarcation between reflex and other varieties of neuro-muscular action. It has been useful in the genetic theory of volition; for example, in Ziehen's (549, 552) theory, the deflex is a stage between the true reflex and a voluntary reaction.   The difficulty of distinguishing between the involuntary and the voluntary action, that is, the point in the series at which the involuntary aspect of the action appears, is inherent in this theory.

Mitchell, for example, (360) attempts to differentiate between reflex and non-reflex activities.   Consciousness and memory he does not consider reliable criteria; predictability, however, he regards as the most satisfactory distinguishing mark of the reflex.

There is a wide difference between a purely unconscious, involuntary reflex, such as those which affect the constriction of arterial muscles, and the strictly conscious, voluntary acts, such as those done in response to the dictates of acquired aesthetic tastes.   The typical reflex can be predicted; these other acts cannot.   *All gradations between these two extremes are to be found.*[9]   But, in general, the physiological definition of a reflex lays stress upon its predictable certainty.   The more mechanical and certain the act the more typical of reflexes it is said to be.

Reflexes may take place through the brain.   These are modified by past experience of the animal and are much more difficult to study than spinal reflexes.   Habits (automatisms) are regarded as "developed reflexes."

Morat (367) distinguishes between reflexes and voluntary acts, although he regards the distinction a superficial one.   From the simplest reflex to a cerebral act the series is continuous.

Voluntary movement is nothing more than the elaborated form of reflex action; muscular movement is itself merely a differentiated form of organic movement usually hidden and invisible.

Just as, in the order of movement, we proceed from the simple reflex act, from the ganglionic or spinal reflex, to the most complex cerebral act, so, from this extremely perfected act we re-descend, in the psychical order, without solution of continuity, to the nervous act, the fundamental base of all the others, and we meet the traces of this consciousness and of this choice, which only appear in their plenitude and a marked form in those superior systematizations which are effected in the brain.   Three chief degrees may be distinguished in this succession, corresponding (1) to the reflex act, (2) to the instinctive act, (3) to the voluntary act.   (pp. 217–8)

Herrick (223) states that the reflex act "is usually" defined by physiologists as being mechanical, involuntary, and adaptive.   He does not, however, place undue emphasis on the reflex arc as an explanatory principle in nervous physiology.   Two important aspects of nervous action are distinguished, "legislative" and "executive."

[9] Italics not in the original.

The first determines what shall be the response to the particular stimulus or complex of stimuli which initiates the activity; the second is concerned wholly with the task of executing the reaction thus determined. Both of these aspects of the reaction may be very complex, but the complexity is of different type and the apparatus employed may be very dissimilar . . . . In short, in both reflex and deliberative (including voluntary) reactions we may say that the nature of the neural process is abruptly changed when it "turns the corner" from the afferent to the efferent limb of the arc. (p. 235)

The functioning of the brain and central nervous system is associated with the correlative aspect; in the higher animals the mnemonic function is the most important characteristic of the cortex. At these higher levels "true learning" takes the place of "physiological habit," "psychological memory of physiological memory, association of correlation."[10] On this basis physiological processes may be divided into the following classes: (1) immediate response of excited protoplasm to external stimuli, (2) preservation of paths thus formed, or physiological habit, (3) permanent changes in organization maintained by biological heredity, that is, fixed, uniform reflexes, (4) individually acquired correlations, conditioned reflexes, etc., growing out of individual experience, (5) cortical memories of specific experiences, "intelligent" behavior, (6) ideation, abstraction, confined probably to the human type.

A distinction between voluntary and involuntary is not fundamental in a classification of physiological or psychological action, and the reflex is regarded by Herrick merely as a system of correlation.

Sherrington, the publication of whose book (441) in 1906 was from many points of view the most important event in the recent history of reflex action, makes the reflex act the unit of functional integration. It is basically different from "voluntary" action on the one hand, and simple conduction in the nerve trunk on the other. It consists in the reception of a stimulus, conduction of an impulse, and a motor effect. This kind of conduction is different from conduction in a simple nerve trunk in certain respects.

Conduction in reflex-arcs exhibits (1) slower speed as measured by the latent period between application of stimulus and appearance of end-effect, this difference being greater for weak stimuli than for strong; (2) less close correspondence between the moment of cessation of stimulus and the moment of cessation of end-effect, i.e., there is a marked "after-discharge;" (3) less close correspondence between rhythm of stimulus and rhythm of end-effect; (4) less close correspondence between grading of intensity of the stimulus and the grading of intensity of the end-effects; (5) considerable resistance to passage of a single nerve impulse, but a resistance easily forced by a succession of impulses (temporal summation); (6) irreversibility of direction instead of reversibility as in nerve-trunks;

---

[10] *Op. cit.*, p. 245.

(7) fatigability in contrast with the comparative unfatigability of nerve-trunks; (8) much greater variability of the threshold value of stimulus than in nerve-trunks; (9) refractory period, "bahnung," inhibition, and shock, in degrees unknown for nerve-trunks; (10) much greater dependence on blood-circulation, oxygen; (11) much greater susceptibility to various drugs—anaesthetics. (p. 14)

Reflexes are machine-like in nature and occur without consciousness.

Pure reflexes are admirably adapted to certain ends. They are reactions which have long proved advantageous in the phylum of which the existent individual is a representative embodiment. Perfected during the course of ages, they have during that course attained a stability, a certainty, and an ease of performance beside which the stability and facility of the most ingrained habit acquired during an individual life is presumably small. But theirs is of itself a machine-like fatality. Their character in this stands revealed when the neural arcs which execute them are separated, e.g., by transection of the spinal cord, from the higher centres of the nervous system . . . . To these ancient invariable reflexes, consciousness, in the ordinary meaning of the term, is not adjunct. The subject as an active agent does not direct them and cannot introspect them. (pp. 387–8)

Reflexes are, however, under control of mechanisms of which consciousness is an adjunct. Sherrington regards it as "urgently necessary" for physiology to know how this volitional control is operative upon the reflex machinery.

How is the convergence of the eyeballs, innately associate to visual fixation of a near object, initiated voluntarily without recourse to fixation on an object? Or how is the innate respiratory rhythm voluntarily modified to meet the passing requirements of vocal utterance? No exposition of the integrative action of the nervous system is complete, even in outline, if this control is left without consideration. Reflexes ordinarily ouside its pale can by training be brought within it. (pp. 388–9)

Reflexes may be brought under voluntary control, and volitional actions may become involuntary. Certain ancestral coördinations may by training be brought under the control of the "will," e.g., the ring finger can be brought to act independently of the other fingers by "training." On the other hand the training process in the case of actions originally volitional results in a loss of the conscious accompaniments.

The transition from reflex action to volitional is not abrupt and sharp. Familiar instances of individual acquisitions of motor coördination are furnished by the cases in which short, simple movements, whether reflex or not, are by practice under volition combined into new sequences and become in time habitual in the sense that though able to be directed they no longer require concentration of attention upon them for their execution. As I write, my mind is not preoccupied with how my fingers form the letters; my attention is fixed simply on the thought the words express. But there was a time when the formation of the letters, as each one was written, would have occupied my whole attention. (pp. 389–90)

Sherrington points out that the knowledge of volitional control is inadequate, but that it seems always to be associated with consciousness.

Luciani (320) states that in the widest sense any immediate reaction of a living and excitable element to an external stimulus may be called a reflex act.

In a narrower sense, however, as applied to the nervous system, the reflex act is the involuntary transformation of a centripetal into a centrifugal nerve impulse, by means of a central organ, represented by a group of ganglion cells. We say "involuntary transformation" to distinguish the reflex act from the voluntary act, which may also follow on, and be evoked by, an afferent impulse . . . .

But in experiments upon animals it is difficult to distinguish "reflex" acts from the "voluntary" acts which result from conscious sensations. In order to establish the purely reflex nature of spinal acts the influence of the will is cut out in animals, either by narcosis, or by decapitation or removal of the cerebrum. (p. 310)

Luciani believes these methods designed to eliminate the influence of the will are for the most part inadequate, and a sharp distinction between "reflex" and "voluntary" acts may not even be made in the spinal animal. The "purposive" character of the actions of the spinal animal are not qualitatively different from the purposive character of voluntary acts. It is necessary then to make objective studies of the reflex acts which the spinal cord is able to carry out independently of the brain.

Luciani is able to conceive the possibility of a rudimentary spinal consciousness which may accompany the reactions of the spinal animal. In this he agrees with Foster (155) and Pflüger (404).

Though direct confirmation of Foster's hypothesis on the nature of the spinal psychical functions is wanting, it appears to us to be logical and generally admissible. Those who take the manifestations of perception and memory as the distinguishing signs of consciousness, and absolutely deny the psychical character of coördinated reflexes, do not reflect that the spinal cord is not claimed as the seat of the *higher* intellectual functions, but only that of a simple rudimentary intelligence due to the synthesis of a small group of elementary sensations . . . . But from our point of view, these facts—even if they show that the spinal frog exhibits no sign of perception and memory—do not exclude the possibility of its possessing transitory flashes of consciousness, arising from a psychical synthesis of elementary sensations. (p. 340)

The difficulties in formulating an "adequate theory of reflexes" are expressed as follows:

An adequate theory of reflexes must throw light on the process by which the centripetal or afferent excitation becomes centrifugal or efferent; it must tell us why the reflex is sometimes confined to a few muscles, and at other times spreads to more muscles in various combinations; why the efferent impulses travel along certain paths and not others; lastly, how the coördination and adaptation of the reflexes to the nature and localization of the stimulus is attained.   At present we can only give vague and inadequate replies to these questions, though a few hypothetical but certainly ingenious attempts have been made towards a partial solution of the problem on the basis of the neurone theory.   (p. 337)

Parker (393) concludes that reflexes may or may not be associated with consciousness.   A nervous reaction in which a sensory stimulation is followed by a motor response is a reflex "irrespective of the association of the action with voluntary or conscious operations."

Our own reflexes are sometimes associated with consciousness and sometimes not. When we pass from a region of dim light to one of bright light the pupils of our eyes contract without our being conscious of the fact.   In a similar way, when food is introduced into the digestive tract, a whole succession of reflex movements is called forth without any direct relation to our consciousness.   On the other hand, if we burn a finger, it is usually withdrawn with full recognition of the sensation and the response.   Thus a reflex may or may not be in association with a conscious state.   (p. 75)

Although Parker's statement is not positive, it seems clear that he does not differentiate sharply between reflexes and voluntary reactions.   For this reason he has been placed in the "genetic" group.

THE "MECHANICAL" GROUP

From a third point of view the characteristics of the reflex are regarded as the characteristics of all neuro-muscular action.   The earmarks of the reflex act, *e.g.*, specificity, innateness, as described from the traditional point of view are, by implication at least, extended to all types of action. For want of a better name we may designate this the "mechanical" concept, since the most universally accepted characteristic of the response from this point of view is its machine-like nature.   Bayliss (21), for example, regards the reflex as the functional unit of the "nervous mechanism."   No clear distinction is made between voluntary and reflex action; the former is not specifically discussed and the assumption is that the reflex is the prototype of all nervous action.   The brain is described as having "control" over the rest of the nervous system, and consciousness is "in some way" associated with its action, although its exact relation to reflex action is not made clear. Brain action is apparently adequately described in the phenomena of the conditioned reflex.

The difference between spinal reflexes and those in which the higher centres, and especially the cerebral cortex, take part is the regularity of the former and the ease with which the latter are modified or abolished by events in other parts of the central nervous system.   For this reason, Pavlov calls the former "unconditioned" and the latter "conditioned" reflexes.   (p. 508)

The conditioned reflex technique is welcomed as a method of investigation of the functions of the higher centers, without an "appeal to consciousness." However, consciousness is not to be eliminated but used "as an indicator only."

Starling (464) also regards the reflex as typical of all nervous action. He says:

The movements of the muscles are carried out in response to changes aroused in the central nervous system by events occurring in the environment and acting on the surface of the body. Every movement of an animal is thus in its most primitive form a reflex action, and involves changes in a peripheral sense organ, in an afferent nerve fibre, before the actual process of contraction occurs . . . . (p. 177)

All portions of this arc have the property of excitability. At a later point he speaks of certain muscles as being voluntary, *i.e.*, under the control of the "will," but does not make clear the neural relation of this type of action to the reflex arc.

The universality of the application of the reflex concept is further emphasized in the following:

A reflex act has often been distinguished from other reactions, described as conscious or purposive, by its fatality—i.e., by the invariability with which it results on a given stimulus, whether the reaction be for the good of the animal as a whole or not. Thus a decapitated eel will wind itself with equal readiness around a stick or a hot poker. *All* reactions are however purposive. The machinery for them has been evolved and the paths laid down in the spinal cord under the action of natural selection, so that they must act, at any rate *in the average of cases*, towards the well-being of the animal as a whole. Since the nerve path involved in any reaction includes a number of synapses, each of which may be influenced from other parts of the body in a positive or negative direction, an absolute uniformity of response cannot be predicated for any one reaction. There will be changes in the facility with which it is evoked and changes in its extent, and these will become the more operative the greater the complexity of the arc, and the larger the number of other impulses to which it may be subject. The fatality of response is therefore shown only at its best in the very simplest of reflexes, or the most lowly organized nervous systems. (p. 344)

These reactions—the term "reaction" becomes synonymous with reflex—carried out through the intervention of the central nervous system are wholly determined by the properties of neurones. These common properties are localization, delay (intervening synapses), summation, fatigue, "block" or resistance, facilitation and inhibition.

In this brief examination of contemporary physiological opinion with regard to the concept of reflex action, the attempt has been made to classify the points of view into three groups. In the first, the reflex is recognized as a specific kind of action, qualitatively distinct from volitional action.

It is variously described as being automatic, involuntary, unconscious, machine-like, adaptive, predictable, in a word, as a constant inheritable characteristic. Its anatomical bases are a receptor mechanism, afferent conduction, efferent conduction and an effector mechanism. In the second conception, the simple reflex is regarded as a type of organic action differing from "willed" actions only in the absence of certain characteristics which mark voluntary actions—these characteristics disappear from the series not suddenly but gradually. From the "willed" action to the reflex are a series of steps, and a given response may be classified with reference to the functional affinity which it bears to a volitional act on the one hand, or a reflex on the other. Reflexes may be regarded as degenerated volitional acts, or volitional acts may be regarded as a recent development in the phylogenetic series. According to the third conception, the reflex is a prototype of all nervous action. It is characteristic of this point of view that the "simple" reflex is described as it appears in the lower animals or in the spinal animal, and there is a tacit assumption that these characters are the same for the more complicated types of nervous action, e.g., those involving the cerebrum.

Although the reflex is diagrammatically and, in the case of the spinal animal, experimentally simple, various accessory phenomena have been observed which the physiologist is constrained to include in the formulation of any adequate theory of reflex action. Especially important are the various ways in which the reflex is modified by concurrent activities, those just preceding, during, and immediately following the occurrence of a given response. This modification either takes the form of facilitating the reflex (Bahnung), or inhibiting it (Hemmung). These coincident activities may take place in the cerebral cortex; Sherrington's statement regarding the importance of studying the effect of volitional activity on reflex activity is pertinent in this connection.[11] Modifying factors most frequently referred to by the physiologist are drugs, fatigue, and functional rhythm. The effect of repeated function as a modifying factor has received little or no attention on the part of the physiologist, although this factor is emphasized in connection with the establishment of the so-called "brain reflex."

PSYCHOLOGICAL INTERPRETATIONS

The psychologist has in large part borrowed his conceptions of reflex action from the physiologist, and as a result the contribution of psychology

---

[11] *Cf.* Sherrington (441), p. 388 *ff.*

to the theory of reflex action has been relatively small.   The consideration of the problems of reflex action from the point of view of psychology almost inevitably leads into the discussion of the nature and location of consciousness, the nature of mind and its relation to the body, problems which are primarily metaphysical and philosophical.   We may, however, limit ourselves to the consideration of the place of reflex action in systematic psychology.

THE "MECHANICAL" GROUP

James (249) though difficult to classify seems to regard reflex action as the prototype of *all* action.

In the "loop-line" along which the memories and ideas of the distant are supposed to lie, the action, so far as it is a physical process, must be interpreted after the type of the action in the lower centres.   If regarded here as a reflex process, it must be reflex there as well. The current in both places runs out into the muscles only after it has first run in; but whilst the path by which it runs out is determined in the lower centres by reflections few and fixed amongst the cell-arrangements, in the hemispheres the reflections are many and instable.   This, it will be seen, is only a difference of degree and not of kind, and does not change the reflex type.   The conception of *all* action as conforming to this type is the fundamental conception of modern nerve-physiology.   (I, p. 23)

However, in another place[12] he distinguishes reflex, semi-reflex, and volitional acts, a distinction which would classify him with our "genetic" group.   A man runs to catch a train, stumbles and thrusts out his hand to keep from falling, and gets a cinder in his eye with a resulting flow of tears. The first act is "voluntary," the thrusting out of the hand is partly instinctive and partly voluntary ("semi-reflex"), and the flow of tears is wholly involuntary and hence reflex.

In discussing the reaction-time experiment, James concludes that the reactions in these experiments are pure reflexes.

Feeling of the impression, attention to it, thought of the reaction, volition to react, would, undoubtedly, all be links of the process under other conditions, and would lead to the same reaction—after an indefinitely longer time.   But these other conditions are not those of the experiments we are discussing; and it is mythological psychology . . . to conclude that because two mental processes lead to the same result they must be similar in their inward subjective constitution . . . .   The reaction whose time is measured is, in short, a reflex action pure and simple, and not a psychic act.   (I, p. 90)

He procedes to point out that a psychic condition is necessary for the operation of this reflex.   In the well-known chapter on "Habit" the

[12] *Vide* I, p. 13.

automatic and involuntary character of this class of reactions is stressed and their identity with reflexes indicated.

For, of course, a simple habit, like every other nervous event—the habit of snuffling, for example, or of putting one's hands into one's pockets, or of biting one's nails—is, mechanically, nothing but a reflex discharge; and its anatomical substratum must be a path in the system. The most complex habits, as we shall presently see more fully, are, from the same point of view, nothing but concatenated discharges in the nerve-centres, due to the presence there of systems of reflex paths, so organized as to wake each other up successively . . . . (I, pp. 107–8)

Regarding the establishment of such a path in the nervous system, James points out:

While habitual action may once have been voluntary, the voluntary action must before that, at least once, have been impulsive or reflex. (I, footnote, p. 109)

Automatisms, then, for James are merely acquired reflexes. They presumably take place through the cerebral cortex, at least in the earlier stages. It is not clear whether with the decrease in conscious accompaniments there is some sort of neural short-circuiting which would no longer involve the cerebrum.

For Watson (527) the reflex arc is the functional unit of conduction, and it is a "convenient abstraction in both physiology and behavior." Reflexes do not take place in isolation but involve other parts of the body.

The term reflex, however, is an extremely convenient one and by it we mean the simplest type of activity that can ordinarily be produced. Theoretically we might have a pure reflex if we were to stimulate a single neuro-fibrillar ending of an afferent neurone and had a single neuro-fibrillar strand of a motor neurone connected with a single muscle fiber. (p. 254)

An instinct may be analyzed into simple reflexes. In the case of habit no "new path-ways" are formed; instinct and habit are composed of the same elementary reflexes.

They [instinct and habit] differ so far as concerns the origin of the pattern (number and localization of the simple reflex arcs involved) and the order (temporal relation) of the unfolding of the elements composing the pattern. In instinct the pattern and order are inherited, in habit both are acquired during the lifetime of the individual. We can define habit then as we did instinct as a complex system of reflexes which functions in a serial order when the child or adult is confronted by the appropriate stimulus, provided we add the statement that in habit the pattern and order are acquired, whereas in instinct they are inherited. (pp. 293–4)

Weiss (534) refers to the "sensori-motor arc" as the unit of physiological function which is composed of

A sense organ, a sensory neuron, a connecting neuron, a motor neuron, and a motor or secretory organ. Its simplest form is that of a reflex arc made up of inherited paths of low resistance between relatively few sensory and motor organs, and grading imperceptibly in complexity to the most recently acquired and most complicated behavior, involving hundreds of sense organs; hundreds of sensory, connecting, and motor neurons; and hundreds of motor organs. (pp. 163–4)

Every action is the result of these sensori-motor processes. Volition is no longer a problem.

The freedom of the will is an illusion that is based upon the inability to discriminate the origin of the implicit reactions. To regard voluntary behavior or volition as a category of human behavior seems hardly worth while. Volition has a social significance only if we assume the existence of some psychical or mental selecting agency. If this is denied voluntary behavior is no different from any other form of behavior. (pp. 361–2)

Bechterev (25), seems to belong in the present group. The chief distinction between the simple reflex and the *neuropsychische Reflexe* lies in the fact that the former is innate, while the latter is dependent upon individual experience. The *neuropsychische Prozess* consists in (1) a centripetal conduction, (2) formation of impressions and leaving behind a trace of these impressions, (3) associative reproduction of earlier traces through stimulation, (4) centrifugal conduction. All neuro-psychical action is essentially reflex in nature.

Unsere ganze neuropsychische Tätigkeit ist ein verwickelter Komplex von Reflexen höherer Ordnung oder Psychoreflexen, die durch Assoziations-vorgänge in Wechselbeziehung stehen, wodurch einerseits Hemmungs- und Depressions-vorgänge, anderseits Bahnungs- und Belebungsprozesse bewirkt werden. (p. 40)

Parmelee (394) distinguishes three levels of reflex action. The first is the spinal level in which the impulse passes from the receptor mechanism to the effector mechanism. The second is one in which various levels of the spinal cord may be involved so that reflexes may influence one another. The third level is reached when the brain is involved. Nervous integration is made possible by reflexes.

All or most of the behavior of the higher animals is therefore reflex, because all or most of it is integrated by the nervous system. (p. 162)

In a later chapter Parmelee points out that in animals ˙with a highly developed nervous system, consciousness is an adjunct of action and volition, but the contents of consciousness serve only the purpose of facilitating or inhibiting action through the influence of memory images. He regards reflexes as simple responses which are usually combined into larger units of behavior which are called instincts.

An interesting example of the "mechanistic" approach is found in Holt (238). Holt makes the reflex the physiological foundation of the "wish," and makes the integration of reflexes the basis of purposive action. In his chapter on "The Physiology of Wishes" he elaborates his theory.

In order to look at this more closely we must go a bit down the evolutionary series to the fields of biology and physiology. Here we find much talk of nerves and muscles, sense-organs, reflex arcs, stimulation, and muscular response, and we feel that somehow these things do not reach the core of the matter, and that they never can: that spirit is not nerve or muscle, and that intelligent conduct, to say nothing of conscious thought, can never be reduced to reflex arcs and the like; . . . If, then, we insist on there being a soul which nevertheless, the biologist says that he cannot discover anywhere in the living tissues of the animal he studies, we are right. And the biologist has only himself to thank if he has overlooked a thing which lay directly under his nose. He has overlooked the *form of organization* of these his reflex arcs, as we shall presently see, into an intelligent conscious creature. Evolution took this important little step of organization ages ago, and thereby produced the rudimentary "wish." (p. 50)

The author proceeds to point out that the single reflex is meaningless, but the organization of several reflexes produces specific behavior which is meaningful.

It is not surprising, then, that in animals as highly organized reflexly as are many of the invertebrates, even though they should possess no other principle of action than that of specific response, the various life-activities should present an appearance of considerable intelligence. And I believe that in fact this intelligence is solely the product of accumulated specific responses. Our present point is that the specific response and the "wish," as Freud uses the term, are one and the same thing.

This thing, in its essential definition, is a *course of action which the living body executes or is prepared to execute with regard to some object or some fact of its environment.* (pp. 56–7)

For Holt the traditional parallelistic doctrine of psychology is "mischievous."

It totally ignores the work of integration, and to assuage this ignorance it fabricates a myth. With that view falls also the entire subject of 'psychophysical parallelism'; which was a complete misapprehension from the outset. It is not that we have two contrasted worlds, the 'objective' and the 'subjective'; there is but one world, the objective, and that which we have hitherto not understood, have dubbed therefore the 'subjective,' are the subtler workings of integrated objective mechanisms. (pp. 92–3)

These objective mechanisms are reflexes. Their integration for Holt results in "behavior," which as an object of scientific investigations, embraces a field which extends beyond the limits of traditional physiology and biology. Mind, Holt regards as merely integrated reflex behavior, and the traditional mental functions and processes of psychology are explained on the basis of integrated reflex arcs.

THE "GENETIC" GROUP

The "genetic" approach to reflex theory has been especially productive in psychology. Certain psychologists by its use have been enabled to account for the existence of the various types of animal responses. It has permitted them to offer an intelligible interpretation of the observed relationship between motor habits (automatisms) and reflexes. The problem of volition, always difficult, may also be considered from this point of view.

Wundt (545) developed a reflex concept as an accessory to his theory of action.[13] Reflexes are assumed to be originally volitional, and the movements of lower animals are simple willed acts. Automatic and impulsive action are steps in this process.

When complex volitions with the same motive are often repeated, the conflict between the motives grows less intense; the opposing motives which were overcome in earlier cases grow weaker and finally disappear entirely. The complex act has then passed into a simple, or *impulsive act* . . . .

This regressive development is but one step in a process which unites all the external acts of a living being, whether they are volitional acts or automatic reflex movements. When the habituating practice of certain acts is carried further, the determining motives finally become, even in impulsive acts, weaker and more transient. The external stimulus originally aroused a strongly affective idea which operated as a motive, but now the stimulus causes the discharge of the act before it can arouse an idea. In this way the impulsive movement finally becomes an *automatic* movement. The more often this automatic movement is repeated, the easier, it in turn, becomes, even when the stimulus is not sensed, as for example in deep sleep or during complete diversion of the attention. The movement now appears as a pure physiological reflex, and the volitional process has become a simple *reflex process*. (pp. 213–4)

The purposive character of reflexes points to the presence, at one stage, of purposive ideas.

This retrogradation of volitional acts receives experimental confirmation, in the view of Wundt, in the investigations on reaction time. Volitional acts are demonstrated in reactions of the so-called "sensorial" type. "Muscular" reactions, on the other hand, are reflex; the objective evidence being in the form of shortened reaction times.

In this form (shortened reactions) of reaction the preparatory expectation is directed entirely toward the external act which is to be executed as rapidly as possible, so that voluntary inhibition or execution of the act in accordance with the special character of the impression can here not take place . . . . On the other hand, it is easy by practice so to habituate one's self to the invariable connection of an impression and a particular move-

---

[13] *Cf.* Wundt (545, 546). Perrault (*supra*, Chapter III, p. 33) presented a point of view in many respects similar to that of Wundt and the "genetic" group.

ment, that the process of perception fades out more and more or takes place after the motor impulse, so that finally the movement becomes just like a reflex movement. This reduction of volition to a mechanical process, shows itself most clearly in the shortening of the objective time to that observed in pure reflexes, and shows itself subjectively in the fact that for psychological observation there is a complete coincidence in point of time, of impression and reaction, while the characteristic feeling of resolution gradually disappears entirely.   (pp. 221–2)

Wundt established two important criteria of reflexes as organically distinct types of movement; consciousness and immediacy. Consciousness may *accompany* a true reflex, but it must not cause it.

A movement mediated in the central organ by way of response to sensory stimulation, if it is to be denominated a reflex movement, may not bear upon it the marks of *psychical causation;* i.e., the idea aroused by the stimulus may not constitute, for the agent's own consciousness, the *motive* to the external movement . . . . In the individual case it may, naturally, be difficult to decide, especially if the observations are made from the outside, whether a given movement is or is not a reflex. But this practical difficulty does not justify our setting aside altogether the criterion that distinguishes the reflexes from other forms of action, and leaving out of account the fact that, while related by their purposiveness to psychically conditioned movements, they differ from them clearly and definitely, in the lack of conscious intermediaries. It is precisely this criterion that makes reflexes an easily distinguishable and characteristic class of organic movements.   (p. 251)

In the second criterion Wundt referred to the fact that in the case of reflexes the response follows immediately upon the stimulus, in the case of psychically conditioned reactions, a longer time intervenes.

In consequence Wundt excluded reflex action from the cortex, since in cortical action psycho-physical intermediaries are, of necessity, included; he concluded that in the higher animals reflex action probably does not take place beyond the mesencephalic region. He objected to using the term "reflex" in the wide sense of applying it to every movement in response to stimulation, and he specifically objected to the use of the term "cortical reflex."

It is also clear that the retention of the term in its stricter meaning is extremely important; for the origin of a class of movements that are at once purely physiological and yet purposive in character is a real and distinct problem . . . . We may, however, point out, in view of the following discussion of the functions of the different central regions, that what holds of man in this connection does not necessarily hold of the animals. We may lay it down as a general proposition that, in man, the centre at which the idea of the reflex gives way to the idea of the psychically conditioned action is the cerebral cortex.   (p. 252)

Titchener (482) follows Wundt in assuming that reflexes have developed from voluntary actions, and that the first organic movements were conscious. He points out that it is important to remember that all movement, biologically considered, is mechanical.

It is very important that the issue here involved be correctly understood. The alternatives are: movement with consciousness, movement without consciousness. They are not—as they are often stated to be—conscious action, mechanical reflex. All actions, biologically regarded, are "mechanical"; all, that is, may by hypothesis be explained (and in all probability will, some day, be explained) in physico-chemical terms. The antithesis of the conscious is not the mechanical, but the unconscious action; the antithesis of the reflex is not the conscious or voluntary action, but the complex coördinated action. A great deal of controversy would have been avoided if this elementary point had been kept clear. (p. 451)

Four lines of evidence are adduced. First, in becoming skilled there is gradual automatization with a decrease of conscious accompaniment; voluntary action degenerates into "secondary reflexes." Second, all reflexes, secondary or primary, may be brought under or modified by consciousness. Third, there are certain reflex movements which express emotion that would be altogether unintelligible if we did not assume "a remote conscious ancestry." Finally, we note that they primarily resemble the secondary reflexes in that they are definite, clear-cut, precise; characters which come with a lapse of consciousness in the case of the secondary reflexes.[14]

Külpe (274) regards consciousness as the chief ground of distinction between voluntary and "automatic or reflex movement." In the case of the simple reaction of the muscular type he doubts if a "sharp line of distinction can be drawn between the reflex and the simple reaction," and regards this type of reaction as essentially "physiological in nature."

The recent paper by Dodge on the "Protopraxic and Epicritic Stratification of Human Adjustments" (113) presents a point of view more or less consistent with that of the group under discussion. The author rejects the "traditional classification of human responses as reflex, instinctive, habitual, and voluntary," since such a classification involves a "simplification fallacy" and gives a wholly artificial picture of human behavior. On the contrary, every adjustment of the organism to the environment involves both crude protopraxic responses of short latency and more finely elaborated epicritic reactions.

Our simplest reflex acts are seldom or never simple muscle twitches of uniform duration and extent. Each stimulus to a reflex operates on a neural center that is already more or less excited from the interaction of various levels. As it gains control of the final common

---

[14] *Cf.* Titchener (481).

path, the reflex stimulus never finds the system on which it acts exactly twice alike except by accident . . . .

In the second place, the effect of any reflex stimulus may be prolonged through the action of intersegmental delay-paths into a series of efferent stimuli with more or less protracted contraction of the reacting muscle, resulting in a subsequent complication of reflex response by intersegmental action. Such response would be illustrated by the voluntary extension of the leg at the knee in reaction to the same stimulus that evokes the knee-jerk. The overt act in such a case originated as a reflex, but developed in voluntary behavior. (p. 149)

Reactions are constantly passing from the protopraxic to the epicritic form of adjustment. This "behavior flux" denies the existence of mutually exclusive categories of behavior; the epicritic phase may pass into the protopraxic or the direction of change may be in the reverse order.

THE "SPECIFIC" GROUP

In McDougall (348) we find a vigorous reaction from the mechanistic interpretations of the Behaviorists. Instead of reflex action as a corner stone, he places purposive action as the fundamental category of psychology. He does not, of course, deny the existence of reflexes. He points out that "they do not exhibit the characteristic marks of behavior, the objective criteria of purpose." The reflex lacks spontaneity, persistency; it is stereotyped, it does not appear to seek a goal, it is not improved by repetition, it does not involve the whole organism, and it does not show preparation for the coming situation.

Warren (523) describes the reflex as a separate and distinctive category of movement. It is characterized as follows:

The distinctive characteristic of the 'pure' reflex is that the neural paths which constitute its arc are definite and the resulting response very precise—the motor outgo is not diffuse. Hence, the form of response depends almost wholly upon the nature of the present stimulus, and not upon the retention effect of preceding impulses which have affected the same arc. (p. 99)

Warren defines the reflex as the "original form of behavior among creatures possessing a nervous system." He distinguishes simple and compound reflexes. The former are due to the action of a simple nervous arc; the latter occur when two or more sensory impulses are combined, or when a single sensory impulse finds multiple expression. The compound reflex always involves higher centers. Warren attempts an elaborate classification of human reflexes. He makes use of five categories: (1) pure reflexes —those least subject to central modification, e.g., the pupillary reflex, trembling, shivering, myenteric reflexes; (2) largely pure—subject to inhibition or reinforcement, *e.g.*, winking, sneezing, knee-jerk, yawning, salivation, plantar reflex, vasomotor reflexes; (3) occasionally pure—more often centrally modified, *e.g.*, coughing, swallowing, sobbing, stretching, sex reflexes; (4) pure in infancy, centrally modified in the adult, *e.g.*, sucking, hunger and thirst reflexes, lip and tongue reflexes, vocal reflexes, grasping; (5) postural reflexes, *e.g.*, holding head erect, standing.

Ladd and Woodworth (277) point out that there are many prompt reactions to stimuli which involve volition or previous learning, that are not to be classed as reflex.

A true reflex should be not learned, but innate. A good example of the true reflex is afforded by the contraction of the pupil in response to bright light entering the eye. This is not an acquired reaction, nor is it dependent on the will. Of some of] the true reflexes we are wholly unconscious; in the case of others, such as flushing, shivering, starting, the secretion of saliva, we are aware of their occurrence, but have no voluntary control over them; in the case of still others, such as coughing, sneezing, winking, we have some degree of control, and yet there can be no doubt that they were never learned by the individual. There are yet other reactions, of which a good example is afforded by the turning of the eyes toward any "attractive" object, which appear at a very early age in the infant, and without any evidence that they are learned; but which are very closely interwoven with our conscious life, and which are controllable, to a large extent, by the adult animal. (p. 145)

THE "GESTALT" INTERPRETATION

A re-examination of the concepts of physiological psychology has taken place at the hands of the proponents of the "new" psychology, the so-called "gestalt" or configuration psychology. This school has reacted vigorously against both mechanistic and atomistic psychology.

It is a fundamental tenet of this school that the properties of organic life are not adequately explained by special properties—either inherited or acquired—which enforce order. In particular they reject the concept, which is a fundamental postulate of mechanistic physiology, that inherited typographical arrangements compel the course of organic processes, for example, the nervous impulse, to follow a fixed and predetermined path. Köhler, in his recent book on configuration psychology (270), says:

In the time of Descartes, his so-called mechanical interpretation of organic functions may have been bold enough; still he was absolutely conservative in assuming without a moment's hesitation that—apart from the influence of one engineer, the soul—all delicate, vital processes were enforced by special arrangements, connections and channels throughout the whole body of man. Figuratively, the organism was for him what the sky had been for Aristotle—full of crystal spheres. (p. 110)

In place of the order imposed by inherited and acquired arrangements, a third type of functional interpretation is proposed which Köhler calls "dynamical self-distribution." According to this theory, there is a dynamical interaction within the system itself which is a fundamental factor in determining the distribution of forces. The organism is regarded as an adjusting, self-regulating apparatus in which order is enforced, not by pre-existing neural arrangements, but by dynamic factors involved in constant inter-action between the processes in the organism itself in relation to the environment These factors are physically predictable and do not involve the mysterious "life force" of the Vitalists.[15] The effect of typographical arrangements within the organism is not eliminated.

In this connection Köhler says:

> Though the direction of local process in a system is not altogether determined by local arrangement, the result of dynamical self-distribution as a whole may still depend upon typographical conditions. Thus the electric current in a network of wires is distributed dynamically; yet the actual distribution as a whole depends upon the position of the electrodes and upon the conductivities in all the conductors. Similarly, the totality of processes in the optical part of the nervous system will depend upon given conditions in each case. For the moment, though this will prove to be an inexact assumption when it is examined more closely, I shall suppose that in the interior of the optical network the general conditions of conduction remain constant. But, then, as a set of peripheral conditions we have the patterns of different chemical reactions on the retina, as they are produced in each case by actual stimulation. Upon these varying conditions self-distribution of process will depend primarily. (p. 141)

Koffka (269) has given especial attention to the concept of reflex action. He discusses a group of movements in response to external stimuli which have the following peculiarities: (1) they are relatively simple, (2) they take place with uniformity, (3) variation of the stimulus is not necessarily accompanied by an alteration in the reaction—the reaction may suddenly become qualitatively different without a corresponding change in the stimulus, (4) they belong to the inherited disposition of the individual, (5) they serve a protective, defensive, and adjustive purpose, (6) they exhibit facilitation or inhibition when an additional stimulus is applied at the same point. These movements are reflexes.

> We might ask the question: How must an organ be constructed whose function is destined to be reflexive? The usual answer to this question is very simple. We know two kinds of nerves, anatomically and physiologically—namely, sensory and motor nerves. Furthermore, we know that sensory nerves possess a terminal arborization which, either directly or through the mediation of other neurones, approaches the terminals of the motor nerves; and we know, finally, that an injury at any point of this more or less complicated

---

[15] The reader is referred to Köhler (270), Koffka (269), Helson (216), and the issues of the *Psych. Forschung*, for a complete statement of the Gestalt theory.

series of neurones involved in the arousal of a movement interferes with the movement itself. The function of the reflex also indicates the double nature of the stimulation and response. The organ of the reflexes is therefore quite obviously a more or less complicated chain of neurones which, in the limiting case, may consist of but two neurones. Always beginning with a sensory neurone and ending with a motor neurone, this apparatus is called a *reflex-arc*. (p. 68)

The characteristic feature of this arc is the connection between the centripetal and centrifugal branches, a connection conceived to be "predetermined, inherited." The stimulus serves the purpose of releasing energy in the nerve cells, the result of which is that a series of dynamic, inter-acting physical processes are set up which results in a re-adjustment of the organism. The channels through which these processes take place are not necessarily inherited or otherwise pre-determined.

Koffka does not believe that the sensory arm of the reflex arc serves merely the function of releasing the motor function. In the case of the eye and the fixation reflex, the organ of vision becomes a self-regulating apparatus, a single system in which the sensory and motor functions act in a unitary manner.

I can perhaps illustrate this self-regulatory process by a simple example. The centre of the field of vision, which corresponds to the *fovea centralis*, is phenomenally as well as functionally a point of outstanding character and significance. Assume an infant lying on its back in a totally dark room, as described in Watson's tests, and allow a light to fall on the peripheral region of its retinae The infant's optical system will then be in a state of dis-equilibrium occasioning eye-movements which continue in a certain direction until equilibrium has been reestablished. This will be the case when the light falls upon the fovea of each eye—that is, upon the centres of gravity, as it were, in each optical field, which condition the fixation of the light by the eyes. (pp. 80–1)

The essential point of the hypothesis is that a relation between the motor and sensory functions is posited which does *not provide for a special connecting mechanism*. This interpretation Koffka applies to all reflexes. He points out, however, that the neurone is not necessarily eliminated.

Yet it does not necessarily follow that the reflexive apparatus of the older theory with its system of neurones must in all cases disappear from the explanation; for it is still conceivable that the fixation of function may go hand in hand with the fixation of an organ as it develops a system within which the process can take place in a relatively independent manner. But even so, the apparatus itself would not be the cause but the consequence of this kind of functioning. The existence of such an apparatus therefore lends no weight to any argument for the older theory, or against the newer one. (p. 109)

The utility of the reflex, then, is not determined by fixed, inherited connections between stimulus and response, but by certain physiological processes which for physical and chemical reasons proceed towards a definite end. Koffka makes it clear the physical does not necessarily signify mechanical.

The experiments of A. Marina (333), first published in 1905 and 1910, demonstrate the inadequacy of the traditional theory that function is determined by pre-existing neural pathways. Koffka discusses these experiments as follows:

> Marina operated upon apes, first by exchanging the medial rectus and lateral rectus muscles of an eye, and later so as to substitute the superior rectus for the lateral rectus. In the first case, therefore, the eye was moved outward by the previously inward-moving muscle, and *vice versa*. In the second case the muscle moving the eye outward was eliminated and its place taken by a lifting muscle. If a definite impulse were conducted from the centre through the pathway to each muscle, the animal must have made the most remarkable eye-movements after the wound had healed. But, instead, the voluntary and automatic sideward movements of the eyes were carried out in a normal manner as soon as the cicatrization was complete. From this and other results the author concludes 'that the anatomical association-pathways from the centres to the eye-muscles are not fixed,' and that the *conduction pathways have no predetermined function*. Considering the results of other operations of transplantation, he seeks to justify his attribution of a very general significance to this conclusion, and demands a new foundation for the physiology of the brain. (p. 363)[16]

These results seem to indicate that the traditional theory of innate neural pathways or specific mechanisms as determining response is incompetent to account for the observed facts.

It is interesting to note that Dewey in 1896 has critically discussed the reflex arc concept from a point of view which bears a recognizable resemblance to that presented by the configurationists. In this paper (105) the reflex arc is discussed from the point of view of its inadequacy as a description of *unified* behavior. This concept is regarded as being particularly inappropriate as a designation for certain coordinated responses where its application demands the splitting up of the total response into artificially simplified parts. Dewey does not believe that sensory stimuli and motor responses are distinct and separate existences, "in reality they are always inside a coordination and have their significance purely from the part played in maintaining or re-constituting that coordination." While pointing out that it is an "undoubted fact that movement as a response follows sensation as a stimulus," Dewey indicates that these terms refer to a "flexible function" only and not a "fixed existence." The stimulus and the response do not have an existence.

[16] *Cf.* Marina (333) and Ziehen's discussion of these results (551).

The sensation or conscious stimulus is not a thing or existence by itself; it is a phase of a coördination requiring attention because, by reason of the conflict within the coördination, it is uncertain how to complete it. It is to doubt as to the next act . . . which gives the motive to examining the act. The end to follow is, in this sense, the stimulus. It furnishes the motivation to attend to what has just taken place; to define it more carefully. From this point of view the discovery of the stimulus is the 'response' to possible movement as 'stimulus.' . . .

In other words, sensation as stimulus does not mean any particular psychical *existence*. It means simply a function, and will have its value shift according to the special work requiring to be done. At one moment the various activities of reaching and withdrawing will be the sensation, because they are that phase of activity which sets the problem, or creates the demand for, the next act. At the next moment the previous act . . . will furnish the sensation, being, in turn, that phase of activity which sets the pace upon which depends further action. Generalized, sensation as stimulus, is always that phase of activity requiring to be defined in order that a coördination may be completed. (p. 368)

The reflex should be regarded not as an arc but a circle "some of whose members have come into conflict with each other," and thus stand in need of a reconstitution; this takes the form of a smooth coordination.

The stimulus is that phase of the forming coördination which represents the conditions which have to be met in bringing it to a successful issue; the response is that phase of one and the same forming coördination which gives the key to meeting these conditions, which serves as instrument in effecting the successful coördination. They are therefore strictly correlative and contemporaneous. The stimulus is something to be discovered; to be made out; if the activity affords its own adequate stimulation, there is no stimulus save in the objective sense already referred to. As soon as it is adequately determined, then and then only is the response complete. To attain either, means that the coördination has completed itself. (p. 370)

It is clear that Dewey is rejecting the traditional view of the mechanical reflex and in its place is describing an adjusting organism which responds in terms of completed acts. He has taken a position which is not inconsistent with, and to some extent anticipates, that of Gestalt psychology.

Regarding the claims of the Behaviorist, who is *par excellence* an exponent of the mechanical point of view, for the general efficacy of the reflex plus the principle of conditioning, to account for the organism as a constantly adjusting entity, Köhler in the previously mentioned book (270) says:

If I feel a little disappointed by the work of behaviorism, the reason is not so much a certain innocence in its treatment of direct experience and in its imitation of adult physics, but its astounding sterility in the development of productive concepts about functions underlying observable behavior. As an imitation of physics it is scarcely a satisfactory achievement for the behaviorist to have taken the old concept of reflex action from physiology (including the reflexes of inner secretion) and to give us no further comprehension into the formation of new individual behavior than is offered by his concepts of positive and negative "conditioning." Why should behaviorism be so utterly negativistic in its characteristic statements? "Thou shalt not acknowledge direct experience in science" is the first commandment and "Thou shalt not conceive of other functions but reflexes and conditioned reflexes" is the second. (p. 55)

SUMMARY OF CHARACTERISTICS OF THE CONCEPT OF REFLEX ACTION

The summary of physiological and psychological opinion regarding reflex action which has been attempted is not exhaustive, but the major points of view have been presented. It seems clear that a simple unqualified definition of reflex action is not feasible in the present state of our knowledge of the subject. We may note, however, that some concept of reflex action has played an important rôle in all physiological and psychological systems. There would seem to be some warrant for the statement that there is no other single physiological principle which has attained a like position of dominance in explaining integrated animal behavior.

The examination of reflex theory as expressed in representative physiological and psychological texts and treatises resulted in a three-fold[17] classification which may be summarized as follows.

1. Reflex action under the first ("specific") concept is regarded as possessing certain physiological and psychological characteristics which distinguish it from all other kinds of action. There is disagreement as to the nature of these criteria, but a list made up from various sources is as follows: (1) the reflex is not conditioned by *consciousness*, (2) it is *involuntary*, (3) the *time* from the reception of the stimulus to the beginning of the response is short as compared with the "voluntary" or "willed" reactions, (4) neurologically the reflex does not involve the *cerebral cortex*, (5) it is a type of behavior which is *unlearned, i.e.*, it is based on inherited neural mechanisms, (6) it is *predictable*, uniform and definite, *i.e.*, given a certain type of stimulus and a certain receptor organ, the response is relatively *invariable*, (7) reflex action serves some adjustive or protective *purpose*, (8) structurally, the reflex involves a receptor, afferent and efferent conduction in a synaptic nervous system, and an effector.

2. Reflex action under the second ("genetic") concept has certain definite characteristics in its simple form, but there is no sharp break in the series of responses in which the reflex or other primitive type of response represents one extreme and complex "volitional" responses, the other. According to Wundt reflex action is genetically derived from voluntary action; intermediate steps are impulsive and automatic action. The most

---

[17] Strictly, we have presented a four-fold classification since the Gestalt interpretation forms a separate group.

important change in this series is with respect to consciousness. For Wundt the reflex is not conditioned by consciousness; Luciani suggests the possibility of extending consciousness even to the spinal animal. It would seem that this concept of reflex action is mainly serviceable in connection with the problem of the genetic development of the "higher" (more complex) forms of response from the "lower" types of response.

3. Reflex action under the third ("mechanical") concept is based on a fixed neural mechanism, including afferent and efferent conduction and receptor and effector organs; this neural arrangement is assumed to underlie and pre-determine *all* behavior. The characteristics of the simple spinal reflex, *e.g.*, invariability, innateness, are applied to all behavior. It is usually the functioning of the simple reflex arc that is described, and it is by implication that the characteristics of this functioning are carried over to all action.

Under the "mechanical" theory automatisms and "volition" are explained in terms of fixed mechanisms. Habits (automatisms) are merely certain reflex responses which have become attached to certain stimuli by a process of conditioning. Watson makes it clear that no "new paths are formed in the establishment of a habit. This conditioning process cannot take place without the cerebrum, but cerebral action involves only the element of increased complexity; hence, volition in the sense of centrally "controlled" acts no longer exists.

The problem which consciousness presents, is ignored under this conception. If centrally excited action is eliminated, "choice" and "purpose" disappear as factors in the control of action. Consciousness becomes a mere accompaniment to the functioning of reflex arcs.

PROBLEMS FOR INVESTIGATION IN REFLEX ACTION

In connection with the concept of reflex action as reviewed in the previous pages, certain problems seem to emerge, the experimental consideration of which might clarify the situation. These questions are not so much problems, perhaps, as points of stress, *i.e.*, issues around which the conflict of theory and interpretation seems to be sharpest. It is suggested that it is in the direction of these problems that the solution of some of the inconsistencies and inadequacies of present day reflex theory may lie. The problems are of necessity stated in general terms.

1. The nature of voluntary action and its relation to the reflex. We may raise here the whole question of centrally excited action. This does not concern any hypothetical "will," but is concerned with the objective and subjective conditions of a type of action which appears to be conscious,

deliberative, and unlearned. Reaction time experiments have made a notable contribution to this problem in calling attention to certain characteristic features of "voluntary" action, namely, "mental set," "determining tendency," *Einstellung*, etc. It is necessary to know more of the neurological nature and limits of "mental set." Golla and Hetwer (174), for example, using the action-current technique, found that "the time relations of the coordination of various muscles in certain voluntary movements is the same as when a similar movement is elicited as a spinal reflex response." They believed that an analogous voluntary movement in the case of the knee-jerk merely innervated "previously existing reflex patterns."

2. The nature of automatisms. Certain actions which are originally "voluntary" become automatic with repetition. This automatization is characterized by (a) elimination of certain "unnecessary" movements, (b) decrease in latency, and (c) decrease in the conscious accompaniments. In certain respects it thus appears to approach the "typical" reflex. In the behavioristic interpretation this is a process of conditioning; nothing "new" is established—one reflex "path" becomes functionally favored. From the point of view of Wundt, a "new" path by reason of frequent use is taking on the functional characteristics of a reflex arc. It is essential to know more of the psychological and physiological characteristics of automatisms. Lashley (288) has recently made an important contribution to the problem of cerebral localization in relation to automatization in the rat.

3. The modification of the reflex. Sherrington has called attention to the urgent necessity for the solution of the problem of "volitional" control of the reflex. By this Sherrington means conscious control.

In other words, the reactions of reflex-arcs are controllable by mechanisms to whose activity consciousness is adjunct. By these higher centres, this or that reflex can be checked, or released, or modified in its reaction with such variety and seeming independence of external stimuli that the existence of a spontaneous internal process expressed as "will" is the naïve inference drawn. Its spring of action is not now our question; its seat in the nervous system seems to correspond with that of processes of perceptual level. It is urgently necessary for physiology to know *how* this control—volitional control—is *operative* upon reflexes, that is, how it intrudes and makes its influence felt upon the running of the reflex machinery. (441, p. 388)

This involves the whole problem of variability. Dodge's recent study (114) presents a program of investigation and describes techniques which should prove profitable in this field. The study of the interaction between simultaneously functioning reaction systems has been insufficiently pursued.

Modification seems to be brought about psychologically by at least two methods: (a) concomitant psychic process, (b) repeated functioning of the reflex arc. Under (a) we may include the physiological phenomena of *Bahnung* and *Hemmung*. We know less about the effects of (b) except that there is some experimental evidence to indicate that the reflex may entirely "disappear" with repeated function. Repeated functioning is important in connection with the establishment of automatisms, and we might logically expect it to have some effect on the "inviolable" reflex arc. There are also a large number of factors that may modify the reflex, about which little is known. Among these should be mentioned fatigue, pharmaco-psychological factors, and functional rhythms or periodicities.

4. Careful consideration of the phenomena called reflex from the point of view of their rôle in the functioning of the intact organism. In the past the tendency has been to conceive of the reflex as an isolated segment of behavior. This conception has received its chief support from the experimental procedures of the physiologists who dealt with neuro-muscular preparations artificially isolated from the rest of the organism.

The question arises as to just what type of behavior the term "reflex" is applicable. Those aspects of the reflex included under such terms as invariability, predictability, etc., do not apply to the response of the intact organism. In such an organism the most persistent aspect of the so-called reflex is its variability. The work of Dodge, Child, Herrick and many other investigators bear out this generalization. When the reflex arc is artificially simplified by operative procedures, or when some particular aspect of the arc is isolated for study, as, for example, the latency as recorded by the galvanometric techniques, this variability tends to be reduced. In these procedures, however, we are dealing with the "reflex" in an atypical situation—a situation which is of great significance to the study of neural latencies, spinal integration, the phenomena of neural conduction, etc.,—but which is only indirectly related to the understanding of the integrated responses of the intact organism.

Strictly speaking, of course, the simple *reflection* of the centripetal impulses back to the periphery does not occur in the complex nervous system. Is the term "reflex" to be limited only to the responses of the spinal animal, or is it to include all responses involving centripetal-centrifugal conduction? It is clear that we are facing terminological difficulties greatly in need of clarification.

From the point of view of physiological psychology we are concerned with the reflex act as a part of the total response pattern of the functioning organism, rather than with the analysis of the functional components of the isolated reflex arc.   Experimental studies proceeding from this stand-point will not be concerned primarily with the analysis of the latencies of the various hypothetical components of the reflex arc, the study of the action currents in the muscle, the form of the electrical response of the muscle as recorded by the galvanometric technique, etc., important as these studies are from the point of view of neural physiology.   But, on the con-trary, it will proceed to the examination of the reflex *in relation to all the concomitant events in the integrated nervous system,* and the object of the experimental technique will be the control of these variables.

That the organism functions as an integrated unit, that in the normal individual there are no isolated neuro-muscular segments—these are truisms which all of us are doubtless inclined to accept.   Yet it not infre-quently appears that in experimentation and theoretical discussion, a functional independence is tacitly ascribed to the reflex which, in reality, it does not possess.

The division of animal responses into arbitrary classes has tended to result in an assumption that these classes are independant functional entities.   Such classifications as habitual acts, reflex acts, volitional acts, automatic acts, etc., present a wholly artificial picture of the adjusting organism.   The arbitrary distinction between voluntary and involuntary action which, as we have seen, came from the Greek physiologists, was translated into an artificial neurology by Descartes and erected by him into a dogma which has become a basic principle of physiological psychology. The distortion which this principle introduces into our picture of the responding organism was pointed out by Dewey in 1896.   The recent dis-cussion of Dodge of protopraxic and epicritic types of human adjustment voices the same protest against the artificial stratification of animal responses.

The interpretations of the Configurationists are pertinent to this point of view.   Koffka's interpretation of reflex action in physical rather than mechanical terms is suggestive, and his objections to the emphasis on a ready-prepared "mechanism" as a controlling factor needs careful con-sideration.   The analogies between machines and the functioning organism have been fruitful in the development of physiological psychology, and have exerted a fascination for the scientific mind since the time of Des-cartes; indeed, they have resisted with measurable success every onslaught. Their vigour is still undiminished, and, if we are to believe the naïve enthusiasms of the Behaviorists, success is assured.   It is possible, how-ever, that in the interpretation of behavior in terms of integrated totalities, we have an hypothesis which offers a more comprehensive and intelligible theory of the complexities of behavior and experience. Although we must proceed with the greatest caution, at least we may take hope that the sterility of the faith that mind and behavior can be envisaged by number and measure has been exposed. Important as these modes of approach are, they do not yield a complete account of experience and behavior.

BIBLIOGRAPHY

1. ACH, N. Über die Willenstätigkeit und das Denken. Göttingen, 1905.
2. ———. Über den Willensakt und das Temperament. Leipzig, 1910.
3. ADRIAN, E. D. Some recent work on inhibition. Brain, 1924, 47: 399–416.
4. ———, AND FORBES, A. The all-or-nothing response of sensory fibers. Jr. Physiol., 1922, 56: 301–330.
5. ———, AND OLMSTEAD, J. M. D. The refractory phase in a reflex arc. Jr. Physiol., 1922, 56: 426–443.
6. ALECHSIEFF, N. Reactionzeiten bei Durchgangsbeobachtungen. Phil. Stud., 1900, 16: 1.
7. ALLBUTT, SIR T. CLIFFORD. Greek Medicine in Rome. London, 1921.
8. D'ALLONES, G. R. Lecture de la pensée par un procédé nouveau d'enrégistrement des contractions automatiques de la main. Bull. de l'inst. gén. psychol., 1905, 5: 261–272.
9. ANGELL, J. R. Psychology. Fourth edition. New York, 1908.
10. ARISTOTLE. On the Common Motions of Animals. On Youth and Old Age, Life and Death. In The Treatises of Aristotle, tr. by Thomas Taylor. London, 1808.
11. ARNOLD, JOHANN WILHELM. Die Lehre von der Reflex-function für Physiologen und Aerzte. Heidelberg, 1842.
12. AUERBACH, L. Über psychische Tätigkeiten des Rückenmarks. Günsburgs Med. Z., 1856, 4: 452–496.
13. AVERY, GEORGE TRUE. Responses of foetal guinea pigs prematurely delivered. Genet. Psychol. Mon., 1928, 3, No. 4.
14. BAGLIONI, S. Zur Analyse der Reflex-funktion. Weisbaden, 1907.
15. BAILLET, A. La Vie de M. Descartes. Paris, 1691.
16. BAIN, ALEXANDER. The Senses and the Intellect. Third Edition. New York, 1868.
17. BALDWIN, J. M. Handbook of Psychology. Parts III and IV. New York, 1891.
18. ———. Dictionary of Philosophy and Psychology. New York, 1901.
19. BANCROFT, C. P. Automatic muscular movements of insane. Am. Jr. Psychol., 1890, 3: 437–452.
20. BAUDIN, E. Psychologie. Paris, 1917.
21. BAYLISS, W. M. Principles of General Physiology. Third Edition. London, 1920.
22. BEAUNIS, H. Le Somnambulisme provoque. Paris, 1887.
23. VON BECHTEREW, W. Ueber eine neue Untersuchungsmethode der Sehnenreflexe und über die Veränderungen letzterer bei Geisteskrankheiten und bei Epileptikern. Neurog. Cent., 1892, 34.
24. ———. Was ist Psychoreflexologie? Deutsch. Med. Wochenschr. Jahrg., 1912, 38: 1481–1487.
25. ———. Objektive Psychologie oder Psychoreflexologie. Leipzig, 1913.

26. Beer, Th., Bethe, A., und von Uexküll, J. Vorschläge z. einer Objektivirender Nomenclatur in der Physiologie des Nervensystems. Biol. Cent., 1899, 19: 517.

27. Beevor, C. E. On the condition of the knee-jerk, ankle clonus, and plantar reflex after epileptic fits. Brain, 1882, 5: 56–62.

28. Bell, Charles. Idea of a New Anatomy of the Brain; submitted for the observations of his friends. London, 1811.

29. ———. An Exposition of the Natural System of the Nerves of the Human Body with a republication of the papers delivered to the Royal Society, on the subject of the nerves. Philadelphia, 1825.

30. ———. The Nervous System of the Human Body; embracing the Papers to the Royal Society on the Subject of the Nerves. Washington, 1833.

31. (Anonymous). [Review of] The Nervous System of the Human Body, by Sir Charles Bell, third edition, 1836. London Quarterly Rev., 1843, 72: 192.

32. Benedict, F. S., Miles, W. R., Roth, P., and Smith, H. M. Human Vitality and Efficiency under Prolonged Restricted Diet. Carnegie Institution, No. 280, Washington, 1919.

33. Bentley, Madison. The Field of Psychology. New York, 1924.

34. Bergemann, Robert. Reaktionem auf Schalleindrücke, nach der Methode der Haüfigskeitskurven bearbeitet. Psych. Stud., 1906, 1: 179–218.

35. Berger, O. Ueber Sehnenreflexe. Cent. f. Nervenheilkunde, 1879, 73.

36. Bernard, Claude. Leçons sur la physiologie et la pathologie du système nerveaux. Vol. II. Paris, 1858.

37. ———. Phenomenes de la Vie. Vol. II. Paris, 1879.

38. Bernhard, E. A. Psychische Vorgänge betrachtet als Bewegungen. Berlin, 1923.

39. Bernheim, H. Hypnotisme, Suggestion, Psychothérapie. Paris, 1891.

40. ———. Automatisme et Suggestion. Paris, 1917.

41. Bethe, A. Dürfen wir den Ameisen u. Beinen psychische Qualitäten zuschreiben? Pflüger's Arch., 1898, 70: 15.

42. Bichat, Xavier. De l'influence Nerveuse dans les Sympathies. Jr. de Méd. Chirurgie, Pharmacie, etc., 1801, 472.

43. Biedermann, W. Ueber die Innervation der Krebsscheere. Sitz. Ber. Wien. Akad., 1887, 95 Abth. 3: 8–48.

44. Binet, Alfred. Alternations of Personality. New York, 1896.

45. ——— et Féré, C. Le Magnétisme Animal. Paris, 1887.

46. ——— et ———. Recherches expérimentales sur la physiologie des mouvements chez les hystériques. Arch. de Physiol., 1887, 10: 320–373.

47. Bischoff, T. L. W. Einige Physiologisch-anatomische Beobachtungen aus einem Enthaupeteten. Arch. f. Anat. Physiol. und Wissensch. Med., 1838, 486–502.

48. Blane, Sir Gilbert. Select Dissertations on Several Subjects of Medical Science. London, 1822.

49. Bliss, Charles B. Investigation in reaction time and attention. Studies from the Yale Psy. Lab., 1892–1893, 1–55.

50. Bloch, E. Neuropathische Diathese und Kniephänomen. Arch. f. Psy. und Nervenkrank., 1882, 12: 471–479.

51. Boerhaave, H. Dr. Boerhaave's Academical Lectures on the Theory of Physic, being a genuine translation of his Institutes and explanatory comments. London, 1753.

52. BOLTON, T. L.   The relation of motor power to intelligence.   Am. Jr. Psychol., 1903, 14: 351.

53. "Book of Medicines"—Syrian anatomy, pathology and therapeutics.   Author unknown.   English translation by E. A. Wallis Budge.   Oxford University Press, 1913.

54. BORELLI, G. A.   De Motu Animalium.   Rome, 1680.

55. BORING, E. G.   The problem of originality in science.   Am. Jr. Psychol., (Washburn Commemorative Volume), 1927, 39: 70–90.

56. BOWDITCH, H. P.   The reinforcement and inhibition of the knee-jerk.   Boston Med. and Surg. Jr., 1888, 118: 542–543.

57. ———, AND WARREN, J. W.   The knee-jerk and its physiological modification. Jr. Physiol., 1890, 11: 25–64.

58. BOYLE, ROBERT.   The Works of the Honourable Robert Boyle.   Five vols.   London, 1744.

59. BRAID, JAMES.   On Hypnotism, Neurypnology; or The Rationale of Nervous Sleep. London, 1899.

60. BRAUNE, C. W., AND FISCHER, O.   Ueber den Schwerpunkt des Menschlichen Körpers mit Rücksicht auf die Ausrüstung des deutschen Infanteristen.   Abhand. der Math.-phys. Klasse der König. Sächs. Gesell. der Wissensch. Leipzig, 1889, 559–672.

61. BRETT, G. S.   A History of Psychology.   Vol. II and vol. III.   London, 1921.

62. BRISSAUD, E.   Recherches anatomo-pathologiques et physiologiques sur la contracture permanente des hémiplégiques.   Paris, 1880.

63. BRONDGEEST, P. J.   Onderzoekingen over den tonus der Willekeurige spieren, Hollandisch.   Beitr. z. physiol. Wissensch., 1860.   German summary in Arch. f. Anatomy u. Physiol., 1860, 703–4.

64. BROWN-SEQUARD, M.   Recherches expérimentales et cliniques sur l'inhibition et la dynamogénie.   Paris, 1882.

65. BRUNTON, T. LAUDER.   On the nature of inhibition, and the action of drugs upon it. Nature, 1883, 27: 419–422, 436–439, 467–468, 485–487.

66. BUCHANAN, FLORENCE.   On the time taken in transmission of reflex impulses in the spinal cord of the frog.   Quart. Jr. Exper. Physiol., 1908, 1: 1–66.

67. BULLARD, W. N., AND BRACKETT, E. G.   Observations on the steadiness of the hand and on static equilibrium.   Boston Med. and Surg. Jr., 1888, 119–595.

68. BURCKHARDT, G.   Ueber Sehnenreflexe.   Festschrift dem Andenken an Albrecht v. Haller dargebracht von den Aerzten der Schweiz am 12 December, 1877. Bern, 1877.

69. BURNHAM, WM. H.   The Normal Mind.   New York, 1924.

70. BURTT, H. E.   The perception of slight changes of equilibrium, with especial reference to problems of aviation.   Jr. Appl. Psychol., 1918, 2: 101–115.

71. ———, AND TUTTLE, W. W.   The patellar tendon reflex and affective tone.   Amer. Jr. Psychol., 1925, 36: 553–561.

72. BUZZARD, THOMAS.   On "tendon-reflex" as an aid to diagnosis in diseases of the spinal cord.   Lancet, 1880, 2: 842–844, 884–885.

73. ———.   Patellar tendon reflex and cerebellar disease.   Med. Press.   Nov., 1880.

74. ———.   An address on the significance and value of tendon reflex.   Lancet, 1888, 1: 159–163.

75. CABANIS, PIERRE JEAN GEORGE. Rapports du physique et du moral de l'homme. 1799.

76. CALMEIL, L. F. De la paralysie considérée chez les aliénés; recherches faites dans le service de feu M. Royer-Collard et de M. Esquirol. Paris, 1826.

77. ———. Recherches sur la structure, les fonctions et le ramollissement de la moelle épinière. Jr. des Progrès et Inst. Méd., 1828, 11: 77.

78. CARMICHAEL, LEONARD. Sir Charles Bell: A contribution to the history of physiological psychology. Psychol. Rev., 1926, 33: 188.

79. ———. Robert Whytt: A contribution to the history of physiological psychology. Psychol. Rev., 1927, 34: 287.

80. CARPENTER, W. B. On the voluntary and instinctive actions of living beings. Edin. Med. and Surg. Jr., 1837, 11: 22–44.

81. ———. Reflex Action in the Nervous System of Invertebrata. London, 1839.

82. ———. Principles of Mental Physiology; with their applications to the training and discipline of the mind, and the study of morbid conditions. Fourth ed. New York, 1877.

83. CASON, HULSEY. The conditioned eyelid reaction. Jr. Exper. Psychol., 1922, 5: 153–196.

83a. ———. The conditioned reflex or conditioned response as a common activity of living organisms. Psychol. Bull., 1925, 22: 445–472.

84. CATTELL, J. M. The time taken up by cerebral operations. Mind, 1886, 11: 220, 377, 524.

85. CAYRADE, JULES. Recherches critiques et expérimentales sur les mouvements réflexes. Thèse pour le doctorat en médicine. Paris, 1864.

86. CHARCOT, J. M., ET RICHER, P. Contribution à l'étude de l'hypnotisme chez les hystériques. Comp. rend. d. l. Soc. de Biol., 1881, 133.

87. CHARDELS, C. Essai de psychologie physiologique, I. Aufl., 1831.

88. CHILD, C. M. Physiological Foundations of Behavior. New York, 1924.

89. CLEGHORN, A. M. The reinforcement of voluntary muscular contractions. Amer. Jr. Physiol., 1898, 1: 336–345.

90. ———. Equilibrium and Equilibration. A Reference Handbook of the Medical Sciences. New York, 1901, 3: 857.

91. COBB, STANLEY. Review on the tonus of skeletal muscle. Physiol. Rev., 1925, 5: 518–550.

92. COOVER, J. E. Experiments in Psychical Research. Psychical Res. Mon. No. 1., Stanford Univ., California, 1917.

93. CORY, CHAS. E. A subconscious phenomenon. Jr. Abnor. Psychol., 1920, 14: 369–375.

94. COURTNEY, J. W. On the clinical differentiation of the various forms of ambulatory automatism. Jr. Abnor. Psychol., 1906, 1: 123–134.

95. CROONE, WILLIAM. De ratione motus musculorum. London, 1667.

96. CRUIKSHANK, WILLIAM. Experiments on the nerves, particularly on their reproduction; and on the spinal marrow of living animals. Phil. Trans., 1795, 85: 177–189.

97. V. CYON, E. Hemmungen und Erregungen in Centralnervensystem der Gefässnerven. Bull. de l'acad. de St. Petersberg, 1870.

98. ———. Zur Hemmungstheorie der reflektorischen Erregungen. Fest. f. C. Ludwig. Leipzig, 1874.

99. DELACROIX, H. De l'automatisme dans l'imitation. Jr. de psychol., 1921, 18: 97–139.

100. DELMAS-MARSALET, P. Les réflexes de posture élémentaires (étude physioclinique). Paris, 1927.

101. DESCARTES, RENÉ. Oeuvres, Tannery Edition. Paris, 1897–1909.

102. ———. Traité de l'Homme. 1662.

103. ———. Philosophical Works rendered into English by Elizabeth S. Haldane and G. R. T. Ross. 2 vols. Cambridge University Press, 1911.

104. DESPINE, —. Étude scientifique sur le somnambulisme. Paris, 1880.

105. DEWEY, J. The reflex arc concept in psychology. Psychol. Rev., 1896, 3: 357–370.

106. DODGE, R. A systematic exploration of a normal knee-jerk, its technique, the form of muscle contraction, its amplitude, its latent time and its theory. Zsch. f. Allg. Physiol., 1910, 12: 1–58.

107. ———. The refractory phase of the protective reflex wink. Amer. Jr. Psychol., 1913, 24: 1–7.

108. ———. The latent time of compensatory eye movements. Jr. Exper. Psychol., 1921, 4: 247–269.

109. ———. Habituation to rotation. Jr. Exper. Psychol., 1923, 6: 1–35.

110. ———. The hypothesis of inhibition by drainage. Proc. Nat. Acad. Sciences, 1925, 11: 689–691.

111. ———. The problem of inhibition. Psychol. Rev., 1926, 33: 1–12.

112. ———. Theories of inhibition. Psychol. Rev., 1926, 33: 106–122, 167–187.

113. ———. Protopraxic and epicritic stratification of human adjustments. Amer. Jr. Psychol., (Washburn Commemorative Vol.), 1927, 39: 145–157.

114. ———. Elementary Conditions of Human Variability. New York, 1927.

115. ———, AND BENEDICT, F. S. Psychological Effects of Alcohol. An experimental investigation of the effects of moderate doses of ethyl alcohol on a related group of neuro-muscular processes in man. Carnegie Inst. pub., No. 232, 1915.

116. ———, AND BOTT, E. A. Antagonistic muscle action in voluntary flexion and extension. Psychol. Rev., 1927, 34: 241–286.

117. DONDERS, F. C. Die Schnelligkeit psychischer Prozesse. Arch. f. Anat. u. Physiol., 1868, 657–681.

118. DOWNEY, J. E. Automatic phenomena of muscle reading. Jr. Phil., Psychol., etc., 1908, 5: 650–651.

119. ———, AND ANDERSON, J. E. Automatic writing. Amer. Jr. Psychol., 1915, 26: 99–129.

120. DUNCAN, JAMES. Memoir of Swammerdam, in Naturalist's Library, vol. 34, ed. by Sir Wm. Jardine, Edinburgh, 1843.

121. DUNLAP, K. Nystagmus test and practice. Jr. Amer. Med. Ass., 1919, 73: 54–55.

122. ———. Elements of Scientific Psychology. St. Louis, 1922.

123. DUSSER DE BARENNE, J. G. Once more the innervation and the tonus of the striped muscles. Proc. Konin. Akad. v. Wet. Amsterdam, 1919, 21: 1238–1248.

124. DUVERNY, G. J. De la Structure et du Sentiment de la Moelle. Mém. de l'Académ. des Sc. de Paris, 1700.

125. ECKHARD, C. Geschichte der Entwickelung der Lehre von den Reflexerscheinungen. Beit. z. Anat. und Physiol., 1881, 9: 31–192.

126. EMERY, F. E.   The effect of temperature upon the tonus of skeletal muscle.   Amer. Jr. Physiol., 1925, 63: 296–303.

127. ERB, W. H.   Ueber Sehnenreflexe bei Gesünden und Rückenmarkskranken.   Archiv. f. Psychiat. und Nervenkrankh., 1875, 5: 792.

128. ERLANGER, J. AND GASSER, H. S.   The compound nature of the action current of nerve as disclosed by the cathode ray oscillograph.   Amer. Jr. Physiol., 1924, 70: 624–666.

129. EULENBURG, A.   Ueber Sehnenreflexe bei Kindern.   Deutsche Zeit. f. prakt. Medicin, 1878, 31.

130. EWALD, J. R.   Physiologische Untersuchungen über das Endorgan das Nervus Octavus.   Wiesbaden, 1890.

131. EXNER, S.   Experimentelle Untersuchung der enfachsten psychischen Processe.   Pflüg. Arch., 1873, 7: 601–660; 1874, 8: 526–537.

132. ———.   Entwurf einen physiologischen Erklärung psychischer Erscheinungen. 1894.

133. FARR, SAMUEL.   A Philosophical Enquiry into the Nature, Origin, and Extent of Animal Motion, Deduced from the Principles of Reason and Analogy.   1771.

134. FEARING, F.   The factors influencing static equilibrium.   An experimental study of the influence of height, weight, and position of the feet on amount of sway, together with the analysis of the variability in the records of one reagent over a long period of time.   Jr. Comp. Psychol., 1924, 4: 90.

135. ———.   The factors influencing static equilibrium.   An experimental study of the effects of practice upon amount and direction of sway.   Jr. Comp. Psychol., 1924, 4: 162.

136. ———.   The experimental study of the Romberg sign.   Jr. Nerv. and Ment. Dis., 1925, 61: 449–465.

137. ———.   Factors influencing static equilibrium.   An experimental study of the effect of controlled and uncontrolled attention apon amount and direction of sway.   Jr. Comp. Psychol., 1925, 5: 1–24.

138. ———.   Motor automatisms and reflex action.   Psychol. Bull., 1926, 23: 457–481.

139. ———.   Post-rotational head nystagmus in adult pigeons.   Jr. Comp. Psychol., 1926, 6: 115–131.

140. ———.   A critique of the experimental studies of cortical inhibition with special reference to the knee-jerk.   Jr. Comp. Psych., 1927, 7: 285–296.

141. ———.   A history of the experimental study of the knee-jerk.   Amer. Jr. Psychol., 1928, 40: 92–111.

142. ———.   Jan Swammerdam: A study in the history of comparative and physiological psychology of the 17th century.   Amer. Jr. Psych., 1929, 39: 442–455.

143. ———.   René Descartes: A study in the history of the theories of reflex action.   Psychol. Rev., 1929, 36: 375–388.

144. FÉRÉ, CHARLES.   Sensations et Mouvement.   Paris, 1900.

145. FERRIER, DAVID.   The Functions of the Brain.   Second ed.   London, 1886.

146. FLEXNER, S.   Jacques Loeb and his period.   Science, 1927, 66: 333–337.

147. FLOURENS, P.   Recherches expérimentales sur les propriétés et les fonctions du système nerv. dans les animaux vertébrés.   Paris, 1824.

148. ———.   Éloge Historique de Francois Magendie.   Paris, 1858.

149. FODERA, MICHEL.   Recherches sur les sympathies et sur d'autres phénomènes qui sont ordinairement attribués comme exclusifs au système nerveux.   Paris, 1822.

150. FORBES, ALEXANDER. Reflex inhibition of skeletal muscle. Quart. Jr. Exp. Physiol., 1912, 5: 149–187.

151. ———. The interpretation of spinal reflexes in terms of present knowledge of nerve conduction. Physiol. Rev., 1922, 2: 361.

152. FORDYCE, GEORGE. The Croonian Lecture on muscular motion. Phil. Trans., 1788, 78: 23.

153. FOSTER, M. Effects of temperature on reflex action. Reply to Lewes. Nature, 1873, 9: 101.

154. ———. On the effects of a gradual rise in temperature on reflex actions in the frog. Studies from the Physiological Laboratory of Cambridge, 1873, pt. 1.

155. ———. A Text Book of Physiology. Part III. Seventh Edition. London and New York, 1897.

156. ———. Lectures on the History of Physiology during the 16th, 17th, and 18th Centuries. Cambridge University Press, 1901.

157. ———. European Science in the 17th and Earlier Years of the 18th Centuries. Cambridge Modern History, 1908, 5: 723–741.

158. FRANZ, S. I. On the functions of the cerebrum. Amer. Jr. Physiol., 1902, 8: 1–22.

159. VON FREY, MAX. Über die Wirkungsweise der erschlaffenden Gerfäss-Nerven. Ludwig's Arbeiten, 1876, 11: 89–107.

160. FRITSCH, G., AND HITZIG, E. Ueber die elektrische Erregbarkeit des Grosshirns. Arch. f. Anat. u. Physiol., 1870, 300–332.

161. FULTON, J. F. Muscular Contraction and the Reflex Control of Movement. Baltimore, 1926.

162. GARRISON, FIELDING H. An Introduction to the History of Medicine. Philadelphia, 1914.

163. GARTEN, S. Über die Grundlagen unserer Orientierung im Raume. XXXVI. Bandes der Abhandl. der Math.-Physischen Klasse der Sächsischen Akademie der Wissenschaften, No. 4.

164. GASKELL, W. H. On the structure, distribution, and functions of the nerves which innervate the visceral and vascular Systems. Jr. Physiol., 1886, 7: 1–80.

165. GAULT, R. H. A sketch of the history of reflex action in the latter half of the nineteenth century. Amer. Jr. Psychol., 1904, 15: 526–568.

166. GEISSLER, L. R. The measurement of attention. Amer. Jr. Psychol., 1909, 20: 473–529.

167. GEORGE, J. D. Contribution to the history of the nervous system. Lond. Med. Gazette, 1837–38, 22: 40–47, 93–96.

168. ———. Letter to Medical Gazette regarding Marshall Hall. Lond. Med. Gazette, 1837–38, 22: 252–254.

169. GLEY, E. Essais de Philosophie et d'Histoire de la Biologie. Paris, 1900.

170. GLISSON, FRANCIS. De Hepate, 1654.

171. ———. Tractatus de ventriculo et intestinis, Cui praemittitur alius, de partibus continentibus in genere; et in specie, de iis abdominis. London, 1677.

172. GOLGI, C. Untersuchungen über den feineren Bau des centralen und peripherischen Nervensystems. (Collected Papers, 1871–1893.) Jena, 1894.

173. GOLLA, F., AND HETTWER, J. The influence of various conditions on the time relations of tendon reflexes in the human subject. Proc. Roy. Soc., 1922, 94 B: 92–98.

174. GOLLA, F., AND HETTWER, J. A study of the electromyogram of voluntary movement. Brain, 1924, 47: 57–69.

175. GOLTZ, F. L. Beiträge zur Lehre von den Functionen der Nervencentren des Frosches. Berlin, 1869.

176. ———. Ueber den Einfluss der Nervencentren auf die Aufsaugang. Arch. f. d. ges. Physiol., 1872, 5: 53.

177. ———. Der Hund ohne Grosshirn. Arch. f. d. ges. Physiol., 1892, 51: 570.

178. GOTCH, F. Note on the so-called tendon reflex. Jr. Physiol., 1896, 20: 322–333.

179. GOWERS, W. R. A study of the so-called tendon reflex phenomena. Med. Chirurgical Trans., 1879, 62: 269.

180. ———. A study of the so-called tendon reflex phenomena. Lancet, 1879, 1: 156–158.

181. GRAINGER, R. D. Observations on the Structure and Functions of the Spinal Cord. London, 1837.

182. GRAINGER, STEWART. Tendon Reflex. A Clinical Lecture. Med. Times and Gazette, London, 1878, Feb. 2.

183. GRIESINGER, W. Ueber psychische Reflexactionen mit einen Blick auf das Wesen der psychischen Krankheiten. Arch. f. Physiol. Heilkunde, 1843, 2: 76–113.

184. GRIFFITH, C. R. Concerning the effect of repeated rotation upon nystagmus. Laryngoscope, 1920, 30: 22–25.

185. ———. The cumulative effect of rotational increments. Proc. Ill. Acad. Sci., 1920, 13: 122–134.

186. ———. The effect upon the white rat of continued bodily rotation. Amer. Natur., 1920, 54: 524.

187. ———. An experimental study of dizziness. Jr. Exper. Psychol., 1920, 3: 89–125.

188. ———. The organic effects of repeated bodily rotation. Jr. Exper. Psychol., 1920, 3: 15–46.

189. ———. An historical survey of vestibular equilibration. Univ. of Ill. Bull., 1922, 20, No. 5.

190. ———. A note on the persistance of the "practice effect" in rotation experiments. Jr. Comp. Psychol., 1924, 4: 137.

191. GURNEY, EDMUND. The problems of hypnotism. Mind, 1884, 9: 477–508.

192. HALDANE, E. S. Descartes, His Life and Times. Cambridge, 1905.

193. HALL, CHARLOTTE. Memoirs of Marshall Hall, M.D., F.R.S., by his widow. London, 1861.

194. HALL, G. STANLEY. A sketch of the history of reflex action. Amer. Jr. Psychol., 1890, 3: 71–86.

195. ———. Life and Confessions of a Psychologist. New York, 1923.

195a. HALL, MARSHALL. On a particular function of the nervous system. Proc. of Zool. Soc., 1832.

196. ———. On the reflex function of the medulla oblongata and medulla spinalis. Phil. Trans. Roy. Soc., 1833, 123: 635–665.

197. ———. Memoirs on the Nervous System. Memoir II. On the true spinal marrow and the excito-motory system of nerves. London, 1837.

198. ———. On Professor Müller's account of the reflex function of the spinal marrow. Lond. and Edin. Phil. Mag., 1837, 10: 192.

199. ———. Letter to the London Medical Gazette inclosing letter from Librarian of Med. Chirur. Society. Editorial Reply. Lond. Med. Gazette, 1837–38, 22: 160.

200. HALL, MARSHALL. Abhandlungen über das Nervensystems. Übersetzt von G. Kürschner. Marburg, 1840.

201. ———. Synopsis of the diastaltic nervous system: or the system of the spinal marrow, and its reflex arcs; as the nervous agent in all the functions of ingestion and of egestion in the animal economy. London, 1850.

202. HALLER, ALBERT VON. First Lines of Physiology. Tr. from third Latin edition. Edinburgh, 1801.

203. HAMEL, IGNATIUS A. A study and analysis of the conditioned reflex. Psychol. Mon., No. 118, 1919, 27: 6–65.

204. HANCOCK, J. A. A preliminary study of motor ability. Ped. Sem., 1894, 3: 9.

205. HARRIS, D. F. The seats of the soul in history. Science Progress, 1913, 8: 145–153.

206. ———. History of the views of nervous activity. Science Progress, 1914, 8: 505–510.

207. HARRISON, R. G. The outgrowth of the nerve fiber as a mode of protoplasmic movement. Jr. Exper. Zool., 1910, 9: 787–846.

208. HART, B. The conception of the subconscious. Jr. Abnor. Psychol., 1909–10, 4: 351.

209. HARTLEY, David. Observations on Man, his frame, his duty, and his expectations. 1749.

210. HARVEY, N. A. A device by which physiological concepts may be employed in teaching psychological functions. Western Jr. of Educ., 1909, 4: 182.

211. HEAD, H. Studies in Neurology. London, 1920.

212. HEIDENHAIN, RUDOLPH. Historisches und Experimentelles über Muskeltonus. Müller's Arch. f. Anat., Physiol., und Wiss. Medicin., 1856, 200–229.

213. ———. Hypnotism or animal magnetism. Physiological observations. Tr. from 4th German edition. London, 1906.

214. HELMHOLTZ, HERMANN. Bericht über die zur Bekanntmachung geeigneten Verhandlungen. Der Königl. Preuss. Akad. d. Wiss. zu Berlin aus dem Jahre 1845, 328.

215. VAN HELMONT, J. B. Ortus Medicinae. 1655.

216. HELSON, H. The psychology of Gestalt. Amer. Jr. Psychol., 1925, 36: 342–370; 494–526. 1926, 37: 25–62; 189–216.

217. HERING, EWALD. Zur Lehre vom Lichtsinne. 2nd Aufl., Wien, 1878.

218. ———. Zur Theorie der Vorgänge in der lebendigen Substanz. Lotos, 1889, 9: 37–70. Translation in Brain, 1897, 20: 232–258.

219. ———. On Memory As a General Function of Organized Matter. Chicago, 1895.

220. HERING, H. E. Beitrag zur Frage der gleichzeitigen Thätigkeit antagonistisch wirkender Muskeln. Zeit. f. Heilkunde, 1895, 16: 129–143.

221. ———. Die intrazentralen Hemmungsvorgänge in ihre Beziehung zur Skelett-Muskulatur. Ergebn. d. Physiol., 1902, 1, Jahrg., 2nd Abth.

222. HERMANN, L. Lehrbuch der Physiologie. Berlin, 1910.

223. HERRICK, C. Judson. Neurological Foundations of Animal Behavior. New York, 1924.

224. ———. Brains of Rats and Men. Chicago, 1926.

225. Herzen, Alexandre. Expériences sur les centres modérateurs de l'action réflexe. Turin, 1864.

226. ———. Über die Hemmungsmechanismen der Reflexthätigkeit. Untersuchungen Zur Naturlehre, 1864, 9: 423.

227. HEYMANS, G. Untersuchungen über psychische Hemmung. Zeit. f. Psychol., Bd. 21, 26, 34, 41, und 53.

228. HINSDALE, G. The Station of man, considered physiologically and clinically. Amer. Jr. Med. Sc., 1887, N. S., 93: 478.

229. ———. Observations on station with reference to respiration, N. Y. Med. Jr., 1890, 51: 292.

230. HIPPOCRATES. Aphorisms. London, 1831.

231. DE LA HIRE. De quelques faits d'Optique, et de la manière dont se fait la Vision. Histoire de L'Académie Royale des Sciences, 1709, 95.

232. HODGE, C. F. A sketch of the history of reflex action. Amer. Jr. Psychol., 1890, 3: 149–167; 343–363.

233. HOFF, HANS, AND SCHILDER, PAUL. Die Lagereflexe des Menschen. Wien, 1927.

234. HOFFMANN, PAUL. Untersuchungen über die Eigenreflexe (Sehnenreflexe) Menschlicher Muskeln. Berlin, 1922.

235. ———. Über die Natur der Sehnenreflexe (Eigenreflexe) und ihr Verhältnis zur sensomotilität. Deutsche Ztschr. f. Nervenheilk., 1924, 82: 269–280.

236. HOLSOPPLE, J. Q. Factors affecting the duration of post-rotation nystagmus. Jr. Comp. Psychol., 1923, 3: 283–303.

237. ———. An explanation for the unequal reductions in post rotation nystagmus following rotation practice in only one direction. Jr. Comp. Psychol., 1924, 4: 185–193.

238. HOLT, E. B. The Freudian Wish and Its Place in Ethics. New York, 1916.

239. HORSLEY, V. Note on the patellar knee-jerk. Brain, 1883, 6: 368.

240. HOUGH, THEODORE. The classification of nervous reactions. Science, 1915, 41: 407–418.

241. HOWELL, W. H. A Textbook of Physiology. 8th ed. Philadelphia and London, 1922.

242. ———. Inhibition. Physiol. Rev., 1925, 5: 161–181.

243. HULL, C. L., AND BAERNSTEIN, H. D. A mechanical parallel to the conditioned reflex. Science, 1929, 70: 14–15.

244. VON HUMBOLDT, A. Versuche über die gereite Muskel- und Nerven-faser, nebst Vermuthungen über den chemischen des Lebens in der Thiere und Pflanzenwelt. Berlin, 1797.

245. HUMPHREY, G. E. The conditioned reflex and the elementary social reaction. Jr. Abnor. Psychol. and Soc. Psychol., 1922, 17: 113–119.

246. HUNTER, J. I. The postural influence of the sympathetic nervous system. Brain, 1924, 47: 261–274.

247. HUXLEY, THOMAS H. Methods and Results. V. On the hypothesis that animals are automata, and its history. 1874. New York, 1896.

248. JAMES, ALEXANDER. The reflex inhibitory centre theory. Brain, 1881, 4: 287–302.

249. JAMES, WILLIAM. The Principles of Psychology. Vol. I. New York, 1890.

250. ———. A case of automatic drawing. Pop. Sci. Mo., 1904, 44: 195–201.

251. JANET, PIERRE. L'Automatisme Psychologique. Paris, 1889.

252. ———. The Mental State of Hystericals. New York, 1901.

253. JARISCH, A., UND SCHIFF, E. Untersuchungen über das Kniephänomen. Med. Jahrbücher d. Gesellsch. d. Aerzte. Wien, 1882.

254. JASTROW, JOSEPH. A further study of involuntary movements. Amer. Jr. Psychol., 1892–3, 5: 223–231.

255. JASTROW, JOSEPH. The Subconscious. Boston, 1906.

256. ———, AND WEST, H. A study of involuntary movements. Amer. Jr. Psychol., 1892, 4: 398–407.

257. JEITELES, ANDREAS LUDWIG. Wer ist der Begründer der Lehre von den Reflexbewegungen? Vierteljahrschrift für prakt. Heilkunde, 1858, 4: 50–72.

258. JENDRASSIK, E. Beitrage zur Lehre von den Sehnenreflexen. Deutsches Archiv. f. Klin. Med., 1883, 33: 177.

259. ———. Zur Untersuchungsmethode des Kniephänomens. Neurol. Centrabl., 1885, 412.

260. JENNINGS, H. S. The work of J. von Uexküll on the physiology of movements and behavior. Jr. Comp. Neurol. and Psychol., 1909, 29: 330.

261. ———. Behavior of the Lower Organisms. New York, 1915.

262. ———. Experimental determinism and human conduct. Jr. Phil., Psychol., etc., 1919, 16: 180–183.

263. JOHNSTON, J. B. The central nervous system of vertebrates. Ergebnisse und Fortschritte der Zoologie, 1910, 2: 1–170.

264. JOLLY, W. A. The knee-jerk and simple reflexes. Brit. Med. Jr., 1910, 2: 1259–1260.

265. ———. The time relations of the knee-jerk and simple reflexes. Jr. Exper. Physiol., 1911, 4: 67–88.

266. ———. The reflex times in the South African clawed frog. Proc. Roy. Soc., 1921, 92 B: 31–51.

267. VON KEMPEN, E. M. Essai expérimental sur la nature fonctionelle nerf pneumogastrique précédé de considerations sur les mouvements réfléchis. Louvain, 1842.

268. KLENCKE, HERMANN. Swammerdam oder die Offenbarung der Natur. 3 vols. Leipzig, 1860.

269. KOFFKA, K. The Growth of the Mind, tr. by R. M. Ogden. New York, 1924.

270. KÖHLER, WOLFGANG. Gestalt Psychology. New York, 1929.

271. KRASNOGORSKÏ, N. Ueber die Bedingungsreflexe im Kindesalter. Jahrbuch für Kinderheilkunde, 1909, 69: 1–24.

272. KRIES, J. W., UND AUERBACH, FELIX. Die Zeitdauer einfachster psychisches Vorgänge. Arch. für Physiol., 1877, 298–378.

273. KRONECKER, H. Das characterische Merkmal der Herzmuskelbewegung. Fest. f. Carl Ludwig. Leipzig, 1874.

274. KÜLPE, OSWALD. Outlines of Psychology, 1893. Tr. by E. B. Titchener, 1901.

275. ———. The problem of attention. Monist, 1902, 13: 38–68.

276. LACROIX, A. Considérations pathologiques et thérapeutiques sur l'attitude de l'homme. Paris, 1824.

277. LADD, G. T., AND WOODWORTH, R. S. Elements of Physiological Psychology. New York, 1911.

278. LAEHR, H. Die Literatur der Psychologie, Neurologie, und Psychiatrie von 1459–1799. Berlin, 1900.

279. LALLEMAND, F. Observations patholog. propres à éclarer plusieurs points de physiologie. Inaug. Diss., Paris, 1818. 2nd ed., 1825.

280. LA METTRIE, JULIAN OFFRAY. Man a Machine. Chicago, 1912.

281. LANGE, FREDERICK ALBERT. The History of Materialism. Tr. By E. C. Thomas. 3rd edition. London and New York, 1925.

282. LANGE, L. Neue Experimente über den Vorgang der einfachen Reaction auf Sinneseindrücke. Phil. Stud., 1888, 4: 479–510.

283. LANGELAAN, J. W. On muscle tonus. Brain, 1915, 38: 235–381.

284. LANGENDORFF, O. Die Beziehungen des Sehorgans zu den reflexhemmenden Mechanismen des Froschgehirns. Du Bois Reymond's Archiv. f. Anat. u. Physiol. Physiol. abtl., 1877, 435.

285. ———. Physiologie des Rücken- und Kopfmarks. Nagel's Handbuch. Bd. IV, 1909.

286. LASHLEY, K. S. The human salivary reflex and its use in psychology. Psychol. Rev., 1916, 23: 446–464.

287. ———. Studies of cerebral function in learning. Psychobiology, 1920, 2: 55–135.

288. ———. The effects of long continued practice upon cerebral localization. Jr. Comp. Psychol., 1921, 1: 453–468.

289. ———. The motor areas. Brain, 1921, 44: 255–285.

290. ———. Vicarious function after destruction of the visual area. Amer. Jr. Physiol., 1922, 59: 44–71.

291. ———. The behavioristic interpretation of consciousness. Psychol. Rev., 1923, 30: 237–277, 329–353.

292. ———. The retention of motor habits after destruction of the so-called motor areas in primates. Arch. Neurol. Psychiat., 1924, 12: 249–276.

293. ———. The theory that synaptic resistance is reduced by the passage of the nervous impulse. Psychol. Rev., 1924, 31: 369–375.

294. ———. The relation between cerebral mass, learning and retention. Jr. Comp. Neur., 1926, 41: 1–59.

295. LAYCOCK, T. Reflex function of the brain. Brit. and Foreign Med. Rev., 1845, 19: 298–311.

296. LEE, M. A. M., AND KLEITMAN, N. Studies in the physiology of sleep. II. Attempts to demonstrate functional changes in the nervous system during experimental insomnia. Amer. Jr. Physiol., 1923, 67: 141–152.

297. LEGALLOIS, J. J. C. Oeuvres. Tome premier. Expériences sur le principe de la vie, notamment sur celui des mouvements du coeur et sur le siege de ce principe. Avec des notes de M. Pariset. Paris, 1824.

298. LEITERSDORFFER, . Das militarische Training. Stuttgart, 1894.

299. LEWES, GEORGE HENRY. The spinal cord a sensational and volitional centre. Report of the 28th meeting of the Brit. Ass. Adv. Sci., 1859, 135.

300. ———. Sensation in the spinal cord. Nature, 1873, 9: 83–84.

301. ———. The Physical Basis of Mind. Problems of Life and Mind. Boston, 1877

302. LILLIE, R. S. The nature of protoplasmic and nervous transmission. Jr. Phys. Chem., 1920, 24: 165–191.

303. ———. Protoplasmic Action and Nervous Action. Chicago, 1923.

304. LINDLEY, E. H. A preliminary study of some of the motor phenomena of mental effort. Amer. Jr. Psychol., 1895, 7: 491.

305. LOCY, W. A. Malpighi, Swammerdam, and Leeuwenhoek. Pop. Sci. Mon., 1900–1901, 58: 561.

306. LOEB, JACQUES. Comparative Physiology of the Brain and Comparative Psychology. New York, 1903.

307. ———. The Mechanistic Conception of Life. Chicago, 1912.

308. Loeb, Jacques. Forced Movements, Tropisms, and Animal Conduct. Philadelphia, London, 1918.

309. Lombard, W. P. A new method of testing the knee-kick. New York Med. Jr. 1887, Jan. 2.

310. ———. Is the knee-kick a reflex act? Amer. Jr. Med. Sci., 1887, 88.

311. ———. The variations of the normal knee-jerk and their relation to the activity of the central nervous system. Amer. Jr. Psychol., 1888, 1: 5–71.

312. ———. Fatiguing voluntary work. Jr. Physiol., 1893, 14: 117.

313. London Medical Gazette. [Editorial] Intemperance of Medical Controversialists. Reflex Function, an Old Discovery. 1837–38, 22: 72–73.

314. Longet, F. A. Anatomie et Physiologie du Système Nerveux de l'Homme et et des Animaux Vertébrés. 2 vols. Paris, 1842.

315. Lorry, M. Sur les mouvemens du Cerveau, second mémoire. Sur les mouvemens centre de ce viscère, et sur les organs qui sont le principe de son action. Mém. de Math. et de Physique. Preséntés à l'Académie Royal des Sciences, 1760, 3: 344.

316. Lotze, R. H. Instinct. Wagner's Handwörterbuch, II, 1844.

317. ———. Medicinische Psychologie oder Physiologie der Seele. Leipzig, 1852.

318. ———. [Review of] Die sensorischen Functionen des Rückenmarks der Wirbelthiere nebst einer neuen Lehre über die Leitungsgesetzte der Reflexionen. Göttingische gelehrte Anzeiger, 1853, 3: 1737–1776.

319. Lucas, K., and Adrian, E. D. The Conduction of the Nervous Impulse. London, 1917.

320. Luciani, L. Human Physiology. Vol. III, Muscular and Nervous System. Tr. from 4th Italian edition. New York, 1915.

321. Mach, Ernst. Popular Scientific Lectures. Tr. by T. J. McCormack, Chicago, 1897.

322. ———. Contribution to the Analysis of the Sensations. Chicago, 1910.

323. Magendie, F. A Summary of Physiology. Tr. from the French by John Revere. Baltimore, 1822.

324. ———. Mémoire sur quelques découvertes récentes relatives aux fonctions du système nerveux. Lu a la séance publique de l'Academie des Sciences. Paris, 1823.

325. Magnus, R. Körperstellung und Labyrinthreflexe beim affen. Pflüger's Arch., 1922, 193: 396–448.

326. ———. Körperstellung. Berlin, 1924.

327. ———. Animal Posture. Proc. Roy. Soc., 1925, 98 B: 339–353.

328. ———. Some results of studies in the physiology of posture. Lancet, 1926, 211: 531–536, 585–588.

329. Mahaffy, J. P. Descartes. Philadelphia, 1881.

330. Maloney, W. J. M. A. Locomotor Ataxia (Tabes Dorsalis). New York, 1918.

331. ———, and Knauer, Alwyn. The Cephalograph: a new instrument for recording and controlling head movements. Jr. Ment. Nerv. Dis., 1914, 41: 75–80.

332. Marey, E. J. Travaux du Laboratoire Paris, 1876.

333. Marina, A. Die Relationem des Palaeencephalons (Edinger) sind nicht fix. Neurol. Centralbl., 1915, 34: 338–345.

334. Martius, Götz. Ueber die muskuläre Reaction und die Aufmerksamkeit. Phil. Stud., 1891, 6: 167–216.

335. MAST D. O. Light and the Behavior of Organisms. New York, 1911.
336. MATEER, FLORENCE. Child Behavior: A Critical and Experimental Study of Young Children by the Method of Conditioned Reflexes. Boston, 1917.
337. MAUDSLEY, HENRY. Physiology and Pathology of Mind. New York, 1867.
338. ———. Body and Mind. New York, 1871.
339. ———. Reflex Action, Instinct, and Reason. Brain, 1897, 20: 201–219.
340. MAXWELL, J. Rapports de l'automatisme et de la personalité normale. Bull. Instit. Gen. Psy., 1916, 16: 101–110.
341. MAXWELL, S. S. Labyrinth and Equilibrium. Philadelphia, 1923.
342. ———, BURKE, U. L., AND RESTON, C. The effect of repeated rotation on the duration of after-nystagmus in the rabbit. Amer. Jr. Physiol., 1922, 58: 432.
343. MAYO, HERBERT. Anatomical and Physiological Commentaries. London, 1822.
344. MAYOW, JOHN. Medico-Physical Works, being a Translation of Tractatus Quinque Medico-Physici. Fourth Treatise. On Muscular Motion and Animal Spirits. Edinburgh, 1907.
345. MCCARTHY, D. J. Epileptic ambulatory automatism. Jr. Nerv. and Ment. Dis., 1900, 27: 143–149.
346. MCDOUGALL, WILLIAM. The nature of inhibitory processes within the nervous system. Brain, 1903, 26: 153.
347. ———. Body and Mind. 3rd edition. London, 1915.
348. ———. Outlines of Psychology. New York, 1922.
349. ———. The hypothesis of inhibition by drainage. Psychol. Rev., 1926, 33: 370–374.
350. ———. Outline of Abnormal Psychology. New York, 1926.
351. MELTZER, S. J. Inhibition. New York Med. Jr., 1899.
352. TER MEULEN, G. Zum Verhalten der Reflexerregbarkeit und der Sehnenreflexe der paretischen Seite bei Cerebraler Hemiplegie. Zeit. f. klin. Med., 1882–1883, 5: 89–106.
353. MEYER, M. F. The comparative value of various conceptions of nervous function based on mechanical analogies. Amer. Jr. Psychol., 1913, 24: 555–563.
354. MEYNERT, T. Psychiatrie. Wien, 1889.
355. MILES, W. R. Effects of Alcohol on Psycho-physiological Functions. Carnegie Inst. Publ., No. 266, Washington, 1918.
356. ———. Static equilibrium as a useful test of motor control. Jr. of Indus. Hyg., 1922, 3: 316–331.
357. ———. Alcohol and Human Efficiency. Carnegie Inst. Publ., No. 333, Washington, 1924.
358. ———, AND MILES, C. C. Eight letters from G. Stanley Hall to H. P. Bowditch with introduction and notes. Amer. Jr. Psychol., 1929, 41: 326–335.
359. MINKOWSKI, M. [Precocious movements, reflexes and muscular reactions of the human foetus and their relations to the foetal nervous and muscular system.] Schweiz. Med. Wochen., 1922, 29: 731–751.
360. MITCHELL, P. H. A Textbook of General Physiology. Ist edition. New York, 1923.
361. MITCHELL, S. W., AND LEWIS, M. J. Physiological studies of the knee-jerk and of the reactions of muscles under mechanical and other excitants. Phil. Med. News, 1886, 13: 20.

362. MITCHELL, S. W., AND LEWIS, M. J.   Tne tendon jerk and muscle jerk in disease, especially in posterior sclerosis.   Amer. Jr. of Med. Sci., 1886, N. S., 92: 363.
363. MOLL, ALBERT.   Hypnotism.   11th edition.   London, 1900.
364. MONRO, ALEXANDER (1697–1767).   The Works of Alexander Monro, M.D.   Edinburgh, 1781.
365. MONRO, ALEXANDER (1733–1817).   Observations on the Structure and Functions of the Nervous System.   Edinburgh, 1783.
365a. ———.   Bemerkungen über die Struktur und Verrichtungen des Nervensystems.   Leipzig, 1787.
366. MOORE, T. V.   Dynamic Psychology.   Philadelphia, 1924.
367. MORAT, J. P.   Physiology of the Nervous System.   English edition tr. and ed. by H. W. Syers.   London, 1914.
368. MORGULIS, S.   Pavlov's theory of the function of the central nervous system and a digest of some of the more recent contributions to the subject from Pavlov's laboratory.   Jr. Anim. Behav., 1914, 4: 362–379.
369. MOTT, F. W.   Importance of stimulus in repair and decay of the nervous system.   Jr. Ment. Sci., 1902, 48: 667–681.
370. MÜHL, A. M.   Automatic writing as an indicator of the fundamental factors underlying personality.   Jr. Abn. and Soc. Psychol., 1922, 17: 162–183.
371. MÜLLER, G. E.   Zur Theorie der sinnlichen Aufmerksamkeit.   Leipzig, 1873.
372. MÜLLER, J.   Handbuch der Physiologie des Menschen.   Coblenz, 1844.
373. MÜNSTERBERG, H.   Die Willenshandlung.   Freiburg, 1888.
374. ———.   Contribution to symposium on the subconscious.   Jr. Abnor. Psychol., 1907–8, 2: 25–33.
375. MURPHY, GARDNER.   An Historical Introduction to Modern Psychology.   New York, 1929.
376. MYERS, CHARLES G.   A Textbook of Experimental Psychology, New York and London, 1909.
377. MYERS, F. W. H.   Automatic Writing.   Proc. Soc. Psych. Res., 1885, 3: 1–63.
378. ———.   The Subliminal Consciousness.   Proc. Soc. Psych. Res., 1892.
379. ———.   Recent Experiments in Normal Motor Automatism.   Proc. Soc. Psych. Res., 1896–7, 12: 316.
380. ———.   De la Conscience Subliminale.   Ann. de Sc. Psych., 1898, 8: 88–126, 170–185, 196–227.
381. ———.   Human Personality and Its Survival of Bodily Death.   2 vols.   London, 1904.
382. NAGEL, W.   Handbuch der Physiologie des Menschen.   III, 1905; IV, 1909.
383. NETTER, HERMANN.   Zur Geschichte der Lehre vom Kniephänomen bei Geisteskranken nebst Beobachtungen über diesen Gegenstand aus der Freiburger Psychiatr. Klinick.   Freiburg, 1897.
384. NEUBURGER, MAX.   Die historische Entwicklung des experimentellen Gehirn- und Rückenmarks- physiologie vor Flourens.   Stuttgart, 1897.
385. NEWHOLD, W. R.   Experimental induction of automatic processes.   Psychol. Rev., 1895, 2: 348–362.
386. NICHOLSON, N. C.   Notes on muscular work during hypnosis.   Johns Hopkins Hospital Bull., 1920, 31: 89–91.
387. NOTHNAGEL, H.   Bewegungshemmende Mechanismen im Rückenmark des Frosches.   Centralbl. f. die. Med. Wissensch., 1869, 211.

388. OBERSTEINER,, HEINRICH. Experimental Researches on Attention. Brain, 1879, 1: 439–453.

389. ———. The maintenance of equilibrium as a function of the central nervous system. Tr. by G. M. Winslow. Amer. Natur., 1899, 33: 313–330.

390. OLLIVIER, D'ANGERS. Traité de la moelle épinière et de ses maladies contenant l'histoire anatom. physiol. et pathologique de ce centre nerveux chez l'homme. Paris, 1823.

391. OTT, J. Notes on inhibition. Jr. Physiol., 1881, 3: 163–164.

392. PALMER, DOROTHY E. Jacques Loeb: A contribution to the history of psychology. Jr. Gener. Psychol., 1927, 2: 97–113.

393. PARKER, G. H. The Origin and Evolution of the Nervous System. The Harvey Lectures, 1913–1914.

394. PARMELEE, M. The Science of Human Behavior. New York, 1913.

395. PARSONS, JAMES. The Croonian Lecture on muscular motion. Phil. Trans., 1744–1745, 43: supplement.

396. PATON, GEORGE. On the perceptive power of the spinal cord as manifested by cold-blooded animals. Edin. Med. Surg. Jr., 1846, 65: 251.

397. PATRIZI, L. M. La simultanéité et la succession des impulsions voluntaires symetriques. Arch. Ital. de Biol., 1893, 19: 126–139.

398. PAVLOV, I. P. Wie die Muschel ihre Schaale öffnet. Versuche und Fragen zur allgemeinen Muskel- und Nervenphysiologie. Arch. f. d. ges. Physiol., 1885, 37: 6–31.

399. ———. New Researches on Conditioned Reflexes. Science, 1923, 58: 359–361.

400. ———. Conditioned Reflexes. An Investigation of Physiological Activity of the Cerebral Cortex. Tr. and ed. by G. V. Anrep. Oxford Univ. Press, 1927.

401. ———. Lectures on Conditioned Reflexes. New York, 1928.

402. PELIZAEUS. Ueber das Kniephänomen bei Kindern. Arch. f. Psy. und Nervenkrank., 1883, 14: 402–410.

403. PERRAULT, C., AND P. Oeuvres diverses de Physique et de Mechanique. 1721.

404. PFLÜGER, EDUARD. Die sensorischen Functionen des Rückenmarks der Wirbelthiere nebst einer neuen Lehre über die Leitungsgesetze der Reflexionen. Berlin, 1853.

405. ———. Ueber d. Hemmung-nervensystem f. d. peristaltischen Bewegungen d. Gedärme. Berlin, 1857.

406. PHILLIP, A. P. WILSON. Experiments made with a view to ascertain the principle on which the action of the heart depends and the relation which subsists between that organ and the nervous system. Phil. Trans., 1815, 65.

407. ———. Some additional experiments and observations on the relation which subsists between the nervous and sanguiferous systems. Phil. Trans., 1815, 424.

408. PIKE, F. H. The nervous mechanism of motor learning and habit formation. Trans. 4th Internat. Cong. on Sch. Hyg., Buffalo, 1913.

409. PILLSBURY, W. B. Attention. London, 1908.

410. ———. The Fundamentals of Psychology. New York, 1923.

411. PORTERFIELD, WILLIAM. Treatise on the Eye. 2 vols. Edinburgh, 1759.

412. PRESTON, CHARLES. An account of a child born alive without a brain, and the observables in it on dissection. Phil. Trans., 1697, 19: 457–467.

413. PREVOST, . Contribution à l'étude des phénomènes nommées réflexes tendineux. Rev. Méd. de la Suisse, Romande, 1881.

414. PRINCE, MORTON. Experiments to determine conconscious (subconscious) idea. Jr. Abnor. Psychol., 1908, 3: 33–42.

415. ———. The Unconscious. New York, 1914.

416. PROCHASKA, GEORGE. Dissertation on the Functions of the Nervous System. 1784. Tr. for the Sydenham Society by Thomas Laycock, London, 1851.

417. PURKINJE, J. E. Neueste Untersuchungen aus der Nerven- und Hirn-Anatomie. Bericht Vers. deutsch. Naturf. Aerzte (Prag.), 1838.

418. RAMÓN Y CAJAL, S. Histologie du Système nerveux de l'homme et les vertébrés. Paris, 1909.

418a. RANSON, S. W. Studies on Muscle Tonus. Jr. Comp. Neurol., 1926, 40: 1–32.

419. Record of the Royal Society, The. 3rd edition. London, 1912.

420. RIBOT, TH. The Psychology of Attention. Tr. of 3rd edition. Chicago, 1896.

421. RICHET, CHARLES. Les Réflexes Psychiques. Rev. Philos., 1888, 25: 224–237, 387–422, 500–528.

422. ———. Dictionaire de Physiologie. Paris, 1895.

423. RIMATHE, FREDERIC. Contribution a l'Étude de L'Ergographie Bilaterale et Simultance. Arch. de Psy., 1924, 19: 128–162.

424. ROMANES, GEORGE G. Further observation on the locomotor system of medusae. Phil. Trans. Roy. Soc., 1877, 157: 659–753.

425. ROMBERG, M. H. A Manual of the Nervous Diseases of Man. Sydenham trans., London, 1853.

426. ROSENBACH, OTTOMAR. Das Verhalten der Reflexe bei Schlafenden. Zeit. f. Klin. Med., 1879–1880, 1: 358–374.

427. ROSENHEIM, TH. Experimentelle Untersuchung der unter dem Namen "Sehnenphänomene" bekannten Ersheinungen unter Möglichster Berücksichtigung von Versuchen an Menschen und pathologischen Beobachtungen. Arch. f. Psych. u. Nervenkrankh., 1884, 15: 184–201.

428. ROUNDS, GEORGE H. Is the latent time in the archilles tendon reflex a criterion of speed in mental relations? Arch. Psychol., 1928, 95: 5–91.

429. RUSSELL, S. BENT. A practical device to simulate the working of nervous discharges. Jr. Anim. Behav., 1913, 3: 15–35.

430. SALMON, A. D'un interessant phénomène d'automatisme qu'on remarque après les efforts musculaires chez les sujets sains. Rev. Neurol., 1916, 1: 8.

431. SANFORD, E. C. History of reaction time. Amer. Jr. Psychol., 1888–9, 2: 3; 271; 403.

432. SCHÄFER, E. A. Textbook of Physiology, vol. II. Edinburgh, 1900.

433. SCHIFF, J. M. Lehrbuch der Physiologie des Menschen. Lahr., 1858–1859.

434. SCHLOSBURG, HAROLD. A study of the conditioned patellar reflex. Jr. Exp. Psychol., 1928, 11: 468–494.

435. SCHULTZE, FR., UND FURBRINGER, P. Experimentelles über die Sehnenreflexe. Centralbl. f. d. Med. Wissens., 1875, 54: 929.

436. SELLER, WILLIAM. Memoir of the life and writings of Robert Whytt. Trans. Roy. Soc. Edin., 1864, 23: 99.

437. SENATOR, H. Ueber Sehnenreflexe und ihre Beziehung zum Muskeltonus. Arch. f. Anat. und Physiol. Physiol. Abth., 1880, 197–208.

438. SETSCHENOW, J. Physiologische Studien über die Hemmungsmechanismen für die Reflexthätigkeit des Rückenmarks im Gehirne des Frosches. Berlin, 1863.

439. SHERRINGTON, C. S. Decerebrate rigidity and reflex coördination of movements. Jr. Physiol., 1898, 22: 319–332.

440. ———. On reciprocal innervation of antagonistic muscles Proc. Roy. Soc., 1905, 76 B: 269.

441. ———. The Integrative Action of the Nervous System. New York, 1906.

442. ———. Reciprocal innervation of antagonistic muscles. Thirteenth Note. On the antagonism between reflex inhibition and reflex excitation. Proc. Roy. Soc., 1908, 80 B: 565–578.

443. ———. On plastic tonus and proprioceptive reflexes. Quart. Jr. Exper. Physiol., 1909, 2: 109–156.

444. ———. Reflex inhibition as a factor in the coördination of movements and postures. Quart. Jr. Exper. Physiol., 1913, 6: 251–308.

445. ———. Postural activity of muscle and nerve. Brain, 1915, 38: 191–234.

446. ———. Note on the history of the word "Tonus" as a physiological term. Contributions to Medical and Biological Research, dedicated to Sir William Osler, 1919.

447. ———. Problem of muscular receptivity. Linacre Lecture. Nature, 1924, 113: 892–894, 929–932.

448. ———. Anniversary Address by President of the Royal Society at the Anniversary Meeting, December 1, 1924. Proc. Roy. Soc., 1925, 97 B: 262–263.

449. ———. Some aspects of reflex inhibition. Proc. Roy. Soc., 1925, 97 B: 528.

450. ———, AND LIDDELL, E. G. T. Reflexes in response to stretch (myotatic reflexes). Proc. Roy. Soc., 1924, 96 B: 212–242.

451. ———, AND ———. Further observations on myotatic reflexes, Proc. Roy. Soc., 1925, 97 B: 267–283, 488–518.

452. SIMONOFF, L. N. Die Hemmungsmechanismen der Säugetiere experimentall bewiesen. Arch. f. Anat. u. Physiol., 1866: 545–564.

452a. SIMSON, TH. An Inquiry How Far the Vital and Animal Actions of the More Perfect Animals Can be Accounted for Independent of the Brain. Edinburgh. 1752.

453. SINGER, H. D. A case of ambulatory automatism. Arch. Neur. and Psychiat., 1923, 9: 347–357.

454. SNYDER, C. D. The latency of knee-jerk response in man as measured by the thread galvanometer. Amer. Jr. Physiol., 1910, 26: 474–482.

455. SOLLY, SAMUEL. The Human Brain: Its Structure, Physiology and Diseases. 2nd. edition, London, 1847.

456. SOLOMONS, L. M. Automatic reactions. Psychol. Rev., 1899, 6: 376–394.

457. ———, AND STEIN, G. Normal motor automatism. Psychol. Rev., 1896, 3: 492–512.

458. SOURY, J. Le système nerveux centrale structure et fonctions. Histoire des doctrines psychologie physiologique contemporaires. Paris, 1891.

459. SPENCER, HERBERT. Principles of Psychology. Vol. I, 2nd edition. New York, 1872.

460. SPENCER, L. T. Central inhibition in the albino rat. Jr. Comp. Psychol., 1923, 3: 381–408.

461. ———. The concept of the threshold and Heymans' law of inhibition. Jr. Exp. Psychol., 1928, 11: 88–97.

462. ———. The validity of Heymans' law. Amer. Jr. Psychol., 1925, 36: 427–433.

463. SPIEGEL, ERNST A. Der Tonus der Skelettmuskulatur. Berlin, 1927.
464. STARLING, E. H. Principles of Human Physiology. 3rd. edition. Philadelphia, 1920.
465. STEIN, G. Cultivated motor automatisms: a study of character in its relation to attention. Psychol. Rev., 1898, 5: 295–306.
466. STENSON, N. Discours sur L'Anatomie du Cerveau. 1668. In Anatomy, by J. B. Winslow, Paris, 1749.
467. STERNBERG, M. Sehnenreflexe bei Ermüdung. Centralbl. f. Phys., 1887.
468. ———. Die Sehnenreflexe und ihre Bedeutung für die Pathologie des Nervensystems. Leipzig, 1893.
469. STIEDA, L. Geschichte der Entwickelung der Lehre von den Nervenzellen und Nervenfasern während des XIX Jahrhunderts. Jena, 1899.
470. STILLING, B. Untersuchungen über den Bau und die Verrichtungen des Gehirns. Jena, 1846.
471. ———. Neue Untersuchungen über den Bau des Rückenmarks. Cassel, 1859.
472. STIRLING, W. Some Apostles of Physiology. London, 1902.
473. STOUT, G. F. A Manual of Psychology. New York, 1899.
474. STUART, ALEXANDER. Three Lectures on Muscular Motion. (1st Croonian Lectures.) Suppl. to Phil. Trans., 1737, 40.
475. SULLY, JAMES. The Human Mind. Vol. II. New York, 1892.
476. SWAMMERDAM, JAN. Bybel der Natur. Amsterdam or Leyden, 1737; Leipzig, 1752.
477. ———. The Book of Nature; or the History of Insects: reduced to distinct classes, confirmed by particular instances, displayed in the anatomical analysis of many species. With Life of the Author, by Herman Boerhaave. Tr. from the Dutch and Latin original Editions by Th. Flloyd. Revised and improved by notes from Reamur and others, by John Hill, 1758.
477a. Anonymous. Half hours with the old naturalists. I. John Swammerdam. Jr. of Science, 1884, 6: 198–206.
478. TALMA, S. Eine Psychische Function des Rückenmarks. Pflüger's Archiv, 1885, 37: 617–623.
479. THÉVENIN, P. Conscience et Automatisme. Paris, 1899.
480. TIGERSTEDT, ROBERT. A Text-book of Human Physiology. Tr. and ed. from 3rd German edition. New York and London, 1906.
481. TITCHENER, E. B. Were the earliest organic movements conscious or unconscious? Pop. Sci. Mon., 1901, 60: 458.
482. ———. A Textbook of Psychology. New York, 1919.
483. ———. Experimental Psychology. Vol. II, Quantitative Experiments, Part II, Instructor's Manual. New York, 1923.
484. TORREY, HENRY P. The Philosophy of Descartes in Extracts from his Writings. 1892.
485. TRAVIS, L. E. The correlation between intelligence and speed in conduction of the nerve impulse in a reflex arc. Science, 1928, 67: 41–43.
486. ———, AND HUNTER, T. A. The Relation between Intelligence and Reflex Conduction Rate. Jr. Exp. Psychol., 1928, 11: 342–354.
487. ———, TUTTLE, W. W., AND HUNTER, T. A. The tetanic nature of the knee-jerk response in man. Amer. Jr .Physiol., 1927, 81: 670–678.

488. Tschirjew, S. Ursprung und Bedeutung des Kniephänomens und verwandter Erscheinungen. Arch. f. Psych. u. Nervenkrankh., 1878, 8: 689.

489. Tucker, M. A. Comparative observations on the involuntary movements of adults and children. Amer. Jr. Psychol., 1896–1897, 8: 394–481.

490. Tuke, H. A Dictionary of Psychological Medicine. London, 1892.

491. Türck, Ludwig. Ueber den Zustand der Sensibilität nach theilweiser Trennung des Rückenmarks. Zeit. der k. R. Gesellschaft der Aerzte zu Wien, 1851, 189.

492. Tuttle, W. W. An apparatus for eliciting and recording the patellar tendon reflex. Amer. Jr. Physiol., 1924, 68: 338–344.

493. ———. The effect of adrenalin upon the patellar tendon reflex. Amer. Jr. Physiol., 1924, 69: 446–454.

494. ———. The effect of alcohol on the patellar tendon reflex. Jr. Pharmacology and exper. Therapeutics, 1924, 23: 163–172.

495. ———. The effect of attention or mental activity on the patellar tendon reflex. Jr. Exper. Psychol., 1924, 7: 401–419.

496. ———. The effect of sleep upon the patellar tendon reflex. Amer. Jr. Physiol., 1924, 68: 345.

497. ———. Factors influencing the knee-jerk. Amer. Jr. Physiol., 1925, 72: 50.

498. ———, and Travis, L. E. A comparative study of the extent of the knee jerk and achilles jerk. Amer. Jr. Physiol., 1927, 82: 147–152.

499. ———, Travis, L. E., and Hunter, T. A. A study of the reflex time of the knee jerk and the achilles jerk. Amer. Jr. Physiol., 1927, 82: 99–105.

500. Twitmyer, E. B. A Study of the Knee-jerk. Philadelphia, 1902.

501. Unzer, John Augustus. The Principles of Physiology. 1771. Tr. and ed. by T. Laycock for Sydenham Society, 1851.

502. Verworn, Max. Die einfachsten Reflexwege im Rückenmark. Centralbl. Physiol., 1909, 23: 281–284.

503. ———. Irritability. A Physiological Analysis of the General Effect of Stimuli in Living Substance. Yale University Press, 1913.

504. Vierordt, Karl. Grundriss der Physiologie des Menschen. Tübingen, 1862.

505. Villiger, Emil. Brain and Spinal Cord. Tr. from 3rd German edition by George A. Piersol. Philadelphia, 1912.

506. Volkmann, A. W. Ueber Reflexbewegungen. Archiv für Anat. Physiol. und Wissens. Med., 1838, 15–43.

507. ———. Nervenphysiologie. Wagner's Handwörterbuch, Bd. II, 1846.

508. Vulpian, M. A. Recherches Expérimentales sur la tendance à l'attitude normale. (1) Chez les astéries. Compte Rendu des Séances de La Société de Biologie, 1861, 3: 189–213.

509. Wagner, R. Handwörterbuch. 1844–1846.

510. Waldeyer, W. Ueber einige neure Forschungen im Gebeite der Anatomie des Centralnervensystems. Deutsch. med. Wochenschr., 1891.

511. Waller, Augustus. Experiments on the section of the Glosso-Pharyngeal and Hypoglossal nerves and observation on the alterations produced in the structure of their primitive fibres. Phil. Trans., 1850, 423.

512. ———. On muscular spasms known as "tendon reflex." Brain, 1880, 3: 179.

513. ———. On the physiological mechanism of the phenomenon termed tendon reflex. Jr. Physiol., 1890, 11: 384–395.

514. WALLER, AUGUSTUS. On the inhibition of voluntarily and of electrically excited muscular contractions. Brain, 1892, 15: 35–65.

515. WALLER, A. D. On the time taken in transmission of reflex impulses in the spinal cord of the frog. Quart. Jr. Exper. Physiol., 1908, 1: 251–256.

516. WALLIN, J. E. W. Experimental studies of mental defectives: A critique of the Binet-Simon tests and a contribution to the psychology of epilepsy. Educ. Psychol. Mon., No. 7, Baltimore, 1912.

517. WALSHE, F. M. R. [Review of] Körperstellung, by R. Magnus. Brain, 1924, 47: 383–390.

518. WARDEN, C. J. The historical development of comparative psychology. Psychol. Rev., 1927, 34: 57–85, 135–168.

519. ———, AND WARNER, L. H. The development of animal psychology in the United States during the past three decades. Psychol., Rev., 1927, 34: 196.

520. WARREN, H. C. Sensations of rotation. Psychol. Rev., 1895, 2: 273–276.

521. ———. Mechanism vs. vitalism in the domain of psychology. Phil. Rev., 1918, 27: 597–615.

522. ———. A classification of reflexes, instincts, and emotional phenomena. Psychol. Rev., 1919, 26: 197–203.

523. ———. Human Psychology. New York, 1919.

524. WASHBURN, M. F. The Animal Mind. 3rd edition, New York, 1926.

525. ———. Movement and Mental Imagery. Boston, 1916.

526. WATSON, J. B. The place of the conditioned reflex in psychology. Psychol. Rev., 1916, 23: 89–116.

527. ———. Psychology from the Standpoint of a Behaviorist. 2nd edition. Philadelphia, 1924.

528. DE WATTEVILLE, A. On reflexes and pseudoreflexes. Brit. Med. Jr., 1882, 1: 736–757.

529. ———. Ueber sehnen Phänomene. Centralbl. für Nervenk., 1886, 9: 353.

530. WEBER, E. Muskelbewegung. Wagner's Handwörterbuch, Bd. III. 1846.

531. WEBER, WILHELM, AND WEBER, EDUARD. Mechanik der Menschlichen Gehwerkzeuge. Göttingen, 1836.

532. WEDENSKY, N. Ueber einige Beziehungen zwischen der Reizstärke und der Tetanushöhe bei indirecter Reizung. Arch. f. d. ges. Physiol., 1885, 37: 69–72.

533. ———. Die Erregung, Hemmung und Narkose. Arch. f. d. ges. Physiol., 1903, 100: 1–144.

534. WEISS, A. P. A Theoretical Basis of Human Behavior. Columbus, Ohio, 1925.

535. WESTPHAL, C. I. O. Ueber einige Bewegungserscheinungen an gelähmten Gliedern. Arch. f. Psych. und Nervenkrankh., 1875, 5: 803–834.

536. WHEWELL, WILLIAM. History of the Inductive Sciences from the Earliest to the Present Time. 2 vols. New York, 1888.

537. WHYTT, ROBERT. An Essay on the Vital and Other Involuntary Motions of Animals. 2nd edition, Edinburgh, 1763. (Introduction dated October 1, 1751.)

538. ———. Physiological Essays, containing (1) An Inquiry into the Causes which Promote the Circulation of the Fluid in the very Small Vessels of Animals. (2) Observations on the Sensibility and Irritability of the Parts of Men and other Animals. 1st edition, 1755, 2nd edition 1759, 3rd edition, 1766.

539. WHYTT, ROBERT. Observations on the Nature, Causes and Cure of those Disorders which are commonly called Nervous, Hypochondriac, or Histeric. 1st edition, 1764, 2nd edition, 1765, 3rd edition, 1767.

540. WIERSMA, E. D. Die psychologische Auffassung einiger Reflexe. Zeit. f. d. ges. Neurol. u. Psychiatrie, 1921, 72: 254–266.

541. WILLIS, THOMAS. The remaining Medical Works of that famous and renowned Physician, Dr. Thomas Willis, tr. by S. Pordage. V. Of Musculary Motion. VI. Of the Anatomy of the Brain. VII. Of the Description and Use of the Nerves. London, 1681.

542. WUNDT, W. Die Lehre von der Muskelbewegung. Braunschweig, 1858.

543. ———. Über den Reflexvorgang und das Wesen der centralen Innervation. Stuttgart, 1876.

544. ———. Principles of Physiological Psychology. Vol. I, tr. from 5th German edition, 1902.

545. ———. Outlines of Psychology. Third English edition, tr. from 7th German edition. Leipzig, 1907.

546. ———. Grundzüge der Physiologische Psychologie. 6th edition, Leipzig, 1911.

547. YERKES, R. M., AND MORGULIS, S. The method of Pavlov in animal psychology. Psychol. Bull., 1909, 6: 257–273.

548. ZEIZING, EMIL. Ueber das Kniephänomen mit specieller Berüchsichtigung des normalen und pathologischen Verhaltens desselben im Kindesalter. Halle, 1887.

549. ZIEHEN, TH. Introduction to Physiological Psychology. Tr. by C. C. Van Lieu and Dr. Otto Beyer, 1892.

550. ———. Die Diagnostiche Bedeutung der Steigerung des Kniephänomens und des Fussklonus. Correspondenz-Blätter des allg. ärztl. Vereines von Thüringen, 1889. No. 1.

551. ———. [Review of] "Die Relationen des Palaencephalons (Edinger) sind nicht fix." A. Marina. Zeit. f. Psychol. u. Physiol., 1915, 73: 142–3.

552. ———. Leitfaden der Physiologischen Psychologie. 12th Aufl. Jena, 1924.

553. ZUNTZ, N., AND LOEWY, A. Lehrbuch der Physiologie des Menschen. Leipzig, 1909.

554. ZWAARDEMAKER, H., UND LANS, L. J. Ueber ein Stadium relativer unerregbarkeit als Ursache des intermittirenden charakters des Lidschlagreflexes. Centralbl. f. Physiol., 1899, 13: 325–329.

NAME INDEX

339

SUBJECT INDEX